BLAST

Other resources from O'Reilly

Related titles   Beginning Perl for Bioinformatics

Developing Bioinformatics Computer Skills

Mastering Perl for Bioinformatics

Sequence Analysis in a Nutshell: A Guide to Common Tools and Databases

Bioinformatics Books Resource Center   *bio.oreilly.com* is a complete catalog of O'Reilly's books on bioinformatics and related technolgies, including sample chapters and code examples.

oreilly.com   *oreilly.com* is more than a complete catalog of O'Reilly books. You'll also find links to news, events, articles, weblogs, sample chapters, and code examples.

   *oreillynet.com* is the essential portal for developers interested in open and emerging technologies, including new platforms, programming languages, and operating systems.

Conferences   O'Reilly & Associates bring diverse innovators together to nurture the ideas that spark revolutionary industries. We specialize in documenting the latest tools and systems, translating the innovator's knowledge into useful skills for those in the trenches. Visit *conferences.oreilly.com* for our upcoming events.

   Safari Bookshelf (*safari.oreilly.com*) is the premier online reference library for programmers and IT professionals. Conduct searches across more than 1,000 books. Subscribers can zero in on answers to time-critical questions in a matter of seconds. Read the books on your Bookshelf from cover to cover or simply flip to the page you need. Try it today with a free trial.

BLAST

Ian Korf, Mark Yandell, and Joseph Bedell

O'REILLY®

Beijing · Cambridge · Farnham · Köln · Sebastopol · Tokyo

BLAST
by Ian Korf, Mark Yandell, and Joseph Bedell

Published by O'Reilly & Associates, Inc., 1005 Gravenstein Highway North, Sebastopol, CA 95472.

O'Reilly & Associates books may be purchased for educational, business, or sales promotional use. Online editions are also available for most titles (*safari.oreilly.com*). For more information, contact our corporate/institutional sales department: (800) 998-9938 or *corporate@oreilly.com*.

Editor:	Lorrie LeJeune
Production Editor:	Mary Anne Weeks Mayo
Cover Designer:	Emma Colby
Interior Designer:	David Futato

Printing History:

July 2003:	First Edition.

ISBN: 978-0-596-00299-2

[LSI]

[2011-03-25]

Table of Contents

Part I.   Introduction

Part II.   Theory

Part III. Practice

Part IV.   Industrial-Strength BLAST

Part V. BLAST Reference

Part VI. Appendixes

Foreword

Reading a book such as this brings home how much BLAST—now in its teenage years—has grown, and provides an occasion for fond reflection. BLAST was born in the first months of 1989 at the National Center for Biotechnology Information (NCBI). The Center had been created at the National Institutes of Health in November 1988, by an act of the U.S. Congress, to foster the development of a field that then had no widely accepted name, but which has since come to be known as "Bioinformatics." In early 1989, David Lipman, my post-doctoral advisor, who at the time was perhaps best known as a codeveloper of the FASTA program, was appointed director of NCBI. On the first of March we moved into new offices at the National Library of Medicine. The NCBI was small, but had large ambitions, and already a number of friends. Several of these well-wishers made it a point to drop by for a visit. Gene Myers, a computer scientist then at Arizona, arrived during a week in which *Science* was hyping a special-purpose computer chip for sequence comparison. He and David, software partisans both, were unimpressed and over dinner resolved to do better. Their original idea was to find not subtle sequence similarities, but fairly obvious ones, and to do it in a flash. Gene pursued a rigorous approach at first, but David, with a fine Darwinian wisdom, was willing to settle for imperfection. If one were to gamble, what kind of match could one expect a strong alignment to contain? Detailed algorithmic and code development on BLAST by Webb Miller—later to be joined by Warren Gish—had hardly begun before Sam Karlin, a Stanford mathematician, came calling. I had approached him a few months earlier with a conjecture concerning the asymptotic behavior of optimal ungapped local sequence alignments. Since then, he had spun this conjecture into a beautiful theory. Now, for the first time, rigorous statistics were available for alignment scoring systems of more than academic interest, and the essential nature of amino acid substitution matrices also began to come into clear focus. This theory dovetailed perfectly with the work that had just started on BLAST: both informing the selection of its algorithmic parameters, and yielding units for the alignment scores produced.

Although David chose BLAST's name as a bit of a pun on "FASTA" (it was only later that I realized "BLAST" to be an acronym), the new program was never intended to vie with the earlier one. Rather, the idea was to turn the "threshold parameter" way up, to find undoubted homologies before you take more than one sip of coffee. It surprised us all when BLAST started returning most weak similarities as well. Thus was born a sort of friendly competition with Bill Pearson's and David's earlier creation. From the start, BLAST had two major advantages to FASTA and one major disadvantage. In the plus column, BLAST was indeed much the faster, and it also boasted Sam's new statistics, which turned raw scores into E-values. However, BLAST could only produce ungapped local alignments, thereby often eliding large regions of similarity and sometimes completely missing weak alignments that FASTA, in its most sensitive but slowest mode, was able to find. These points of comparative advantage were healthy for both programs. In time, FASTA fit its scores to the extreme value distribution, yielding reliable statistical evaluations of its output. And by the mid '90s, Warren Gish's WU-BLAST from Washington University, and NCBI's BLAST releases, introduced gapped alignments, using differing algorithmic strategies. The result, at least for protein sequence comparisons, is that BLAST and FASTA have converged in many important ways, although there still remain significant differences.

The programs comprehended by the name "BLAST" have multiplied astonishingly in the nearly 15 years since the first one was conceived. Learning the best way to use these various programs for research can be a challenge, and this book is a significant aid. While BLAST's developers have done their best to make the programs' default behavior the most generally applicable, a sophisticated user still has many issues to consider.

To achieve speed, BLAST is a heuristic program. It isn't guaranteed to find every local alignment that passes its reporting criteria, and there are an array of parameters that control the shortcuts it takes. With the introduction of gapped alignments, the programs' complexity increased, as did the number of parameters that influence BLAST's tradeoff of speed and sensitivity. In a certain sense, however, these mechanics are the least important for a user to understand because, except for the occasional appearance or disappearance of a weak similarity, they don't greatly effect the programs' output. Perhaps of more importance is an understanding of attendant matters that are relevant to the effective use of any local alignment search method, such as the filtering of "low-complexity" sequence regions, the proper choice of scoring systems, and the correct interpretation of statistical significance. This book deals with these and many other matters, and nicely combines theoretical considerations with practical advice informed by these considerations.

The BLAST programs have been the fruit of much hard work by scores of talented programmers and scientists. This work continues, linking BLAST output to other databases, improving alignment formatting options, refining the types of queries that may be performed. Newer offshoots, such as PSI-BLAST for protein profile searches, also continue under development, and BLAST is thus a moving and a growing target. This book should prove a valuable guide for those wishing to use the programs to best effect.

—Stephen Altschul
June 26, 2003

Preface

The second half of the 20th century was witness to incredible advances in molecular biology and computer technology. Only 50 years after identifying the chemical structure of DNA (1953), the sequence of the human genome has been determined and can be downloaded to a computer small enough to fit in your hand. The pace of science can be truly dizzying. So what do you do when you literally have the book of life in the palm of your hand? Well, you read it of course. Unfortunately, it's much easier to read the book of life than to understand it, and one of the great quests of the 21st century will be unraveling its mysteries. One particularly fruitful approach to deciphering the book of life has been through comparative studies, such as those between mouse and human.

Comparisons between the human and mouse genomes show how little has changed since humans and mice last shared a common ancestor around 75 million years ago. Very few genes are unique to humans or mice, and in general the genes are more than 80% identical at the sequence level. However, genes account for a small fraction of these genomes and the majority of sequence is not recognizably similar. This is where BLAST, the Basic Local Alignment Search Tool, comes in. BLAST is useful for finding similarities between biological sequences, be they DNA, RNA, or protein. Sequence similarity is often an indication of conserved function, and you can use comparative sequence analysis to understand biological sequences in much the same way that ancient Greeks used comparative anatomy to understand the human body or that linguists used the Rosetta Stone to understand Egyptian hieroglyphs.

Audience for This Book

People interested in BLAST come from many disciplines including biology, chemistry, computer science, law, mathematics, medicine, physics, etc. One reason for this is that knowledge of genes and genomes is becoming increasingly useful in a variety of settings. Another reason is that bioinformatics is this century's rocket science. Researchers from many disciplines are being drawn into its fascinating and rapidly growing orbit. So if you've recently become interested in bioinformatics, understanding BLAST is a great place to start. And if you're already a bioinformatics student or professional, this book can help you get more out of BLAST.

Structure of This Book

This book is divided into six parts: An Introduction to BLAST, Theory, Practice, Industrial-Strength BLAST, Reference, and the Appendixes. The quick start guide in Chapter 1 is the best place to begin if you've never run BLAST before. You won't need sophisticated hardware or software, just a web browser connected to the Internet. In Part II, we begin by exploring the molecular biology, computer science, and statistics that form the foundation of BLAST searches. We then describe the BLAST algorithm in detail. You will find that a sound theoretical understanding is essential when you put BLAST into practice. In Part III, we present practical advice to help you design and interpret BLAST experiments intelligently and efficiently. Whether you're a complete novice or a seasoned pro, you'll find the tutorials and protocols a valuable resource. Part IV discusses using BLAST in a high-throughput setting where the goal is to get as much BLAST as possible for your buck. Here, we integrate the information usually found scattered among systems administrators, database administrators, and advanced BLAST users into a few sensible chapters. Part V contains reference chapters for NCBI-BLAST and WU-BLAST with detailed descriptions of each parameter.

Here's a chapter-by-chapter breakdown:

Part I, *Introduction*

Chapter 1, *Hello BLAST*, gives a quick introduction to BLAST by exploring Internet search pages.

Part II, *Theory*

Chapter 2, *Biological Sequences*, gives some background molecular and evolutionary biology to help you understand why biological sequences are similar to one another.

Chapter 3, *Sequence Alignment*, explains how global and local sequence alignment works and describes common algorithms for aligning sequences of letters.

Chapter 4, *Sequence Similarity*, explains how scores are used to determine the best alignmentand discusses the statistical significance of sequence similarity in a database search.

Part III, *Practice*

Chapter 5, *BLAST*, discusses BLAST itself. Understanding the theoretical framework of the BLAST suite of programs will help you design and interpret BLAST experiments and give you a foundation for troubleshooting when your search produces unexpected results.

Chapter 6, *Anatomy of a BLAST Report*, explores the standard format of the BLAST report.

Chapter 7, *A BLAST Statistics Tutorial*, shows how to calculate the numbers in a BLAST report and use this knowledge to better understand the results of a BLAST search.

Chapter 8, *20 Tips to Improve Your BLAST Searches*, is a summary of the previous seven chapters as well as the authors' expertise, and is designed to help you get the most from your BLAST searches.

Chapter 9, *BLAST Protocols*, contains "recipes" for the most common BLAST searches; it describes what to do and why to do it.

Part IV, *Industrial-Strength BLAST*

Chapter 10, *Installation and Command-Line Tutorial*, shows how to install NCBI-BLAST and WU-BLAST software on your own computer. This is necessary if you want to use BLAST in a high-throughput setting or develop specialized applications.

Chapter 11, *BLAST Databases*, shows how to create and maintain BLAST databases—one of the most neglected yet important aspects of using BLAST.

Chapter 12, *Hardware and Software Optimizations*, explores how to optimize BLAST searches for maximum throughput and will help you get the most out of your current and future hardware and software.

Part V, *BLAST Reference*

Chapter 13, *NCBI-BLAST Reference*, describes the parameters and options for the NCBI suite of BLAST programs.

Chapter 14, *WU-BLAST Reference*, describes the parameters and options for the WU-BLAST program.

Part VI: *Appendixes*

Appendix A, *NCBI Display Formats*, gives a brief description of each NCBI-BLAST sequence alignment display option, followed by a detailed explanation and example.

Appendix B, *Nucleotide Scoring Schemes*, shows the target frequencies and simple gap costs for pairs of sequences of length 100, 500, and 1,000.

Appendix C, *NCBI-BLAST Scoring Schemes*, shows the default values for several combinations of NCBI-BLAST matrices and gap costs.

Appendix D, *blast-imager.pl*, is a Perl script that creates a graphical summary of a BLAST report using Thomas Boutell's GD graphics library, which has been ported to Perl by Lincoln Stein.

Appendix E, *blast2table.pl*, is a Perl script that converts standard WU-BLAST or NCBI-BLAST output to the NCBI tabular format (-m 8) described in Appendix A.

There is also a Glossary of BLAST terms.

A Little Math, a Little Perl

Certain parts of this book are mathematical or algorithmic in nature, so you will find various equations and computer programs throughout the book. If these notations are unfamiliar to you, don't panic. To make this book accessible to a general audience, we have included graphical examples and descriptive text along with the equations. The programming examples are written in Perl, one of the most popular programming languages and one that has an especially strong following in bioinformatics. While we could have relied on pseudocode for our examples, using a real language means that you can run the programs on your own computer and edit them as you wish.

Conventions Used in This Book

The following conventions are used in this book:

Constant width
> Used for Perl programs, parameters, and BLAST output

Italics
> Used for program names, databases, for emphasis, and for new terms where they are defined

URLs Referenced in This Book

For more information about the URLs referenced in this book and for additional material about BLAST, see this book's web page, which is listed in the next section.

Comments and Questions

Please address comments and questions concerning this book to the publisher:

> O'Reilly & Associates, Inc.
> 1005 Gravenstein Highway North
> Sebastopol, CA 95472
> (800) 998-9938 (in the United States or Canada)
> (707) 829-0515 (international or local)
> (707) 829-0104 (fax)

There is a web page for this book, which lists errata, examples, or any additional information. You can access this page at:

> *http://www.oreilly.com/catalog/blast*

To comment or ask technical questions about this book, send email to:

bookquestions@oreilly.com

For more information about books, conferences, Resource Centers, and the O'Reilly Network, see the O'Reilly web site at:

http://www.oreilly.com

Acknowledgments

As a group, the authors would like to thank O'Reilly & Associates for their patience and support, and especially their editor Lorrie LeJeune. The book owes a lot to its technical reviewers: Scott Markel, Tony Palombella, and staff of the NCBI. Special thanks go out to Scott McGinnis, Tom Madden, and Stephen Altschul for all their insightful comments.

Ian

I thank my wife Karen (whose critical comments improved the readability of the book) and daughter Zoe for putting up with the extra hours required to write this book. (Sorry, I had no idea it was going to take this much time.) I'd also like to thank my former mentors, especially Warren Gish and Susan Strome, for their scientific guidance and high standards. Writing a book in the wee hours can be arduous work, so I appreciate Apple Computer for making things simple and WeakLazyLiar and Trespassers William for musical companionship. My coauthors deserve a lot of credit for tolerating my tyranny and helping to make a dream come true. Lastly, I'd like to say a special thanks to Mom and Dad.

Mark

Thanks to my coauthors, Ian and Joey. Special thanks to Stephen Altschul for all his patience with my frequent telephone calls and emails, and to Tom Madden for help with the BLAST code. I'd also like to thank Karen Eilbeck for putting up with me; Suzi Lewis for her patience; and yes, Martin, it is finished now! Finally, I'd like to dedicate my portion of the book to Dr. Marc Perry for showing me my first BLAST report.

Joey

If you are reading this, it means that I'm an O'Reilly author—wow! I'd like to first and foremost thank O'Reilly for putting out a great line of books that have allowed me to make the transition from the bench to the keyboard and, ultimately, to the bookshelves! I also thank my coauthors, Ian and Mark. It is truly amazing that we were able to put this together without even being on the same continent for the last year and a half. This is a testament to Ian's great organizational skills, his grand (yet ever-changing) vision for the book, and his unrelenting quest for perfection. I thank my wife Alison and daughter Lauren for their love and support. Thanks for putting up with the late BLAST nights and early BLAST mornings. I owe you both a lot for your patience and understanding.

Finally, I'd like to thank the members of the Blueberry Hill dart league for their support and friendship.

I'd like to dedicate this book to the memory of David Jagor and to the BBBs, the best group of friends a guy could have!

## PART I

Introduction

## CHAPTER 1

Hello BLAST

Welcome to BLAST! This chapter offers a quick start guide to BLAST by exploring some Internet search pages. Throughout the chapter, you may encounter unfamiliar (or even frightening) terms. Don't panic. The terms are fully explained in later chapters or in the Glossary. You don't need to understand all the concepts to get the most out of this chapter. If you're already a seasoned BLAST user, feel free to skip this introduction and dive right into the later sections.

What Is BLAST?

BLAST is an acronym for Basic Local Alignment Search Tool. Despite the adjective "Basic" in its name, BLAST is a sophisticated software package that has become the single most important piece of software in the field of bioinformatics. There are several reasons for this. First, sequence similarity is a powerful tool for identifying the unknowns in the sequence world. Second, BLAST is fast. The sequence world is big and growing rapidly, so speed is important. Third, BLAST is reliable, from both a rigorous statistical standpoint and a software development point of view. Fourth, BLAST is flexible and can be adapted to many sequence analysis scenarios. Finally, BLAST is entrenched in the bioinformatics culture to the extent that the word "blast" is often used as a verb. There are other BLAST-like algorithms with some useful features, but the historical momentum of BLAST maintains its popularity above all others.

Although BLAST originated at the National Center for Biotechnology Information (NCBI), its development continues at various institutions, both academic and commercial. This can be a little confusing, especially because people often put prefixes or suffixes on the acronym to come up with names like XYZ-BLAST-PDQ. We have aimed to keep this book as simple as possible, and therefore we concentrate on the two most popular versions: NCBI-BLAST and WU-BLAST (pronounced "woo blast"). NCBI-BLAST, as the name suggests, is the version available from the NCBI. WU-BLAST comes from Washington University in St. Louis and is developed by Warren Gish, one of the original authors of BLAST.

Using NCBI-BLAST

This book begins by exploring the BLAST pages on the NCBI web site. The NCBI, part of the National Institutes of Health, is a U.S. government-funded center for the curation and presentation of public biological knowledge. The NCBI is a public repository for DNA and protein sequences (GenBank), but it's far more than just a data storehouse. The NCBI also maintains a comprehensive medical publication archive (PubMed), distributes many tools for biological analyses (NCBI toolbox), and puts together its own tools for making the most use of the data that it stores (LocusLink, UniGene, RefSeq, Taxonomy browser). Most importantly, for our purposes, it's where the BLAST algorithm was first developed (Altschul et al., 1990) and where it can be obtained, distributed, and used for free without restrictions. Anyone with access to the Internet can run a BLAST search and explore the plethora of genetic resources that have been amassed and curated by the NCBI over the years.

You'll get the most out of this chapter if you follow along with a web browser. Begin by going to the BLAST homepage at *http://www.ncbi.nlm.nih.gov/BLAST*.

Choosing the BLAST Program

Without explaining all of the options presented on the homepage, let's get right into it with a default BLASTN search. Choose "Standard nucleotide-nucleotide BLAST [blastn]" as shown in Figure 1-1. BLASTN is a program that compares a nucleotide query sequence to a database of nucleotide sequences.

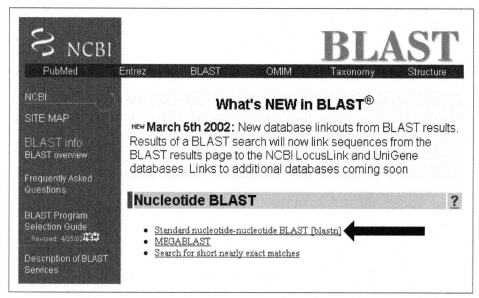

Figure 1-1. NCBI BLAST home page

Entering the Query Sequence

After choosing the kind of search you want to perform, the next step is to define the sequence with which to search. There are three options for this: paste in the bare sequence, paste in a file in FASTA format, or enter a valid NCBI identifier. You can just start typing a sequence in the search box; however, when the search is done, there will be no identifier to describe the sequence you entered. After several such searches, the lack of an identifier will make it difficult to keep track of which results go with which sequence. The second option allows you to define the sequence using the FASTA format. The FASTA format is described in detail in Chapter 11, but the basic specifications are that it's a text file beginning with a greater than sign (>) followed by an identifier and a definition line, which is then proceeded by the one-letter nucleotide or peptide sequence on subsequent lines. Let's use the following sequence:

```
>gi|11611818|gb|AF287139.1|AF287139 Latimeria chalumnae Hoxa-11 gene, partial cds
TACTTGCCAAGTTGCACCTACTACGTTTCGGGTCCCGATTTCTCCAGCCTCCCTTCTTTTTTGCCCCAGACCCCGTCTTCTCGCC
CCATGACATACTCCTATTCGTCTAATCTACCCCAAGTTCAACCTGTGAGAGAAGTTACCTTCAGGGACTATGCCATTGATACATC
CAATAAATGGCATCCCAGAAGCAATTTACCCCATTGCTACTCAACAGAGGAGATTCTGCACAGGGACTGCCTAGCAACCACCACC
GCTTCAAGCATAGGAGAAATCTTTGGGAAAGGCAACGCTAACGTCTACCATCCTGGCTCCAGCACCTCTTCTAATTTCTATAACA
CAGTGGGTAGAAACGGGGTCCTACCGCAAGCCTTTGACCAGTTTTTCGAGACGGCTTATGGCACAACAGAAAACCACTCTTCTGA
CTACTCTGCAGACAAGAATTCCGACAAAATACCTTCGGCAGCAACTTCAAGGTCGGAGACTTGCAGGGAGACAGACGAGAAGGAG
AGACGGGAAGAAAGCAGTAGCCCAGAGTCTTCTTCCGGCAACAATGAGGAGAAATCAAGCAGTTCCAGTGGTCAACGTACAAGGA
AGAAGAGGTGC
```

Before you try to type all this into the search text box, let's look at identifiers, which are an easier and more reliable way to enter queries. The previous example of the coelacanth (*Latimeria chalumnae*) Hoxa-11 gene has three valid NCBI identifiers that can be entered into the search box. The three identifiers are separated by pipes (|) and designate the GI (11611818), the accession number and version (AF287139.1), and the locus (AF287139). These identifiers are explained in detail in Chapter 11. For the current search (Figure 1-2), use the locus identifier, AF287139.

Using the locus, BLAST pulls out the FASTA file from the NCBI databases and uses it in the search just as if you had entered it all in the search box. If you are dealing with public sequence, this is the fastest and most reliable way to enter the query.

Choosing the Database to Search

For this search, we'll leave the default database as *nr* (Figure 1-3). Historically, the database was curated to contain a nonredundant set of nucleotide sequences (hence *nr*); however, it's no longer screened to be nonredundant. Because of its comprehensive nature, *nr* is usually a good first start when trying to identify a novel sequence or when determining if related sequences have been described previously. The database is curated by the NCBI and consists of nucleotide sequences from all of GenBank, RefSeq, EMBL, and DDBJ. You don't need to be concerned about the details of these /-sequence sources now but just know that they provide a comprehensive set of

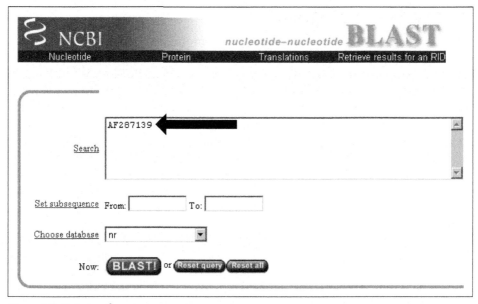

Figure 1-2. Entering the query sequence

sequences. As of January 2003, the *nr* database contained more than 1.5 million entries consisting of more than 7.5 billion nucleotides.

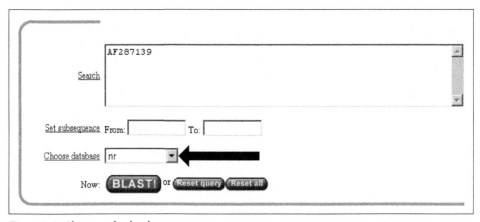

Figure 1-3. Choosing the database

Choosing the Parameters of the Search

Once you enter a query sequence and choose a database, the next step is to decide on the parameters of the search (Figure 1-4). For this test case, just use the default parameters, which are low-complexity filtering, an Expect value of 10, and a word size of 11. There is also a default reward of +1 and a penalty of -3, which isn't apparent on this submission form but makes a big difference in the results you obtain. A full explanation of these parameters and how they relate to the expected results are discussed in Chapters 4, 7, and 9.

Options for advanced blasting

Limit by entrez query [   ] or select from: (none) [▼]

Choose filter ☑ Low complexity ☐ Human repeats ☐ Mask for lookup table only ☐ Mask lower case

Expect [10]

Word Size [11 ▼]

Other advanced [   ]

Figure 1-4. Selecting parameters

Choosing the Format

Once you have entered the query, selected the database, and chosen the appropriate search parameters, you must then choose the desired results format (Figure 1-5).

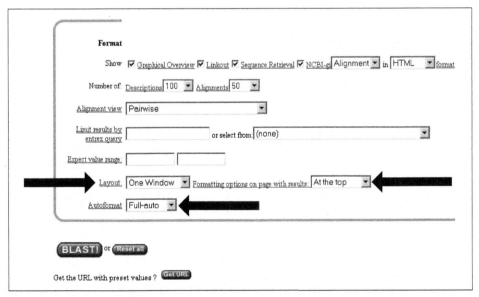

Figure 1-5. Choosing the format

These options allow you to format the results in a number of ways. For this quick start guide, you need to change the three bottom options: "Layout," "Formatting options on page with results," and "Autoformat." "Layout" should be changed from "Two Windows" to "One Window." This keeps all the results in the current window instead of launching a separate window. The "Formatting options on page with results" should be set to "At the top." Because the NCBI has set up the BLAST pages so that the search is separate from the results, using "At the top" lets you easily explore all the different formatting options once you get your results. Now you can run the compute-intensive search once and then format it rapidly in a number of ways. The final change is to set "Autoformat" to "Full-auto." This automatically updates and formats the results page when the search is done.

Submitting the Search

Once you select the BLAST! button, the window changes to show the Request Identifier (RID) and the estimated time to completion (below the Format options section). The web page will update itself periodically until the search is complete (Figure 1-6).

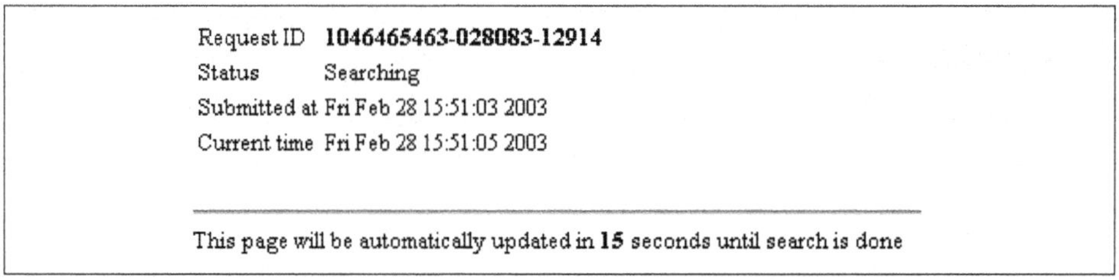

Request ID   **1046465463-028083-12914**
Status   Searching
Submitted at Fri Feb 28 15:51:03 2003
Current time Fri Feb 28 15:51:05 2003

_____

This page will be automatically updated in **15** seconds until search is done

Figure 1-6. Waiting for results

Viewing the Results

Once the search is complete, a results window appears. To understand all the parts of a BLAST report, break down the results window into pieces. The header of the report, shown in Figure 1-7, contains important bookkeeping information. For example, at the top is the BLAST version and date of compilation (Version 2.2.5, compiled on November 16, 2002). Also shown is the reference for the Nucleic Acids Research article, which should be used in any publication arising from using NCBI-BLAST. Following the reference is the RID, which can be copied and used to retrieve these results for up to 24 hours. Next, the query definition line and sequence length are reported along with a description of the database and its size. Also included in the header is a link to "Taxonomy reports," which shows the lineage and taxonomic breakdown of all the database matches.

Looking further down in the report (Figure 1-8), you can see that the body of the report begins with a graphical display of the database hits (the result of setting the

```
BLASTN 2.2.5 [Nov-16-2002]

Reference:
Altschul, Stephen F., Thomas L. Madden, Alejandro A. Schäffer,
Jinghui Zhang, Zheng Zhang, Webb Miller, and David J. Lipman (1997),
"Gapped BLAST and PSI-BLAST: a new generation of protein database search
programs", Nucleic Acids Res. 25:3389-3402.

RID: 1046465463-028083-12914

Query= gi|11611818|gb|AF287139.1|AF287139 Latimeria chalumnae
Hoxa-11 gene, partial cds.
        (606 letters)


Database: All GenBank+EMBL+DDBJ+PDB sequences (but no EST, STS,
GSS, or phase 0, 1 or 2 HTGS sequences)
           1,704,979 sequences; 7,927,210,239 total letters


If you have any problems or questions with the results of this search
please refer to the BLAST FAQs

Taxonomy reports
```

Figure 1-7. Header of a BLAST report

Graphical Overview option) as they align to the query. At the top of the display, you can see that 72 BLAST hits passed the threshold of your search criteria (you may see more than 72 because of the rapid database growth). After the color key, the top line represents the query sequence as a solid red line with the sequence coordinates. Each line below represents one subject match with its position in relation to the query and the color-coded relative strength of the similarity. You can move your mouse over each line to see the definition line, and if you click on it, you will be taken to the actual alignment.

The next part of the body is the summary (see Figure 1-9), which lists the one-line descriptions (set with the Descriptions option) of the database matches (also known as hits or subjects) along with the score and the E value. The hits are listed from best to worst, with high scores and low E values being better. Also included in this part, and set with the Linkout option, are links to other NCBI curated databases with more information about each hit. In this case some sequences have links in Locus-Link (L) and/or UniGene (U).

At the heart of the report are the actual alignments (the number of alignments displayed is controlled by the Alignments option). The definition line is listed for each subject, and then some statistics about the alignment are given (Score, Expect (E) value, Identities, and Strand), followed by the actual sequence alignment. The letters of the sequences involved in the alignment are shown with the sequence coordinates and vertical bars connecting identical letters.

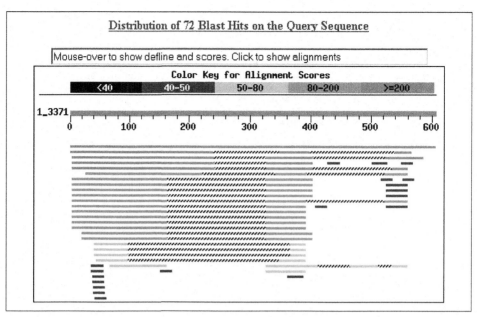

Figure 1-8. The body: graphical overview

```
                                                         Score    E
Sequences producing significant alignments:             (bits)  Value

gi|11611818|gb|AF287139.1|AF287139  Latimeria chalumnae Hoxa...  1201   0.0
gi|211938|gb|M81250.1|CHKHOXB  Gallus gallus homeodomain-con...   216   3e-53
gi|13249168|gb|AF327372.1|AF327372  Gallus gallus transcript...   216   3e-53
gi|11611820|gb|AF287140.1|AF287140  Silurana tropicalis Hoxa...   204   1e-49
gi|20278974|gb|AF479755.1|  Heterodontus francisci homeobox ...   188   6e-45
gi|6754225|ref|NM_010450.1|  Mus musculus homeo box A11 (Hox...   161   1e-36  L U
gi|664837|gb|U20371.1|MMU20371  Mus musculus homeobox protei...   161   1e-36  L
gi|664835|gb|U20370.1|MMU20370  Mus musculus homeobox protei...   161   1e-36  L U
gi|664831|gb|U20366.1|MMU20366  Mus musculus Hoxa11 locus an...   161   1e-36  L U
gi|26454732|gb|BC040948.1|  Homo sapiens, homeo box A11, clo...   153   4e-34  L
gi|24497552|ref|NM_005523.4|  Homo sapiens homeo box A11 (HO...   153   4e-34  L
gi|19848424|gb|AC116608.1|  Papio hamadryas chromosome , clo...   153   4e-34
gi|14589643|gb|AC004080.2|  Homo sapiens PAC clone RP1-17001...   153   4e-34  L
gi|3930576|gb|AF071164.1|AF071164  Homo sapiens homeobox A11...   153   4e-34  L
gi|2745850|gb|AF039307.1|AF039307  Homo sapiens homeobox A11...   153   4e-34  L
gi|25050005|ref|XM_149724.3|  Mus musculus homeo box A11, op...   143   3e-31  L
gi|664832|gb|U20367.1|MMU20367  Mus musculus Hoxa11 locus an...   143   3e-31  L U
gi|18858818|ref|NM_131147.1|  Danio rerio homeo box A11b (ho...    80   4e-12  L U
gi|18308323|gb|AC107364.1|  Danio rerio, clone -10019, compl...    80   4e-12
gi|11611814|gb|AF287137.1|AF287137  Danio rerio Hoxa-11b gen...    80   4e-12  L
gi|11611812|gb|AF287136.1|AF287136  Danio aequipinnatus Hoxa...    66   6e-08
```

Figure 1-9. The body: one-line descriptions

Figure 1-10 shows one database match alignment from this search. The query (your input) is aligned to the subject (a chicken homeodomain-containing gene) with all high-scoring local alignments shown. Each alignment is a high-scoring segment pair (HSP) that has its own alignment statistics. There are three HSPs in this case, each with a very significant score and Expect value. Some subject sequences have an associated link "D" that allows you to download just the part of the subject that aligns with the query, plus up to 1,000 bases flanking the HSP.

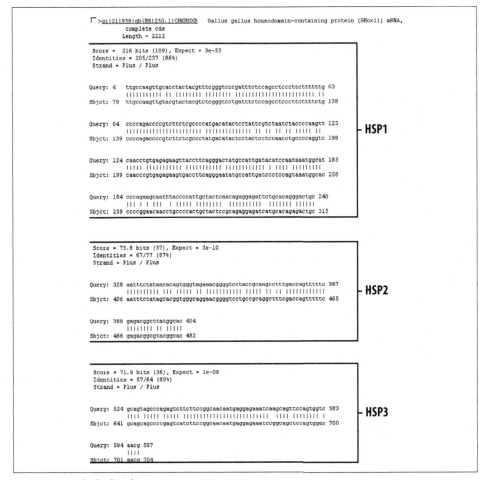

Figure 1-10. The body: alignments

Finally, at the bottom of the report, after all significant alignments are shown, comes the footer containing a detailed description of the search parameters (Figure 1-11). The footer contains information about the database, including a brief description, the date posted, and the size. The footer also lists the values of the lambda, K, and H variables used in calculating E values, bit scores, and other statistics about the alignments. The significance of all these numbers are explained in detail in Chapters 4 and 7.

```
        Database: All GenBank+EMBL+DDBJ+PDB sequences (but no EST, STS, GSS,
        or phase 0, 1 or 2 HTGS sequences)
          Posted date:  Feb 26, 2003  9:19 PM
        Number of letters in database: 7,927,210,230
        Number of sequences in database:  1,704,979

    Lambda     K       H
        1.37     0.711     1.31

    Gapped
    Lambda     K       H
        1.37     0.711     1.31


    Matrix: blastn matrix:1 -3
    Gap Penalties: Existence: 5, Extension: 2
    Number of Hits to DB: 2,672,883
    Number of Sequences: 1704979
    Number of extensions: 2672883
    Number of successful extensions: 43823
    Number of sequences better than 10.0: 44
    Number of HSP's better than 10.0 without gapping: 44
    Number of HSP's successfully gapped in prelim test: 0
    Number of HSP's that attempted gapping in prelim test: 43730
    Number of HSP's gapped (non-prelim): 93
    length of query: 606
    length of database: 7,927,210,239
    effective HSP length: 21
    effective length of query: 585
    effective length of database: 7,891,405,680
    effective search space: 4616472322800
    effective search space used: 4616472322800
    T: 0
    A: 0
    X1: 6 (11.9 bits)
    X2: 15 (29.7 bits)
    S1: 12 (24.3 bits)
    S2: 20 (40.1 bits)
```

Figure 1-11. The footer

Alternate Output Formats

This chapter showed the default HTML format, which is obviously best for viewing in a web browser. But what if you wanted to parse the output or store it in a database? HTML is not the best format for these choices. The NCBI also supports Plain Text, eXtensible Markup Language (XML), and ASN.1 formats. To see these different formats, just scroll back to the top of the report, choose another format under the Format option, and then resubmit using the Format! button. You can try this for all the formats, and then just hit the browser Back button to return to the HTML formatted page.

Alternate Alignment Views

The default Pairwise view shown in Figure 1-10 is the classic BLAST output style, but other options are available for other purposes. These options, described in the NCBI reference section and in Appendix A, include pairwise, query-anchored with identities, query-anchored without identities, flat query-anchored with identities, flat query-anchored without identities, and Hit Table. The most friendly option for text parsers is the Hit Table, which is viewed in plaintext format. This displays all the results in a tab-delimited table, which can be parsed easily. You can select this at the top of the page by changing "Format" to "Plain text" and "Alignment view" to "Hit Table" (Figure 1-12).

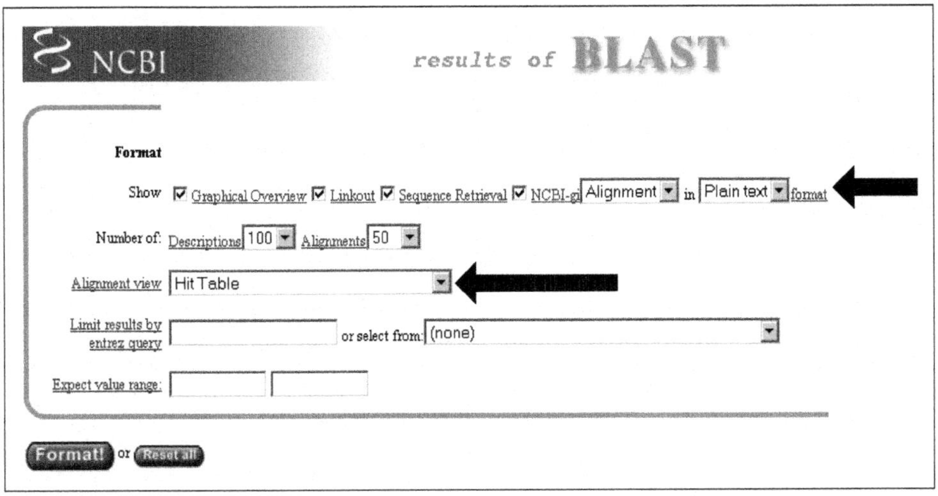

Figure 1-12. Changing format options

The Hit Table alignment view is shown in Figure 1-13. The first five lines start with # and are comments about the BLAST program, the query, and the database, followed by a description of the reported fields. The lines after the comments are the alignments in table format. The Hit Table contains all the necessary data to judge a hit without displaying the actual sequence being aligned.

```
# BLASTN 2.2.5 [Nov-16-2002]
# Query: gi|11611818|gb|AF287139.1|AF287139 Latimeria chalumnae Hoxa-11 gene, partial cds.
# Database: nr
# Fields: Query id, Subject id, % identity, alignment length, mismatches, gap openings, q. start, q. end, s.
start, s. end, e-value, bit score
# Query: gi|11611818|gb|AF287139.1|AF287139 Latimeria chalumnae Hoxa-11 gene, partial cds.

gi|11611818|gb|AF287139.1|AF287139 gi|11611818|gb|AF287139.1|AF287139 100.00 606 0 0 1 606 1 606 0.0 1201.8
gi|11611818|gb|AF287139.1|AF287139 gi|21699164|gb|AC126321.1| 89.12 239 26 0 1 239 9736 9498 9.0e-69 268.1
gi|11611818|gb|AF287139.1|AF287139 gi|21699164|gb|AC126321.1| 92.00 50 4 0 349 398 9391 9342 1.7e-08 67.89
gi|11611818|gb|AF287139.1|AF287139 gi|21699164|gb|AC126321.1| 100.00 26 0 0 541 566 9199 9174 0.001 52.03
```

Figure 1-13. Hit Table alignment

The other available alignment options allow a multiple sequence alignment view of the BLAST hits. One of these multiple alignment options, query-anchored with identities, is shown in Figure 1-14. In this view, the full sequence of the query is shown on the top line with a unique identifier (1_18852, in this case). Subsequently, each line shows the alignment for one database hit. Identical residues are represented with a dot (.), while nucleotide differences are shown explicitly. This alignment option is useful for quickly identifying changes common to a group of sequences. For example, you can see from the part of the alignment shown in Figure 1-14 that the bottom four sequences (6754225, 664837, 664835, and 664831) have common shared differences. A deeper look into these sequences reveals that they are actually different database entries for the same mouse Hoxa11 gene, which is homologous to the coelacanth Hoxa11 gene.

```
ALIGNMENTS
1_18852   1      tacttgccaagttgcacctactacgtttcgggtcccgatttctccagcctcccttctttt 60
11611818  1      ............................................................ 60
21699164  9736   .....a..c.....t..t........g....c...t......................... 9677
211938    79     ...........t..g........c........t........................... 135
13249168  8516   ...........t..g........c........t........................... 8572
11611820  7      ...............t........c........t..............t.....a..c 63
20278974  30055           ........g..............g......... 30087
6754225   94     ...........t..t........c........a........................... 150
664837    4753   ...........t..t........c........a........................... 4809
664835    93     ...........t..t........c........a........................... 149
664831    432    ...........t..t........c........a........................... 376


1_18852   61     ttgccccagaccccgtcttctcgccccatgacatactcctattcgtctaatctaccccaa 120
11611818  61     ............................................................ 120
21699164  9676   ..a.....a...................t......g.....t..c..........c.......g 9617
211938    136    c...........................t...........c..c..c..c..g.....g 195
13249168  8573   c...........................t...........c..c..c..c..g.....g 8632
11611820  64     c.....a.....a........t..........t.......t..c..c..c.....g 123
20278974  30088  ..a.....a..a..g..................t..c....c...a..c.....g 30147
6754225   151    ..................g.....a...............c..c..c..c..g.....g 210
664837    4810   ..................g.....a...............c..c..c..c..g.....g 4869
664835    150    ..................g.....a...............c..c..c..c..g.....g 209
664831    375    ..................g.....a...............c..c..c..c..g.....g 316
```

Figure 1-14. Query-anchored with identities view

The other multiple sequence alignment views are similar to this one, but differ on whether or not they show identical residues (with or without identities) and whether the gaps are displayed in the query sequence or in the subjects (flat or not). You'll find a detailed explanation of these alignment options in Appendix A.

The Next Step

This chapter has taken you through a simple BLASTN search at the NCBI database; however, more than two dozen specialized BLAST pages are available, and they let you do anything—from screening for vector sequence, to identifying protein family members, to mapping a sequence to the human genome. For a quick guide to these specialized pages, the NCBI presents a convenient reference to these tools at *http://www.ncbi.nlm.nih.gov/BLAST/producttable.html.*

Further Reading

Altschul, S.F., T.L. Madden, A.A. Schaeffer, J. Zhang, Z. Zhang, W. Miller, and D.J. Lipman (1997). "Gapped BLAST and PSI-BLAST: a new generation of protein database search programs." *Nucleic Acids Research*, 25, pp. 3389-3402.

## PART II

Theory

## CHAPTER 2

Biological Sequences

Sequence similarity is a powerful tool for discovering biological function. Just as the ancient Greeks used comparative anatomy to understand the human body and linguists used the Rosetta stone to decipher Egyptian hieroglyphs, today we can use comparative sequence analysis to understand genomes, RNAs, and proteins. But why are biological sequences similar to one another in the first place? The answer to this question isn't simple and requires an understanding of molecular and evolutionary biology.

The Central Dogma of Molecular Biology

Most courses in molecular biology begin with the Central Dogma of Molecular Biology, which describes the path by which information contained in DNA is converted to protein molecules with specific functions. Stated simply, the Central Dogma is: "from DNA to RNA to protein." Figure 2-1 shows a more complete diagram of this process and will be referenced throughout this section.

DNA

The hereditary material that carries the blueprint for an organism from one generation to the next is called deoxyribonucleic acid. It is much more commonly referred to by its acronym, DNA. Every time cells divide, the DNA is duplicated in a process called *DNA replication*. The entire DNA of an organism is called its *genome*, and genomes are sometimes called "the book of life" (especially with respect to the human genome). Reading and understanding the various books of life is one of the most important quests of the genomic age. Modern medicine, agriculture, and industry will increasingly depend on an intimate knowledge of genomes to develop individualized medicines, select and modify the most desirable traits in plants and animals, and understand the relationships among species.

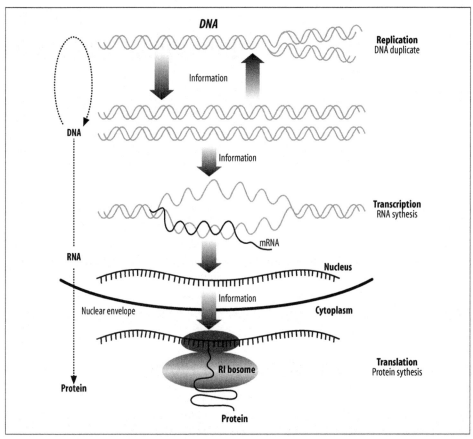

Figure 2-1. The Central Dogma of Molecular Biology: DNA to RNA to protein

The language of DNA is complicated. Over the last 50 years, scientists have begun to decipher it, but it is still largely a mystery. Although the language is elusive, the alphabet is simple, consisting of just four nucleotides: adenine, cytosine, guanine, and thymine. For simplicity in both speech and on the computer, they are usually abbreviated as A, C, G, and T. DNA usually exists as a double-stranded molecule, but we generally talk about just one strand at a time. Here's an example of a DNA sequence that is six nucleotides (nt) long:

    GAATTC

DNA has polarity, like a battery, but its ends are referred to as 5-prime (5′) and 3-prime (3′) rather than plus and minus. This nomenclature comes from the chemical structure of DNA. While it isn't necessary to understand the chemical structure, the terminology is important. For example, when people say "the 5′ end of the gene," they mean the beginning of the gene. We usually display DNA sequence as we read text, left to right, and the convention is that the left side is the 5′ end and the right side is the 3′ end.

In addition to the 4-letter alphabet, there is also a 15-letter DNA alphabet used to describe nucleotide ambiguities (Table 2-1). The most common noncanonical DNA symbol is N, which stands for an unknown nucleotide. Other common ones include R and Y.

Table 2-1. Nucleotide ambiguity codes

Symbols	Nucleotides	Mnemonic
R	A or G	puRine
Y	C or T	pYrimidine
W	A or T	Weak hydrogen bonds
S	G or C	Strong hydrogen bonds
K	G or T	Keto in major groove
M	A or C	aMino in major groove
B	C, G, or T	not A
D	A, G, or T	not C
H	A, C, or T	not G
V	A, C, or G	not T
N	A, C, G, or T	aNy

The pairing rule of DNA is that A pairs with T, and C pairs with G. It is very easy to determine the sequence of the complementary strand of any DNA sequence. In double-stranded form, the 6 base pairs (bp) of DNA above looks like this:

```
GAATTC
CTTAAG
```

In this example, if you read the bottom strand backward, it is the same as the top strand read forward. Such *palindromes* are often of biological interest. This particular one is the recognition site for an enzyme called *EcoRI* that cuts DNA at this sequence. This is an example of how information can be gleaned simply from analyzing the primary sequence. Palindromes and other patterns often give clues to the function of small stretches of DNA.

But why is DNA double stranded? The answer is because the molecule is chemically more stable that way, and the double-stranded structure also allows some error correction if a base is accidentally damaged—for example by UV irradiation from too much sunlight. (This is a good reason to wear sunscreen.) DNA by itself doesn't do much. It's just a storehouse for information. For the computer scientists in the audience: think of the genome as a hard disk with RAID mirroring that stores A's, C's, G's, and T's instead of 1s and 0s.

Before we continue with the Central Dogma, we'll discuss genes. What is a gene? Like many complicated problems, this is a question for which five experts would give you six different answers. For our purposes, a *gene* is a functional unit of the genome (a purposefully vague definition). Most genes contain instructions for producing proteins at a certain time and in a certain space. Some genes have very narrow windows of activity, while others are ubiquitous. Not all genes code for proteins, however. Some genes produce RNAs that aren't translated into proteins and are therefore called noncoding RNAs (ncRNA). So we've already deviated from the Central Dogma. Molecular biology is filled with rules that are constantly violated. (In fact, that's one of the first rules!) Molecular biology is also filled with names and acronyms that may be new to you. To help you keep track of them, this book includes most of them in the Glossary.

RNA

As mentioned earlier, DNA doesn't do much on its own. The excitement starts when DNA is copied into RNA by a protein called *RNA polymerase* in a process called *transcription*. Chemically, RNA is a lot like DNA except that it uses uracil instead of thymine and is single stranded instead of double stranded. The RNA alphabet is A, C, G, and U, and an RNA molecule might look like this:

GAAUUC

What happens to the RNA transcript from a gene? If it is a transfer RNA (tRNA), ribosomal RNA (rRNA), or other ncRNA, it may undergo some chemical modifications, but the gene product remains as an RNA molecule. RNAs corresponding to protein coding genes are called messenger RNAs (mRNA).

Protein

Proteins make up the "buildings" and "machines" inside a cell. They are chemically very different from DNA and RNA because they are composed of amino acids (often abbreviated aa) rather than nucleic acids. Proteins have a useful property: they can fold into very specific three-dimensional shapes that are dependent on their amino acid sequences. Thus, the amino acid sequence determines the shape of the protein and the shape determines the function. A protein shaped like a stiff rod may be used as a structural support. Collagen and keratin are such proteins and make skin and hair durable. A protein with a hook may be used as a part of a ratcheting motor. A good example of this is myosin, which is found in muscle cells. Therefore, while DNA and RNA are largely used to store and send information, proteins make things happen.

The protein alphabet commonly contains 20 symbols, A, C, D, E, F, G, H, I, K, L, M, N, P, Q, R, S, T, V, W, and Y. The names, abbreviations, and structures of the amino acids are shown in Table 2-2.

Table 2-2. Amino acids

Amino acid	Abbreviation	Symbol	Properties	Structure
Alanine	Ala	A	Hydrophobic	
Cysteine	Cys	C	Neutral; forms disulfide bridges	
Aspartate	Asp	D	Negatively charged	
Glutamate	Glu	E	Negatively charged	
Phenylalanine	Phe	F	Hydrophobic; aromatic	
Glycine	Gly	G	Neutral; smallest amino acid	
Histidine	His	H	Positively charged; aromatic	
Isoleucine	Ile	I	Hydrophobic	
Lysine	Lys	K	Positively charged	
Leucine	Leu	L	Hydrophobic	
Methionine	Met	M	Hydrophobic; start amino acid	

Table 2-2. Amino acids (continued)

Amino acid	Abbreviation	Symbol	Properties	Structure
Asparagine	Asn	N	Neutral ; hydrophilic	
Proline	Pro	P	Hydrophobic	
Glutamine	Gln	Q	Neutral ; hydrophilic	
Arginine	Arg	R	Positively charged	
Serine	Ser	S	Neutral; hydrophilic	
Threonine	Thr	T	Neutral ; hydrophilic	
Valine	Val	V	Hydrophobic	
Tryptophan	Trp	W	Hydrophobic; aromatic	
Tyrosine	Tyr	Y	Hydrophobic; aromatic	

Using one-letter symbols, a protein sequence might be written like this:

```
MLVGSRA
```

Like DNA and RNA, proteins also have polarity, and the nomenclature comes from the chemical structure. Here again, the convention is to display the sequence from left to right. In proteins, the left end is called the *N-terminus* and the right end is called the *C-terminus*. Thus, when people say, "the N-terminus is often removed after translation," they're talking about the beginning of the protein. Remember that all proteins start with the amino acid methionine (M). This is another of the universal laws of molecular biology, and like all biological laws, it is occasionally violated.

The sequences of proteins are one-dimensional, but their shapes are three-dimensional, or four-dimensional if you take into account that they're not frozen in time and can change their shape depending on their environment. It's worth remembering because most of this book talks about proteins as one-dimensional sequences and not shapes, and this approximation is frequently at odds with reality. Let's take a brief sojourn into protein folding and structure to see why this is.

First, just to make sure you get your daily dose of jargon, the sequence of amino acids is called the 1° structure of the protein (this is read as "primary structure," not "1st degree"). Proteins in aqueous solution usually have a globular structure; that is, they aren't sprawled out all over the place but adopt a compact structure. How do they get this way? Many proteins fold into their final structure by themselves because it represents the "easiest" shape they can adopt. But some proteins need a little help, and they receive assistance from other proteins in the cell called *chaperones*. Amino acid chemistry is beyond the scope of this chapter, but note that amino acids can be classified as *hydrophobic* ("fears water") or *hydrophilic* ("likes water"). Hydrophobic amino acids are like oils: they don't mix well with water and prefer to clump together in blobs rather than disperse. When a protein folds, the hydrophobic parts tend to aggregate. This creates a globular structure in which the inside is composed of hydrophobic amino acids, and the exterior is composed of hydrophilic amino acids. Of course, the complete story is much more complicated, but this provides a convenient way to think about protein folding and structure.

Although proteins come in many different shapes and sizes, if you look closely at the structure, you can find recurring structural themes that biologists call 2° (secondary) structure. The most common themes are the α-helix, β-sheet, and random coil. In Figure 2-2, these themes are represented as cylinders, arrows, and squiggly lines.

The Genetic Code

How is the information in DNA and RNA translated to protein sequence? A complex machine composed of proteins and ncRNAs called the *ribosome* reads an mRNA sequence and writes a protein sequence. The mRNA is read three nucleotides at a time. The nucleotide triplets are called *codons*. Each codon corresponds to a single amino acid. The mapping from codons to amino acids is called the *genetic code*, and its discovery is one of the great achievements in molecular biology. The genetic code is one of the universal laws of molecular biology (and, as you should expect, is sometimes broken).

Because codons are three nucleotides long and there are four possible nucleotides at each position, it follows that there are 64 (4^3) possible codons. However, there are

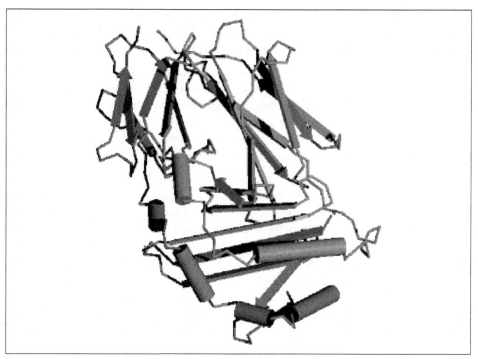

Figure 2-2. Structure of immunoglobulin domain

only 20 amino acids. Thus there is redundancy in the genetic code and in turn, the code is often described as degenerate. Figure 2-3 shows the standard nuclear genetic code (there are more than a dozen different genetic codes, mostly from different mitochondrial genomes). If you look closely at the redundancies, you will find patterns. For example, the third position of a codon is often insignificant; A, C, G, or T all lead to the same translation. When this isn't the case, A and G are usually synonymous, as are C and T. It so happens that A and G belong to the same chemical class, called *purines*, and C and T belong to another class, called *pyrimidines*, so this makes sense in a biochemical way. There are other neat patterns, such as any codon with a T in the middle translates to a hydrophobic amino acid. In addition to the amino acids, there are three *stop codons*. When a ribosome sees a stop codon, translation terminates, and the protein is released to go about its business. As mentioned before, all proteins start with the amino acid methionine. This has only one codon, ATG, and so ATG is often called the *start codon*.

Consider the following nucleotide sequence.

```
TTTATATCACAC
```

If you translate this from the first letter, you get the protein sequence:

```
FISH
```

	T	**C**	**A**	**G**
T	TTT Phe (F) TTC " TTA Leu (L) TTG "	TCT Ser (S) TCC " TCA " TCG "	TAT Tyr (Y) TAC TAA Ter TAG Ter	TGT Cys (C) TGC TGA Ter TGG Trp (W)
C	CTT Leu (L) CTC " CTA CTG "	CCT Pro (P) CCC " CCA " CCG "	CAT His (H) CAC " CAA Gin (Q) CAG "	CGT Arg (R) CGC " CGA " CGG "
A	ATT Ile (I) ATC " ATA " ATG Met (M)	ACT Thr (T) ACC " ACA " ACG "	AAT Asn (N) AAC " AAA Lys (K) AAG "	AGT Ser (S) AGC " AGA Arg (R) AGG "
G	GTT Val (V) GTC " GTA " GTG "	GCT Ala (A) GCC " GCA " GCG "	GAT Asp (D) GAC " GAA Glu (E) GAG "	GGT Gly (G) GGC " GGA " GGG "

Figure 2-3. Standard codon translation

But what if you translate it from the second nucleotide? You get a different protein sequence (note that the fractional codon AC at the end of the DNA translates to threonine no matter what the next nucleotide is):

    LYHT

Because codons are three nucleotides long, you can translate DNA in three different *reading frames*. Since DNA is double stranded, there are really six reading frames for every piece of DNA. So if someone hands you a DNA sequence and asks you to translate it, you may have a little trouble.

Evolution

BLAST works because evolution is happening. Biological sequences show complex patterns of similarity to one another. In this regard, they mirror the external morphologies of the organisms in which they reside. You'll notice that birds, for example, show natural groupings. You don't have to be a biologist to see that ducks, geese, and swans comprise a reasonably natural group called the waterfowl, and that the similarities between ducks and geese seem too great to explain by mere coincidence. Biological sequences are no different. After all, the reason why ducks look like ducks and geese look like geese is because of their genes. Many molecular biologists are convinced that understanding sequence evolution is tantamount to understanding evolution itself.

Sequences change over time due to three forces: mutation, natural selection, and genetic drift. If you use BLAST, it's important to understand these forces because they form the biological foundation of similarity searches. The biological and mathematical foundations aren't the same, and are sometimes at odds. You need to understand both theories in order to knowledgeably interpret the sequence alignments in a BLAST report.

Mutation

A *mutation* is simply a change in a DNA sequence. What causes mutation? Many chemicals and conditions damage DNA, so its sequence either changes or ceases to be recognizable. Mutagenic agents are often called *carcinogens* because cancer is caused by the accumulation of mutations in genes that control cell division. But even in a world without carcinogens there would still be mutation because the process of DNA replication isn't perfect. Every time a cell divides, it must duplicate its DNA. The human genome is about three billion letters long, and the error rate of DNA replication is about one error in every 300 million letters, so you can expect about 10 mutations per genome duplication. Genome size varies, as does the replication error rate, so don't take the 10 mutations per genome replication as any kind of biological truth. Human beings are composed of about a trillion cells, and you might take a moment now and consider just how much mutation is going on in your own body. Whatever that large number is, it's infinitesimal compared to what's happening in the biosphere as a whole.

What happens when a mutation occurs in the protein-coding portion of a gene? Because the DNA is mutated, the mRNA is also mutated. This in turn *may* lead to a different protein, but not necessarily, because the genetic code is degenerate. Take a look at an example for which you mutate just one letter in a coding sequence. If the mutation changed a codon from TTA to TTG, for example, the protein would be unchanged because both codons translate to the amino acid leucine. Such mutations are called *silent*, *synonymous*, or *same-sense* because they don't affect the protein sequence in any way. If the mutation changed a TTA to a TTT, however, the codon would code for a different amino acid, phenylalanine. Such substitutions are called *mis-sense* mutations. Molecular biologists will often classify mis-sense mutations into either conservative or nonconservative substitutions, depending on whether the two amino acids are chemically similar to one another. Leucine and phenylalanine are both hydrophobic amino acids, and such a substitution would be considered conservative. Bioinformaticists, however, give a more rigorous and quantifiable definition of conservative (see Chapter 4). If the TTA codon is mutated to TAA, the codon becomes a stop codon, which causes the ribosome to stop translating the mRNA. This represents the most destructive kind of mutation, and is called a *non-sense* mutation. Non-sense mutations cause translation to terminate prematurely, and the result is a truncated protein that may function partially, not function at all, or be poisonous to the cell.

Not all mutations substitute one nucleotide for another. Some mutations may insert or remove nucleotides. In addition, there are duplications, inversions, and other large-scale rearrangements that destroy genes or even fuse them together. Insertions and deletions are often destructive because they change the reading frame of translation if they aren't additions/subtractions of a multiple of three (a whole codon). After such a *frame-shift mutation*, there are usually several mis-sense mutations caused by the out-of-frame codons, and then a premature stop codon that was not previously in frame. Insertions and deletions are therefore usually as disruptive as mis-sense mutations.

What happens to an organism with mutations? It depends on a lot of factors. A mutation may have disastrous consequences, it might prove beneficial, or it might have no effect at all. To understand the forces that govern sequence evolution, let's take a close look at natural selection and genetic drift.

Natural Selection

The theory of natural selection was developed to explain why organisms look the way they do and why they seem to "fit" their environments so well. For example, why do giraffes have such long necks? Historically, there have been a lot of explanations, but we'll skip those debates and focus on the theory of natural selection because it is simple and fits the data well. The theory has only three assumptions.

- There must be variation within a population.
- The variation must be heritable.
- There must be differential reproduction based on variation.

In the case of the giraffe ancestor, those individuals with slightly longer necks were at an advantage because they could reach leaves higher in the trees. This advantage translates to more surviving offspring, and since the variation is heritable, they too will tend to have longish necks. Now, within this population of longish necked pre-giraffes, there is still more variation, and the cycle of selecting for longer-necked individuals can persist until you have something that looks like a modern giraffe. People often look at the organisms today and think that their form is "complete." But all organisms are undergoing change from one generation to the next. When you look at a giraffe, try thinking about it as a particular form at a snapshot in time, on its way to something perhaps taller, or shorter, or with wings and horns and a penchant for breathing fire.

When Charles Darwin formulated the theory of natural selection, he had no idea about mutations, DNA, proteins, or the genetic code. The theory was based solely on observation; there was no known mechanism. In the last 50 years, the advances in molecular biology have revolutionized our understanding of natural selection. We now understand why there is variation and what is being selected for and against.

The *why* is that variation exists at the DNA level (called *alleles* by geneticists). The *what* is differences in genes.

Consider how protein structure is selected for or against. What if a mutation causes an amino acid in the hydrophobic core of a protein to be changed to something hydrophilic? Well, it probably wouldn't fold the same way anymore because the hydrophobic core of the globular structure now has a part that wants to be in an aqueous environment. In most cases, changes in protein structure are unfavorable and therefore selected against; however, sometimes they result in altered function, which is favorable in certain conditions. Such is the case with sickle cell anemia. A charged amino acid (glutamate) is changed to a hydrophobic one (valine), causing altered protein interactions at the surface. Disease results when both alleles of the gene have this change, but it offers some protection against malaria when present in only one allele. As natural selection would predict, the sickle cell allele, and therefore sickle cell anemia, is prominent in certain parts of the world where malaria is common.

Several take-home messages are worth stating quite clearly. First, there is an *inexhaustible* source of variation because mutation is constantly happening. Natural selection isn't going to run out of variation. Evolution isn't going to stop. Second, a mutation can't be declared either good or bad on its own. Even a mutation that introduces a stop codon can be beneficial. Look at seedless oranges. It might seem an abomination of nature that they can't reproduce by themselves, but it is this very fact that makes humans breed them. To the seedless orange, genes that allow seeds to form are the kiss of death.

Genetic Drift

The interplay between mutation and natural selection that was just outlined makes a nice story. Like most stories, though, the truth is a lot more complicated. Reading the previous section, you may have concluded that natural selection is an all-powerful force, responsible for determining every nucleotide in a DNA sequence. In such a world, you would expect proteins to be perfectly functioning machines and the DNA sequences that encode them to be the best possible sequence for the job. This might be true in a mathematical model involving infinite population size and limitless generations, but the real biological world is a harsh place subject to happenstance. Even if the highly advantageous mutation enabling X-ray vision were to arise in some individual, it might not end up in the gene pool if that person thinks he's Superman and tries to stop a runaway train.

Darwin was not aware of how variation is transmitted from generation to generation; he didn't have the concept of genes. Genes were introduced by Gregor Mendel to explain how hereditary information is transmitted from one generation to the next. Combining Mendelian genetics and natural selection led to the field of population genetics, which is chiefly concerned with the changes in allele frequencies over time. Mathematical simulations show quite clearly that allele frequencies can change by purely random processes. This behavior is called *genetic drift*, and it's based on the fact that populations aren't infinitely large.

Let's demonstrate genetic drift with an example. For simplicity, let's ignore new mutations and just consider an anonymous site that has no consequence in natural selection. Assume there are only 10 individuals in the population, and that 5 have a C at this position and 5 have a T. Keeping the population fixed, in the next generation, the allele frequencies may change to C=0.6 and T=0.4 due to a runaway train or, less spectacularly, sampling error. All things being equal, in the next generation, there's a greater chance that the C will increase and the T will decrease. If this trend continues for a few generations, the T's may disappear from the population entirely at which point the C allele is considered *fixed* in the population. Alleles can be fixed very rapidly if some individuals move away to form a new population. This is called the *founder effect*. As you can see, changes in allele frequencies don't require mutation or natural selection.

The Neutral Theory of Evolution

Molecular biology and the discovery of the genetic code had a profound effect on evolutionary biology. One shocking realization was that many sites for mutation—for example, the third position in a codon or a nucleotide in the middle of an intron (a term defined later), are expected to be invisible to natural selection. This led Motoo Kimura to propose the neutral theory of evolution. It was somewhat heretical when first proposed because it deemphasized the role of natural selection, but the theory states that the majority of sequence evolution is purely random, the product of mutation and drift.

Imagine what happens to a sequence as it accumulates random mutations over time. At first, the sequence is nearly identical to the original. If the rate of mutation is relatively consistent, you can count the number of mismatches to determine how much time has passed. This turns out to be very useful and forms the basis for determining the probability that a DNA sample matches a particular person, for example. Eventually, the number of mutations becomes so great that the sequence is no longer recognizably similar to the original. At this point, the sequence is *saturated* for mutation. Saturated sequences can't be used to measure time, but they are still very useful because they indicate which sequences aren't under selective pressure. By inference, those that remain similar over long periods of time are under selective pressure. As a practical example, when comparing the human and puffer fish genomes, you find that most of the conserved sequence is in genes.

One of the great debates of evolutionary biology is the relative importance of natural selection and neutral evolution in the formation of species. We don't need to be overly concerned with this argument because we're more interested in how sequences change over time, and for this we can observe actual sequence data.

Molecular Clocks

If you compare the sequences from related organisms, it is clear that certain positions don't change much over time while others change very rapidly. For example, parts of the ribosomal RNA are identical in every organism sequenced to date, from bacteria to humans. These subsequences are so important that if they change, the organism dies. Clearly, these are under intense selective pressure. There are other sites, such as third codon positions, that are only mildly affected by selection and tend to drift. There are even sequences, such as viral coat proteins, in which selection acts to promote variation, and these change very rapidly. Regardless of the underlying mechanism, it is possible to use the rate of change as a molecular clock.

If you know the mutation rate for a particular sequence, you can use it to determine how long ago two sequences diverged. Suppose you have the same protein sequence from both cats and dogs, and there are 10 differences between them. From the fossil record, you estimate that cats and dogs had a common ancestor 50 million years ago. Now when you compare the cat sequence to the same sequence in humans, you find 12 differences. You can now estimate that carnivores and humans shared a common ancestor 60 million years ago. We're using a very simple model here that treats all positions identically and we're not using real data, but this is the general idea behind molecular clocks.

The key to using molecular clocks is that the sequences must "tick" at the appropriate rate. The hypothetical protein in the last example is a poor choice for determining how long ago humans and chimps last shared a common ancestor because one difference here or there would lead to a large difference in the estimated time. Sequences that tick too fast are also not appropriate because they are prone to saturation.

Homology, Phylogeny, and Trees

When looking at the biological world around you, you see only what exists today. You can't get a clear picture of what the world looked like 100 million years ago. However, you can see relationships between organisms and make inferences. For example, you don't know what the last common ancestor of humans, chimpanzees, and gorillas looked like, but you can guess that it looked more like an ape than a bird. This is also the case at the sequence level; proteins from humans and chimps are much more similar to each other than either is to a bird. The study of relationships between organisms is called *phylogenetics*.

By definition, two sequences are *homologous* if they share a common ancestor. Two sequences are either homologous or they aren't. However, people often misuse the term and say something like "these two sequences are 80 percent homologous." What they usually mean is that two sequences are 80 percent identical and not that there is an 80 percent chance that they have a common ancestor. Determining if two sequences are indeed homologous requires making inferences. This isn't always a simple task; sometimes homology can be stated with near certainty, but not always. Sequences may appear to be related from chance similarity (or *convergent evolution*).

Sequence homology is further refined by the terms orthologous and paralogous. Sequences separated by speciation are called *orthologs,* while sequences separated by duplication are called *paralogs.* The genes for myoglobin in humans and mice are orthologs; they are the same gene in different species. If the myoglobin gene is duplicated in humans, the two myoglobins will be paralogs of each other. It's somewhat confusing, but both human paralogs would be considered orthologous to the mouse myoglobin. It is generally the case that the most similar genes between species are orthologs, and this is often used as an operational definition.

The Tree of Life

An introduction to molecular evolution would be incomplete without an overview of life on Earth. You may have learned in an introductory biology class that there are five taxonomic kingdoms (animals, plants, fungi, monera, and protista). This is based largely on what can be seen with your eyes or a microscope. Molecular biology opened up a new way to classify organisms based on sequences rather than external features. Figure 2-4 shows a tree for various organisms based on ribosomal DNA sequence. There are three obvious domains that Carl Woese called the Bacteria, Archaea, and Eucarya. Note that the arrow in the figure points to the root of the plants, animals, and fungi. From this perspective, the traditional five kingdoms are a bit nearsighted.

gIn terms of genomes and overall cell structure, there are only two major divisions: the *prokaryotes* (bacteria and archaea) and *eukaryotes.* Except in rare cases, prokaryotes are microscopic organisms that are usually shaped like rods or spheres. Some of the more famous prokaryotes include *Escherichia coli* (a bacterium that lives in your gut and is a favorite model organism for microbiologists) and *Yersinia pestis* (the bacterium that causes bubonic plague). The major distinguishing feature of prokaryotes is that DNA replication, transcription, and translation all take place in the same compartment of the cell because there is only one compartment in the cell.

Eukaryotes come in many shapes and sizes, primarily because they can form multicellular organisms such as birds and trees. But some eukaryotes are simple, single-celled organisms such as *Saccharomyces cereviseae* (the yeast used for making beer). All eukaryotes have a nucleus (*karya* is Greek for nucleus) in which DNA is stored, in addition to other membranous organelles. Interestingly, most eukaryotes contain *mitochondria.* These organelles have their own genome and are descended from bacteria that long ago entered a cooperative relationship with eukaryotes. This is also true of *chloroplasts*, which are responsible for photosynthesis in plants. It is thought that eukaryotes are a fusion of two bacteria, one a Eubacteria and one an Archaebac-

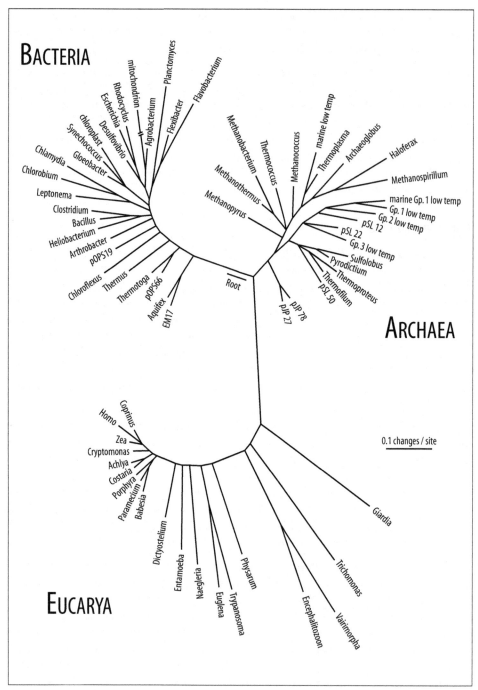

Figure 2-4. Tree of life based on rRNA sequence (Diagram courtesy of Norman Pace. Used with permission.)

teria. So the next time you munch on a carrot, you might consider how many genomes are really in there.

So far, this chapter has neglected viruses. Where do they fit in? By most definitions, viruses aren't even alive; they don't grow or have repair processes. Viruses seem to break every rule of biology. Some viruses infect prokaryotes and others that parasitize eukaryotes. Viruses come in many different shapes and have wildly different lifestyles. Some have genomes made from RNA instead of DNA, and others have single-stranded rather than double-stranded genomes.

Genomes and Genes

In general, the genomic structure of prokaryotes is very different from that of eukaryotes (Figure 2-5). Genomes are organized into chromosomes. Prokaryotes often have a single circular chromosome, and eukaryotes usually have multiple linear chromosomes. People are sometimes surprised to find that genome size and chromosome number aren't reflected in organismal complexity. For example, the single-celled *Amoeba dubia* has a genome that is about 200 times larger than the human genome. Although dogs and cats have very similar genome sizes, dogs have twice as many chromosomes. One rule to keep in mind when thinking about genomic organization is that genomes of viruses and prokaryotic organisms generally contain little noncoding sequence, whereas the genomes of more complex organisms usually contain a much higher percentage of noncoding sequence.

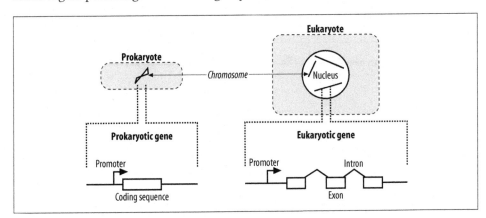

Figure 2-5. Prokaryote and eukaryote cells

Prokaryotic Genes

Prokaryotic genes are relatively simple. They contain a promoter that determines when the gene is transcribed and a coding region that contains the DNA sequence for a protein. It is relatively easy to find genes in prokaryotic genomes. Since stop codons are expected about every 21 triplets (there are three stop codons out of 64 total triplet combinations), long open reading frames (ORFs) should be very rare, at least from an unbiased random model. On average, proteins are 300 amino acids long, so finding an ORF that is 900 nucleotides long is really unexpected and a pretty clear signal that the ORF codes for a real protein. Of course, some genes encode small proteins, and finding these is a bit more difficult.

Eukaryotic Genes

Eukaryotic gene structure is more complicated than prokaryotic gene structure. Unlike prokaryotic genes, eukaryotic genes are often broken into pieces that are assembled before they are translated. Like prokaryotes, eukaryotes also have promoters to regulate when genes are turned on, but they are often much larger and may exist a great distance from the start of translation. In addition, many genes respond to additional sequences called *enhancers* and *suppressors* that aren't necessarily upstream of a gene and may be many kilobases away.

In eukaryotes, mRNAs are processed before they are translated (Figure 2-6). Two kinds of processing are common: splicing and poly-adenylation. *Splicing* brings together the coding sequences and throws out the intervening stuff. The sequences that end up in the mature mRNA are called *exons,* and the intervening stuff is called *introns*. The part of the mRNA that codes for protein is called the *coding sequence* (CDS), and the parts at either end are called *untranslated regions* (UTRs). The other common post-transcriptional modification is *poly-adenylation*. In this process, 50 or more adenine nucleotides are added to the end of the mRNA, which is called a *poly-A tail*.

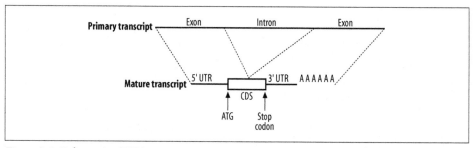

Figure 2-6. Eukaryotic mRNA processing

Transcripts

To many people, the most interesting parts of a genome are its genes. However, genes may account for a small fraction of a genome. In the human genome, for example, only 1 to 2 percent of the sequence codes for proteins. So why not just sequence the proteins? This procedure turns out to be much more difficult than sequencing nucleotides, but you can sequence the transcripts that code for proteins. Using some clever molecular biology techniques, it's possible to separate mRNAs from the rest of the cellular material and in this way specifically select for protein-coding genes. However, the mRNAs aren't sequenced directly. First they are copied into complementary DNA (cDNA) by an enzyme called *reverse transcriptase*. This enzyme converts mRNA into DNA, flouting the first rule, which is the Central Dogma of Molecular Biology. A collection of cDNAs is called a *cDNA library*, and it is common to have cDNA libraries from many kinds of tissues. The mRNAs present in the liver may be very different from those in the brain (the tissues have very different properties due to different collections of proteins). If you're interested in certain cancers, for example, you might develop and sequence cDNA libraries derived from specific types of tumors.

In the world of sequencing, it is therefore common to find cDNA sequencing projects in addition to, or instead of, genome sequencing projects. The downside to cDNA sequencing is that many interesting sequences aren't transcribed, and those that are transcribed may be difficult to capture if they aren't abundant. In your quest for jargon compliance, note that sequencing reads from cDNA sequences are often called *expressed sequence tags* (ESTs). You will probably come across this term frequently in your BLAST searches.

Repeats

Repeats are one of the most mysterious features of genomes. All genomes sequenced to date contain some form of repeat, but the big eukaryotic genomes are richest. About half the human genome is easily recognized as repetitive. Understanding repeats is critical to BLAST users because if they aren't dealt with properly, they can tie up your computer for days, dominate your report, invalidate your statistics, and obscure your findings.

The words "repeat" and "repetitive sequence" are used very loosely in genomics, and this causes a lot of confusion for novices. Broadly speaking, repeats can be classified as simple and complex. *Simple repeats* generally consist of low-complexity sequences (see Chapter 4); examples include runs of a single nucleotide such as A^n, T^n, G^n, and C^n; dinucleotide repeats such as $[CA]^n$; tri-nucleotide repeats in the form of $[CAG]^n$; and so on. The strange thing about these sequences is that they occur much more frequently in genomes than you'd expect by chance. Simple sequence repeats occur just about everywhere in the genome, even in the protein coding exons of genes, but they are especially common in heterochromatic, pericentromeric, and telomeric regions of eukaryotic chromosomes that play structural roles and don't contain many genes.

The term *complex repeat* usually describes any genomic repeat that doesn't consist of low complexity/low entropy sequence. Noncoding RNAs, such as rRNAs and tRNAs, comprise one commonly encountered class of complex repeat, but because they have known important functions, they are often not lumped together with the rest of the repeats. The term *complex repeat* can also denote some form of mobile genetic element or *selfish DNA* (a phrase coined by Francis Crick). These entities are a bit like the fleas and ticks of the genome: they copy and spread themselves within and between genomes and are generally believed to do little for the host genome. Selfish DNAs are usually further classified into three subcategories: transposons, retroviruses, and retrotransposons. If you see these names in a BLAST report, you may need to use a repeat filter.

Pseudogenes

One of the most confounding problems in similarity searches is the presence of pseudogenes. As the name suggests, pseudogenes are "fake genes"; that is, they look like they could encode a protein, but they aren't functional. Pseudogenes come from a variety of sources. A mutation that introduces a stop codon into a gene creates a pseudogene, but more commonly, pseudogenes are created from some kind of duplication event. Sometimes, through various mechanisms, regions of a chromosome may become duplicated. The extra copies of genes are generally free of selective pressures and may become pseudogenes as they accumulate mutations. Duplication may also result from repetitive elements that include neighboring DNA as they copy themselves into new locations. In eukaryotes, a very common form of pseudogene is the retro-pseudogene, in which the mRNA from a gene is reverse-transcribed into DNA and inserted back into the genome. Because retro-pseudogenes come from mRNA, they contain the hallmarks of transcripts, notably an absence of introns and the presence of a poly-A tail. They are therefore easy to detect if you know what to look for. Most retro-pseudogenes come from highly transcribed genes such as the protein components of the ribosome.

Biological Sequences and Similarity

The beginning of this chapter asked why biological sequences are similar to one another. Let's answer that question now. You've seen that biological sequences like proteins may have important functions necessary for the survival of an organism. You've also seen that DNA sequence can mutate randomly, and this may change how a sequence functions. Over time, both functional constraints and random processes impact the course of sequence evolution. The degree to which a sequence follows a functional or random path depends on natural selection and neutral evolution. So the reason why sequences are similar to one another is because they start out similar to one another and follow different paths. When you read a BLAST report, you will find that your knowledge of molecular and evolutionary biology will help you interpret the similarities and differences you see.

Further Reading

Genetics, molecular biology, and evolution aren't especially difficult topics, but they are filled with many potentially unfamiliar terms. The following books are recommended for those just getting started in these fields. They are informative and entertaining, and can help more experienced readers communicate effectively with novices.

Clark, David P. and Lonnie D. Russell, *Molecular Biology Made Simple and Fun* (Cache River Press).

Gonick, Larry and Mark Wheelis, *The Cartoon Guide to Genetics* (Perennial).

Tagliaferro, Linda and Mark Vincent Bloom, *The Complete Idiot's Guide to Decoding Your Genes* (Alpha Books).

The following are typical textbooks for college-level courses in molecular biology, genetics, and evolution:

Alberts, Brooks et al., *Molecular Biology of the Cell* (Garland).

Futuyma, Douglas J., *Evolutionary Biology* (Sinauer Associates, Inc.).

Graur, Dan and Wen-Hsiung Li, *Molecular Evolution* (Sinauer).

Hartl, Daniel L. and Elizabeth W. Jones, *Genetics: Analysis of Genes and Genomes,* (Jones & Bartlett).

Lewin, Benjamin, *Genes VII* (Oxford University Press).

Lodish, Harvey et. al., *Molecular Cell Biology* (W.H. Freeman & Co.).

Page, Roderic D. M. and Edward C. Holmes, *Molecular Evolution: A Phylogenetic Approach* (Blackwell Science).

Watson, James D. and Joan Steitz. *Molecular Biology of the Gene* (Addison-Wesley).

CHAPTER 3

Sequence Alignment

BLAST finds statistically significant similarities between sequences by evaluating alignments, but how are sequences aligned? In principle, there are many ways to align two sequences, but in practice, one method is used more often than any other. This chapter explains this technique with the biologist in mind, without using the mathematical notation and jargon that is usually employed to describe such algorithm. Divested of unfamiliar language and notation, these algorithms are quite simple.

Finding the optimal alignment between two sequences can be a computationally complex task. Fortunately, a technique called *dynamic programming* (DP) makes sequence alignment tractable as long as you follow a few rules. Rather than have you struggle with a confusing definition of DP, this chapter demonstrates how the technique works for sequence alignment and then gets back to the generalities. There are fundamentally two kinds of alignment: global and local. In *global alignment*, both sequences are aligned along their entire lengths and the best alignment is found. In *local alignment*, the best subsequence alignment is found. For example, if you want to find the two most similar sentences between two books, you use local alignment. If you want to compare the sentences end to end, use global alignment. This chapter describes global alignment, then local alignment. The example uses English words instead of biological sequences and the algorithms are quite general.

Global Alignment: Needleman-Wunsch

The global alignment algorithm described here is called the Needleman-Wunsch algorithm. We will explain it in a way that seems natural to biologists, that is, it tells the end of the story first, and then fills in the details. (This is why biologists make terrible comedians; they always tell the punch line first.) We will align the words COELANCANTH and PELICAN using a simple scoring scheme: +1 for letters that match, −1 for mismatches, and −1 for gaps. The alignment will eventually look like one of the following, which are equivalent given our scoring scheme:

```
COELACANTH          COELACANTH
P-ELICAN--          -PELICAN--
```

Note that every letter of each sequence is aligned to a letter or a gap. In local alignments, discussed later, this isn't the case.

The alignment takes place in a two-dimensional matrix in which each cell corresponds to a pairing of one letter from each sequence. To get an intuitive understanding of the alignment algorithm, look at Figure 3-1, which shows where the maximum scoring alignment lies in the matrix. The alignment starts at the upper left and follows a mostly diagonal path down and to the right. When two letters are aligned, the path follows a diagonal trajectory. There are several places in which the letters from COELACANTH are paired to gap characters. In this case, the graph is followed horizontally. Although not shown here, the path may be also be followed vertically when the letters from PELICAN are paired with gap characters. Gap characters can never be paired to each other. Note that the first row and column are blank. The reason for this will become clear shortly.

	C	O	E	L	A	C	A	N	T	H
P	C P	O								
E			E E							
L				L L						
I					A I					
C						C C				
A							A A			
N								N N	T -	H -

Figure 3-1. Example of an alignment matrix

In reality, you don't store letters in the matrix as shown in Figure 3-1. Each cell of the matrix actually contains two values: a score and a pointer. The score is derived from the scoring scheme. Here, this means +1 or −1, but when aligning biological sequences, the values come from a scoring matrix (a topic of the next chapter). The pointer is a directional indicator (an arrow) that points up, left, or diagonally up and left. The pointer navigates the matrix, and its use will become clearer later in the chapter. Now, let's look at the algorithm in detail. There are three major phases: initialization, fill, and trace-back.

Initialization

In the initialization phase, you assign values for the first row and column (Figure 3-2). The next stage of the algorithm depends on this. The score of each cell is set to the gap score multiplied by the distance from the origin. Gaps may be present at the beginning of either sequence, and their cost is the same as anywhere else. The arrows all point back to the origin, which ensures that alignments go all the way back to the origin (a requirement for global alignment).

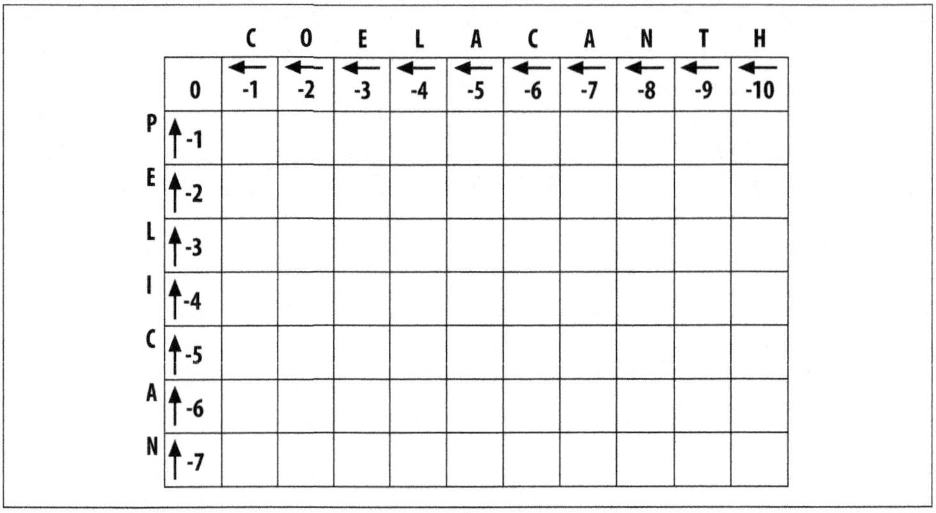

		C	O	E	L	A	C	A	N	T	H
	0	← -1	← -2	← -3	← -4	← -5	← -6	← -7	← -8	← -9	← -10
P	↑ -1										
E	↑ -2										
L	↑ -3										
I	↑ -4										
C	↑ -5										
A	↑ -6										
N	↑ -7										

Figure 3-2. Initialization of the alignment matrix

Fill

In the fill phase (also called *induction*), the entire matrix is filled with scores and pointers using a simple operation that requires the scores from the diagonal, vertical, and horizontal neighboring cells. You will compute three scores: a match score, a vertical gap score, and a horizontal gap score. The *match score* is the sum of the diagonal cell score and the score for a match (+1 or –1). The *horizontal gap score* is the sum of the cell to the left and the gap score (–1), and the *vertical gap score* is computed analogously. Once you've computed these scores, assign the maximum value to the cell and point the arrow in the direction of the maximum score. Continue this operation until the entire matrix is filled, and each cell contains the score and pointer to the best possible alignment at that point.

If you look at the initialized matrix, you'll find that there's only one cell where you can compute the maximum score because there's only one cell with the required 3 neighbors. Now you can see why you needed to leave one extra column and row and why you needed the initialization phase. Without them, you wouldn't be able to start the fill. Ignoring the rest of the table, compute this cell (the one that matches C to P).

The match score is the sum of the preceding diagonal cell (score = 0) and the score for aligning C to P (−1). The total match score is −1. The horizontal gap score is the sum of the score to the left (−1) and the gap score (−1). The horizontal gap score is therefore −2. The same is true for the vertical gap score. Your maximum score is therefore the diagonal score (−1), and the pointer is set to the diagonal (Figure 3-3). Now that this first cell is computed, you can compute the cell to the right or the cell below. Calculate one more cell, the right neighbor (the one that aligns O and P).

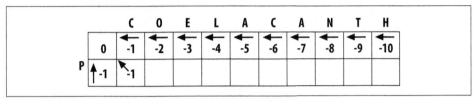

Figure 3-3. Beginning to fill the alignment matrix

The match score is the sum of the preceding diagonal cell (−1) and the mismatch score (−1), which equals −2. The horizontal gap score is the score of the cell to the left (−1) and the gap penalty (−1), which is also −2. The vertical gap score is the cell above (−2) and the gap penalty (−1), which totals −3. The maximum score is −2, but this can come from the diagonal or from the left. This is where you must make a consistent, arbitrary choice—for example, always choose the diagonal over a gap.

The matrix up to this point is shown in Figure 3-4. It may seem rather trivial, but the maximum global alignment between CO and P can be calculated. It has a score of −2 and has either of the following equivalent forms:

```
CO    CO
-P    P-
```

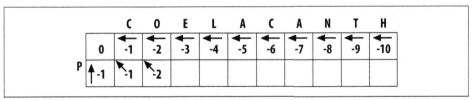

Figure 3-4. Second cell filled in the alignment matrix

Using the same maximizing procedure for each cell, you can fill the entire matrix. At the end of the fill, the matrix appears as in Figure 3-5.

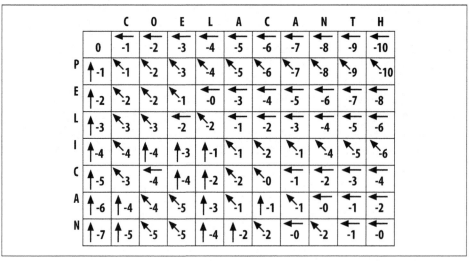

Figure 3-5. Filled alignment matrix

Trace-Back

The trace-back lets you recover the alignment from the matrix. Like the other parts of this algorithm, it's pretty simple. Start at the bottom-right corner and follow the arrows until you get to the beginning. To produce the alignment, at each cell, write out the corresponding letters or a hyphen for the gap symbol. Since you're following it from the end to the start, the alignment will be backward, and you just reverse it. The final alignment looks like this:

```
COELACANTH
-PELICAN-
```

Example 3-1 shows a Perl script.

Example 3-1. Trace-back with Needleman-Wunsch algorithm

```
# Needleman-Wunsch  Algorithm

# usage statement
die "usage: $0 <sequence 1> <sequence 2>\n" unless @ARGV == 2;

# get sequences from command line
my ($seq1, $seq2) = @ARGV;

# scoring scheme
my $MATCH    =  1; # +1 for letters that match
my $MISMATCH = -1; # -1 for letters that mismatch
my $GAP      = -1; # -1 for any gap

# initialization
my @matrix;
```

Example 3-1. Trace-back with Needleman-Wunsch algorithm (continued)

```perl
$matrix[0][0]{score}   = 0;
$matrix[0][0]{pointer} = "none";
for(my $j = 1; $j <= length($seq1); $j++) {
    $matrix[0][$j]{score}   = $GAP * $j;
    $matrix[0][$j]{pointer} = "left";
}
for (my $i = 1; $i <= length($seq2); $i++) {
    $matrix[$i][0]{score}   = $GAP * $i;
    $matrix[$i][0]{pointer} = "up";
}

# fill
for(my $i = 1; $i <= length($seq2); $i++) {
    for(my $j = 1; $j <= length($seq1); $j++) {
        my ($diagonal_score, $left_score, $up_score);

        # calculate match score
        my $letter1 = substr($seq1, $j-1, 1);
        my $letter2 = substr($seq2, $i-1, 1);
        if ($letter1 eq $letter2) {
            $diagonal_score = $matrix[$i-1][$j-1]{score} + $MATCH;
        }
        else {
            $diagonal_score = $matrix[$i-1][$j-1]{score} + $MISMATCH;
        }

        # calculate gap scores
        $up_score   = $matrix[$i-1][$j]{score} + $GAP;
        $left_score = $matrix[$i][$j-1]{score} + $GAP;

        # choose best score
        if ($diagonal_score >= $up_score) {
            if ($diagonal_score >= $left_score) {
                $matrix[$i][$j]{score}   = $diagonal_score;
                $matrix[$i][$j]{pointer} = "diagonal";
            }
            else {
                $matrix[$i][$j]{score}   = $left_score;
                $matrix[$i][$j]{pointer} = "left";
            }
        } else {
            if ($up_score >= $left_score) {
                $matrix[$i][$j]{score}   = $up_score;
                $matrix[$i][$j]{pointer} = "up";
            }
            else {
                $matrix[$i][$j]{score}   = $left_score;
                $matrix[$i][$j]{pointer} = "left";
            }
        }
    }
}
```

Example 3-1. Trace-back with Needleman-Wunsch algorithm (continued)

```perl
# trace-back

my $align1 = "";
my $align2 = "";

# start at last cell of matrix
my $j = length($seq1);
my $i = length($seq2);

while (1) {
    last if $matrix[$i][$j]{pointer} eq "none"; # ends at first cell of matrix

    if ($matrix[$i][$j]{pointer} eq "diagonal") {
        $align1 .= substr($seq1, $j-1, 1);
        $align2 .= substr($seq2, $i-1, 1);
        $i--;
        $j--;
    }
    elsif ($matrix[$i][$j]{pointer} eq "left") {
        $align1 .= substr($seq1, $j-1, 1);
        $align2 .= "-";
        $j--;
    }
    elsif ($matrix[$i][$j]{pointer} eq "up") {
        $align1 .= "-";
        $align2 .= substr($seq2, $i-1, 1);
        $i--;
    }
}

$align1 = reverse $align1;
$align2 = reverse $align2;
print "$align1\n";
print "$align2\n";
```

Local Alignment: Smith-Waterman

The local alignment algorithm we describe here, the Smith-Waterman algorithm, is a very simple modification of Needleman-Wunsch. There are only three changes:

- The edges of the matrix are initialized to 0 instead of increasing gap penalties.
- The maximum score is never less than 0, and no pointer is recorded unless the score is greater than 0.
- The trace-back starts from the highest score in the matrix (rather than at the end of the matrix) and ends at a score of 0 (rather than the start of the matrix).

These simple changes have a profound effect on the behavior of algorithm. Using the same words and scoring scheme as you did in global alignment, look at the filled matrix in Figure 3-6.

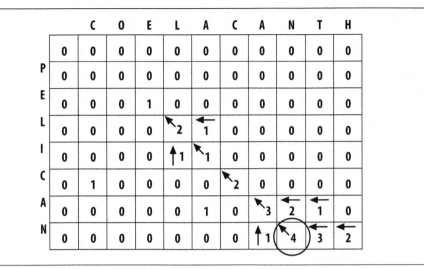

Figure 3-6. Filled Smith-Waterman alignment matrix

As you can see, there are a lot of zeroes. That's because there are a lot of places where you can't get a positive score. Also note that one cell is circled. This is the cell with the maximum score in the matrix. There may be more than one place in the matrix with the same maximum score, and in this case, some kind of arbitrary decision must be made. Start your trace-back from the maximum score and follow it to a score of zero, creating your alignment as you step backward, just as you did with global alignment. At the end, you have an alignment with a score of 4 that looks like this:

```
ELACAN
ELICAN
```

Example 3-2 shows the Perl code.

Example 3-2. Local alignment with the Smith-Waterman algorithm

```perl
# Smith-Waterman  Algorithm

# usage statement
die "usage: $0 <sequence 1> <sequence 2>\n" unless @ARGV == 2;

# get sequences from command line
my ($seq1, $seq2) = @ARGV;

# scoring scheme
my $MATCH    =  1; # +1 for letters that match
my $MISMATCH = -1; # -1 for letters that mismatch
my $GAP      = -1; # -1 for any gap

# initialization
my @matrix;
```

Example 3-2. Local alignment with the Smith-Waterman algorithm (continued)

```
$matrix[0][0]{score}   = 0;
$matrix[0][0]{pointer} = "none";
for(my $j = 1; $j <= length($seq1); $j++) {
    $matrix[0][$j]{score}   = 0;
    $matrix[0][$j]{pointer} = "none";
}
for (my $i = 1; $i <= length($seq2); $i++) {
    $matrix[$i][0]{score}   = 0;
    $matrix[$i][0]{pointer} = "none";
}

# fill
my $max_i     = 0;
my $max_j     = 0;
my $max_score = 0;

for(my $i = 1; $i <= length($seq2); $i++) {
    for(my $j = 1; $j <= length($seq1); $j++) {
        my ($diagonal_score, $left_score, $up_score);

        # calculate match score
        my $letter1 = substr($seq1, $j-1, 1);
        my $letter2 = substr($seq2, $i-1, 1);
        if ($letter1 eq $letter2) {
            $diagonal_score = $matrix[$i-1][$j-1]{score} + $MATCH;
        }
        else {
            $diagonal_score = $matrix[$i-1][$j-1]{score} + $MISMATCH;
        }

        # calculate gap scores
        $up_score   = $matrix[$i-1][$j]{score} + $GAP;
        $left_score = $matrix[$i][$j-1]{score} + $GAP;

        if ($diagonal_score <= 0 and $up_score <= 0 and $left_score <= 0) {
            $matrix[$i][$j]{score}   = 0;
            $matrix[$i][$j]{pointer} = "none";
            next; # terminate this iteration of the loop
        }

        # choose best score
        if ($diagonal_score >= $up_score) {
            if ($diagonal_score >= $left_score) {
                $matrix[$i][$j]{score}   = $diagonal_score;
                $matrix[$i][$j]{pointer} = "diagonal";
            }
            else {
                $matrix[$i][$j]{score}   = $left_score;
                $matrix[$i][$j]{pointer} = "left";
            }
        } else {
            if ($up_score >= $left_score) {
```

Example 3-2. Local alignment with the Smith-Waterman algorithm (continued)

```
                $matrix[$i][$j]{score}   = $up_score;
                $matrix[$i][$j]{pointer} = "up";
            }
            else {
                $matrix[$i][$j]{score}   = $left_score;
                $matrix[$i][$j]{pointer} = "left";
            }
        }

        # set maximum score
        if ($matrix[$i][$j]{score} > $max_score) {
            $max_i     = $i;
            $max_j     = $j;
            $max_score = $matrix[$i][$j]{score};
        }
    }
}

# trace-back

my $align1 = "";
my $align2 = "";

my $j = $max_j;
my $i = $max_i;

while (1) {
    last if $matrix[$i][$j]{pointer} eq "none";

    if ($matrix[$i][$j]{pointer} eq "diagonal") {
        $align1 .= substr($seq1, $j-1, 1);
        $align2 .= substr($seq2, $i-1, 1);
        $i--; $j--;
    }
    elsif ($matrix[$i][$j]{pointer} eq "left") {
        $align1 .= substr($seq1, $j-1, 1);
        $align2 .= "-";
        $j--;
    }
    elsif ($matrix[$i][$j]{pointer} eq "up") {
        $align1 .= "-";
        $align2 .= substr($seq2, $i-1, 1);
        $i--;
    }
}

$align1 = reverse $align1;
$align2 = reverse $align2;
print "$align1\n";
print "$align2\n";
```

Dynamic Programming

Now that you've seen the typical approach to global and local alignment, consider the generality of dynamic programming. The advantage of DP can be seen in the fill phase. Each cell represents the maximum scoring alignment between the two sequences up to that point. When you calculate the next cell, you use previously stored values. In other words, DP is an optimizing function whose definition is extended as the algorithm proceeds.

Algorithmic Complexity

The complexity of algorithms is often described in big-O notation, a shorthand for the asymptotic behavior of the algorithm. For example, searching for a name in a phone book by starting at the beginning and going name-by-name takes on average, $n/2$ operations, where n is the number of names in the phone book. Such a search has $O(n)$ time complexity (constants are dropped from the notation). It scales linearly in time; a phone book twice as long takes twice as long to search. An approach that scales more efficiently successively splits the phone book in half based on the alphabetical order. This is called a *binary search* and has $O(\log_2 n)$ complexity. For example, a phone book eight times longer takes only three times longer to search. The alignment algorithms as described have $O(nm)$ complexity in both time and memory, where n and m are the lengths of the sequences. It's also common to label such algorithms as $O(n2)$ and speak of them as scaling quadratically.

Global Versus Local

Although global and local alignment are mechanistically similar, they have very different properties. Consider the alignment between the genomic sequence of two eukaryotic genes from distantly related organisms. You'd expect the exons to remain the same because their coding sequences are evolutionarily constrained, but the introns may no longer be recognizably similar, especially if they have acquired many insertions or deletions. The problem is that exons may account for only 1 to 2 percent of the sequence. As a result, a global alignment between these sequences is an alignment of mostly random letters. In such a scenario, it's very likely (especially if introns change size, as they often do) that the exons will not align to one another because their score contribution is very small compared to the rest of the sequence. In contrast, local alignment can pick out conserved exons, but unfortunately, just the maximum scoring one. The shortcomings of the standard alignment algorithms have been addressed by numerous variants.

Variations

The algorithms as described and implemented earlier are rarely used. Over the years, important innovations have made the general algorithms more applicable to aligning biological sequences and running efficiently in a computer.

Gap Modifications

Most alignment algorithms employ *affine gaps*. The previous description used a simple gap-scoring scheme in which every letter inserted or deleted cost the same amount. This isn't a very good model of biology because large gaps tend to occur fairly often. To better model this phenomenon, affine gaps are used where there is a greater penalty for opening a gap than extending the gap. Figure 3-7 shows a graphical view.

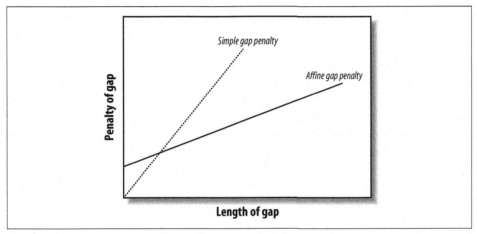

Figure 3-7. Comparison of simple and affine gap scoring schemes

Affine gap penalties are a simple modification to either algorithm. All you need to do is to record a third value in each cell of the matrix that keeps track of whether a gap has already been opened or not and then assign the appropriate gap penalty. Some algorithms even allow multiple gap scoring schemes so that very long gaps are not penalized as much. You can visualize how this works by following the minimal penalty in Figure 3-7. These algorithms are slightly more complicated because scores for each affine gap must be tracked. Usually two affine penalties are employed, and the algorithms are labeled *double affine*.

Reduced Memory

You shouldn't attempt to align long sequences (e.g., genomic DNA) with the versions of Needleman-Wunsch and Smith-Waterman described in Examples 3-1 and

3-2. The number of cells in the alignment matrix is the product of the sequence lengths, and each cell may take 8 bytes or more of memory. Therefore, aligning two 100,000-bp DNA sequences requires approximately 80 gigabytes (GB) of RAM. Fortunately, there are linear-memory versions of the algorithms.

You may have noticed during the fill phase of the algorithms that you use only two rows at a time. The other rows just sit there, either waiting to be calculated or waiting for the trace-back. Why not just use two rows at a time and not allocate the whole matrix? If you do this, you can calculate the score of the maximum scoring alignment and record its ending coordinates. By reversing direction, you can then compute the starting coordinates. Unfortunately, you lose the ability to perform a trace-back. But the memory required is now just two times the length of one of the sequences rather than the product of the two sequences. Using this approach, you can compare two 100,000-bp DNA sequences in just 1.6 megabytes (MB) of RAM. The alignment algorithm is now $O(n)$ in memory, but still $O(nm)$ in time.

How do you get the actual alignment? Given the coordinates of the maximum scoring alignment you can restrict the search space to a region between the two endpoints (Figure 3-8). With this approach, a diagonal line is drawn between the endpoints, and the search space is restricted to a certain number of cells on either side of the diagonal. The width of the search space is called the bandwidth. If the bandwidth is too small, the alignment will walk along the edge of the band and may no longer follow the path of the maximum score. If the bandwidth is needlessly large, both memory and computation are wasted. Now that the search space is sufficiently small, you can perform a complete fill and trace-back. However, if the alignment is especially large, even this restricted space can be quite large. For this reason, it is common to use a divide-and-conquer strategy that requires twice the computation, but very little memory.

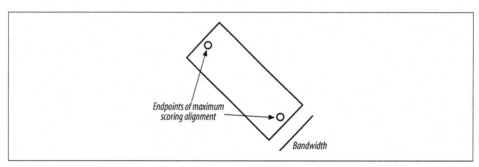

Figure 3-8. Banded alignment

In Example 3-2, most of the cells had a score of zero. Doesn't it seem a waste of time and memory to explore regions in which the score is poor? Why not make alignments only where positive scores are likely? That's exactly the thinking behind BLAST, as discussed in Chapter 5.

Aligning Transcripts to Genomic Sequence

Determining the correct exon-intron structure of genes isn't always easy. One very successful approach is to align transcripts back to their origin in a genome. However, this isn't as simple as it may appear. Several solutions to this problem use either global or local techniques.

A global alignment between a transcript and a genomic sequence is expected to have huge gaps corresponding to the introns. In eukaryotic genomes, such as the human genome, exons may account for only 1 to 2 percent of a genome. As a result, the gap scores may completely dominate the scoring function, and the alignment may be of little consequence. If the gap costs are too low, the alignment may spread out, and exons may not be faithfully aligned. These problems are largely solved by gapping with double affine penalties, but there are still potential problems with short exons and introns.

A standard local alignment between a transcript and a genome typically identifies the longest exon as the maximum scoring pair. This isn't as useful, but many local alignment algorithms, like BLAST, produce more than one alignment. With these variants, mapping a transcript back to a genome is simply a matter of chaining the individual alignments together. This turns out to be another tricky problem, but it works well most of the time

Final Thoughts

When you use the Needleman-Wunsch or Smith-Waterman algorithms to find the maximum scoring alignment, you're playing by computational, not biological, rules. As a result, the maximum scoring alignment only approximates the truth. However, even if all the nuances of biology were clear and you could code this in a computer algorithm, you might still favor the approximation because the computational cost of the correct algorithm can be excessive. In any case, the fact that you can align the unrelated words pelican and coelacanth merits consideration. It's possible to align any sequence; finding proper meaning in alignments is up to the user, not the algorithm.

Further Reading

For more information on the Perl programming language, consider these books:

Christiansen, Tom and Nathan Torkington, *Perl Cookbook* (O'Reilly & Associates).

Schwartz, Randal L. and Tom Phoenix, *Learning Perl* (O'Reilly).

Tisdall, James, *Beginning Perl for Bioinformatics* (O'Reilly).

Wall, Larry, Tom Christiansen, and Jon Orwant, *Programming Perl* (O'Reilly).

The following texts are indispensable resources for information on sequence alignment and algorithms in general:

Cormen, Thomas H. et al., *Introduction to Algorithms* (MIT Press).

Gusfield, Dan, *Algorithms on Strings, Trees, and Sequences: Computer Science and Computational Biology* (Cambridge University Press).

## CHAPTER 4

Sequence Similarity

The fact that the human genome is often referred to as the Book of Life is an apt description because nucleic acids and proteins are often represented (and manipulated) as text files. Chapter 3 described common algorithms for aligning sequences of letters, and *score* is the metric used to determine the best alignment. This chapter shows what scores really are. Some of the introduced terms come from information theory, so the chapter begins with a brief introduction to this branch of mathematics. It then explores the typical ways to measure sequence similarity. You'll see that this approach fits well with the sequence-alignment algorithms described in Chapter 3. The last part of the chapter focuses on the statistical significance of sequence similarity in a database search. The theories discussed in this chapter apply only to local alignment. There is currently no theory for global alignment.

Introduction to Information Theory

In common usage, the word *information* conveys many things. Forget everything you know about this word because you're going to learn the most precise definition. Information is a decrease in uncertainty. You can also think of information as a degree of surprise.

Suppose you're taking care of a child and the response to every question you ask is "no." The child is very predictable, and you are pretty certain of the answer the next time you ask a question. There's no surprise, no information, and no communication. If another child answers "yes" or "no" to some questions, you can communicate a little, but you can communicate more if her vocabulary was greater. If you ask "do you like ice cream," which most children do, you would be informed by either answer, but more surprised if the answer was "no." Qualitatively, you expect more information to be conveyed by a greater vocabulary and from surprising answers. Thus, the information or surprise of an answer is inversely proportional to its probability. Quantitatively, information is represented by either one of the following equivalent formulations shown in Equation 4-1.

$$H(p) = \log_2 \frac{1}{p} \qquad\qquad H(p) = -\log_2 p$$

Equation 4-1.

The information, H, associated with some probability p, is by convention the base 2 logarithm of the inverse of p. Values converted to base 2 logarithms are given the unit *bits*, which is a contraction of the words *binary* and *digit* (it is also common to use base e, and the corresponding unit is *nats*). For example, if the probability that a child doesn't like ice cream is 0.25, this answer has 2 bits of information (liking ice cream has 0.41 bits).

It is typical to describe information as a *message* of *symbols* emitted from a *source*. For example, tossing a coin is a source of head and tail symbols, and a message of such symbols might be:

```
tththttt
```

Similarly, the numbers 1, 2, 3, 4, 5, and 6 are symbols emitted from a six-sided die source, and the letters A, C, G, and T are emitted from a DNA source. The symbols emitted by a source have a frequency distribution. If there are n symbols and the frequency distribution is flat, as it is for a fair coin or die, the probability of any particular symbol is simply $1/n$. It follows that the information of any symbol is $\log_2(n)$, and this value is also the average. The formal name for the average information per symbol is *entropy*.

But what if all symbols aren't equally probable? To compute the entropy, you need to weigh the information of each symbol by its probability of occurring. This formulation, known as Shannon's Entropy (named after Claude Shannon), is shown in Equation 4-2.

$$H = -\sum_{i}^{n} p_i \log_2 p_i$$

Equation 4-2.

Entropy (H) is the negative sum over all the symbols (n) of the probability of a symbol (p_i) multiplied by the log base 2 of the probability of a symbol ($\log_2 p_i$). Let's work through a couple of examples to make this clear. Start with the flip of a coin and assume that h and t each have a probability 0.5 and therefore a $\log_2$ probability of -1. The entropy of a coin is therefore:

```
- ( (0.5)(-1) + (0.5)(-1) ) = 1 bit
```

Suppose you have a trick coin that comes up heads 3/4 of the time. Since you're a little more certain of the outcome, you expect the entropy to decrease. The entropy of your trick coin is:

```
- ( (0.75)(-0.415) + (0.25)(-2) ) = 0.81 bits
```

A random DNA source has an entropy of:

```
- ( (0.25)(-2) + (0.25)(-2) + (0.25)(-2) + (0.25)(-2) ) = 2 bits
```

However, a DNA source that emits 90 percent A or T and 10 percent G or C has an entropy of:

```
- ( 2(0.45)(-1.15) + 2(0.05)(-4.32) ) = 1.47 bits
```

In these examples, you've been given the frequency distribution as some kind of truth. But it's rare to know such things *a priori*, and the parameters must be estimated from actual data. You may find the following Perl program informative and entertaining. It calculates the entropy of any file.

```perl
# Shannon Entropy Calculator
my %Count;      # stores the counts of each symbol
my $total = 0;  # total symbols counted

while (<>) {                          # read lines of input
    foreach my $char (split(//, $_)) { # split the line into characters
        $Count{$char}++;              # add one to this character count
        $total++;                     # add one to total counts
    }
}

my $H = 0;                   # H is the entropy
foreach my $char (keys %Count) {  # iterate through characters
    my $p = $Count{$char}/$total;  # probability of character
    $H += $p * log($p);           # p * log(p)
}
$H = -$H/log(2);             # negate sum, convert base e to base 2
print "H = $H bits\n";       # output
```

Amino Acid Similarity

Molecular biologists usually think of amino acid similarity in terms of chemical similarity (see Table 2-1). Figure 4-1 depicts a rough qualitative categorization. From an evolutionary standpoint, you expect mutations that radically change chemical properties to be rare because they may end up destroying the protein's three-dimensional structure. Conversely, changes between similar amino acids should happen relatively frequently.

In the late '60s and early '70s, Margaret Dayhoff pioneered quantitative techniques for measuring amino acid similarity. Using sequences that were available at the time, she constructed multiple alignments of related proteins and compared the frequencies of amino acid substitutions. As expected, there is quite a bit of variation in amino acid substitution frequency, and the patterns are generally what you'd expect from the chemical properties. For example, phenylalanine (F) is most frequently paired to itself. It is also found relatively frequently with tyrosine (Y) and tryptophan (W), which share similar aromatic ring structures (see Table 2-1), and to a lesser

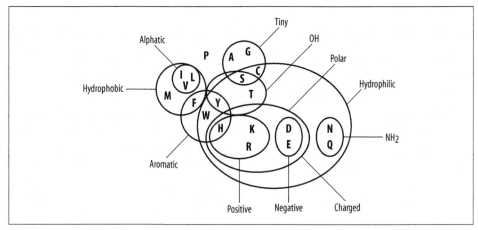

Figure 4-1. Amino acid chemical relationships

extent with the other hydrophobic amino acids (M, V, I, and L). Phenylalanine is infrequently paired with hydrophilic amino acids (R, K, D, E, and others). You can see some of these patterns in the following multiple alignment, which corresponds to a portion of the *cytochrome b* protein from various organisms.

```
PGNPFATPLEILPEWYLYPVFQILRVLPNKLLGIACQGAIPLGLMMVPFIE
PANPFATPLEILPEWYFYPVFQILRTVPNKLLGVLAMAAVPVGLLTVPFIE
PANPMSTPAHIVPEWYFLPVYAILRSIPNKLGGVAAIGLVFVSLLALPFIN
PANPLVTPPHIKPEWYFLFAYAILRSIPNKLGGVLALLFSILMLLLVPFLH
PANPLSTPAHIKPEWYFLFAYAILRSIPNKLGGVLALLLSILVLIFIPMLQ
PANPLSTPPHIKPEWYFLFAYAILRSIPNKLGGVLALLLSILILIFIPMLQ
IANPMNTPTHIKPEWYFLFAYSILRAIPNKLGGVIGLVMSILIL..YIMIF
ESDPMMSPVHIVPEWYFLFAYAILRAIPNKVLGVVSLFASILVL..VVFVL
IVDTLKTSDKILPEWFFLYLFGFLKAIPDKFMGLFLMVILLFSL..FLFIL
```

Dayhoff represented the similarity between amino acids as a $\log_2$ odds ratio, also known as a *lod score*. To derive the lod score of an amino acid, take the $\log_2$ of the ratio of a pairing's observed frequency divided by the pairing's random expected frequency. If the observed and expected frequencies are equal, the lod score is zero. A positive score indicates that a pair of letters is common, while a negative score indicates an unlikely pairing. The general formula for any pair of amino acids is shown in Equation 4-3.

$$S_{ij} = \log(q_{ij}/p_i p_j)$$

Equation 4-3.

The score of two amino acids i and j, is s_{ij}, their individual probabilities are p_i and p_j, and their frequency of pairing is q_{ij}. For example, suppose the frequencies of methionine (M) and leucine (L) in your data set are 0.01 and 0.1, respectively. By random pairing, you expect 1/1000 amino acid pairs to be M-L. If the observed frequency of pairing is 1/500, the odds ratio is 2/1. Converting this to a base 2 logarithm gives a lod score of +1, or 1 bit. Similarly, if the frequency of arginine (R) is 0.1 and its frequency of pairing with L is 1/500, the lod score of an R-L pair is -2.322 bits. In computers, using base e rather than base 2 is more convenient. The values of +1 and -2.322 bits are 0.6931 and -1.609 nats, respectively.

If you know the direction of change from an evolutionary tree, the pair-wise scores can be asymmetric. That is, the score of M-L and L-M may not be equal. For simplicity, the direction of evolution is usually ignored, though, and the scores are symmetrical.

Scoring Matrices

A two-dimensional matrix containing all possible pair-wise amino acid scores is called a *scoring matrix*. Scoring matrices are also called substitution matrices because the scores represent relative rates of evolutionary substitutions. Scoring matrices are evolution in a nutshell. Take a moment now to peruse the scoring matrix in Figure 4-2 and compare it to the chemical groupings in Figure 4-1.

	A	R	N	D	C	Q	E	G	H	I	L	K	M	F	P	S	T	W	Y
A	4	-1	-2	-2	0	-1	-1	0	-2	-1	-1	-1	-1	-2	-1	1	0	-3	-2
R	-1	5	0	-2	-3	1	0	-2	0	-3	-2	2	-1	-3	-2	-1	-1	-3	-2
N	-2	0	6	1	-3	0	0	0	1	-3	-3	0	-2	-3	-2	1	0	-4	-2
D	-2	-2	1	6	-3	0	2	-1	-1	-3	-4	-1	-3	-3	-1	0	-1	-4	-3
C	0	-3	-3	-3	9	-3	-4	-3	-3	-1	-1	-3	-1	-2	-3	-1	-1	-2	-2
Q	-1	1	0	0	-3	5	2	-2	0	-3	-2	1	0	-3	-1	0	-1	-2	-1
E	-1	0	0	2	-4	2	5	-2	0	-3	-3	1	-2	-3	-1	0	-1	-3	-2
G	0	-2	0	-1	-3	-2	-2	6	-2	-4	-4	-2	-3	-3	-2	0	-2	-2	-3
H	-2	0	1	-1	-3	0	0	-2	8	-3	-3	-1	-2	-1	-2	-1	-2	-2	2
I	-1	-3	-3	-3	-1	-3	-3	-4	-3	4	2	-3	1	0	-3	-2	-1	-3	-1
L	-1	-2	-3	-4	-1	-2	-3	-4	-3	2	4	-2	2	0	-3	-2	-1	-2	-1
K	-1	2	0	-1	-3	1	1	-2	-1	-3	-2	5	-1	-3	-1	0	-1	-3	-2
M	-1	-1	-2	-3	-1	0	-2	-3	-2	1	2	-1	5	0	-2	-1	-1	-1	-1
F	-2	-3	-3	-3	-2	-3	-3	-3	-1	0	0	-3	0	6	-4	-2	-2	1	3
P	-1	-2	-2	-1	-3	-1	-1	-2	-2	-3	-3	-1	-2	-4	7	-1	-1	-4	-3
S	1	-1	1	0	-1	0	0	0	-1	-2	-2	0	-1	-2	-1	4	1	-3	-2
T	0	-1	0	-1	-1	-1	-1	-2	-2	-1	-1	-1	-1	-2	-1	1	5	-2	-2
W	-3	-3	-4	-4	-2	-2	-3	-2	-2	-3	-2	-3	-1	1	-4	-3	-2	11	2
Y	-2	-2	-2	-3	-2	-1	-2	-3	2	-1	-1	-2	-1	3	-3	-2	-2	2	7
V	0	-3	-3	-3	-1	-2	-2	-3	-3	3	1	-2	1	-1	-2	-2	0	-3	-1

Figure 4-2. BLOSUM62 scoring matrix

Lod scores are real numbers but are usually represented as integers in text files and computer programs. To retain precision, the scores are generally multiplied by some scaling factor before converting them to integers. For example, a lod score of -1.609 nats may be scaled by a factor of two and then rounded off to an integer value of -3. Scores that have been scaled and converted to integers have a unitless quantity and are called *raw scores*.

PAM and BLOSUM Matrices

Two different kinds of amino acid scoring matrices, PAM (Percent Accepted Mutation) and BLOSUM (BLOcks SUbstitution Matrix), are in wide use. The PAM matrices were created by Margaret Dayhoff and coworkers and are thus sometimes referred to as the Dayhoff matrices. These scoring matrices have a strong theoretical component and make a few evolutionary assumptions. The BLOSUM matrices, on the other hand, are more empirical and derive from a larger data set. Most researchers today prefer to use BLOSUM matrices because *in silico* experiments indicate that searches employing BLOSUM matrices have higher sensitivity.

There are several PAM matrices, each one with a numeric suffix. The PAM1 matrix was constructed with a set of proteins that were all 85 percent or more identical to one another. The other matrices in the PAM set were then constructed by multiplying the PAM1 matrix by itself: 100 times for the PAM100; 160 times for the PAM160; and so on, in an attempt to model the course of sequence evolution. Though highly theoretical (and somewhat suspect), it is certainly a reasonable approach. There was little protein sequence data in the 1970s when these matrices were created, so this approach was a good way to extrapolate to larger distances.

Protein databases contained many more sequences by the 1990s so a more empirical approach was possible. The BLOSUM matrices were constructed by extracting ungapped segments, or *blocks,* from a set of multiply aligned protein families, and then further clustering these blocks on the basis of their percent identity. The blocks used to derive the BLOSUM62 matrix, for example, all have at least 62 percent identity to some other member of the block.

Why, then, are the BLOSUM matrices better than the PAM matrices with respect to BLAST? One possible answer is that the extrapolation employed in PAM matrices magnifies small errors in the mutation probabilities for short evolutionary time periods. Another possibility is that the forces governing sequence evolution over short evolutionary times are different from those shaping sequences over longer intervals, and you can't estimate distant substitution frequencies without alignments from distantly related proteins.

Target Frequencies, lambda, and H

The most important property of a scoring matrix is its *target frequencies* and the expected frequencies of the individual amino acid pairs. Target frequencies represent the underlying evolutionary model. While scoring matrices don't actually contain the target frequencies, they are implicit in the scores.

The Karlin-Altschul statistical theory on which BLAST is based (discussed in the next section) states that all scoring schemes for which a positive score is possible (and the expected score is negative) have implicit target frequencies. Thus they are lod-odds scoring schemes; even a simple "+1 match -1 mismatch" scheme is implicitly a log-odds scoring scheme and has target frequencies. You'll learn how to calculate those frequencies in just a bit, but you first need to understand two additional concepts associated with scoring schemes: lambda and relative entropy.

Lambda

Raw score can be a misleading quantity because scaling factors are arbitrary. A *normalized score*, corresponding to the original lod score, is therefore a more useful measure. Converting a raw score to a normalized score requires a matrix-specific constant called *lambda* (or λ). Lambda is approximately the inverse of the original scaling factor, but its value may be slightly different due to integer rounding errors. Let's now derive lambda.

When calculating target frequencies from multiple alignments, the sum of all target frequencies naturally sums to 1 (see Equation 4-4).

$$\sum_{i=1}^{n} \sum_{j=1}^{i} q_{ij} = 1$$

Equation 4-4.

Recall from Equation 4-3 that the score of two amino acids is the log-odds ratio of the observed and expected frequencies. The same equation is presented in Equation 4-5, but the lod score is replaced by the product of lambda and the raw score (in other words, lambda had a value of 1 in Equation 4-3).

$$\lambda S_{ij} = \log_e(q_{ij}/p_i p_j)$$

Equation 4-5.

Equation 4-6 rearranges Equation 4-5 to solve for pair-wise frequency.

$$q_{ij} = p_i p_j e^{\lambda S_{ij}}$$

Equation 4-6.

From Equation 4-6, you can see that a pair-wise frequency (q_{ij}) is implied from individual amino acid frequencies (p_i and p_j) and a normalized score (λS_{ij}). The key to solving for lambda is to provide the individual amino acid frequencies (p_i and p_j) and find a value for lambda where the sum of the implied target frequencies equals one. The formulation is given in Equation 4-7 and later in Example 4-1.

$$\sum_{i=1}^{n}\sum_{j=1}^{i} q_{ij} = \sum_{i=1}^{n}\sum_{j=1}^{i} p_i p_j e^{\lambda S_{ij}} = 1$$

Equation 4-7.

Normally, once lambda is estimated, it is used to calculate the Expect of every HSP in the BLAST report. Unfortunately, the residue frequencies of some proteins deviate widely from the residue frequencies used to construct the original scoring matrix. Recently, some versions of PSI-BLAST and BLASTP have therefore begun to use the query and subject sequence amino acid compositions to calculate a *composition-based lambda*. These "hit-specific" lambdas have been shown to improve BLAST sensitivity, so this approach may see wider use in the near future.

Relative Entropy

The *expected score* of a scoring matrix is the sum of its raw scores weighted by their frequencies of occurrence (see Equation 4-8). The expected score should always be negative.

$$E = \sum_{i=1}^{20}\sum_{j=1}^{i} p_i p_j S_{ij}$$

Equation 4-8.

The *relative entropy* of a scoring matrix (*H*) conveniently summarizes the general behavior of a scoring matrix. Its formulation is similar to the expected score (see Equation 4-9) but is calculated from normalized scores. *H* is the average number of bits (or nats) per position in an alignment and is always positive.

$$H = -\sum_{i=1}^{20}\sum_{j=1}^{i} q_{ij}\lambda S_{ij}$$

Equation 4-9.

H of PAM1 is greater than the *H* PAM120. Recall that the PAM120 matrix is derived from mutation probabilities for PAM1 extrapolated to 120 PAMs. The PAM120 matrix is therefore less specific, contains less information, and thus has a lower *H*. Similarly, BLOSUM80 has a greater *H* than BLOSUM62. This makes sense since BLOSUM80 was made from sequences that were more similar to one another than BLOSUM62.

Which PAM matrix is most similar to BLOSUM45? To answer this, you only need to determine the PAM matrix with an *H* closest to that of the BLOSUM45 matrix. By relative entropy, PAM250 is closest to BLOSUM45, PAM120 to BLOSUM80, and PAM180 to BLOSUM62.

Match-Mismatch Scoring

Now let's determine the target frequencies of a +1/-1 scoring scheme. We will explore this in the case of DNA alignments where match/mismatch scoring is frequently employed. For generality, assume that all nucleotide frequencies are equal to 0.25. This fixes the previous p_i and p_j terms. Example 4-1 shows a Perl script that contains an implementation for estimating lambda by making increasingly refined guesses at its value. Table 4-1 displays the expected score, lambda, H, and the expected percent identity for several nucleotide scoring schemes. Note that the match/mismatch ratio determines H and percent identity. As the ratio approaches 0, lambda approaches 2 bits, and the target frequency approaches 100 percent identity. Intuitively, this makes sense; if the mismatch score is -∞, all alignments have 100 percent identity, and observing an A is the same as observing an A-A pair.

Table 4-1. Nucleotide scoring schemes

Match	Mismatch	Expected score	λ (bits)	H (bits)	% ID
+10	-10	-5	0.158	0.793	75
+1	-1	-0.5	1.58	0.791	75
+1	-2	-1.25	1.92	1.62	95
+1	-3	-2	1.98	1.89	99
+5	-4	-1.75	0.277	0.519	65

Example 4-1. A Perl script for estimating lambda

```perl
#!/usr/bin/perl -w
use strict;
use constant Pn => 0.25; # probability of any nucleotide

die "usage: $0 <match> <mismatch>\n" unless @ARGV == 2;
my ($match, $mismatch) = @ARGV;
my $expected_score = $match * 0.25 + $mismatch * 0.75;
die "illegal scores\n" if $match <= 0 or $expected_score >= 0;

# calculate lambda
my ($lambda, $high, $low) = (1, 2, 0); # initial estimates
while ($high - $low > 0.001) {        # precision

    # calculate the sum of all normalized scores
    my $sum = Pn * Pn * exp($lambda * $match)    * 4
            + Pn * Pn * exp($lambda * $mismatch) * 12;

    # refine guess at lambda
    if ($sum > 1) {
        $high = $lambda;
```

Example 4-1. A Perl script for estimating lambda (continued)

```perl
        $lambda = ($lambda + $low)/2;
    }
    else {
        $low = $lambda;
        $lambda = ($lambda + $high)/2;
    }
}

# compute target frequency and H
my $targetID = Pn * Pn * exp($lambda * $match) * 4;
my $H = $lambda * $match     *       $targetID
      + $lambda * $mismatch * (1 -$targetID);

# output
print "expscore: $expected_score\n";
print "lambda:   $lambda nats (", $lambda/log(2), " bits)\n";
print "H:        $H nats (", $H/log(2), " bits)\n";
print "%ID:      ", $targetID * 100, "\n";
```

Sequence Similarity

Sequence similarity is a simple extension of amino acid or nucleotide similarity. To determine it, sum up the individual pair-wise scores in an alignment. For example, the raw score of the following BLAST alignment under the BLOSUM62 matrix is 72. Converting 72 to a normalized score is as simple as multiplying by lambda. (Note that for BLAST statistical calculations, the normalized score is $\lambda S - \ln k$.)

```
Query:   885 QCPVCHKKYSNALVLQQHIRLHTGE 909
             +C VC K ++     L++H RLHTGE
Sbjct:   267 ECDVCSKSFTTKYFLKKHKRLHTGE 291
```

Recall from Chapter 3 that the score of each pair of letters is considered independently from the rest of the alignment. This is the same idea. There is a convenient synergy between alignment algorithms and alignment scores. However, when treating the letters independently of one another, you lose contextual information. Can you assume that the probability of A followed by G is the same as the probability of G followed by A? In a natural language such as English, you know that this doesn't make sense. In English, Q is always followed by U. If you treat these letters independently, you lose this restriction. The context rules for biological sequences aren't as strict as for English, but there are tendencies. For example, low entropy sequences appear by chance much more frequently than expected. To avoid becoming sidetracked by the details, accept that you're using an approximation, and note that in practice, it works well.

Karlin-Altschul Statistics

In 1990, Samuel Karlin and Stephen Altschul published a theory of local alignment statistics. Karlin-Altschul statistics make five central assumptions:

- A positive score must be possible.
- The expected score must be negative.
- The letters of the sequences are independent and identically distributed (IID).
- The sequences are infinitely long.
- Alignments don't contain gaps.

The first two assumptions are true for any scoring matrix estimated from real data. The last three assumptions are problematic because biological sequences have context dependencies, aren't infinitely long, and are frequently aligned with gaps. You now know that both alignment and sequence similarity assume independence, and that this is a necessary convenience. You will soon see how sequence length and gaps can be accounted for. For now, though, let's turn to the Karlin-Altschul equation (see Equation 4-10):

$$E = kmne^{-\lambda S}$$

Equation 4-10.

This equation states that the number of alignments expected by chance (*E*) during a sequence database search is a function of the size of the search space (*m*n*), the normalized score (λS), and a minor constant (*k*).

In a database search, the size of the search space is simply the product of the number of letters in the query (*m*) and the number of letters in the database (*n*). A small adjustment (*k*) takes into account the fact that optimal local alignment scores for alignments that start at different places in the two sequences may be highly correlated. For example, a high-scoring alignment starting at residues 1, 1 implies a pretty high alignment score for an alignment starting at residues 2, 2 as well. The value of *k* is usually around 0.1, and its impact on the statistics of alignment scores is relatively minor, so don't bother with its derivation. According to Equation 4-10 the relationship between the expected number of alignments and the search space (*mn*) is linear. If the size of the search space is doubled, the expected number of alignments with a particular score also doubles. The relationship between the expected number of alignments and score is exponential. This means that small changes in score can lead to large differences in *E*.

Gapped Alignments

In practice, gaps reduce the stringency of a scoring scheme. In other words, an alignment score of 30 occurs more often in collection of gapped alignments than it does in a similar collection of ungapped alignments. How much more often depends on the cost of the gaps relative to the scoring matrix values. To determine the statistical significance of gapped alignments with Karlin-Altschul statistics (Equation 4-10), you must find values for lambda, k, and H for a particular scoring matrix and its associated gap initiation and extension costs. Unfortunately, you can't do this analytically, and the values must be estimated empirically. The procedure involves aligning random sequences with a specific scoring scheme and observing the alignment properties (scores, target frequencies, and lengths). The ungapped scoring matrix whose behavior is most similar to the gapped scoring scheme provides values for lambda, k, and H.

In the Karlin-Altschul theory, the distribution of alignment scores follows an extreme value distribution, a distribution that looks similar to a normal (Gaussian) distribution but falls off more quickly on one side and more slowly on the other side. Experiments show that gapped alignment scores fit the extreme value distribution as well. This fit is important because it strongly suggests that applying empirically derived values for lambda, k, and H to gapped alignment is statistically valid. Table 4-2 shows how much the parameters change by allowing gaps given the BLOSUM62 scoring matrix (also see Appendixes A and C).

Table 4-2. Effect of gaps on BLOSUM62

Gap open	Gap extend	λ	k	H (nats)
No gaps allowed	No gaps allowed	0.318	0.134	0.40
11	2	0.297	0.082	0.27
10	2	0.291	0.075	0.23
7	2	0.239	0.027	0.10

Length Correction

The Karlin-Altschul equation (Equation 4-10) gives the search space between two sequences as $m*n$, but not all this space can be effectively explored because some portion of it lies at either end of the sequences. As discussed in Chapter 5, BLAST operates by extending seeds in the alignment space. It can't effectively extend seeds near the ends of the sequences, though, because it runs out of room.

Karlin-Altschul statistics provides a way to calculate just how long a sequence must be before it can produce an alignment with a significant Expect. This minimum length, l, is usually referred to as the *expected HSP length* (see Equation 4-11)

$$l = \ln(kmn)/H$$

Equation 4-11.

Note that the expected HSP (high scoring pair) length is dependent on the search space (m^*n) and the relative entropy of the scoring scheme, H, so it varies from search to search.

To take edge effects into account when calculating an Expect, the expected HSP length is subtracted from the actual length of the query, m, and the actual number of residues in the database, n, to give their *effective* lengths, usually denoted by m' and n', respectively (see Equations 4-12 and 4-13).

$$m' = m - l$$

Equation 4-12.

$$n' = n - (l \cdot \text{number\_of\_squences\_in\_db})$$

Equation 4-13.

In a large search space, the expected HSP length may be greater than the length of the query, resulting in a negative effective length, m'. In practice, if the effective length is less than $1/k$, it is set to $1/k$, as doing so cancels the contribution of the short sequence to the Expect; setting $m' = 1/k$ for example, gives $E = n'e^{-\lambda S}$, a formulation independent of m'.

Unfortunately, effective lengths of less than $1/k$ aren't uncommon today. Because $l \alpha n$, the large size on many sequence databases can result in large expected HSP lengths. In fact it's not uncommon to see expected HSP lengths approaching 200 when searching some of the larger protein databases. Keep in mind that the average protein is ~300 amino acids long; thus, for many searches, m' is being set to $1/k$ routinely. Recent work by S.F. Altschul and colleagues has suggested that part of the problem may be that Equation 4-11 overestimates l. They have proposed another way to calculate this value that results in shorter effective HSP lengths. Thus, the method used to calculate l may change in the not so distant future.

Sum Statistics and Sum Scores

BLAST uses Equation 4-14 to calculate the normalized score of an individual HSP, but it uses a different function to calculate the normalized score of group of HSPs (see Chapter 7 for more information about sum statistics).

$$S'_{nats} = \lambda S - \ln k$$

Equation 4-14.

Before tackling the actual method used by BLAST to calculate a sum score, it's helpful to consider the problem from a general perspective. One simple and intuitive approach for calculating a sum score might be to sum the raw scores, s_r for a set of HSPs, and then convert that sum to a normalized score by multiplying by λ, or in mathematical terms (see Equation 4-15).

$$S'_{sum} = \lambda \sum_{i=1}^{r} S_r$$

Equation 4-15.

The problem with such an approach is that summing the scores for a collection of r HSPs, always results in a higher score, even if none or those HSPs has a significant score on its own. In practice, BLAST controls for this by penalizing the sum score by a factor proportional to the product of the number of HSPs, r, and the search space as shown in Equation 4-16.

$$S'_{sum} = \lambda \sum_{i=1}^{r} S_r - r\ln(kmn)$$

Equation 4-16.

Equation 4-16 is sometimes referred to as an *unordered-sum score* and is suitable for calculating the sum score for a collection of noncollinear HSPs. Ideally, though, you should use a sum score formulation that rewards a collection of HSPs if they are collinear with regards to their query and subject coordinates because the HSPs comprising real BLAST hits often have this property. BLASTX hits for example often consist of collinear HSPs corresponding to the sequential exons of a gene. Equation 4-17 is a sum score formulation that does just that.

$$S'_{sum} = \lambda \sum_{i=1}^{r} S_r - r\ln(kmn) + \ln(r!)$$

Equation 4-17.

Equation 4-18 is sometimes referred to as a *pair-wise ordered sum score*. Note the additional term $\ln r!$, which can be thought of as a bonus added to the sum score when the HSPs under consideration are all consistently ordered.

One shortcoming of Equations 4-16 and 4-17 is that they invoke a sizable penalty for adding an additional HSP raw score to the sum score. To improve the sensitivity of its sum statistics, NCBI-BLASTX employs a modified version of the pair-wise ordered sum score (Equation 4-17) that is influenced less by the search space and contains a term for the size of the gaps between the HSPs (Equation 4-18). The advantage of this formulation is that the gap size, g, rather than the search space, mn, is multiplied by r. For short gaps and big search spaces, this formulation results in larger sum scores.

$$S'_{sum} = \lambda \sum_{i=1}^{r} S_r - \ln(kmn) - (r-1) \cdot (\ln(k) + 2\ln(g)) - \log(r!)$$

Equation 4-18.

Converting a Sum Score to a Sum Probability

The aggregate pair-wise P-value for a sum score can be approximated using Equation 4-19.

$$P_r \approx e^{-S_{sum}} S_{sum}^{r-1} / r!(r-1)!$$

Equation 4-19.

Thus, when sum statistics are being employed, BLAST not only uses a different score, it also uses a different formula to convert that score into a probability—the standard Karlin-Altschul equation $E = kmne^{-\lambda S}$ (Equation 4-10) isn't used to convert a sum score to an Expect.

BLAST groups a set of HSPs only if their aggregate P-value is less than the P-value of any individual member, and that group is an optimal partition such that no other grouping might result in a lower P-value. Obviously, finding these optimal groupings of HSPs requires many significance tests. It is common practice in the statistical world to multiply a P-value associated with a significant discovery by some number proportional to the number of tests performed in the course of its discovery to give a test corrected P-value. The correction function used by BLAST for this purpose is given in Equation 4-20. The resulting value, P'_r is a *pair-wise test-corrected sum-P*.

$$P'_r = P_r / \beta^{r-1}(1-\beta)$$

Equation 4-20.

In this equation, β is the gap decay constant (its value can be found in the footer of a standard BLAST report).

The final step in assigning an E-value to a group of HSPs to adjust the pair-wise test-corrected sum-P for the size of the database The formula used by NCBI-BLAST (Equation 4-21) divides the effective length of the database by the actual length of the particular database sequence in the alignment and then multiplies the pair-wise test-corrected sum-P by the result.

$$\text{Expect}(r) = (\text{effective\_db\_length}/n)P'_r$$

Equation 4-21.

NCBI-BLAST and WU-BLAST compute combined statistical significance a little differently. The previous descriptions apply to NCBI-BLAST only. The two programs probably have many similarities, but the specific formulations for WU-BLAST are unpublished.

Probability Versus Expectation

While NCBI-BLAST reports an Expect, WU-BLAST reports both the E-value and a P-value. An E-value tells you how many alignments with a given score are expected by chance. A P-value tells you how often you can expect to see such an alignment. These measures are interchangeable using Equations 4-22 and 4-23.

$$P = 1 - e^{-E}$$

Equation 4-22.

$$E = -\ln(1 - P)$$

Equation 4-23.

For values of less than 0.001, the E-value and P-value are essentially identical.

Further Reading

Altschul, S.F. (1991). "Amino acid substitution matrices from an information theoretic perspective." *Journal of Molecular Biology*, Vol. 219, pp. 555-565.

Altschul, S.F. (1997). "Evaluating the statistical significance of multiple distinct local alignments." *Theoretical and Computational Methods in Genome Research*, S. Suhai (ed.), pp. 1-14.

Altschul, S.F. (1993). "A protein alignment scoring system sensitive at all evolutionary distances." *Journal of Molecular Evolution*, Vol. 36, pp. 290-300.

Altschul, S.F., M.S. Boguski, W. Gish, and J.C. Wootton (1994). "Issues in searching molecular sequence databases." *Nature Genet.*, Vol. 6, pp. 119-129.

Altschul S.F., R. Bundschuh, R. Olsen, T. Hwa (2001) "The estimation of statistical parameters for local alignment score distributions." *Nucleic Acids Research*, January 15;29(2), pp. 351-361.

Altschul, S.F. and W. Gish (1996). "Local alignment statistics." *Meth. Enzymol.*, Vol. 266, pp. 460-480.

Dayhoff, M.O., R.M. Schwartz, and B.C. Orcutt (1978). "A model of evolutionary change in proteins." *Atlas of Protein Sequence and Structure*, Vol. 5, Suppl. 3. M. O. Dayhoff (ed.), National Biomedical Research Foundation, pp. 345-352.

Henikoff, S. and J.G. Henikoff (1992). "Amino acid substitution matrices from protein blocks." *Proceedings of the National Academy of Sciences*, Vol. 89, pp. 10915-10919.

Karlin, S. and S.F. Altschul (1993). "Applications and statistics for multiple high-scoring segments in molecular sequences." *Proceedings of the National Academy of Sciences*, Vol. 90, pp. 5873-5877.

Karlin, S. and S. F. Altschul (1990). "Methods for assessing the statistical significance of molecular sequence features by using general scoring schemes." *Proceedings of the National Academy of Sciences*, Vol. 87, pp. 2264-2268.

Schaffer A.A., Aravind L., Madden TL., Shavirin S., Spouge JL., Wolf YI., Koonin EV., Altschul SF. (2001). "Improving the accuracy of PSI-BLAST protein database searches with composition-based statistics and other refinements." *Nucleic Acids Research*, July 15;29(14), pp. 2994-3005.

Schwartz, R.M. and M.O. Dayhoff (1978). "Matrices for detecting distant relationships." *Atlas of Protein Sequence and Structure*, Vol. 5, Suppl. 3. M.O. Dayhoff (ed.), National Biomedical Research Foundation, pp. 353-358.

## PART III

Practice

## CHAPTER 5

BLAST

Previous chapters explored what biological sequences are, how they are aligned, and how similarity is measured. This chapter discusses BLAST itself. What is BLAST? The simple answer is that it is a set of programs that search sequence databases for statistically significant similarities. The details of *how* BLAST searches for similarities aren't so easily answered. Searching requires multiple steps and many controlling parameters. Understanding the theoretical framework will help you design and interpret BLAST experiments, and give you a foundation for troubleshooting when your search produces unexpected results.

The Five BLAST Programs

The five traditional BLAST programs are: BLASTN, BLASTP, BLASTX, TBLASTN, and TBLASTX. BLASTN compares nucleotide sequences to one another (hence the N). All other programs compare protein sequences (see Table 5-1).

Table 5-1. Traditional BLAST programs

Program	Database	Query	Typical uses
BLASTN	Nucleotide	Nucleotide	Mapping oligonucleotides, cDNAs, and PCR products to a genome; screening repetitive elements; cross-species sequence exploration; annotating genomic DNA; clustering sequencing reads; vector clipping
BLASTP	Protein	Protein	Identifying common regions between proteins; collecting related proteins for phylogenetic analyses
BLASTX	Protein	Nucleotide translated into protein	Finding protein-coding genes in genomic DNA; determining if a cDNA corresponds to a known protein
TBLASTN	Nucleotide translated into protein	Protein	Identifying transcripts, potentially from multiple organisms, similar to a given protein; mapping a protein to genomic DNA
TBLASTX	Nucleotide translated into protein	Nucleotide translated into protein	Cross-species gene prediction at the genome or transcript level; searching for genes missed by traditional methods or not yet in protein databases

You'll also find several BLAST derivatives and BLAST wrappers (scripts that run BLAST in a specialized way) with names such as PSI-BLAST, PHI-BLAST, Mega-BLAST, BLASTZ, XBLAST, MPBLAST, HT-BLAST, and GENE-BLAST. This book—and especially this chapter—deals primarily with the five traditional programs. If you are familiar with the details of these algorithms, you will have a solid foundation for understanding the variants.

The BLAST Algorithm

The *search space* between two sequences can be visualized as a graph with one sequence along the X-axis and the other along the Y-axis (Figure 5-1). Each point in this space represents a pairing of two letters, one from each sequence. Each pair of letters has a score that is determined by a scoring matrix whose values were determined empirically. (See Chapter 4 for more about scoring matrices.) An *alignment* is a sequence of paired letters that may contain gaps (See Chapters 3 and 4 for more about gaps). Ungapped alignments appear as diagonal lines in the search space, and the score of an ungapped alignment is simply the sum of the scores of the individual letter pairs. Alignments containing gaps appear as broken diagonals in the search space, and their score is the sum of the letter pairs minus the gap costs, which usually penalize more score points for initiating a gap than extending a gap. How can you tell the difference between two ungapped alignments and a single gapped alignment? In a BLAST report, unaligned regions aren't displayed, and gaps are represented by dashes. However, a simple change in parameters can change one into the other. The diagrams in this chapter show only one gapped alignment, which is indicated in Figure 5-1.

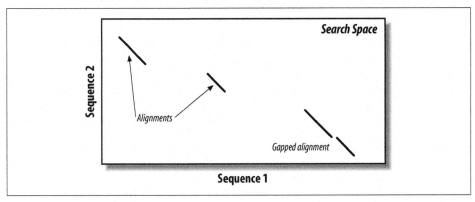

Figure 5-1. Search space and alignment

As you saw in Chapter 3, the Smith-Waterman algorithm will find the maximum scoring alignment between two sequences. Some people feel that this ability makes Smith-Waterman the gold standard of alignment algorithms, but this is true only in theory. When comparing real sequences, you may have several good alignments or none. What you really want reported is all of the statistically significant alignments; this is what BLAST does. However, unlike Smith-Waterman, BLAST doesn't explore the entire search space between two sequences. Minimizing the search space is the key to its speed but at the cost of a loss in sensitivity. You will find that the speed/sensitivity trade-off is a key concept when designing BLAST experiments. How exactly does BLAST find similarities without exploring the entire search space? It uses three layers of rules to sequentially refine potential high scoring pairs (HSPs). These heuristic layers, known as seeding, extension, and evaluation, form a stepwise refinement procedure that allows BLAST to sample the entire search space without wasting time on dissimilar regions.

Seeding

BLAST assumes that significant alignments have words in common. A *word* is simply some defined number of letters. For example, if you define a word as three letters, the sequence MGQLV has words MGQ, GQL, and QLV. When comparing two sequences, BLAST first determines the locations of all the common words, which are called *word hits* (Figure 5-2). Only those regions with word hits will be used as alignment seeds. This way, BLAST can ignore a lot of the search space.

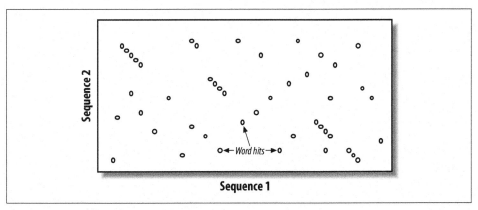

Figure 5-2. Word hits

Let's take a moment to define a word hit. A simple interpretation is that a hit is two identical words. Some significant alignments don't contain any identical words, though. Therefore, BLAST employs a more useful definition of a word hit called the neighborhood. The *neighborhood* of a word contains the word itself and all other words whose score is at least as big as T when compared via the scoring matrix. Therefore, by adjusting T it is possible to control the size of the neighborhood, and therefore the number of word hits in the search space. Table 5-2 shows the neighborhood around the word RGD, and Example 5-1 shows a Perl script for determining the neighborhood for three-letter words.

Table 5-2. The neighborhood near RGD

BLOSUM62		PAM200	
Word	**Score**	**Word**	**Score**
RGD	17	RGD	18
KGD	14	RGE	17
QGD	13	RGN	16
RGE	13	KGD	15
EGD	12	RGQ	15
HGD	12	KGE	14
NGD	12	HGD	13
RGN	12	KGN	13
AGD	11	RAD	13
MGD	11	RGA	13
RAD	11	RGG	13
RGQ	11	RGH	13
RGS	11	RGK	13
RND	11	RGS	13
RSD	11	RGT	13
SGD	11	RSD	13
TGD	11	WGD	13

Example 5-1. Determining the neighborhood for three-letter words

```perl
#!/usr/bin/perl -w
use strict;

die "usage: $0 <matrix> <word> <threshold>\n" unless @ARGV == 3;
my ($matrix_file, $WORD, $T) = @ARGV;
my @W = split(//, $WORD);
die "words must be 3 long\n" unless @W == 3;
my @A = split(//, "ARNDCQEGHILKMFPSTWYVBZX*"); # alphabet
my %S;                                        # Scoring matrix

# Read scoring matrix - use those provided by NCBI-BLAST or WU-BLAST
open(MATRIX, $matrix_file) or die;
while (<MATRIX>) {
    next unless /^[A-Z\*]/;
    my @score = split;
    my $letter = shift @score;
    for (my $i = 0; $i < @A; $i++) {
        $S{$letter}{$A[$i]} = $score[$i];
    }
}

# Calculate neighborhood
my %NH;
```

Example 5-1. Determining the neighborhood for three-letter words (continued)

```
for (my $i = 0; $i < @A; $i++) {
    my $s1 = $S{$W[0]}{$A[$i]};
    for (my $j = 0; $j < @A; $j++) {
        my $s2 = $S{$W[1]}{$A[$j]};
        for (my $k = 0; $k < @A; $k++) {
            my $s3 = $S{$W[2]}{$A[$k]};
            my $score = $s1 + $s2 + $s3;
            my $word = "$A[$i]$A[$j]$A[$k]";
            next if $word =~ /[BZX\*]/;
            $NH{$word} = $score if $score >= $T;
        }
    }
}

# Output neighborhood
foreach my $word (sort {$NH{$b} <=> $NH{$a} or $a cmp $b} keys %NH) {
    print "$word $NH{$word}\n";
}
```

The proper value for T depends on both the values in the scoring matrix and the balance between speed and sensitivity. Higher values of T progressively remove more word hits (see Figure 5-3) and reduce the search space. This makes BLAST run faster, but increases the chance of missing an alignment.

Word size (W) is another variable that controls the number of word hits. It's easy to see why a word size of 1 will produce more hits than a word size of 10. In general, if T is scaled uniformly with W, smaller word sizes increase sensitivity and decrease speed. The interplay between W, T, and the scoring matrix is critical, and choosing them wisely is the most effective way to control the speed and sensitivity of BLAST.

In Figures 5-2 and 5-3, you may have noticed that word hits tend to cluster along diagonals in the search space. The *two-hit algorithm*, as it is known, takes advantage of this property by requiring two word hits on the same diagonal within a given distance (see Figure 5-4). Smaller distances isolate more single word hits and further reduce the search space. The two-hit algorithm is an effective way to remove meaningless, neighborless word hits and improve the speed of BLAST searches.

Implementation details

The descriptions thus far have been mostly theoretical. However, some implementation details are worth discussing. In NCBI-BLAST, BLASTN is very different from the other, protein-based algorithms. BLASTN seeds are always identical words; T is never used. To make BLASTN faster, you increase W and to make it more sensitive, you decrease W. The minimum word size is 7. The two-hit algorithm isn't used in BLASTN searches because word hits are generally rare with large, identical words. BLASTP and the other protein-based programs use word sizes of 2 or 3. To make protein searches faster, you set W to 3 and T to a large value like 999, which removes

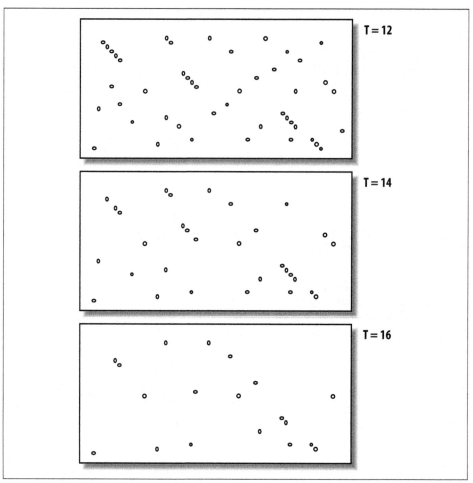

Figure 5-3. How T affects seeding

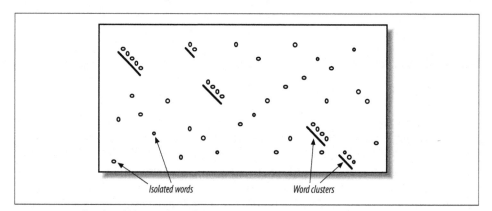

Figure 5-4. Isolated and clustered words

all potential neighborhood words. The two-hit distance is set to 40 amino acids by default, so words don't have to be clustered as closely as they appear in the figures. In principle, setting the two-hit distance to a smaller value also increases speed, but in practice, its effect is insubstantial.

In WU-BLAST, you may set W to any value for any program. If W is set to 5 or more, neighborhood word scores aren't used; they are computed only by explicitly assigning a value for T. High values of W in conjunction with moderate values of T can lead to immense memory requirements, so it is best not to set T when W is 6 or more. To alter the speed/sensitivity of WU-BLAST you can use a variety of combinations of W, and T, and you can also employ the two-hit algorithm.

The statistical model underlying BLAST assumes the letters are independent of one another so that the words MQV and MVQ have the same probability of occurring. However, certain combinations occur in biological sequences much more often than expected. These are usually low-complexity sequences—for example, FFF (see Chapters 2 and 4). Low-complexity sequences are often of little biological interest and aligning them wastes CPU cycles. Masking these regions is therefore common. Both NCBI-BLAST and WU-BLAST let you replace these regions with N's or X's, which have negative scores when aligned with a nucleotide or amino acid. A more useful technique, termed *soft masking*, prevents seeding in such regions, but lets alignments extend through them.

Extension

Once the search space is seeded, alignments can be generated from the individual seeds. We've drawn the alignment as arrows extending in both directions from the seeds (Figure 5-5), and you'll see why this is appropriate. In the Smith-Waterman algorithm (Chapter 3), the endpoints of the best alignment are determined only after the entire search space is evaluated. However, because BLAST searches only a subset of the space, it must have a mechanism to know when to stop the extension procedure.

To make this clearer, we'll try aligning two sentences using a scoring scheme in which identical letters score +1 and mismatches score -1. To keep the example simple, ignore spaces and don't allow gaps in the alignment. Although only extension to the right is shown, it also occurs to the left of the seed. Here are the two sentences:

```
The quick brown fox jumps over the lazy dog.
The quiet brown cat purrs when she sees him.
```

Assume the seed is the capital T, and you're extending it to the right. You can extend the alignment without incident until you get to the first mismatch:

```
The quic
The quie
```

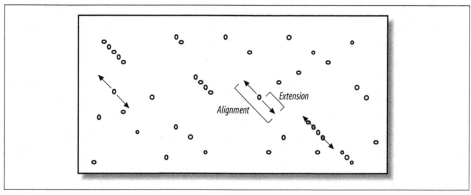

Figure 5-5. Generating alignments by extending seeds

At this point, a decision must be made about whether to continue the alignment or stop. Looking ahead, it's clear that more letters can be aligned, so it would be foolish to stop now. The ends of the sentences, however, aren't at all similar, so we should stop if there are too many mismatches. To do this, we create a variable, X, that represents the recent alignment history. Specifically, X represents how much the score is allowed to drop off since the last maximum. Let's set X to 5 and see what happens. We'll keep track of the sum score and the drop off score as we go. Figure 5-6 shows the graphical interpretation.

```
The quick brown fox jump
The quiet brown cat purr
123 45654 56789 876 5654  <- score
000 00012 10000 123 4345  <- drop off score
```

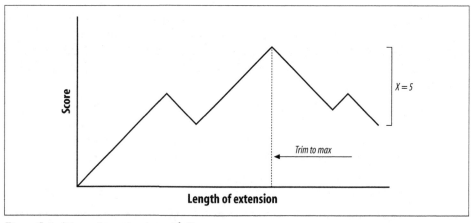

Figure 5-6. Attenuating extension with X

The maximum score for this alignment is 9, and the extension is terminated when the score drops to 4. After terminating, the alignment is trimmed back to the maximum score. If you set X to 1 or 2, the best alignment has a score of 6. If you set X to

3, you can retrieve the longer alignment and save a little computation. A very large value of X doesn't increase the score and requires more computation. So what is the proper value for X? It's generally a good idea to use a large value, which reduces the risk of premature termination and is a better way to increase speed than with the seeding parameters. However, W, I, and 2-hit are better for controlling speed than X.

The gapless extension algorithm just demonstrated is similar to what was used in the original version of BLAST. The algorithms in the current versions of BLAST allow gaps and are related to the dynamic programming techniques described in Chapter 3. Therefore, X not only depends on substitution scores, but also gap initiation and extension costs.

Implementation details

Extension in BLASTN is a little different from BLASTP and the other protein-based programs. The reason for this has to do with how nucleotide sequences are stored in BLAST databases. Because there are only four common nucleotide symbols, nucleotide databases can be stored in a highly compressed state with only two bits per nucleotide. What happens if the sequence contains an N or other ambiguous nucleotide? A random canonical nucleotide is substituted. For example, an N can be randomly changed to A, C, G, or T and a Y changed to a C or T. It is possible, especially with long stretches of ambiguous nucleotides, that the two-bit approximation terminates extension prematurely.

NCBI-BLAST and WU-BLAST take very different approaches to the gapped extension procedure. NCBI-BLAST has three values for X (parameters -X -y -Z) and WU-BLAST has two (parameters -X and -gapX). Some differences, such as the presence of a floating bandwidth (NCBI) rather than a fixed bandwidth, are interesting from an academic viewpoint but less so from a user's perspective. What is important is that altering the extension parameters from their defaults is generally not an effective way to increase the speed or sensitivity of a BLAST search. You might consider adjusting the parameters in two situations:

- If you align sequences that are nearly identical and you want to prevent the extensions from straying into a nonidentical sequence, you can set the various X values very low.

- If you try to align very distant sequences and have already adjusted W, T, and the scoring matrix to allow additional sensitivity, it makes sense to also increase the various X values. That said, when searching for remote homologies, it is often better to employ an algorithm with a position-specific scoring matrix, such as PSI-BLAST or HMMER.

Since gapped extension also depends on the gap initiation and extension costs, you should note that these parameters are interpreted differently in NCBI-BLAST and WU-BLAST. In NCBI-BLAST, the total cost for a gap is the gap opening cost (-G) plus the gap extension cost (-E) times the length of the gap. In WU-BLAST, the total cost of a gap is the cost of the first gap character (-Q) plus all remaining gap characters (-R). The NCBI parameters -G 1 -E 1 are identical to -Q 2 -R 1 in WU-BLAST.

Evaluation

Once seeds are extended in both directions to create alignments, the alignments are evaluated to determine if they are statistically significant (Chapter 4). Those that are significant are termed HSPs. At the simplest level, evaluating alignments is easy; just use a score threshold, S, to sort alignments into low and high scoring. Because S and E are directly related through the Karlin-Altschul equation, a score threshold is synonymous with a statistical threshold. In practice, evaluating alignments isn't as simple, which is due to complications that result from multiple HSPs.

Consider the alignment between a eukaryotic protein and its genomic source. Because most coding regions are broken up by introns, an alignment between the protein and the DNA is expected to produce several HSPs, one for each exon. In assessing the statistical significance of the protein-DNA match, should each exon alignment be forced to stand on its own against the statistical threshold, or does it make more sense to combine the scores of the various exons? The latter is generally more appropriate, especially if some exons are short and may be thrown out if not aided in some way. However, determining the significance of multiple HSPs isn't as simple as summing all the alignment scores because many alignments are expected to be extensions from fortuitous word hits and not all groups of HSPs make sense.

An *alignment threshold* is an effective way to remove many random, low-scoring alignments (Figure 5-7). However, if the threshold is set too high, (Figure 5-7c), it may also remove real alignments. This alignment threshold is based on score and therefore doesn't consider the size of the database. There are, of course, E-value and P-value interpretations, if you consider the size of individual sequences or a constant theoretical search space.

Qualitatively, the relationship between HSPs should resemble the relationship between ungapped alignments. That is, the lines in the graph should start from the upper left and continue to the lower right, the lines shouldn't overlap, and there should be a penalty for unaligned sequence. Groups of HSPs that behave this way are considered consistent. Figure 5-8 shows consistent and inconsistent HSPs. From a biological perspective, you expect the 5′ end of a coding sequence to match the N-terminus of a protein and the 3′ end to match the C-terminus—not vice versa.

The algorithm for defining groups of consistent HSPs compares the coordinates of all HSPs to determine if there are overlaps (a little overlap is actually allowed to account for extensions that may have strayed too far). This computation is quadratic in the number of HSPs and therefore can be costly if there are many HSPs (e.g., when the sequences are long, and the alignment threshold is low).

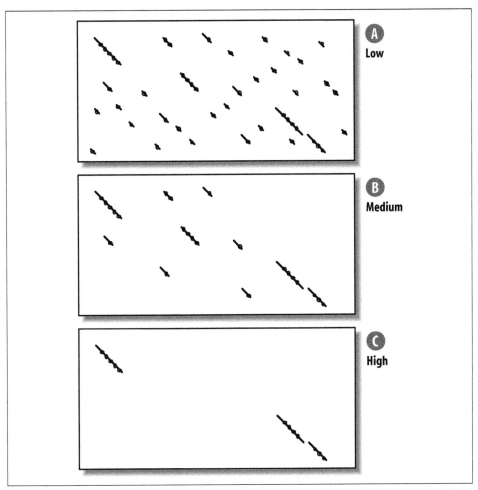

Figure 5-7. Increasing alignment thresholds remove low scoring alignments

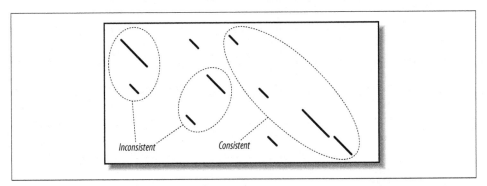

Figure 5-8. Consistent and inconsistent alignment groups

Once HSPs are organized into consistent groups, they can be evaluated with a *final threshold* based on the entire search space and corresponding to the value of *E* set for the search. You can read more about this topic in Chapter 4. BLAST reports any alignment or group of alignments that meets the *E* requirement.

Implementation details

This chapter initially described BLAST as having three phases: seeding, extension, and evaluation. In reality, BLAST isn't so straightforward. There are two rounds of extension and evaluation: ungapped and gapped. Gapped extension and evaluation are triggered only if ungapped alignments surpass the ungapped thresholds. In other words, to find a gapped alignment, you must first find a reasonable ungapped alignment.

In NCBI-BLAST, the command line parameter -e sets the final threshold. The value for the alignment threshold is set by the software and isn't a user-definable parameter. You can find the value for *E* in the footer. For example, if *E* is set with -e 1e-10, *E* is reported as follows:

```
Number of sequences better than 1.0e-10: 4
```

The value for the alignment threshold and its gapped equivalent are displayed respectively as *S1* and *S2* with the raw score listed first. Note that the ungapped threshold is quite a bit lower than the gapped threshold.

```
S1: 41 (21.7 bits)
S2: 158 (65.5 bits)
```

In WU-BLAST, the E or S parameters specify the final threshold (if both are specified, the most stringent one is used). The command-line parameters S2 and its gapped counterpart gapS2 specify the alignment threshold. WU-BLAST includes E-value versions of the alignment threshold based on a constant search space. They may be set via E2 and gapE2. The values for these parameters are shown in the footer. In this example, the alignment threshold (S2) has an ungapped threshold of 33 and a gapped threshold of 36 (one line below).

```
Query
Frame  MatID  Length  Eff.Length    E    S  W   T   X   E2     S2
 +0      0     235       235       10.  65  3  12  22  0.20    33
                                            32  0.21    36
```

While gapped alignments are useful from a biological perspective, they pose a small problem to Karlin-Altschul statistics because there is no known way to calculate lambda with arbitrary gap penalties. However, lambda can be estimated by observing the properties of random alignments in a given scoring scheme. Both NCBI-BLAST and WU-BLAST have internal tables that contain Karlin-Altschul parameters for common matrices and gap penalties. If you try to use an unsupported scoring scheme in NCBI-BLAST, the program will terminate and list the possible gap penalties. Unsupported scoring schemes in WU-BLAST revert to ungapped parameters, but a warning is issued that informs you that you can provide your own values for lambda, k, and H on the command line.

NCBI's version of BLASTN doesn't contain gapped values for lambda; lambda is always calculated directly from the match/mismatch scores. Because of this, equivalent alignments may have much higher bit scores (and lower E-values) in NCBI-BLAST than WU-BLAST, even if their match/mismatch scores are identical.

Further Reading

The following papers describe BLAST algorithms in more detail:

Altschul, Stephen F., Warren Gish, Webb Miller, Eugene W. Myers, and David J. Lipman (1990). "Basic local alignment search tool," *Journal of Molecular Biology*, 215:403-10.

Altschul, Stephen F., Thomas L. Madden, Alejandro A. Schaffer, Jinghui Zhang, Zheng Zhang, Webb Miller, and David J. Lipman (1997), "Gapped BLAST and PSI-BLAST: a new generation of protein database search programs," *Nucleic Acids Research*, 25:3389-3402.

Gish, Warren and David J. States (1993). "Identification of protein coding regions by database similarity search," *Nature Genet.*, 3:266-72.

For the latest information on NCBI-BLAST and other helpful documents, see the official web site at *http://ncbi.nlm.nih.gov/BLAST*.

The WU-BLAST web site (*http://blast.wustl.edu*) has several useful documents on BLAST in general, and includes pages specifically for WU-BLAST users. One of its most interesting documents is a thorough manual for the classic, ungapped version of BLAST 1.4 (*http://blast.wustl.edu/doc/blast1.pdf*).

CHAPTER 6
Anatomy of a BLAST Report

This chapter explores the standard BLAST format. NCBI-BLAST and WU-BLAST are very similar, and their few important differences are described below. NCBI-BLAST offers several additional output options described in Appendix A.

Basic Structure

A standard BLAST report has four parts (see Figure 6-1).

Header

> The first line contains the name of the program, its version, and its build date. If BLAST crashes or has some kind of unexpected behavior, include this information when you report the problem to the authors. The next piece of information is a reference to the scientific literature, which should be cited if you publish research that employed BLAST. The most important information in the header, the names of the query sequence and the database, appear next. The last line is a progress meter that is updated during the search.

One-line summaries

> Each line indicates the name of the sequence, the highest scoring alignment found and the lowest E-value for any HSP or group of HSPs. The one-line summaries are often hyperlinked to the alignments farther below when the output comes from a web page. If you just want to know for example, the names of the top matches, these one-line summaries are convenient.

Alignments

> The alignments usually make up the bulk of the report. Figure 6-1 shows only one alignment. The following section discusses alignments in greater detail and gives examples from the five standard BLAST programs.

Footer

> The footer reports search parameters and various other statistics. The most important features are the word size (W), neighborhood word threshold score (T), Expect (E), and the scoring scheme (scoring matrix or match/mismatch

```
BLASTP 2.2.5 [Nov-16-2002]

Reference: Altschul, Stephen F., Thomas L. Madden, Alejandro A. Schaffer,
Jinghui Zhang, Zheng Zhang, Webb Miller, and David J. Lipman (1997),
"Gapped BLAST and PSI-BLAST: a new generation of protein database search
programs", Nucleic Acids Res. 25:3389-3402.

Query= OO2567 MYOGLOBIN.
        (145 letters)

Database: nr
          1,230,998 sequences; 391,609,117 total letters

Searching................................................done
```
Header

```
                                                          Score    E
Sequences producing significant alignments:              (bits)  Value

gi|7428631|pir||GGGAA globin [validated] - slug sea hare   222   6e-58
gi|2133520|pir||S64703 myoglobin - slug sea hare (fragment) 222  7e-58
gi|70584|pir||GGGA2A globin - Kuroda's sea hare (tentative seque... 217  2e-56
gi|9257039|pdb|1DM1|A Chain A, 2.0 A Crystal Structure Of The Do... 215  7e-56
gi|230148|pdb|1MBA| Myoglobin (Met) (pH 7.0) >gnl|BL_ORD_ID|302... 214  2e-55
gi|121267|sp|P29287|GLB_BURLE Globin (Myoglobin) >gnl|BL_ORD_ID|... 212  8e-55
```
One-line summaries

```
>gi|7428631|pir||GGGAA globin [validated] - slug sea hare
          Length = 146

 Score =  222 bits (566), Expect = 6e-58
 Identities = 112/146 (76%), Positives = 127/146 (86%), Gaps = 2/146 (1%)

Query: 2   ALSAADAGLLAQSWAPVFANSAANGDSFLVALFTQFPESANFFNDFKGKSLADIQASPKL 61
           +LSAA+A L +SWAPVFAN  ANGD+FLVALF +FP+SANFF DFKGKS+ADI+ASPKL
Sbjct: 1   SLSAAEADLAGKSWAPVFANKDANGDAFLVALFEKFPDSANFFADFKGKSVADIKASPKL 60

Query: 62  RDVSSRIFARLNEFVSNAADAGKMGSMLQQFATEHAGFGVGSAQFQNVRSMFPGFVASLS 121
           RDVSSRIF RLNEFV+NAADAGKM +ML QFA EH GFGVGSAQF+NVRSMFPGFVAS++
Sbjct: 61  RDVSSRIFTRLNEFVNNAADAGKMSAMLSQFAKEHVGFGVGSAQFENVRSMFPGFVASVA 120

Query: 122 AP--AGDAAWNSLFGLIISALQSAGK 145
           AP    DAAW  LFGLII AL++AGK
Sbjct: 121 APPAGADAAWTKLFGLIIDALKAAGK 146
```
Alignments

```
  Database: nr
    Posted date:  Jan 18, 2003 11:01 AM
  Number of letters in database: 391,609,117
  Number of sequences in database:  1,230,998

Lambda     K       H
  0.319    0.130    0.371

Gapped
Lambda     K       H
  0.267    0.0410   0.140

Matrix: BLOSUM62
Gap Penalties: Existence: 11, Extension: 1
Number of Hits to DB: 95,320,877
Number of Sequences: 1230998
Number of extensions: 3177411
Number of successful extensions: 8194
Number of sequences better than 10.0: 435
Number of HSP's better than 10.0 without gapping: 271
Number of HSP's successfully gapped in prelim test: 164
Number of HSP's that attempted gapping in prelim test: 7851
Number of HSP's gapped (non-prelim): 453
length of query: 145
length of database: 391,609,117
effective HSP length: 121
effective length of query: 24
effective length of database: 242,658,359
effective search space: 5823800616
effective search space used: 5823800616
T: 11
A: 40
X1: 16 ( 7.4 bits)
X2: 38 (14.6 bits)
X3: 64 (24.7 bits)
S1: 41 (21.8 bits)
S2: 64 (29.3 bits)
```
Footer

Figure 6-1. The four parts of a standard BLAST report

values and the gap costs) because these factors control the sensitivity and specificity of a search. The footer labels these values clearly.

Alignments

The alignments and alignment statistics reported by BLAST differ slightly from program to program. The rest of this chapter describes the details of BLASTP, BLASTN, BLASTX, TBLASTN, and TBLASTX alignments and shows how to recognize alignment groups.

BLASTP

BLASTP alignments are the simplest to understand. Figure 6-2 shows the anatomy of a typical BLASTP alignment.

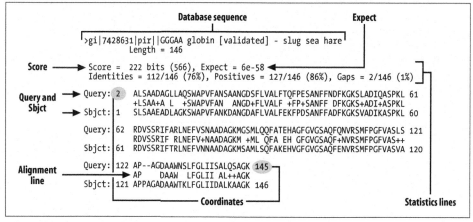

Figure 6-2. A BLASTP alignment

Here are the parts you should pay attention to:

Score
> This value is computed from the scoring matrix and gap penalties. A higher score indicates greater similarity. The raw score is shown without units, and the normalized score is followed by "bits."

Database sequence
> The complete FASTA definition line is reported here along with the length of the sequence. All the alignments between the query and a specific database sequence are collectively called a *hit*. The database in Figure 6-2 has one alignment.

Expect

> The number of alignments expected at random given the size of the search space, the scoring matrix, and the gap penalties. The lower the E-value, the less likely this is a random similarity.

Statistics lines

> Score, E-value, and percent identity always appear here. Depending on the program, percent positive scoring, P-value, group, gaps, strand, and reading frame may also be reported.

Coordinates

> The coordinates of each sequence are indicated at the beginning and ending of each line. The single alignment in Figure 6-2 is long enough that it is reported on three separate lines.

Alignment line

> Letters that are identical between two sequences are reported here. Those that have positive scores in the scoring matrix are displayed with a plus sign. Gaps and nonpositive scores are blank.

Query and Sbjct

> The query sequence is always listed first. The database sequence is abbreviated as Sbjct (subject).

The database sequence may be several lines long if the BLAST database is a nonredundant database with concatenated definition lines. For more on this topic, see Chapter 11. The WU-BLAST format differs slightly from the NCBI format: gaps aren't reported on the statistics line, and the P-value (displayed as P or Sum P) is always reported in addition to the Expect.

BLASTN

DNA is a double-stranded molecule, and genes may occur on either strand. This fact makes BLASTN alignments a little more difficult to interpret than BLASTP alignments. When a query sequence is searched against a database, both strands of the query are examined. The *plus* strand is the sequence in the FASTA file. The *minus* strand is the reverse complement of this sequence. If the similarity between the query and subject sequences is on the same strand, both sequences are labeled as being on the plus strand and the coordinates increase from left to right (Figure 6-3a). Since BLAST just aligns letters and has no model of genes or other features, it is impossible to determine on which strand a gene lies from a BLASTN alignment. Even if an alignment is labeled as "Plus/Plus," the encoded gene may be on the minus strand.

When the minus strand of the query sequence is similar to a database sequence, the alignment is reported with either the subject or query sequence in reversed coordinates. In NCBI-BLAST, the database sequences are flipped (Figure 6-3b), but in WU-BLAST, the query coordinates are flipped (Figure 6-3c).

```
a  Score = 56.4 bits (29), Expect = 4e-08
   Identities = 65/80 (81%), Gaps = 4/80 (5%)
   Strand = Plus / Plus

   Query: 29079 ggtggtttagaacgatctggtcttaccctgctaccaactgttcatcggttattgttggag 29138
                ||||||  |||||  || |||||||||||||  |||||  || ||||| ||||  |  |||
   Sbjct: 35273 ggtggtggagaac-atttggtcttaccctgaaaccaattgctcatcagtta--g-gggac 35328

   Query: 29139 attgttctctgaaatgggaa 29158
                |||| |||||||||||||||
   Sbjct: 35329 attggtctctgaaatgggaa 35348


b  Score = 48.8 bits (25), Expect = 8e-06
   Identities = 59/76 (77%)
   Strand = Plus / Minus

   Query: 34086 ttatctgtacttctcagccagggccagagccacagaggccaggaacttgtccacagccac 34145
                ||||||||||||||||||||| |  || ||| | |||||||||||||| | ||| |
   Sbjct: 50700 ttatctgtacttctcagccagcacagcagacacggcagacaggaacttgtcgaaggcagc 50641

   Query: 34146 atggacctcaggggtg 34161
                ||| || |||||||||
   Sbjct: 50640 atgcacttcaggggtg 50625


c  Score = 25 (48.8 bits), Expect = 1.2e-10, Sum P(5) = 1.2e-10
   Identities = 59/76 (77%), Positives = 59/76 (77%), Strand = Minus / Plus

   Query: 34161 CACCCCTGAGGTCCATGTGGCTGTGGACAAGTTCCTGGCCTCTGTGGCTCTGGCCCTGGC 34102
                ||||||||  || |||| || | ||||||||||||||  | ||| || ||||  |||||
   Sbjct: 50625 CACCCCTGAAGTGCATGCTGCCTTCGACAAGTTCCTGTCTGCCGTGTCTGCTGTGCTGGC 50684

   Query: 34101 TGAGAAGTACAGATAA 34086
                ||||||||||||||||
   Sbjct: 50685 TGAGAAGTACAGATAA 50700
```

Figure 6-3. BLASTN alignments: (a) NCBI-BLAST, same strand; (b) NCBI-BLAST, different strand; (c) WU-BLAST, different strand

Table 6-1 shows how strand is displayed in the five standard BLAST programs.

Table 6-1. Strandedness

Program	Plus / Plus	Plus / Minus	Minus / Plus	Minus / Minus
BLASTP	Always	Never, proteins don't have strand		
BLASTN	Same strand	NCBI-BLAST flips the subject sequence	WU-BLAST flips the query sequence	Never
BLASTX	The query sequence is labeled as Frame +1, +2, +3	Never	The query sequence is labeled as Frame -1, -2, -3	Never
TBLASTN	The subject sequence is labeled as Frame +1, +2, +3	The subject sequence is labeled as Frame -1, -2, -3	Never	Never
TBLASTX	Any combination of positive or negative frames for either the query or subject sequence.			

Here are a few minor notes:

- Both NCBI-BLAST and WU-BLAST change the alignment format for BLASTN to represent matches as vertical bars. Because match/mismatch scoring is used, positive scoring mismatches are not displayed.

- NCBI-BLAST displays nucleotide sequences in lowercase, whereas WU-BLAST displays them in uppercase.

BLASTX

Alignments from BLASTX are complicated by both strand and reading frame. The query sequence is translated in three frames on both the plus and minus strands. Chapter 2 discusses the reading frame in more detail. With three nucleotides per codon, the coordinates of the query sequence increase by threes (Figure 6-4a). On the plus strand, the reading frame is computed relative to the start of the plus strand; reading frame 1 starts at position 1 and reading frame 2 starts at position 2. On the minus strand, the reading frame is calculated relative to the reverse complement of the plus strand; the last letter of the FASTA file starts frame –1 and the second-to-last letter starts frame –2. Minus strand matches invert the query coordinates (Figure 6-4b).

```
a  Score = 74.7 bits (182), Expect = 1e-10
   Identities = 26/61 (42%), Positives = 38/61 (61%)
   Frame = +3

Query: 21813 SQITRIPLNGLGCEHFQSCSQCLSAPPFVQCGWCHDRCVHLEECPTGAWTQEVCLPAIYE 21992
             ++IT++PL G GC+H  +C+ CL +      +CGWC  RC    +CP   WTQE C P + +
Sbjct: 517   NKITKVPLIGPGCDHLTTCTSCLVSSRVTECGWCEGRCTRANQCPPSVWTQEYCTPVVTK 576

Query: 21993 V 21995
             V
Sbjct: 577   V 577


b  Score = 169 (64.5 bits), Expect = 1.7e-258, Sum P(14) = 1.7e-258
   Identities = 30/34 (88%), Positives = 34/34 (100%), Frame = -1

Query: 1071 SQVGPAGSQFGILACLFVELFQSWQILAQPWKAF 970
            ++VGPAGSQFGILACLFVELFQSWQILA+PW+AF
Sbjct:  722 AEVGPAGSQFGILACLFVELFQSWQILARPWRAF 755
```

Figure 6-4. BLASTX alignments (ovals indicate that nucleotide coordinates increase by threes (a) and are reversed for minus strand matches (b))

TBLASTN

TBLASTN alignments are very similar to BLASTX alignments, except that the database and query are exchanged. Therefore, the database sequence increases in threes, and the database sequence has flipped coordinates on the minus strand.

TBLASTX

TBLASTX has more complicated alignments because both the query and the database have strand and frame. Figure 6-5 shows examples of all strand combinations.

One of the most confusing aspects of TBLASTX alignments is that a number of different frames may represent the same region from both the query and subject. A TBLASTX alignment between two genomic sequences often highlights shared coding sequences. However, the correct frame of the encoded proteins can't be determined from a TBLASTX report. Chapters 8 and 9 discuss techniques that make TBLASTX more discriminate.

```
a  Score = 57.9 bits (120), Expect(2) = 9e-17
   Identities = 23/43 (53%), Positives = 32/43 (73%)
   Frame = +3 / +3

   Query: 25221 VFISCAGLILARRHHQADVGVQLDQQAPLKHPHHHLDQLSLGS 25349
                 VFI   L+L R HHQ DV V+L+++  L+HP+HHL++LSL S
   Sbjct: 6492  VFILGTELLLVRGHHQTDVRVELNEEPVLEHPYHHLNELSLQS 6620

b  Score = 49.6 bits (102), Expect = 5e-07
   Identities = 23/42 (54%), Positives = 27/42 (63%)
   Frame = +1 / -1

   Query: 34471 TLKLAGSTRRVKACSSLRLKRPPFRSSILDTESPMAFMMVIP 34596
                 TLK  GST R+ ACSSL L + P  SS+  T SPMAF  + P
   Sbjct: 47195 TLKFTGSTLRM*ACSSLSLAKAPLMSSMFFTASPMAFRTLEP 47070

c  Score = 74.8 bits (157), Expect(2) = 2e-18
   Identities = 30/54 (55%), Positives = 38/54 (69%)
   Frame = -2 / +1

   Query: 34631 DQSPTSASAKKHGITIMNAIGDSVSKIDDLKGGLFNLSELHAFTLRVDPANFKV 34470
                 D S  S  + HG ++NAIG++V  IDD++ L  LSELHA+ LRVDP NFKV
   Sbjct: 47035 DVSQGSVQLRGHGSKVLNAIGEAVKNIDDIRGALAKLSELHAYILRVDPVNFKV 47196

d  Score = 84.0 bits (177), Expect(2) = 2e-24
   Identities = 33/43 (76%), Positives = 37/43 (85%)
   Frame = -2 / -1

   Query: 25343 QAQLIQMVVWMLQRRLLIQLHTYVCLMVPPSEDEPSTRDEDPP 25215
                 Q QLIQMV+WMLQ RLLIQLHTYVCLMVPP+E+E   +DED P
   Sbjct: 6614  QTQLIQMVIWMLQHRLLIQLHTYVCLMVPPNEEEFRAQDEDMP 6486
```

Figure 6-5. TBLASTX alignments (coordinates increase by threes and may have any combination of frames)

Alignment Groups

Alignment groups are one of the most confusing aspects of the BLAST report. Chapters 4 and 5 discuss how and why alignments are sometimes grouped to increase their statistical significance. However, the standard BLAST format doesn't make this structure easy to see. Figure 6-6 shows the scores reported for various alignments in a single database hit. The groups can be inferred from the Expect values. If several alignments have the same E-value, it is more difficult to determine which alignments belong to which groups.

By default, WU-BLAST alignment groups are just as difficult to recognize as NCBI-BLAST groups. WU-BLAST has a very useful command-line option called topcomboN that organizes and limits the number of groups. Chapter 8 discusses topcomboN in more detail. Figure 6-7 shows how groups are organized by strand and then by Sum

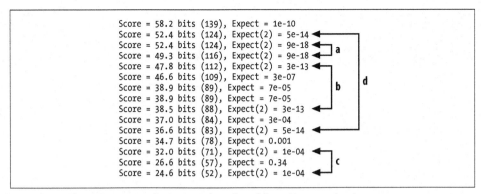

```
Score = 58.2 bits (139), Expect = 1e-10
Score = 52.4 bits (124), Expect(2) = 5e-14
Score = 52.4 bits (124), Expect(2) = 9e-18
Score = 49.3 bits (116), Expect(2) = 9e-18      a
Score = 47.8 bits (112), Expect(2) = 3e-13
Score = 46.6 bits (109), Expect = 3e-07               d
Score = 38.9 bits (89), Expect = 7e-05         b
Score = 38.9 bits (89), Expect = 7e-05
Score = 38.5 bits (88), Expect(2) = 3e-13
Score = 37.0 bits (84), Expect = 3e-04
Score = 36.6 bits (83), Expect(2) = 5e-14
Score = 34.7 bits (78), Expect = 0.001
Score = 32.0 bits (71), Expect(2) = 1e-04
Score = 26.6 bits (57), Expect = 0.34           c
Score = 24.6 bits (52), Expect(2) = 1e-04
```

Figure 6-6. Alignment groups (groups can be inferred from Expect values)

P-value for a single database hit. Groups are labeled and need not be inferred. Notice that some groups contain only one alignment.

```
Score = 130 (50.8 bits), Expect = 6.5e-14, Sum P(2) = 6.5e-14, Group = 1
Score = 128 (50.1 bits), Expect = 6.5e-14, Sum P(2) = 6.5e-14, Group = 1
Score = 130 (50.8 bits), Expect = 1.3e-09, Sum P(3) = 1.3e-09, Group = 2
Score = 86 (35.3 bits), Expect = 1.3e-09, Sum P(3) = 1.3e-09, Group = 2
Score = 61 (26.5 bits), Expect = 1.3e-09, Sum P(3) = 1.3e-09, Group = 2
Score = 120 (47.3 bits), Expect = 5.6e-09, Sum P(2) = 5.6e-09, Group = 3     Plus
Score = 90 (36.7 bits), Expect = 5.6e-09, Sum P(2) = 5.6e-09, Group = 3
Score = 142 (55.0 bits), Expect = 8.5e-09, P = 8.5e-09, Group = 4
Score = 109 (43.4 bits), Expect = 9.2e-09, Sum P(2) = 9.2e-09, Group = 5
Score = 99 (39.9 bits), Expect = 9.2e-09, Sum P(2) = 9.2e-09, Group = 5
Score = 90 (36.7 bits), Expect = 0.0030, P = 0.0030, Group = 7
Score = 71 (30.1 bits), Expect = 0.32, P = 0.27, Group = 9
Score = 89 (36.4 bits), Expect = 6.5e-05, Sum P(2) = 6.5e-05, Group = 6
Score = 81 (33.6 bits), Expect = 6.5e-05, Sum P(2) = 6.5e-05, Group = 6     Minus
Score = 89 (36.4 bits), Expect = 0.0038, P = 0.0038, Group = 8
```

Figure 6-7. WU-BLAST alignment groups with topcomboN=9

## CHAPTER 7

A BLAST Statistics Tutorial

BLAST statistics are everywhere in biology today. In fact, it's hard to find a molecular-biology paper, grant proposal, patent application, or biotech business plan that doesn't refer to the Expect or P-value of a BLAST result. The BLAST Expect has so permeated biological thinking in recent years that for many scientists it has become synonymous with biological truth. Tell a colleague that you've just cloned a gene that's homologous to something trendy, and odds are that he will ask what the Expect of its alignment was in a BLAST search.

Of course, what some see as a sweeping change, others label a fad. While some researchers consider BLAST statistics a welcome injection of mathematical rigor into the biological world, others lament the abandonment of biological insight for faith in a number. No matter where you stand on this issue, there is no avoiding the reality of BLAST statistics in today's bioinformatics workplace. Understanding what the numbers in a BLAST report mean and how they are derived isn't just for mathematicians; it's a real-world survival skill for biologists and bioinformatics professionals in academia and industry alike.

The material covered in this chapter is practical rather than theoretical in nature. Chapter 4 summarized some of the theory behind local alignment statistics. Read that chapter to learn more about the basic parameters of BLAST: λ, k, and H. This chapter shows how to calculate the numbers in a BLAST report and use this knowledge to better understand the results of a BLAST search.

Basic BLAST Statistics

Primary BLAST literature doesn't focus on the arithmetic involved in calculating an Expect. Understandably, the papers discuss the theoretical underpinnings of Karlin-Altschul statistics, leaving BLAST users without the kinds of examples found in a text book. This chapter provides this missing information.

Figure 7-1 summarizes the basic operations involved in converting the raw score of a high-scoring pair into an Expect, or P-value. The following discussion explains how to perform each calculation and any accessory operations required to derive an Expect.

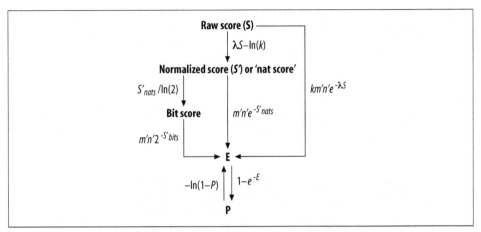

Figure 7-1. The essential calculations involved in converting an HSP's raw score into a probability

Calculating Karlin-Altschul statistics isn't easily done with a pencil, paper, and calculator. Applying Karlin-Altschul statistics to an HSP and avoiding a migraine requires code. We use simple Perl subroutines to take the grind out of the calculations and help clarify the equations. Hopefully these subroutines will also provide a basis for further investigations of your own BLAST results. If you'd like to add these subroutines to your codebase, you can download them from this book's web site; the module name is *BlastStats.pm*.

Example 7-1 shows a sample HSP from a BLASTP search. Use this alignment as a reference to check your calculations.* For our present purposes, the details of the search aren't important, but the values given in the header and footer of the report are. The header and footer are omitted from the search that generated this alignment.

Example 7-1. A sample HSP from a BLASTP search

```
>CT12121 translation from_gene[CG3603 CG3603 FBgn0029648]
        seq_release:2  mol_weight=18568
        cds_boundaries:(X:2,699,992..2,700,667[+]) aa_length:176
        transcript_info:[CT12121  seq_release:2] gene_info:[gene
        symbol:CG3603 FBgn0029648
```

---

* If you plan to perform the calculations described in this chapter and have searched the NCBI web site (*http://www.ncbi.nlm.nih.gov/BLAST*), make sure you don't select the composition-based statistics in the Advanced Options checkbox because the values of the composition-based lambdas aren't given in the report. Currently, it's selected by default for BLASTP, and you unselect it by clicking on it.

Example 7-1. A sample HSP from a BLASTP search (continued)

```
        gene_boundaries:(X:2,699,935..2,700,670[+]) (GO:0016614
        "oxidoreductase, acting on CH-OH group of donors")]
        Length = 176

 Score = 70.9 bits (172), Expect = 8e-13
 Identities = 49/170 (28%), Positives = 85/170 (49%), Gaps = 6/170 (3%)

Query: 50   IAGEVAVVTGAGHGLGRAISLELAKKGCHIAVVDINVSGAEDTVKQIQDIYKVRAKAYKA 109
            +AG+VA+VTGAG G+GRA   LA+ G  +  VD N+  A++TV   Q++   R+ A +
Sbjct: 6    LAGKVALVTGAGSGIGRATCRLLARDGAKVIAVDRNLKAAQETV---QELGSERSAALEV 62

Query: 110  NVTNYDDLVELNSKVVEEMGPV-TVLVNNAGVMMHRNMFNPDPADVQLMINVNLTSHFWT 168
            +V++  +   ++ +++    T++VN+AG+     +   D  + VNL   F
Sbjct: 63   DVSSAQSVQFSVAEALKKFQQAPTIVVNSAGITRDGYLLKMPERDYDDVYGVNLKGTFLV 122

Query: 169  KLVFLPKM--KELRKGFIVTISSLAGVFPLPYSATYTTTKSGALAHMRTL 216
             +   M  ++L  G IV +SS+       A Y  TK+G ++      L
Sbjct: 123  TQAYAKAMIEQKLENGTIVNLSSIVAKMNNVGQANYAATKAGVISFTERL 172
```

Table 7-1 lists only the necessary parameters* and their values.

Table 7-1. The parameters and their values required for Karlin-Altschul statistical calculations

Parameter	Value
λ	0.267 nats (gapped)
k	0.0410 nats (gapped)
H	0.140 nats/aligned residue
m	321 (length of the query sequence)
n	9418064 (number of letters in the database searched)
Effective HSP length	99
Number of sequences in database	17878

Actual Versus Effective Lengths

The Karlin-Altschul equation $E = kmne^{-\lambda S}$ is probably the most recognized equation in bioinformatics. It states that the number of alignments expected by chance (E) during a sequence database search is a function of the size of the search space ($m*n$), the normalized score (λS), and a minor constant (k). (For more information about the Karlin-Altschul equation and its associated parameters, see Chapter 4). The first step toward understanding how to use the Karlin-Altschul equation is to understand what values for m and n BLAST uses when calculating an Expect. Many users assume

---

* The WU-BLAST footer reports both gapped and ungapped values for λ, k, and H. Because the reported P-values and bit scores are based on the gapped parameters by default, use the gapped values for your own calculations.

that the *m* and *n* in the equation refer to the length of the query and subject sequences; this isn't the case. In practice, you use the *effective lengths* rather than actual lengths of the query and database when calculating the Expect of an HSP.

The terms used in the BLAST literature to denote the actual and effective lengths of the query, subject, and database can be confusing. Sometimes *m* and *n* denote actual lengths, and sometimes they denote the effective lengths. To avoid confusion, this chapter uses *m* and *n* to denote actual lengths and *m´* and *n´* to denote effective lengths.

The effective length of the query, *m´*, is its actual length minus the expected HSP length. The effective length of the database, *n´*, is the sum of the effective length of every sequence within it. In other words, if the sequence database used in a BLAST search contains only a single sequence, the actual length of that database, *n*, is the length of that sequence; the effective length, *n´*, of that database is the effective length of the single sequence it contains. If the database contains two sequences, its actual length is the sum of the lengths of those two sequences; the effective length of that database is the sum of those two sequences' effective lengths.

Calculating *m´* and *n´* requires knowing the expected HSP length, which is the length of an HSP that has an Expect of 1. You can find this value in the NCBI-BLAST report footer (where it's called, confusingly, effective HSP length). You can also calculate it, as you'll learn later in this chapter. For now, though, use the value from Table 7-1. Here are two Perl functions used to calculate *m´* and *n´*:

```perl
sub effectiveLengthSeq {
    my $m                 = shift; # actual length sequence
    my $expected_HSP_length = shift;
    my $k                 = shift; # gapped k

    my $m_prime = $m - $expected_HSP_length;

    if ($m_prime < 1/$k){
        return 1/$k;
    }
    else {
        return $m_prime;
    }

}
sub effectiveLengthDb {
    my $n                 = shift; # actual length
    my $expected_HSP_length = shift;
    my $num_seqs_in_db    = shift;
    my $k                 = shift; # gapped k

    my $n_prime = $n - ($num_seqs_in_db*$expected_HSP_length);

        if ($n_prime < 1/$k){
        return 1/$k;
```

```
        }
    else {
return $n_prime;

        }
}
```

Notice that no effective length of the query or the database can ever be less than $1/k$. Setting an effective length to $1/k$ basically amounts to ignoring a short sequence for statistical purposes; in cases when both m and n are less than $1/k$, BLAST searches are ill-advised. For more information about effective lengths and short sequences, see Chapter 4.

Using these functions with the information provided in Table 7-1 gives a value of 222 and 7648142 for m' and n', respectively.

The Raw Score and Bit Score

BLAST reports two scores: the raw score and a normalized score called a *bit score*. The *raw score*, S, is the sum of the alignment's pair-wise scores using a specific scoring matrix (see Chapter 4 for more information). When deriving the bit score for an HSP, first convert its raw score to a nat score using the following equation:

$$S'_{nats} = \lambda S - \ln k$$

Because BLAST reports λ in nats (or more precisely, nats per unit raw score) rather than bits, you must divide the *nat score, S'*, by *ln(2)* to convert it to a bit score. As you become a more critical user and interpreter of BLAST reports, you may find yourself converting nats to bits and raw scores to bit scores regularly. The following two Perl subroutines convert bits to nats, and vice versa:

```
sub nToB {
    my $n = shift;

    return $n/log(2); # converts nats to bits
}
sub bToN {
    my $n = shift;

    return $n*log(2); # converts bits to nats
}
```

Try using λ and k to calculate the bit score for the alignment shown in Figure 7-1. If you use the following Perl function and the values of k and λ given in Table 7-1, you get a bit score of 70.9 for a raw score of 172.

```
sub rawScoreToBitScore {
    my $raw_score = shift;
    my $k         = shift;
    my $l         = shift; #lambda in nats
```

```
# S'_bits = (λ_nats S - ln(k))/ln(2)

return nToB($l*$raw_score - log($k));

}
```

The Expect of an HSP

Now calculate the Expect for the HSP shown in Figure 7-1, recalling that $E = km'n'e^{-\lambda S}$. Again, a simple Perl function is useful:

```
sub rawScoreToExpect {
    my $raw_score = shift;
    my $k         = shift;
    my $l         = shift; # lambda in nats
    my $m         = shift; # effective length of query
    my $n         = shift; # effective length of database

    # E = km'n'e^{-λS}
    return $k*$m*$n*exp(-1*$l*$raw_score);
}
```

Using this function, the values of k and λ, given in Table 7-1, combined with the values m' (222) and n' (7648142) that you calculated in your discussion of effective lengths, gives an Expect of 8e-13 for the alignment shown in Figure 7-1.

You can also calculate the Expect of an alignment with a normalized score, S' (Figure 7-1). The Karlin-Altschul equation $E = km'n'e^{-\lambda S}$ is formulated for the raw score, S, not the normalized score S'. To calculate an Expect using a normalized score S' whose units are nats, use the equation $E = m'n'e^{-S'}$. Note that k doesn't appear in this equation; it has already been accounted for when deriving the normalized (nat) score (e.g., $S' = \lambda S - \ln k$).

To calculate the Expect of an HSP from its bit score (Figure 7-1) use the Perl function shown next. The formula is similar to that used to calculate an Expect from a nat score. However, the base of the exponent is 2 rather than e because you're using bits rather than nats.

```
sub bitScoreToExpect {
    my $bit_score = shift;
    my $m         = shift; # effective length query
    my $n         = shift; # effective length of database

    # reformulated for bits
    # E = m'n'2^{-bit_score}
    return $m*$n*2**(-1*$bit_score);
}
```

The WU-BLAST P-Value

Another important difference between WU-BLAST and NCBI-BLAST is that WU-BLAST reports a P-value as well as an Expect for an alignment. The two functions shown below will convert between these two related measures of statistical significance. Because P is equal to $1 - e^{-E}$, $P \approx E$ if either value is less than 0.001.

```
sub EtoP {
    my $e = shift;

    # P = 1 - e^-E
    return 1-exp(-1*$e);
}
sub PtoE {
    my $p = shift;

    # E = -ln(1 - P)
    return -1*log(1-$p);
}
```

Some of the calculations discussed in this chapter don't apply to sum statistics. The sum score for a set of alignments isn't merely the sum of the raw scores for a set of HSPs. Likewise, the familiar $E = kmne^{-\lambda S}$ equation isn't used when calculating the Expect of a sum score. Thus, the `rawScoreToBitScore`, `rawScoreToExpect`, and `bitScoreToExpect` functions must be modified for sum statistics.

Sum Statistics

Now that you've learned how BLAST calculates the Expect of an individual HSP, let's examine how BLAST assigns an Expect to a group of HSPs. Unlike the Smith-Waterman algorithm, which finds the single maximum scoring alignment, BLAST finds multiple high-scoring pairs. As a result, aligning two sequences often results in multiple HSPs. In some cases, BLAST groups several HSPs in a hit,[*] recalculates, and reports their aggregate statistical significance in place of each HSP's individual Expect. The ubiquitous Karlin-Altschul equation $E = kmne^{-\lambda S}$ isn't used to calculate the aggregate statistical significance of a group of HSPs; instead, a related measure is used that employs a *sum score*.

Many BLAST users are surprised to learn the BLAST employs not one, but two measures of statistical significance. This misconception is understandable, as little in a BLAST report alerts the casual user to this fact. In the default BLAST format, the only indication that sum statistics were applied to a set of HSPs is the presence of the Expect(n) (in an NCBI BLAST report) and the Sum P(n) (in a WU-BLAST report).

---

[*] Here *hit* means one or more HSPs. You'll encounter the word "hit" frequently in the BLAST literature and when using BLAST.

Figure 7-2 provides an overview of the procedure used by NCBI-BLAST to derive an Expect(n), and the following section discusses each calculation in detail.

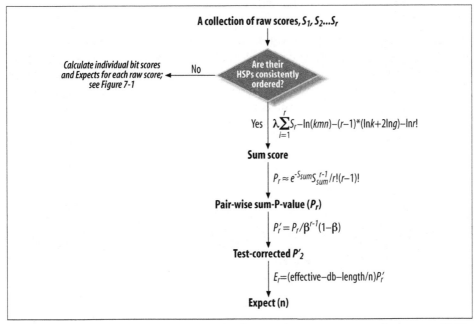

Figure 7-2. *The essential calculations involved in deriving the aggregate Expect for a group of HSPs*

An Expect(n) Means That Sum Statistics Were Applied

Unless you know what to look for, you probably won't notice that the output in Example 7-2 contains two HSPs that were grouped for statistical purposes. The reported Expect(2) for these two alignments is the Expect for their combined or sum score rather than their reported bit scores. As such, it doesn't refer to the actual statistical significance of either alignment's reported bit score.

Example 7-2. *Two BLASTX HSPs to which sum statistics were applied*

```
Score = 71.2 bits (173), Expect(2) = 1e-15
 Identities = 31/59 (52%), Positives = 44/59 (74%)
 Frame = -1

Query: 24837 WLDFLYYCSYVKLTITIIKYVPQALMNYRRKSTSGWSIGNILLLDFTGGTLSMLQMILNA 24661
             WL  +    + +++ +T +KY+PQA MN+ RKST GWSIGNILLDFTGG  + LQM++ +
Sbjct: 148   WLWLISIFNSIQVFMTCVKYIPQAKMNFTRKSTVGWSIGNILLDFTGGLANYLQMVIQS 206

 Score = 38.5 bits (88), Expect(2) = 1e-15
 Identities = 15/34 (44%), Positives = 21/34 (61%)
 Frame = -3
```

Example 7-2. Two BLASTX HSPs to which sum statistics were applied (continued)

```
Query: 24595 DDWVSIFGDPTKFGLGLFSVLFDVFFMLQHYVFY 24494
             + W + +G+  K  L L S+ FD+ FM QHYV Y
Sbjct: 210   NSWKNFYGNMGKTLLSLISIFFDILFMFQHYVLY 243
```

The reported Expect(2) for both alignments is identical, yet their reported raw scores are 173 and 88, respectively. Obviously, the reported Expect for these two alignments can't have been calculated using these raw scores. When BLAST applies sum statistics to a set of HSPs, it uses their sum score to calculate their combined Expect. Unfortunately, this score isn't available anywhere in the report. (For more information about sum scores, see Chapter 4). The sum score, however, can be calculated with the various parameters listed in Table 7-2. These values are taken from the same search as the BLASTX hit shown in Example 7-2. Normally, these values are located in the header and footer of a BLAST report.

Table 7-2. Parameters and their values required for calculating the aggregate statistical significance of HSPs

Parameter	Value
λ	0.267 nats (gapped)
k	0.0410 nats (gapped)
H	0.140 nats/aligned residue
m	40206 (length of the query sequence)
n	270 (length of the subject sequence)
Gap decay constant	0.1
Effective _db_length	78368169
Effective HSP length	144

Sum Statistics Are Pair-Wise in Their Focus

Pair-wise is a term to consider when thinking about sum statistics. Previous discussions of BLAST statistics involved formulations that are most intuitive in the context of database searches; for example, the n in the equation $E = kmne^{-\lambda S}$ refers to the size of the database. Yes, a database may sometimes consist of a single sequence, but in most cases it won't. The published formulations for sum statistics, on the other hand, are pair-wise in their focus; only after all the pair-wise scores and significance values are calculated are adjustments made for database size. In the following discussion, for example, n refers to the actual length of the subject sequence of the alignment, no matter how many sequences make up the database.

The Sum Score

While neither WU-BLAST nor NCBI-BLAST reports the sum score for a group of HSPs anywhere in its output, this invisible number is the basic currency of sum statistics; thus, you should understand how it's calculated. Whether or not sum statistics are applied to a group of HSPs depends on the details of the alignments themselves. If the HSPs are ordered consistently with respect to the subject and query begin and end coordinates, BLAST calculates a sum score. If not, it reports the raw score and individual Expect for each HSP in the BLAST Hit. The following Perl function calculates the (pair-wise-ordered) sum score for a collection of r HSPs. (For more information about sum scores see Chapter 4.)

```perl
sub sumScore {
    my $raw_scores = shift; # raw scores are in an array reference
    my $k          = shift;
    my $l          = shift;
    my $m          = shift; # effective length of query sequence
    my $n          = shift; # effective length of sbjct sequence
    my $g          = shift; # gap_size;for NCBI-BLAST this value is 50


    my $r = @{$raw_scores};

    die "do not take sum for a single score!\n"
    if $r == 1;

    my $total_raw_score = 0;
    foreach my $individual_raw_score (@{$raw_scores}){
        $total_raw_score += $individual_raw_score;
    }
    # sum_score = λ ∑_{i = 1}^{r} S_r − ln(kmn) − (r − 1) · (ln(k) + 2 ln(g)) − log(r!)
    my $n_score = $l*$total_raw_score;

    return
    $n_score - log($k*$m*$n)-($r -1)*(log($k)+2*log($g))-log(fac($r));

}
```

Effective Length of a BLASTX Query

To calculate a sum score, you need to calculate the effective length of the query sequence. Recall, however, that for BLASTX, the query is a nucleotide sequence, and yet a partial translation of that sequence is being aligned. What, then, is its effective length of m', for purposes of sum score calculations? BLASTX considers the effective length of the nucleotide query sequence, m', to be equal to its translated actual length ($m/3$) minus the expected HSP length. The following Perl function calculates the effective length of a BLASTX query:

```perl
sub effectiveLengthOfBlastxQuery {
    my $m    = shift;  # actual nucleotide length of the query
    my $exp  = shift;  # expected HSP length.
    # m' = m/3 − expected_HSP_length
    return $m/3 - $exp;
}
```

Recall that calculating a sum score also requires you to calculate the effective length, n', of the subject sequence. To do so, use the Perl function, effectiveLengthSeq, given earlier in the chapter, because it also applies to the subject sequence for purposes of calculating a sum score.

Calculating a Sum Score

If you look at Example 7-2, you'll see that these two BLASTX HSPs comprise an ordered set. In other words, these two alignments suggest that the query sequence contains a minus strand gene, at least two exons of which are homologous to the subject sequence. Because these two alignments comprise a consistently ordered set, you will calculate their pair-wise ordered sum score. Using the Perl function sumScore that's in the earlier section "The Sum Score," the sum score for these two HSPs is about 53 nats, or 77 bits.

Calculating the Pair-Wise Sum P-Value

The sum score (77 bits) for these two HSPs isn't much more than that of the first HSP's individual bit score (71.2). Why, then, is the resulting Expect (2) for these two HSPs so low: Expect (2) = 1e-15, when the first HSP with only a slightly lower bit score has a much less significant individual Expect of 3.7e-10?

The reason for the discrepancy is that the familiar Karlin-Altschul equation $E = km'n'e^{-\lambda S}$ isn't used when calculating the Expect of a sum score. Sum statistics uses a very different formula. In fact, an Expect isn't calculated, but rather a pair-wise sum P-value. A Perl function for calculating this value is shown next:

```
sub pairwiseSumP {
    my $sumS = shift; # the sum score
    my $r    = shift; # number of HSPs being combined

#  Pr ≈ e^-S_sum S_sum^r-1 /r!(r-1)!

    return (exp(-1*$sumS)*$sumS**fac($r-1))/(fac($r)*fac($r -1));

}
sub fac {
    my $r = shift;

    my $fac;
    for (my $i = $r; $i > 0; $i--){
        $fac = defined($fac) ? $fac*$i: $i;
    }
    $fac = 1 unless defined($fac);
    return $fac;
}
```

Using this function, the pair-wise sum P of a sum score of 53 nats is about 2e-22. That's a lot less than the reported Expect(2) of 1e-15. The discrepancy occurs because

2e⁻²² isn't the Expect(2), but the pair-wise P-value for these two alignments. You must perform two additional calculations using the pair-wise P-value to derive the Expect(n). First, adjust the pair-wise sum P-value for additional significance tests performed when identifying combinations of alignments whose sum P is more significant than any one of its member's individual significance. Second, convert the adjusted P-value into an Expect(n) by correcting for database size.

Correcting for Multiple Tests

BLAST will group a set of HSPs only if the Expect(n) of the group is less than the Expect of any individual member, and if that group is an optimal partition such that no other grouping might result is a lower Expect(n). Identifying these optimal groups is done internally by BLAST and requires testing many potential groups for statistical significance. You must make a correction for these tests. BLAST uses a test-correction function that takes the number of HSPs in the group—the "n" of the Expect(n), rather than the actual number of comparisons made. A function for performing this correction on the pair-wise sum P-value is shown next. In the function, r is simply the number of HSPs being grouped. Because you're dealing with an Expect(2) in Example 7-2, $r = 2$ (again, see Chapter 4 for more information).

```
sub rTestsCorrectedP {
    my $r     = shift;
    my $sum_p = shift;
    my $beta  = shift; # gap decay constant

    # P'_r = P_r/β^(r-1)(1-β)
    return $sumP/($beta**($r-1)*(1-$beta));
}
```

β in the function above is the gap decay constant which, by default, is 0.1 for NCBI-BLASTX. Applying this function to the pair-wise sum P-value gives a test-corrected value of 2.2e⁻²¹. This value isn't very different from the original, as when $r = 2$, so $\beta^{r-1}(1-\beta)$ is equal to 1/11. Notice, however, that for values of $r > 5$, this correction becomes much less trivial.

Correcting for Database Size

Converting the (test-corrected) pair-wise sum P-value to a database-size corrected Expect is the final step in calculating an Expect(n). How best to do this isn't an axiomatic issue, but a practical one. Chapter 4 discusses some of the issues surrounding database size correction in more detail. NCBI-BLASTX applies a size correction that assumes the number of HSPs are proportional to the length of the subject sequence.

```
sub dbSizeCorrectedExpect {
    my $sumP                = shift; # test corrected sumP
```

```
            my $effective_db_length_db = shift;
            my $sbjct_seq_length     = shift; # actual length

            #  = (effective_db_length_db/n)P'
            return ($effective_db_length_db/$sbjct_seq_length)*$sumP;
        }
```

Using this function, the test-corrected, pair-wise sum P-value of 2.2e^{-21} gives an Expect(2) of 7e^{-16}, a fairly close match to the reported value (in Example 7-2) of 1e^{-15}. The difference between the two values can be attributed to rounding and floating-point error.

Frame- and Size-Corrected Expects

BLASTX translates all six frames of the query and uses these translations to search the protein database. At first, you might think that correcting for six frames would entail multiplying the final database-size-corrected Expect by six, but that isn't the case. Neither version of BLASTX applies such a correction. In fact, WU-BLASTX posts a notice in its header stating that it doesn't apply the correction (illustrated in Example 7-3). Like NCBI-BLAST, WU-BLAST searches all six frames by default, but assumes that only one frame was searched when calculating Expects. The reason why is that BLAST statistics assume open reading frames don't overlap. Accordingly, BLASTX statistics assume that the query contains only a single ORF whose frame may change from HSP to HSP.

Example 7-3. The header from a WU-BLASTX report

```
BLASTX 2.0MP-WashU [09-Nov-2000] [linux-i686 19:13:41 11-Nov-2000]

Copyright (C) 1996-2000 Washington University, Saint Louis, Missouri USA.
All Rights Reserved.

Reference:  Gish, W. (1996-2000) http://blast.wustl.edu
Gish, Warren and David J. States (1993).  Identification of protein coding
regions by database similarity search.  Nat. Genet. 3:266-72.

Notice:  statistical significance is estimated under the assumption that the
equivalent of one entire reading frame in the query sequence codes for protein
and that significant alignments will involve only coding reading frames.

Query=  3R 3R.3 [18846615 18886821] flank:20000 length:40206
        (40,206 letters)

  Translating both strands of query sequence in all 6 reading frames

Database:  rscu.fsa
           386,401 sequences; 134,009,913 total letters.
Searching....10....20....30....40....50....60....70....80....90....100% done
```

So far in this chapter, we've just walked through most basic operations of Karlin-Altschul statistics to provide you with the knowledge necessary to calculate bit scores, effective lengths, and Expects. We've explained that BLAST uses one statistical measure to calculate the Expect of an HSP and another to calculate the aggregate Expect of a group of HSPs. Hopefully, you've gained a better understanding of how all of these operations of fit into the larger picture of Karlin-Altschul statistics.

You have also seen that it's possible to use Karlin-Altschul statistics to recover statistical measures that are calculated by BLAST internally, but not included in the report—principally, sum scores and the individual Expect for an HSP for which an Expect(n) has been reported. Learning to calculate these values is the first step toward becoming a power user of BLAST statistics. The remaining sections of this chapter will show you how to use what you've learned to deal with critical questions about BLAST results.

Using Statistics to Understand BLAST Results

Karlin-Altschul statistics is much more than a way to determine the statistical significance of a sequence alignment in the context of a database search. It also provides a framework with which to probe the complex relationships that exist between BLAST parameters and results. Using Karlin-Altschul statistics to ask and answer questions about a BLAST search is much like using stoichiometry at the lab bench; it doesn't require theoretical savvy, just a little algebra. It's also useful; you no longer need to be frustrated when confronted with an inexplicable BLAST result.

Now let's look at a practical application of Karlin-Altschul statistics: using BLASTN to map a PCR primer to a genome. The application is a simple but striking example of how to use Karlin-Altschul statistics to understand the way parameter choice determines BLAST results. Finally, Karlin-Altschul statistics reveal much about BLASTN's strengths and weaknesses and its potential as a tool to detect the conserved, cis-regulatory regions of genes.

Where Did My Oligo Go?

First, try to identify the position of the following oligo-nucleotide in the *Drosophila melanogaster* genome using WU-BLASTN with its default parameters:

TACATCCGGCACTTAGCCGGGCTCG

Example 7-4 shows that the oligo isn't found in the *Drosophila melanogaster* genome that uses WU-BLASTN with default parameters.

Example 7-4. The oligo isn't found

```
Reference:  Gish, W. (1996-2000) http://blast.wustl.edu

Notice:  this program and its default parameter settings are optimized to find
nearly identical sequences rapidly.  To identify weak similarities encoded in
nucleic acid, use BLASTX, TBLASTN or TBLASTX.

Query= oligo
       (25 letters)

Database:  na_whole-genome_genomic_dmel_RELEASE3.FASTA
           7 sequences; 124,181,667 total letters.
Searching....10....20....30....40....50....60....70....80....90....100% done

                                                         Smallest
                                                            Sum
                                                   High  Probability
Sequences producing High-scoring Segment Pairs:    Score  P(N)      N

     *** NONE ***
```

There are, of course, many reasons why you might not be able to identify an oligo in the *Drosophila melanogaster* genome. First, the oligo might contain repetitive sequence and thus be masked out. However, because WU-BLAST doesn't mask by default, that can't be the reason. Second, the assembled genome may be incomplete. Every sequenced genome to date is incomplete to some degree. In fact, a 99 percent complete 124mb genome is still missing 1.24 mega-bases of a euchromatic (nonrepetitive DNA) sequence, leaving plenty of space for an oligo to go missing in. The incompleteness of the genome is a possible explanation for our WU-BLAST result, but is it the correct one? Before concluding that the oligo falls into a sequencing gap, let's try to run NCBI-BLASTN with its default parameters. Aha! The NCBI-BLASTN results in Example 7-5 show that the oligo is present in the *Drosophila melanogaster* genome and the HSP is assigned a significant Expect.

Example 7-5. Using NCBI-BLASTN to find the oligo

```
Sequences producing significant alignments:                (bits) Value

2R 2R.3 assembled 23-11-2001                                  50   1e-06
X X release:2 length:21666217bp Assembled X chromosome arm seque...   32   0.25
3R 3R.3                                                       32   0.25
U GenomicInterval:U                                           30   0.99
3L 3L.3 v.3e  23351213bp BCM HGSC guide:3l-mtp-eval.08apr02   28   3.9
2L 2L release:3 length:22217931bp Assembled 2L chromosome arm se...   28   3.9

>2R 2R.3 assembled 23-11-2001
          Length = 20302755

 Score = 50.1 bits (25), Expect = 1e-06
 Identities = 25/25 (100%)
```

Example 7-5. Using NCBI-BLASTN to find the oligo (continued)

```
Strand = Plus / Plus

Query: 1        tacatccggcacttagccgggctcg 25
                |||||||||||||||||||||||||
Sbjct: 16190927 tacatccggcacttagccgggctcg 16190951
```

Results like these frustrate a lot of BLAST users. Why does NCBI-BLAST find the oligo when WU-BLAST doesn't? The results may seem contradictory, but they make perfect sense, and understanding why this is so will help you use Karlin-Altschul statistics to ask questions about your own BLAST results.

Karlin-Altschul Statistics as a Tool for Further Investigation

Parameter choice seems a likely explanation for the results shown in Examples 7-4 and 7-5. If you assume the failure of WU-BLASTN to report the alignment isn't due to a bug, maybe the hit wasn't significant in the context of the current search. By now you've been exposed to enough Karlin-Altschul statistics to know that BLAST parameters determine the significance of an alignment. The scoring scheme used in a search is the fundamental BLAST parameter, so you should begin your investigation there.

WU-BLASTN and NCBI-BLASTN have very different default scoring schemes. WU-BLASTN uses a +5/–4 scheme to score alignments by default, whereas NCBI-BLASTN uses a +1/–3 scheme. One central theorem of Karlin-Altschul statistics is that every scoring scheme is implicitly a log-odds scoring scheme, and every log-odds scoring scheme implies a target frequency. This insight is significant because it means that a scoring scheme always hunts for alignments having a particular percent identity. One great thing about Karlin-Altschul statistics is they enable you to calculate that percent identity.

Chapter 4 provides a Perl script called Qcalc for calculating various nucleotide scoring scheme target frequencies; Table 4-1 summarizes the λ and percent identity implied by some common scoring schemes. The default +5/–4 scoring scheme used by WU-BLAST implies an ungapped target frequency of 65 percent identity, whereas the +1/–3 default scheme used by NCBI-BLASTN looks for alignments with 99 percent identity. But why would a +5/–4 scoring scheme miss a real alignment with 100 percent identity? The answer to this question lies in the value of λ and the role played by gap penalties.

Table 7-3 gives 0.104 nats for the value of gapped λ associated with the WU-BLASTN default scoring scheme and gap penalties. On the other hand, the λ associated with the NCBI-BLASTN default scoring scheme and gap penalties is 1.37 nats (Table 7-4). The difference between the two values is tenfold. To see how the value of λ impacts your search results, use Karlin-Altschul statistics to delve more deeply into the relationship between raw scores, normalized (bit and nat) scores, and λ.

Table 7-3. Selected WU-BLASTN parameters and values from the search shown in Example 7-5

Parameter	Value
λ	0.104 nats (gapped)
k	0.0151 nats (gapped)
H	0.0600 nats/aligned residue
m	25 (length of the query sequence)
n	124,181,667(number of letters in the database)
Number of sequences in database	7

Table 7-4. Selected NCBI-BLASTN parameters and values from the search shown in Example 7-5

Parameter	Value
λ	1.37 nats (gapped)
k	0.711 nats (gapped)
H	1.31 nats/aligned residue
m	25 (length of the query sequence)
n	124,181,667 (number of letters in the database searched)
Number of sequences in database	7

First, see how the value of λ impacts the expected HSP length. Recall that this value is the length of an alignment that has an Expect=1; more precisely, it's the expected HSP length for E equal to 1 associated with a scoring matrix for a search space of size $m'*n'$. This value is reported in the footer of NCBI-BLAST reports, where it's called "Effective HSP length." However, it's absent from the WU-BLAST footer, so you should calculate it with the Perl function expectedHSPlength and the information from Tables 7-3 and 7-4.

Please note that the following function shows the traditional way to calculate the expected HSP length. Recent work by Altschul and colleagues suggests that this function overestimates the effective HSP length for short sequences, and the manner in which it's calculated may change in the future. Therefore, use the value reported in the BLAST report footer, if it's available. For the purposes here, though, this function is fine.

```
sub expectedHSPlength{
    my $k = shift;
    my $m = shift; # actual length of query
    my $n = shift; # actual length of query
    my $h = shift; # average nats/aligned pair

    # l = ln(kmn)/H
    return  log($k*$m*$n)/$h;

}
```

expectedHSPlength returns an expected HSP-length of about 16 nucleotides for the NCBI defaults. The expected length of the WU-BLASTN HSP with Expect = 1, however, is higher—about 294 nucleotides. That's a big difference. Once again, the reason for the difference lies with the scoring matrix. Recall that the implied target frequency for the NCBI-default +1/–3 scoring scheme was 99 percent, but it was 65% for the WU-BLAST defaults (see Table 4-1). This is why the effective HSP length for the WU-BLAST search is so much longer. The hypothetical 294-nucleotide alignment is expected to have a percent identity of less than 65 percent. In other words, taking into account mismatches and gaps, it needs to be 294 bases long to attain a raw score sufficient to generate an Expect of 1. Thus, the WU-BLAST defaults implicitly assume that nucleotide homologies will have low identity (<65%), but be long—294 nucleotides in the context of the *Drosophila melanogaster* genome. Is this biological assumption valid? Yes and no.

The WU-BLASTN defaults are well suited for detecting long regions of low identity such as poorly conserved exons. On the other hand, the NCBI-BLAST parameters are suitable for finding shorter but nearly identical sequences. Both sets of default parameters will likely fail to detect other kinds of homology, especially short, conserved sequences such as cis-regulatory elements, which tend to be highly conserved and are often less than 10 nucleotides long.

Just how short can an HSP be and still generate a significant hit using WU-BLASTN defaults? Again, Karlin-Altschul statistics provide a basis for answering this question. First you need to know what raw score corresponds to an Expect of 1. The following Perl function calculates this value:

```
sub rawScoreOfExpectOne {
    my $k = shift;
    my $m = shift; # actual length of query
    my $n = shift; # actual length of database
    my $l = shift; # gapped lambda in nats

    # S_{E = 1} = ln(kmn)/λ
    return  log($k*$m*$n)/$l;
}
```

For the ~124 mega-base *Drosophila melanogaster* genome, that raw score is about 15 with the NCBI-BLASTN defaults and about 170 for WU-BLASTN. Recall that the maximum score for aligning an oligo-nucleotide 25 bases long under the +5/–4 scheme is 125 (25*5). Even an alignment with an Expect of 1 has a raw score (170) greater than the maximal attainable score for a 25-mer under the WU-BLAST defaults! This is another reason why WU-BLASTN didn't report a hit.

To determine the length of an ungapped alignment that has 100 percent identity for a given raw score, divide the raw score by the match score. By this calculation, any oligo shorter than about 15 nucleotides (15/1) for NCBI-BLASTN and 34 nucleotides (170/5) for WU-BLASTN will have an Expect > 1. This means that the NCBI-BLASTN defaults are fine for mapping oligo-nucleotides to the *Drosophila melanogaster* genome. On the other hand, it appears that looking for short—less than 15 base-pair—cis-regulatory elements using either version of BLASTN with the default parameters is unlikely to be successful.

So what was the unreported WU-BLASTN Expect? Let's calculate it. With the data in Table 7-3 and the previously calculated effective HSP length of 294, first calculate m' and n' using the Perl functions `effectiveLengthSeq` and `effectiveLengthDB`. Plugging m' and n' together with the WU-BLASTN λ and k and a raw score of 125 into the `rawScoreToExpect` function gives an Expect of 281. Recall that the NCBI-BLASTN Expect was 1e-6. That's a 281-million-fold difference. BLAST is clearly parameter-sensitive! Using the default parameters, you instructed NCBI-BLASTN to search for short highly conserved regions, and it found one. WU-BLASTN, on the other hand, is parameterized to look for large regions of relatively low percent identity. This would be fine for cross-species searches of poorly conserved exons but is inappropriate for finding oligos.

Using BLAST intelligently requires using the correct parameters for the task at hand and not placing too much faith in the reported Expect. See the section on BLAST protocols in Chapter 9 for practical suggestions on BLAST parameter choice. Remember, you get what you look for.

What It All Means

You now know how bit scores, sum scores, Expects, and P-values are calculated. You've also seen first-hand that scoring matrices and target frequencies aren't merely theoretical abstractions but realities that determine the outcome of a BLAST search. In some ways, choosing the right scoring scheme for a BLAST search is like choosing the right pair of eyeglasses. If your scoring scheme is too stringent, BLAST becomes nearsighted and will miss distant homologies. If your scheme is too lenient, BLAST becomes farsighted and fails to detect the obvious. Unfortunately, there's no optimal scoring scheme. As in real life, sometimes the best you can do is put on bifocals.

You've also seen that searching the same sequence and database with varied parameters can result in different alignments having very different Expects. Scores and E-values aren't implicit in a sequence or an alignment; they are solely contingent upon parameter values and the methods used to assess significance. There is nothing absolute about a BLAST significance value; it merely denotes the significance of an alignment in the context of a given search. Like everything else in bioinformatics, the biological implications of a (significant) alignment are inferred by the user and should be tested experimentally, if possible.

Hopefully, you've also learned that there is more to Karlin-Altschul statistics than simply calculating an Expect for an alignment. Karlin-Altschul statistics provide a theoretical framework from which to interpret alignment scores in the context of parameter choice. They also give you the means to tune BLAST for specific purposes.

Without them, you'd have no way of knowing what a given scoring scheme was looking for, and you'd cast around in the dark for the right set of parameters. Karlin-Altschul statistics remove the mystery from parameter choice. BLAST certainly has its limitations, but thanks to its statistical foundation, at least you know what you're looking for.

## CHAPTER 8

20 Tips to Improve
Your BLAST Searches

8.1 Don't Use the Default Parameters

You shouldn't use BLAST the way you use an Internet search engine such as Google. BLAST results are very sensitive to parameters, and the defaults aren't suitable for all searches. Historically, BLAST parameters have changed periodically. In addition, the NCBI-BLAST and WU-BLAST defaults have very different properties, and your results may differ depending on where you perform your BLAST search. Thus, you should get out of the habit of using default parameters. There are situations in which the default parameters are just fine, but using them knowledgeably and accepting them out of ignorance are two very different motivations. If you don't know which settings are appropriate for a particular search, you're not alone; most BLAST users don't know how to set up a search. That's why we wrote this book, so keep reading.

8.2 Treat BLAST Searches as Scientific Experiments

Scientists are often taught to structure their experiments into four parts: the *question* (hypothesis), the *approach* (experimental design), the *results* (data), and the *interpretations* (beliefs). This approach shows that beliefs depend on the experiment's data. Whether or not an experiment is capable of answering the question is one way to separate good science from bad.

When setting up a BLAST experiment, the most important thing to remember is "you get what you look for." In other words, search parameters determine what you find. For example, the BLASTN program from NCBI with the default settings assumes that the alignments you are seeking are nearly identical because the parameters (match +1, mismatch −3) have a target frequency of 99 percent identity. If your experimental question is "How many worm genes are related to my favorite human gene," using the default parameters would be foolish because the approach (looking for nearly identical sequences) isn't expected to answer the question; too many sequences have changed in the 500 million years that separate worms and humans.

8.3 Perform Controls, Especially in the Twilight Zone

Controls are crucial to any scientific experiment. The random model underlying BLAST statistics provides one kind of control, but performing an explicit control can give you greater confidence in your results. This is especially true when looking for weak similarities, commonly called the *twilight zone*. One of the simplest and most effective ways to determine if an alignment is believable is to shuffle your query sequence and repeat the search. If the shuffled sequence returns similar results, the alignment is based on compositional biases or the search parameters aren't specific enough. The following Perl script shuffles a FASTA file:

```
#!/usr/bin/perl -w
use strict;

my ($def, @seq) = <>;
print $def;
chomp @seq;
@seq = split(//, join("", @seq));
my $count = 0;
while (@seq) {
    my $index = rand(@seq);
    my $base = splice(@seq, $index, 1);
    print $base;
    print "\n" if ++$count % 60 == 0;
}
```

Now let's put this script into action. Let's make the dubious hypothesis that ALU repeats aren't specific to primates but are present in all genomes. They haven't been found because people just haven't looked hard enough. Your search parameters use +1/-1 match/mismatch scores and a gap opening cost of 1 and extension cost of 1. (WU-BLAST users would understand this as a cost of 2 for the first gap and 1 for each additional gap). Figure 8-1a shows an alignment between a human ALU (a variety of repeats are available from *ftp://ftp.ncbi.nih.gov/repository/repbase*) and the *Caenorhabditis elegans* genome (see *http://www.wormbase.org*). Without a control, you might be able to convince yourself that you found a match to a *C. elegans* ALU. However, because a shuffled control (Figure 8-1b) produces an alignment that is approximately 100 times more significant, this conclusion isn't very likely.

You might wonder why the alignments in Figure 8-1 seem to have significant E-values. The search employed low gap penalties and ungapped alignment statistics. When using gapped alignment statistics, these alignments are expected at random.

```
a  Score = 36.5 bits (22), Expect = 0.28
   Identities = 57/88 (64%), Gaps = 9/88 (10%)
   Strand = Plus / Minus

   Query: 115   tctacaaaaaatacaaaaattagccg-ggcgt--ggtggcg--cgcgcctgtagtcccag 169
                ||||||||||| | || |||||| ||   ||  ||| ||| | ||| | || ||||
   Sbjct: 66749 tctacaaaaaacagaataattagacgcaaagtccggtagcggcctcgcacgacgttccag 66690

   Query: 170   ctactcgggaggctgaggcaggaggatc 197
                ||    ||    ||  |||||| || ||
   Sbjct: 66689 ct----gggcatttggagcaggtggttc 66666

b  Score = 42.9 bits (26), Expect = 0.003
   Identities = 100/157 (63%), Gaps = 25/157 (15%)
   Strand = Plus / Plus

   Query: 139   tcgaaca-gaatagaccacgcacaatatggarccacaccggcg--tgc-aac-c-gca-- 190
                |||||| | ||| || |||||||||| | || ||||| ||  || | || |||
   Sbjct: 83998 tcgaaaatgaaaag-ccacgcacaatttagaacca-atcggcgacttcgaactctgcacc 84055

   Query: 191   aggggggtcatcgg-aggatagtgtgcgaa--gaa--actgatt-gccgttgactactgg 244
                |  |   | || || ||| ||| || | | |  ||| |||||| | ||| | | ||
   Sbjct: 84056 atccgtttgattggtcggaacgtgggtggagcgaatcgctgattggtcgtgcagttct-- 84113

   Query: 245   catggtcggatgaaca-tgaa---gag-gagtcatgc 276
                ||| | ||| ||| | | ||   ||| || | ||||
   Sbjct: 84114 cat-tttgga-gaaaattcaaaccgagagattaatgc 84148
```

Figure 8-1. Searching (a) an ALU element and (b) a shuffled version against the C. elegans genome

8.4 View BLAST Reports Graphically

BLAST reports can be complicated. Viewing them graphically can help you understand them better, especially when the reports are very long. Appendix D includes a
simple Perl program that converts tabular output from NCBI-BLAST reports into a
GIF, PNG, or JPEG image. Figures 8-2, 8-4, 8-8, and 8-9 were created with this program. Appendix E contains a program that converts the standard BLAST reports to
the NCBI tabular format. The programs are available at this book's O'Reilly web
site.

Figure 8-2 is an example of a BLASTX search. Appendix D contains more information on the display.

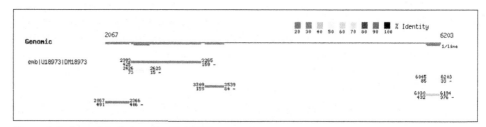

Figure 8-2. A graphical view of a BLASTX report

8.5 Use the Karlin-Altschul Equation to Design Experiments

The Karlin-Altschul equation is very useful for predicting the outcome of a BLAST experiment, especially in large search spaces. Suppose you want to find exons in the human genome by looking for similarities in the pufferfish genome. These genomes last shared a common ancestor about 450 million years ago. You might assume that any similarities at this distance must be due to evolutionary conservation.

Recall from Chapter 4 that the number of alignments expected by chance (E) is a function of the search space (M, N), the normalized score (λS), and a minor constant (K).

$$E = KMNe^{-\lambda S}$$

The typical cross-species parameters +1/-1 match/mismatch have a target frequency of 75 percent identity and 0.55 nats per aligned letter on average (*H*). A 50-bp alignment therefore contains about 27.5 nats. Substituting this normalized score into the Karlin-Altschul equation with K=0.334, M=1.5 GB (assuming half of the human genome contains repeats), and N=450 MB (the size of the repeat-poor pufferfish genome), you expect about 230,000 alignments by chance. That's roughly the same as the number of exons in the human genome. If you want to look for 50-bp exons, you'll have to sift through a lot of false positives.

To change the Karlin-Altschul expectation to something more manageable, either look for larger exons or reduce your search space. A 72-nucleotide alignment is expected only once by chance, and an alignment the size of a typical exon (110 bp) has a probability of about 1 in 1 billion of occurring. An even better approach is to restrict the search to orthologous regions of the size of a typical gene. Here 50-bp alignments have a probability of approximately 1 in 10,000.

8.6 When Troubleshooting, Read the Footer First

Novices usually focus on the one-line summaries, regular users concentrate on the alignments and their statistics, and professionals first read the footer. When it comes to solving the two most common problems, no hits and too many hits, the one-line summaries aren't much help. Regular users can often look at alignments and diagnose compositional biases and unidentified repeats, but determining the cause of no hits isn't easy. Examining the footer to determine what the search was actually looking for is the best way to determine what happened. Always answer the following questions first:

- What are the values for the seeding parameters W, T, and two-hit distance? If the seeding parameters are too stringent, divergent alignments may not be seeded. In NCBI-BLAST, W is unfortunately not displayed in the footer. The value for T and two-hit distance are given as T: and A:, respectively.

- What is the scoring scheme expecting to find (i.e., target frequency)? If the scoring matrix expects nearly identical sequences, highly divergent sequences may be missed.

- What is the alignment threshold? If the alignment threshold is too high, low scoring alignments will be thrown away. The gapped and ungapped values are given after S1: and S2: in NCBI-BLAST. In WU-BLAST, they are on the rows beneath S2.

- What are B and V set to? If they are set too low, the number of one-line summaries and database hits may be truncated.

- What is the score and expected length of a significant alignment? Use the Karlin-Altschul equation to solve for the normalized score and then divide by H to calculate the length.

- Was complexity filtering employed, and if so, was it hard or soft? Complexity filtering is generally a good idea, but may prevent some sequences from generating significant alignments. NCBI-BLAST doesn't not currently report which filters were employed.

8.7   Know When to Use Complexity Filters

Low-complexity sequence occurs much more frequently than expected by chance in both proteins and nucleic acids. When a BLAST search takes longer than expected, it is almost always due to low complexity sequence or repeats. Low-complexity filters can sometimes be destructive. Figure 8-3a shows what happens when a query sequence is filtered: the low complexity region is replaced with Xs (or Ns for nucleotide sequences). This operation always reduces the score and can terminate an alignment extension. For this reason, it is almost always better to use soft-masking (see Figure 8-3b). This technique masks low-complexity sequence in the seeding phase but allows the extension phase to see the sequence normally. See -F in Chapter 13 and wordmask in Chapter 14.

What if your query is almost entirely low-complexity? If soft-masking doesn't work, you may have to perform the search without complexity filters. In this case, expect many false-positive alignments and a slow search. Setting a lower E-value to remove low-scoring alignments can help reduce the size of the output.

```
a  Score = 70.1 bits (170), Expect = 5e-12
   Identities = 35/79 (44%), Positives = 45/79 (56%)

Query: 1   MAVTQXXXXXXXXXXXXXXXXXXXPSEITPEKSFVDDLDIDSLSMVEIAVQTEDKYGVKIP 60
           MA TQ                   ++  +KSF DDLD+DSLSMVE+ V  E+++ VKIP
Sbjct: 1   MAATQEEIVAGLADIVNEIAGIPVEDVQLDKSFTDDLDVDSLSMVEVVVAAEEERFDVKIP 60

Query: 61  DEDLAGLRTVGDVVTYIQK 79
           DED+ L+TVGD   YI K
Sbjct: 61  DEDVKNLKTVGDATEYILK 79

b  Score = 99.0 bits (245), Expect = 1e-20
   Identities = 45/79 (56%), Positives = 60/79 (74%)

Query: 1   MAVTQEEIIAGIAEIIEEVTGIEPSEITPEKSFVDDLDIDSLSMVEIAVQTEDKYGVKIP 60
           MA TQEEI+AG+A+I+ E+ GI   ++  +KSF DDLD+DSLSMVE+ V  E+++ VKIP
Sbjct: 1   MAATQEEIVAGLADIVNEIAGIPVEDVQLDKSFTDDLDVDSLSMVEVVVAAEEERFDVKIP 60

Query: 61  DEDLAGLRTVGDVVTYIQK 79
           DED+ L+TVGD   YI K
Sbjct: 61  DEDVKNLKTVGDATEYILK 79
```

Figure 8-3. Complexity filters (a) hard-masking and (b) soft-masking

8.8   Mask Repeats in Genomic DNA

As mentioned in Chapter 2, genomes may be full of repetitive elements and low-complexity sequence. They can be very problematic in BLAST searches, and if not masked prior to a BLAST search, will waste computer time and inflate BLAST reports with meaningless, redundant information (Figure 8-4).

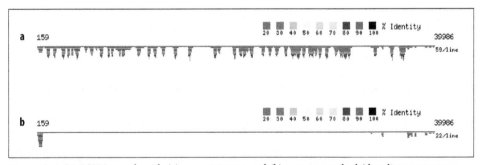

Figure 8-4. BLASTX search with (a) repeats intact and (b) repeats masked (the alignments were removed from the display)

8.9   Segment Large Genomic Sequences

Nucleotide sequences can be very, very long. For example, the shortest human chromosome, number 22, is over 47 million bp. BLAST wasn't designed for large sequences and runs poorly in such an environment. You can easily run out of memory with chromosome-sized sequences. Even if you have a computer with sufficient memory, searching large sequences is inefficient because the procedure for assessing combined statistical significance scales quadratically with the number of alignments.

The simplest way to deal with large sequences is to split them into overlapping fragments. For genomes with high gene density, each fragment should be 100 Kb or less.
For the human genome and others with low gene density, fragments can be larger,
but try not to exceed 1 Mb.

The following Perl script splits a FASTA file into overlapping fragments. Each
sequence fragment is given a unique identifier, and the definition contains the original coordinates and complete definition.

```perl
#!/usr/bin/perl -w
use strict;
die "usage: $0 <fasta file> <size> <overlap>\n" unless @ARGV == 3;
my ($file, $size, $overlap) = @ARGV;

my $def = "";
my $dna = "";
my $sequence = 0;
my $fragment = 0;

open(IN, $file) or die;
while (<IN>) {
    chomp;
    if (/^>(.+)/) {
        segment();
        $def = $1;
        $sequence++;
        $fragment = 1;
        $dna = "";
    }
    else {
        $dna .= $_;
    }
    while (length($dna) > $size) {segment()}
}
segment();

sub segment {
    return unless $dna;
    my $output = substr($dna, 0, $size);
    if (length($output) == $size) {
        $dna = substr($dna, $size - $overlap);
    }
    else {
        $dna = "";
    }
    my $start = ($fragment -1) * ($size - $overlap) + 1;
    my $end = $start + length($output) -1;
    print ">$sequence-$fragment {$start..$end} $def\n";
    for (my $i = 0; $i < length($output); $i+= 80) {
        print substr($output, $i, 80), "\n";
    }
    $fragment++;
}
```

8.10 Be Skeptical of Hypothetical Proteins

Amino acid sequencing is more difficult than nucleic acid sequencing, and therefore, sequences of most proteins are inferred from DNA translations. Some inferences come from gene predictions and others come from transcript translations. Finding the correct structure of genes in genomic DNA is very difficult; algorithms are incomplete approximations, and people make mistakes. Some research groups are conservative and only report proteins when there is good evidence. Others submit hypothetical proteins and hope that they will be useful (and they often are). As a result, many proteins in the public database are slightly incorrect or even fictitious. Unfortunately, hypothetical gene structures aren't always clearly labeled.

The most accurate protein sequences come from translating full-length cDNAs. But determining the protein encoded by a transcript isn't as simple as it sounds. While there is usually only one long open reading frame (ORF), the longest ORF won't necessarily correspond to a real protein. Be suspicious of all short proteins. Even in a full-length cDNA with a very large ORF, determining the start of translation isn't straightforward. The first methionine in the longest ORF is usually picked as the start of translation, but as a rule of convenience, not a biological truth. Many protein sequences have erroneous N-terminal extensions.

8.11 Expect Contaminants in EST Databases

A simple view is that ESTs are sequencing reads from cDNAs, cDNAs are derived from mRNAs, and mRNAs are derived from genes. Theoretically, this is true, but in practice ESTs frequently don't correspond to genes (e.g., rather than match an exon or UTR, they overlap part of a repeat on the wrong strand within an intron). The fraction of nontranscript sequence depends on the way the library was created. Some libraries are nearly devoid of extra-genic material, while others are essentially random shotgun sequence. How can you tell the difference? It's difficult to determine directly from the EST sequences.

Before the human genome was completed, the number of genes was estimated at 100,000 to 200,000. Current estimates are 25,000 to 30,000. One of the reasons for the initial high figure was that EST clustering experiments found many clusters, and people believed each cluster was a gene. One of the best ways to sort out real transcripts from pollutants is to align ESTs back to their genome. See the section "Annotating Genomic DNA with ESTs" in Chapter 9 for more details.

8.12 Use Caution When Searching Raw Sequencing Reads

The largest source of raw sequencing reads comes from the early stages of genome projects and from EST sequencing. Most sequencing reads have an error rate of about 1 percent. This rate isn't uniform; there is a spike near the beginning and a gradual increase towards the end of the read. In addition, some regions have intrinsically high error rates due to compositional properties such as high GC content. DNA sequencing involves several steps, and there are abundant opportunities for mechanical and human error. Thus, you will need to be careful when using large word sizes. For redundant sequence collections, such as 3x shotgun coverage of a genome, large word sizes are fine, but if the absence of a single alignment is troublesome, scale down the word size to keep sequencing errors from preventing seeding.

Raw sequencing reads may be contaminated from a variety of sources. Cloning vectors are one expected source. Depending on the sequencing center, the vectors may or may not have been clipped from the sequence. Other kinds of contamination are also possible. Nuclear DNA is sometimes contaminated with mitochondrial or viral DNA, and any collection of sequence can be contaminated from another organism (genome centers usually sequence more than one entity at a time, and sometimes there's a mix up of who did what and when). ESTs sometimes have their poly-A tail intact, and whether or not this is contamination is a matter of perspective. Taken together, there are many opportunities for contamination, and it's a good idea to be cautious when using raw sequencing reads.

8.13 Look for Stop Codons and Frame-Shifts to find Pseudo-Genes

Stop codons generally aren't found in protein-coding genes. They are common, however, in pseudo-genes. It's important to recognize pseudo-genes early in a sequence-analysis pipeline because they may confound downstream analyses. Pseudo-genes usually have stop codons and insertions or deletions (Figure 8-5). Stop codons are easy to spot in alignments, but insertions and deletions must be inferred from alignment coordinates. Look for HSPs that are in different frames and appear too close to be separated by an intron (< 25 bp).

8.14 Consider Using Ungapped Alignment for BLASTX, TBLASTN, and TBLASTX

The first versions of BLAST produced strictly ungapped alignments but were still very useful. Although gapped alignment has some advantages, it may produce

```
            Score = 1320 (469.7 bits), Expect = 4.8e-152, Sum P(2) = 4.8e-152
            Identities = 247/276 (89%), Positives = 256/276 (92%), Frame = +3

Query:   225 VMRDPNTKRSRGFGFVTYATVEEVDAAMNARPCKVDGRTVEPKRDISREDSRRPGAHLTV 404
             VMRDPNTKRSRGFGFVTYATVEEVDAAMNARP KVDGR VEPKR +SREDS+RPGAHLTV
Sbjct:    45 VMRDPNTKRSRGFGFVTYATVEEVDAAMNARPHKVDGRVVEPKRAVSREDSQRPGAHLTV 104

Query:   405 KKIFVGGVKEDTEEHHLKDYFEQ*GKIEVIEIMTD*GSGKKKGFAFVTFDNHDSVDKTVI 584
             KKIFVGG+KEDTEEHHL+DYFEQ GKIEVIEIMTD GSGKKKGFAFVTFD+HDSVDK VI
Sbjct:   105 KKIFVGGIKEDTEEHHLRDYFEQFGKIEVIEIMTDRGSGKKKGFAFVTFDDHDSVDKIVI 164

Query:   585 QKYCTVSGHNCEARKAL*KQEMARASTSQRGRSGSGNFGGGRGGGFDGNDNFGGGGNFSG 764
             QKY TV+GHNCE RKAL KQEMA AS+SQRGRSGSGNFGGGRGGGF GNDNFG GGNFSG
Sbjct:   165 QKYHTVNGHNCEVRKALSKQEMASASSSQRGRSGSGNFGGGRGGGFGGNDNFGRGGNFSG 224

Query:   765 RGGFGGSHGGGGYGGRGDGYNGCGNDGSSFGGGGSYNDFVNYNNQSSHFGPMKGGNFGGR 944
             RGGFGGS GGGYGG GDGYNG GNDGS+FGGGGSYNDF NYNNQSS+FGPMKGGNFGGR
Sbjct:   225 RGGFGGSRGGGGYGGSGDGYNGFGNDGSNFGGGGSYNDFGNYNNQSSNFGPMKGGNFGGR 284

Query:   945 SSGPYGGGGQYFTKP*NQGGYGSSSSSSSYSSGRRF 1052
             SSGPYGGGGQYF KP NQGGYG SSSSSSY SGRRF
Sbjct:   285 SSGPYGGGGQYFAKPRNQGGYGSSSSSSSYGSGRRF 320

           Score = 197 (74.4 bits), Expect = 4.8e-152, Sum P(2) = 4.8e-152
           Identities = 37/44 (84%), Positives = 42/44 (95%), Frame = +2

Query:    92 LSKSESSKKPEQLRKLFIGVLTFETTDESLRSHFEQWGTLTNCM 223
             +SKSES K+PEQLRKLFIG L+FETTDESLRSHFEQWGTLT+C+
Sbjct:     1 MSKSESPKEPEQLRKLFIGGLSFETTDESLRSHFEQWGTLTDCV 44
```

Figure 8-5. BLASTX alignment of a pseudo-gene (stop codons are circled)

surprising results. When running the translating BLAST programs (BLASTX, TBLASTN, and TBLASTX), you generally look for protein coding regions and therefore don't expect to see stop codons. Stop codons are very frequent in alignments from these programs, and it isn't possible to eliminate stop codons by simply making their scores highly negative. In standard alignment algorithms (see Chapter 3), no match score can be more negative than the cost of two gaps. In Figure 8-6, all stop codon scores are given a value of -999 (for more details, see Chapter 10). Notice how two alternating gaps skip over the stops in this TBLASTX alignment between two noncoding sequences (this is a WU-BLAST alignment; NCBI-BLAST is always ungapped for TBLASTX). You can avoid stop codons only by using ungapped alignment in addition to highly negative stop scores. Doing so segments the alignment in Figure 8-6 into three short alignments with insignificant E-values.

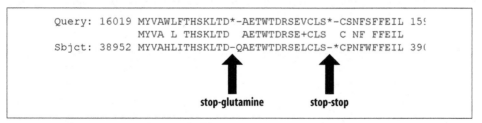

Figure 8-6. Alternating gaps skip over highly negative scores

Figure 8-7 demonstrates another feature of gapped alignment: alignments may extend far beyond the end of an exon because gapped extension is generally less specific. This is especially annoying in genomes with short introns in which gapped alignments can extend between nonadjacent exons and obscure intervening introns and exons. To reduce these lengthy extensions, decrease X, increase the gap extension cost, select a more stringent scoring matrix, or use ungapped alignment.

```
Query: 201 MKLVILLSFVATVAVFG--------EFML*IILFRQKYSCRSRYGNIFVKFEKQ 338
           MKLVILLSFVATVAVF         E  L   L  Q YS    G + VK ++Q
Sbjct: 1   MKLVILLSFVATVAVFAAPSAPAGLEEKL-RALQEQLYSLEKENG-VDVKQKEQ 52
```

Figure 8-7. Extension is sometimes excessive: the real exon region is boxed in this BLASTX alignment

8.15   Look for Gaps in Coverage as a Sign of Missed Exons

The seeding parameters and alignment thresholds may prevent short or highly divergent exons from appearing in BLAST reports. Figure 8-8a shows an alignment between a genomic query and an EST. Most alignments overlap by a few bp, except for the 2 at the 5′ end (left side). Gaps and overlaps in coverage are easier to see by using the reciprocal search shown in Figure 8-8b. To find the missing 7-bp exon in Figure 8-8c, use *bl2seq* (see Chapter 13) with the following command line:

```
bl2seq -i est -I 21,29 -j genomic -J 76047,76744 -pblastn -W 7
```

The -I and -J parameters let you select a specific region of each sequence. What you've done is a BLASTN search between the missing part of the EST and the region between the alignments.

8.16   Parse BLAST Reports with Bioperl

The traditional BLAST output format is meant to be human readable, but when your BLAST report is 1,000 pages long, it isn't much fun to read. Sometimes all you want is the names of all sequences that have alignments above 90 percent identity. Such tasks require a BLAST parser that lets you select only the information you want. Many freely available BLAST parsers can be downloaded from the Internet, but the ones in most common use come from the Bioperl project. Bioperl is an open-source community of bioinformatics professionals that develops and maintains code libraries and applications written in the Perl programming language. If your daily routine finds you running BLAST or other sequence analysis applications, learning to use the Bioperl system can save you many hours of work and frustration.

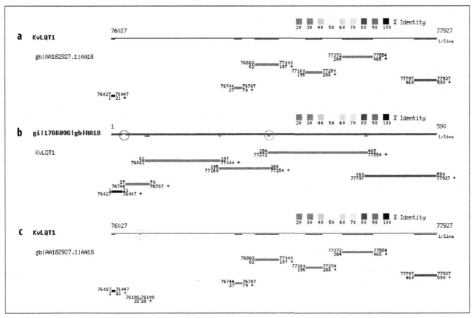

Figure 8-8. Finding missed exons: (a) an alignment between a genomic query and EST, (b) the reciprocal alignment showing a gap (d) and overlap (e) in coverage, (c) the tiny missed exon can be found (f) by changing the word size to 7

Let's see how Bioperl can help solve the problem posed earlier: to report the names of all sequences that are more than 90 percent identical to your query.

```perl
#!/usr/bin/perl -w
use strict;
use Bio::SearchIO;

my $blast = new Bio::SearchIO(
    -format => 'blast',
    -file   => $ARGV[0]);

my %Name;
my $result = $blast->next_result;
while(my $sbjct = $result->next_hit) {
    while(my $hsp = $sbjct->next_hsp) {
        $Name{$sbjct->name} = 1 if $hsp->frac_identical >= 0.9;
    }
}

print join("\n", sort keys %Name), "\n";
```

Pretty simple, huh? With BLAST and Bioperl, it's possible to create all kinds of useful applications.

8.17 Perform Pilot Experiments

Before embarking on a large BLAST experiment, first try some pilot experiments. For example, if you want to compare all human proteins to all nonhuman proteins, try 100 proteins first. Or, if you want to annotate a 5 mb chromosomal region with BLASTX similarities, search 100 Kb first. If you're unsure of which parameters to use, try several and see which ones give you the kinds of results you're looking for. It may seem like a waste of time, but performing pilot experiments will actually save you time in the end.

8.18 Examine Statistical Outliers

In a high-throughput setting, BLAST reports may be huge and number in the thousands. There's no way you can look at all of them, but for quality control, you should examine some of them. Keep global statistics on BLAST reports, such as number of hits per Kb. Statistical outliers may point to general problems that become more apparent in certain sequences.

8.19 Use links and topcomboN to Make Sense of Alignment Groups

WU-BLAST has two very useful parameters for displaying alignment groupings. topcomboN sorts alignments into groups and labels them. The links parameter shows the order of alignments in a group, which is much like the order of a gene's exons. Figure 8-9 displays these features.

8.20 How to Lie with BLAST Statistics

Several techniques can help you massage BLAST statistics to either hide significant alignments or make meaningless alignments appear highly significant. Why would you want to do this? If you have to ask, you're not the intended audience. Dishonest evil doers read on.

The easiest method to adjust the significance of all scores is to set the effective size of the search space either higher or lower. Command-line parameters in both NCBI-BLAST (-Y) and WU-BLAST (Y and Z) are available. You can also alter the scoring scheme by editing the scoring matrices. A more involved approach involves hacking the source code to set your own values for λ, k, and H. WU-BLAST makes it all too easy because you can alter scores or set Karlin-Altschul parameters on the command line. Whatever approach you take, you will, of course, want to edit the footer to cover your tracks. The easiest way to do this is to run the search twice and *diff* the footers to determine what needs fixing.

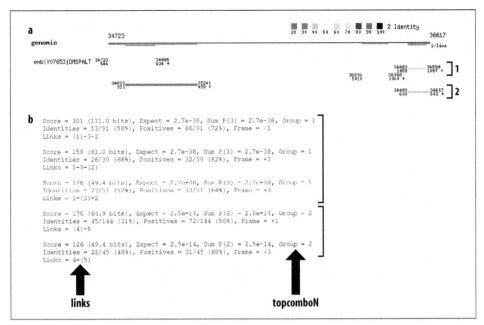

Figure 8-9. WU-BLAST topcomboN and links (the top-to-bottom order of alignments in the graphic (a) are the same as the statistics lines from the BLASTX report (b))

With low gap penalties, you can make alignments between just about anything. For BLASTN, NCBI-BLAST always uses ungapped statistics, so you don't have to do much work to lie. Just hope that nobody notices all the gaps. This works best if you have a supervisor who is either too busy to look at alignments or wouldn't know a decent alignment if it bit him. NCBI-BLAST is very restrictive about what gap penalties you can employ for the protein-based BLAST programs. Your only choice here is to hack and recompile. WU-BLAST is very easy; set your gap costs low and include warnings on the command line to suppress messages about ungapped statistics.

Another way to trick the unobservant is to remove complexity filters. This works especially well when claiming that some anonymous low-complexity region or transcript is a cool gene. You can almost always find a small ORF that has a poor match to something with an interesting definition line. A poor match is only poor if you don't know how to fix the statistics. This approach even works when fooling scientific journals. (It really does. We've seen it happen.)

CHAPTER 9

BLAST Protocols

This chapter contains protocols for the most common BLAST searches. Because every BLAST experiment is unique, you should treat the protocols as a starting point and use your own knowledge about BLAST to modify the procedures. The discussions include what to do, as well as why. Although this approach makes the descriptions more verbose, explaining the logic behind these choices will help you make intelligent choices when creating your own protocols.

Most BLAST experiments fall into one of two categories: mapping and exploring. *Mapping* is the process of finding the position of one sequence within another—for example, finding a gene within a genome. When mapping, you can expect the alignments to be nearly identical, and the coordinates are generally the focus of the results. When *exploring*, the goal is usually to find functionally related sequences. When exploring, your alignment statistics (score, expectation, percent identity, etc.) are often of greatest importance, at least initially. Making functional and phylogenetic inferences, especially between distantly related sequences, often requires inspecting the alignments from a biological rather than a statistical perspective. There is, of course, a continuum between mapping and exploring, but keeping this dichotomy in mind can help you zero in on the fundamental aspects of a search strategy.

The notation used here and in the reference chapters in Section 5 is the command-line interface. If you're unfamiliar with shells and terminals, the command line is where you type in program names and options. It may seem a little odd at first, but it is analogous to filling in a web form and then clicking the submit button. While most people use BLAST via some web interface, not all pages look the same or support the same parameters. Behind the scenes, though, they all interact with a command-line version of BLAST. BLAST pages frequently let you set advanced options; usually it's a text box or boxes in which you can enter the command-line options.

BLASTN Protocols

As we said earlier, most searches can be categorized as either mapping or exploring searches. When sequences are expected to be nearly identical, you should use the +1/-3 match-mismatch parameters, which have a target frequency of 99 percent identity. Cross-species exploration requires a change in the scoring parameters and word size. We like +1/-1 for both its simplicity and its 75 percent identity target frequency. The choice of word size depends on balancing sensitivity and specificity. The default word size of 11 is too risky; use 9, which corresponds to a little more stringency than three identical amino acids because there's no allowance for degenerate codons. The choice of gap costs depends on the size of the expected gap. For simulating sequencing errors, the gap costs should be uniform and relatively high, but for modeling amino acid gaps or nucleotide hybridization bubbles, the cost of extension should be lower.

Mapping Oligos to a Genome

Many kinds of experiments, both molecular and computational, employ short nucleotide sequences called oligonucleotides, or just oligos (*oligo* is Greek for *few*). For example, the polymerase chain reaction (PCR) is a routine laboratory procedure for amplifying a specific nucleotide sequence from DNA or indirectly from RNA. In PCR, oligos are used as templates for DNA replication, and the subsequence between the oligos is amplified. The most important feature of oligos is they may be short enough to give rise to many false-positive matches. In a test tube, we would say the oligo hybridizes nonspecifically, and in a BLAST experiment, we would say the alignments have high expectations.

Approach

Our goal here is to simulate the interaction between an oligo and a genome in a test tube. The thermodynamics of annealing are complex and depending on the conditions of the experiment (temperature, salt concentration, length, and composition of oligo), some mismatches between the sequences and even gaps may be possible. Still, the sequences are expected to be nearly identical, so we use corresponding match-mismatch parameters. The default word size is fine here; we don't increase it because a fortuitous mismatch can prevent seeding for a short oligo. Complexity filtering is turned off because we want the entire oligo to match, and low complexity isn't expected to be a problem with such a short query sequence. Because there is quite a bit of variation from one oligo to the next, we can't set a specific E value. Instead, we use the default and visually inspect the report after the search.

NCBI-BLAST parameters

```
blastall -p blastn -d <genome> -i <oligo> -G 2 -E 1 -F F
megablast -d <genome> -i <oligo> -W 11 -F F -D 2
```

WU-BLAST parameters

```
blastn <genome> <oligo> M=1 N=-3 Q=3 R=1
```

Expected results

There may be several alignments between the oligo and genome, and not all of them may align end to end. If you are simulating PCR, mismatches at the 3′ end of the oligo are of particular interest because they may prevent priming.

If you don't find any hits, the oligo may be too short for its alignments to achieve statistical significance. For short oligos, even a 100 percent matching alignment may have a score that is expected at random in a large search space. Try raising E. Also, make sure that the scoring scheme favors near identity. Otherwise, lambda may transform the score to a very low amount of information, and you may not be able to set E high enough to recover the alignment. Other possibilities include too large a value for W or the use of complexity filters.

If you find too many hits, increase the stringency of the search by decreasing E. The suggested scoring scheme is already pretty strict, but you may want to set the gap penalties higher or turn off gapping entirely if you find too many gapped alignments. It may be that the query is just found in many places. If you don't care about the details of the alignments, tabular format is convenient to parse and takes up much less space. See Appendixes A and E to learn how to report in tabular format.

Optimizations and variations

If you have many oligos to map, a technique called query packing (see Chapter 10) can greatly improve your speed. If you're interested only in exact matches, you can set the word size to the same size as the oligo. This is probably not a good simulation for what happens in a test tube, but it will make the search faster. Here, you might consider using MegaBLAST rather than BLASTN because it automatically packs queries and uses large word sizes but make sure the word size isn't larger than the oligo. If you want to search for oligos cross-species, be prepared to sift through many alignments because the expectation for low-scoring alignments may be very high.

Mapping Nonspliced DNA to a Genome

Many BLASTN searches fall into the same general category in which a moderately sized DNA sequence (usually around 500 bp) is used to query a genome. There are separate protocols for spliced query sequences, searching EST databases, and exploring distantly related sequences.

Approach

Our alignment parameters favor near identity and use a large word size to make the search faster. It is probably not necessary to set a value for E because the word size alone provides specificity. But if you lower the word size, you will want to set E to a small value that depends on your search space. The value presented here is only a suggestion. As with any search involving genomic DNA, you should mask repeats before you begin. See Chapter 7 for more details.

NCBI-BLAST parameters

```
blastall -p blastn -d <genome> -i <dna> -G 1 -E 3 -W 30 -F "m D" -U -e 1e-20
megablast -d <genome> -i <dna> -F "m D" -U -D 2
```

WU-BLAST parameters

```
blastn <genome> <dna> M=1 N=-3 Q=3 R=3 W=30 wordmask=seg lcmask E=1e-20
```

Expected results

True matches between the query and the genome ought to align from end to end with near identity. Because BLAST is a local alignment program, you can't require the alignment to cover the entire length of the sequence, so you just have to look for this property in the output. If the alignment doesn't go end to end, the sequence quality of the query might drop at the ends (which happens with raw sequencing reads).

Even if you mask repeats, they can still cause trouble. Some repeats aren't very abundant, or are limited to a particular region/chromosome and therefore may not be part of your repeat library. If your report is particularly long, look for regions that are over-represented in alignments. Graphical reports are very useful (see Appendix D). You may have to mask or omit troublesome regions by hand if they continue to give you problems.

Low-complexity sequences can also be problematic because not all instances are caught by the default parameters of complexity filters. You can further reduce nonspecific hits by filtering both the query and the database, but since the database is case-insensitive, soft-masking isn't an option. If you find that repeats or low-complexity matches dominate your report, you will probably have to run the report through a parser and select the hits that are nearly full length.

Genomes sometimes have regions of large duplications. While you may expect a single near-identity alignment, you can find multiple matches if your query has paralogs. Depending on how much time has passed since the duplication event, paralogs may be very distant or identical to one another.

Optimizations and variations

If you don't care much about the alignments, tabular output will help you read the report (see Appendixes A and E). If you have a number of query sequences, this is a really good place to use MegaBLAST; it was designed for tasks such as this. For sequences that aren't expected to be identical, see the section "Cross-Species Sequence Exploration."

Mapping a cDNA/EST to a Genome

Determining the correct structure of eukaryotic protein-coding genes isn't an easy task because genes are broken up into exons. One of the most accurate methods for determining exon-intron structure involves mapping transcripts back to their origin in a genome. This procedure sounds simple, but it is actually a bit complicated, and its difficulties shouldn't be underestimated. A related, but more difficult, problem is mapping transcripts between species (see the following protocol). Also see the section "Annotating Genomic DNA with ESTs."

Approach

Most exons are 100-200 bp long, but there is a large range from only a few nucleotides to several kilobases. Generally, 99 percent of exons are larger than 50 bp, so large word sizes work fine. We suggest that you use typical near-identity parameters, but choose a word size that isn't quite as large as the previous protocol because it may be difficult to seed short exons with low quality sequence. As with any DNA search, the query should be repeat-masked prior to the search, and lowercase masking is preferred. Including a low value for E reduces many nonspecific hits. The proper value for E depends on the length of the query and the size of the database. The value given here is only a suggestion.

NCBI-BLAST parameters

```
blastall -p blastn -d <genome> -i <cDNA> -G 1 -E 3 -W 15 -F "m D" -U -e 1e-20
megablast -d <genome> -i <cDNA> -W 12 -F "m D" -U -t 21 -N 0 -D 2
```

WU-BLAST parameters

```
blastn <genome> <cDNA> M=1 N=-3 Q=3 R=3 W=15 wordmask=seg lcmask E=1e-20
```

Expected results

BLAST performs local alignments and doesn't explicitly model exon-intron structure or splice sites. For this reason, HSP endpoints aren't expected to correspond to exon boundaries, though they sometimes do. It is common for the alignment to be a few bps longer than the exon boundary on each side but in a low quality sequence, the alignment may be shorter than the exon. To determine whether you missed a short exon, look for a region of the query that isn't represented in any alignment. A graphical report is useful here (see Appendix D). If you find such a region, you may wish to search just this piece against the intron between neighboring exons with the *bl2seq* program using a shorter word size.

The same issues involving unidentified repeats, low-complexity sequence, and paralogs you encounter when mapping nonspliced sequences also apply here. Pseudo genes may also pose a problem. They are fairly easy to detect because they look like mRNAs embedded in the genome rather than real genes. See the section "Annotating Genomic DNA with ESTs."

Optimizations and variations

If you have several sequences, MegaBLAST is a better choice than BLASTN. If your sequences come from different species, also see the section "Cross-Species Sequence Exploration." Several programs model exon-intron structure, and they often give accurate results. But don't expect them to work every time because small exons, low quality sequence, repeats, gene duplications, etc., also affect these tools. Some of the most popular programs include SIM4, SPIDEY, and EST2GENOME. If you want to align ESTs and genomes from distant species, EST2GENOME is the best choice because it doesn't seed alignments with words.

Cross-Species Sequence Exploration

Comparative sequence analysis is a powerful approach for finding biologically important sequences. You may search for protein-coding genes, regulatory elements, RNA genes, or other regions of interest. In most cases, you expect the sequences to be similar but probably not identical. Most changes will probably be nucleotide substitutions, insertions, or deletions, but some may be more extreme. For example, genes may gain/lose exons or introns, repetitive elements may be inserted/deleted, and large-scale duplications, inversions, and deletions and other rearrangements may occur. Be cautious. This book doesn't include multiple cross-species protocols, so use this one to modify the other BLASTN protocols.

Approach

Because we don't expect the sequences to be identical, we use relaxed parameters for both seeding and alignment. Therefore, we use typical exploration parameters (+1/–1 and word size of 9) with soft masking. These parameters are similar to the following repetitive element identification parameters, but we choose higher gap penalties here because functional sequences usually have few gaps. The choice of E is left to you because there are many appropriate values, depending on your level of stringency. Should you set it high, you may also want to increase the output reporting options (-b and -v in NCBI-BLAST; B and V in WU-BLAST).

NCBI-BLAST parameters

```
blastall -p blastn -d <genome> -i <dna> -r 1 -q -1 -G 1 -E 2 -W 9 -F "m D" -U
```

WU-BLAST parameters

```
blastn <genome> <dna> M=1 N=-1 Q=3 R=2 W=9 wordmask=seg lcmask
```

Expected results

Be on the lookout for repetitive and low-complexity sequence and pseudogenes. Cross-species alignments are difficult to interpret because many factors impact DNA evolution. Not all sequences evolve at the same rate, and it is very easy to confuse signal and noise. It's a good idea to approach your findings with skepticism. Sequences that are nearly identical may indicate a very important biological signal, or they may represent sequencing contamination.

Low-scoring alignments may be coincidental similarities of no biological significance. If your search space is large, even high-scoring alignments are expected by chance. Work out the Karlin-Altschul expectation and search fabricated sequences to appreciate how frequently false positive alignments occur. That said, some biological signals are short and may be buried in the stochastic noise. The best way to deal with them is to reduce your search space. For example, if you are interested in determining if there is a short region of interest within the intron of a gene, try aligning the intron with the orthologous intron from another genome rather than the entire genome.

If you want to identify orthologs between genomes, the most common approach is to label the best reciprocal match to the ortholog. This approach can be confounded by paralogs, so take synteny into account if possible and look for homology that extends to neighboring genes.

Optimizations and variations

Changing word size and scoring parameters are some of the most obvious alterations you can make to the protocol. Adjusting word size by a single point can alter the speed by a factor of 3 (this is a rough estimate and applies only to relatively small word sizes). How seeding affects sensitivity depends on what you're searching for and the expected divergence. Other useful scoring schemes are given in Appendix B.

If you're interested in coding sequence similarities, TBLASTX is a better choice for more distant relationships. But since this program runs relatively slowly, you are better off with BLASTN for closer relatives. As a rule, if the expected identity is less than 70 percent, switch to TBLASTX.

MegaBLAST isn't recommended for cross-species searches. The new discontiguous version is designed for this task, but the effective word size, 14, is too high.

Annotating Genomic DNA with ESTs

Identifying genes in genomic sequence is a difficult and important task. None of the many experimental and computational approaches is foolproof. One useful technique is to identify related transcripts. The most common form of transcript information comes from ESTs.

ESTs are sequencing reads derived from the ends of cDNAs, and they therefore conceptually correspond to the transcripts of protein-coding genes. But not all ESTs encode proteins: mRNAs have untranslated regions at both ends, and many ESTs don't actually correspond to genes. Various techniques are employed to increase the proportion of less abundant transcripts, and while these techniques are useful for discovering genes with low levels of expression, they tend to increase the fraction of nontranscript sequences (otherwise know as "junk"). As a result, some EST collections contain a lot of sequence that doesn't correspond to any protein. Unfortunately, it is no simple task to determine which EST sequences in a database correspond to transcripts and which are junk.

Approach

Even though we expect many ESTs to align to the genomic DNA with near-identity, exploration parameters are often more appropriate than mapping parameters. There may be genes for which matching transcripts haven't yet been isolated but for which similar transcripts are available. These genes may come from the same or different species.

As usual, you should repeat-mask the sequence prior to the search and (preferred, but not necessary) use lowercase masking rather than Ns. Set a low E value to cut down on false positive alignments, and set the output options high because some regions are highly expressed and may prevent the display of real, low-scoring alignments.

After this search is performed, you will probably want to use specialized alignment algorithms to determine the exon-intron boundaries. See the "Optimizations and variations" section in the protocol in "Mapping a cDNA/EST to a Genome."

NCBI-BLAST parameters

```
blastall -p blastn -d <est_db> -i <genomic> -r 1 -q -1 -G 1 -E 2 -W 9 -F "m D" -U -e
1e-20 -b 100000 -v 100000
```

WU-BLAST parameters

```
blastn <est_db> <genomic> M=1 N=-1 Q=3 R=2 W=9 wordmask=seg lcmask E=1e-20 B=100000
V=100000
```

Expected results

The first thing to remember is that not all transcript matches correspond to a gene. There is quite a bit of variability from one region of a genome to the next; some regions have very few nontranscript matches while others are completely covered in junk alignments. Several features can separate transcripts from junk. Here are a few rules to remember:

Multiple HSPs

Eukaryotic genes usually have introns, so if a database match has only one HSP, it may be junk. However, some genes have only one exon, and some exons are longer than sequencing reads, so you can't rely on this rule. If the exon contains coding sequence, there ought to be a large ORF. It is possible for what should be a single HSP to look like multiple HSPs if the extension terminates (low sequence quality and hard-masking cause this). True splicing events are easily identified from their coordinates; there ought to be a large coordinate gap in the genome but not the EST.

Repeat proximity

Exons almost never overlap a repetitive element and are usually at least 20 bp away. If you mask repeats with Ns, you won't find repeat overlaps, so look for HSPs that abut repeats. Low complexity is a completely different issue, and transcripts often overlap short, low-complexity regions.

Conservation

Most real genes are evolutionarily conserved. Therefore, ESTs from multiple species ought to align to a gene if the organisms aren't too diverged. However, just because ESTs pile up on a particular region doesn't mean that a gene is there. Many pseudogenes have this property, as do unmasked repeats and low entropy regions.

cDNA library

cDNA libraries constructed with subtractive/selective hybridization, micro-dissected tissues, or PCR amplification usually have a lot of nontranscript sequences. You may wish to track down the literature references for suspect ESTs to determine how their cDNA libraries were constructed.

Developmental regulation

Genes are regulated in time and space, so not all of them may be present in a particular cDNA library. For example, for ethical reasons, it is more difficult to find genes expressed in the human egg than the chicken egg. Regulation also occurs at the level of splicing, so some exons may be absent at one time or another.

Internal priming

cDNA libraries are usually constructed using poly-T primers to bind to the poly-A tail of mRNAs. If the genomic sequence has a long run of As, the resulting ESTs may all appear to end there; the real transcript may be much longer.

Stacking

> You can often discriminate exons from junk by simply viewing how the alignments stack up on the genome. Exonic regions generally have short HSPs with numerous alignments (except if the exon is very long). Junk regions usually have long alignments with little overlap. Visually, exons look like towers, and junk looks like stepping stones. But internal priming can make junk look like it has a defined endpoint. A graphical report is very handy here (see Appendix D).

Optimizations and variations

If your database is very large, you may consider increasing the word size. This will, of course, reduce sensitivity, but if you're only interested in nearly identical ESTs, you can change to typical mapping parameters, and you may want to change to Mega-BLAST as well. To increase sensitivity, rather than decreasing the word size, you may consider TBLASTX if you are most interested in the coding sequences.

Transcript Clustering and Extension

cDNA libraries are often redundant, with a handful of highly expressed genes making up most transcripts. Clustering transcripts to create a representative set with less redundancy is therefore a common task. A variant of clustering is *extension*, in which ESTs are assembled into larger, more complete entities. Clustering and extension are difficult even for seasoned bioinformatics professionals. Treat this protocol as a starting or learning point. BLASTN isn't the best program for this specific task. Several software packages for clustering and extension already exist, and this protocol can help you understand their features.

Approach

This is an "all versus all BLASTN" procedure, so your computational time may be immense if you have a lot of sequences. It's one of the few cases when hard-masking is preferable because repeats and low complexity can confuse clustering or extension if the wrong associations are made. To err on the side of safety, we recommend masking your sequences before creating your database.

We expect the alignments to be nearly identical, except for sequencing errors and allelic differences (polymorphisms), so we use typical mapping parameters and a very large word size (WU-BLAST parameters use a slightly smaller word size; you can include WINK to reduce the number of seeds because this combination is more efficient). It may seem risky to use large words with data that is expected to contain sequencing errors, but because the dataset is potentially very large and we're primarily interested in long, highly specific alignments, the risk is worth taking. The word size has enough specificity that it is probably not necessary to set E, but we do so just in case. Finally, we set the output options to "high" in case some clusters are particularly deep.

NCBI-BLAST parameters

```
blastall -p blastn -d <db> -i <EST> -G 1 -E 3 -W 30 -U -v 10000 -b 10000 -e 1e-10
```

WU-BLAST parameters

```
blastn <db> <EST> M=1 N=-3 Q=3 R=3 W=15 WINK=15 filter=seg lcmask V=10000 B=10000
E=1e-10
```

Expected results

In the simplest case, EST overlaps can be followed in either direction to create longer, virtual transcripts. For clustering, the representative EST is usually the one with the most matches (the longest). These straightforward expectations have many potential problems. Here are some of the common ones:

Repeats and low complexity
> Alignments may not be able to cross long repetitive regions. It is therefore possible for multiple HSPs to be present for sequences that are 100 percent identical. A second alignment with unmasked sequences can solve this problem.

Multiple isoforms
> Some genes have multiple promoters or undergo alternative splicing and therefore produce multiple forms of transcripts. As a result, transcripts that are identical for much of their length may have discrepancies that correspond to unique or variant exons.

Chimeras
> Cloning artifacts and lane tracking errors may join two sequences artificially. It is difficult to differentiate between chimeric sequences and isoform variants with just transcript alignments. Mapping the ESTs in their source genome is the best way to sort this issue out.

Paralogs
> Some genes exist in multiple copies in a genome. These may be completely identical to one another or quite diverged. Determining if two nearly identical ESTs come from the same gene isn't as simple because it depends on the sequencing error rate and the level of polymorphism. Mapping transcripts to their genomic source can help solve this problem.

Internal priming
> The presence of a poly-A tail is often taken as meaning the end of a transcript, but it may just be a run of A's in the middle of an exon. Real poly-A tails often have an AATAAA consensus sequence upstream, but a more reliable measure examines the genomic source to determine if the A's come from the genome or were added to a transcript.

Clustering with blastclust

Given a database of DNA sequences, it is often necessary to rapidly group related sequences for further analysis or simply identify redundancy at some level. One approach is to use BLASTN with rapid, insensitive search parameters, and then parse the output for the desired properties (e.g., 97 percent identity over at least 90 percent of the sequence length), and finally group all reads that are directly or indirectly (transitively) associated. Bioperl tools can automate such a procedure, but it takes a little work. The NCBI-BLAST distribution includes a standalone program called *blastclust* that is designed for just this task.

Approach

Two protocols are given below—one for clustering ESTs that are expected to be nearly identical across the length of the read (99 percent identity, 90 percent coverage), and another for shotgun sequences that have high identity over a smaller region of the read (97 percent identity, 10 percent coverage). The alignment parameters are preset for near identity, but some differences that may be the result of sequencing errors or polymorphism are allowed. Unlike other BLAST programs, *blastclust* doesn't allow soft masking.

EST clustering

```
blastclust -i <fasta file> -o <output file> -p F -L 0.9 -S 99 -b F
```

Shotgun sequences

```
blastclust -i <fasta file> -o <output file> -p F -L 0.1 -S 97 -b F
```

Expected results

The output from *blastclust* is one line for each cluster. Each line contains the identifiers for sequences in the cluster and may therefore be very long.

Repetitive elements are a problem because they may lead to false associations. This is especially true in the shotgun sequence approach where you're looking for high identity over short stretches. In contrast, the EST approach requires a high-identity match over a large portion of the sequence, making it less prone to small repeat or domain problems.

Vector Clipping

Vectors are DNA sequences used to clone (copy) fragments of DNA. They are commonly used in DNA sequencing. For various reasons, the vector DNA may inadvertently be present in a sequencing read. Therefore, a common practice in sequencing labs is to identify and remove vector sequences. This protocol describes how to identify vectors but not actually clip them. This additional step can be accomplished in many ways and is easily automated using the Bioperl tools.

Approach

Our goal is to take a batch of sequencing reads and search them against a database of vector sequences (a comprehensive database is distributed in GenBank). We expect vector sequences to align with near identity, so our parameters reflect this. The parameters here are almost the same as for oligo mapping because vector contamination may be relatively short. However, we add complexity filters because raw sequencing reads sometimes have an abundance of low complexity sequence, and we change the gap parameters to better simulate sequence error.

NCBI-BLAST parameters

```
blastall -p blastn -d <vector_db> -i <read> -G 1 -E 3 -W 10
```

WU-BLAST parameters

```
blastn <vector_db> <read> M=1 N=-3 Q=3 R=3 W=10 filter=seg
```

Expected results

Vector similarity usually occurs on one end of the query sequence, but it may not extend all the way to the end of the read if the sequence quality drops, and the alignment deteriorates. It's difficult to tell the difference between a short piece of vector contamination and a fortuitous similarity. If the alignment is at the end of the read and longer than 15 nucleotides, it's a good bet that the alignment is to vector.

Overcalling and undercalling are two potential problems in vector clipping. Poor sequence quality may lead to undercalling, so quality clipping usually precedes vector-clipping (this isn't a BLAST-based procedure). Undercalling can also occur if the value of E is set too high. Overcalling can result from believing that all alignments reported are vector similarities when they are really only expected at one end of the sequence.

Optimizations and variations

Query packing speeds up this BLAST search by a factor of 10. The standard vector database has many more vectors than may be used by the sequencing lab, so a good way to increase your efficiency is to minimize the vector database. You can use MegaBLAST here, though the default large word size poses a small risk for short regions of vector contamination.

Repeat Masking

Eukaryotic genomes often contain an abundance of repetitive elements. There are many kinds of repetitive elements, and these sequences may comprise most of a genome. Libraries of repetitive sequences are available from GenBank and elsewhere (*http://www.girinst.org/Repbase_Update.html*), but for newly sequenced organisms, you may have to build your own library.

Approach

Finding repetitive elements requires relaxed search parameters because their sequences are free to drift, and there is usually quite a bit of divergence within a particular family. We recommend soft masking rather than ordinary complexity filtering to ensure that the elements containing a low complexity sequence are aligned over their entire length. When choosing a value for W, we try to balance speed and sensitivity. While it may make sense to choose a very small value to ensure that all repeats are found, doing so isn't practical if you have to process many sequences. For WU-BLAST, we include the kap parameter, which omits calculating scores for combinations of alignments.

NCBI-BLAST parameters

```
blastall -p blastn -d <repeat_db> -i <dna> -r 1 -q -1 -G 2 -E 2 -W 9 -F "m D"
```

WU-BLAST parameters

```
blastn <repeat_db> <dna> M=1 N=-1 Q=2 R=2 W=9 wordmask=seg kap
```

Expected results

Alignments between repeats are expected to range from perfect identity to complete obscurity. The common classification scheme applies a score cutoff to discriminate between repeats and nonrepeats. Identifying the proper score threshold takes some experimentation because each repeat family has its own length and expected divergence. Overall, the score threshold determines the balance between undercalling and overcalling.

Some repetitive elements are mobile and may therefore insert themselves into other elements. If an insertion occurs near the end of an element, the alignment on the shorter side may fall below the score threshold.

Optimizations and variations

RepeatMasker (*http://repeatmasker.genome.washington.edu*) is the standard program used to identify and mask repeats. It uses a range of word sizes, scoring matrices, and cutoffs to optimize the sensitivity for each repeat family. One of its special features is that it clips full-length elements from sequences and performs a second round of searches with a "compressed" sequence. This enables it to find nested repeats. If your favorite genome is supported by RepeatMasker, it is probably better to use this software than write your own. However, if you want/need to do your own repeat masking, you will find that Bioperl tools are an enormous help.

Contaminant Detection

This protocol departs from the usual format because it is especially difficult and requires more than a single BLAST search. Contaminants come in many forms. Some, such as mitochondrial DNA mixed with nuclear DNA, are easily detected with near-identity parameters. But cross-species contamination is very difficult to detect. If you find an exact match between two genomes, is it contamination or a highly conserved region? There's no simple answer. Some genomes, however have specific signatures. For example, the human genome has many primate-specific *Alu* repetitive elements. If you find many *Alu* elements in a database of corn sequence, it's probably a contaminant.

The most critical part of contaminant detection is having representative databases. You can't find contaminants for which you have no sequences. On the other hand, if your sequence database is too large, you may spend an inordinate amount of time looking for contaminants. Repetitive element databases are good representative databases, and a reasonable approach to contaminant detection is to look for repeats that match other genomes better than your genome of interest. This won't catch everything, but it will tell you how much of a contaminant problem you may have.

BLASTP Protocols

Most BLASTP searches fall under the exploring category, which means you're trying to learn about your query sequence by comparing it to other proteins. You might also want to determine if particular regions are highly or not so highly conserved. Or you may want to gather proteins to build a phylogenetic tree. In any case, your main concern is how deeply you want to explore. The following protocols offer three levels of sensitivity.

The Standard BLASTP Search

Probably the most common BLAST search is BLASTP with default parameters. It is used in various settings because it balances speed and sensitivity. For example, if you want to compare all the proteins between two organisms, this is a good place to start. If the proteomes are very distant, the default parameters may not be ideal because alignments containing less than 35 percent identity aren't as easily detected. If the proteomes are very close, the standard search is still a good strategy because not all proteins evolve at the same rate, and some may diverge rather quickly.

Approach

We'll make only one adjustment to the default NCBI parameters. We use soft masking instead of normal complexity filtering so the entire alignment is scored. The WU-BLAST parameters are approximately the same as those of NCBI-BLAST.

NCBI-BLAST parameters

```
blastall -p blastp -d <db> -i <query> -F "m S"
```

WU-BLAST parameters

```
blastp <db> <query> hitdist=40 wordmask=seg postsw
```

Expected results

If you don't find any database hits, your query sequence may correspond to a novel protein. On the other hand, it may be that the parameters of the search are obscuring the similarity. If your query is very short, it may be difficult for it to achieve statistical significance. In this case, first try raising E. However, this step alone may not be enough, and you may have to change to a scoring matrix with a higher value of H (bits per aligned letter), such as BLOSUM80.

If you want to find remote homologies with short query sequences, be prepared for many false-positive alignments. If your sequence has a long, low-complexity region, be sure to have soft masking turned on. It's difficult to find collagens, for example, if complexity filters are destroying most of the alignment. Finally, try the slower, more sensitive search described later.

If you find that you have hundreds of database hits, you may be overrunning the output reporting parameters (-b and -v in NCBI-BLAST and V and B in WU-BLAST). If this is a concern, simply increase these values. However, if you're interested in only the top hits, you can either set E higher or use a search strategy designed for more similar sequences (below).

Optimizations and variations

The two protocols below offer speed-sensitivity tradeoffs. For more subtle changes, try altering T. If you use WU-BLAST, set W=4 and scale up T appropriately.

Fast, Insensitive Search

Increased speed is one reason to use an insensitive search. This is particularly true when performing multiple searches. Another reason is to increase the information content in the alignments, which is helpful for short query sequences whose alignments might otherwise fall below the significance threshold. As a rule, the insensitive search shouldn't be used for sequences that are expected to have less than 50 percent identity.

Approach

A simple way to make BLASTP faster is to ignore neighborhood words and require that seeds be formed from identical words. Because the sequences are expected to be very similar, we choose the BLOSUM80 scoring matrix and set a low value for E. The proper value for E depends on the query length and database size, so treat the value given next as a starting point.

NCBI-BLAST parameters

```
blastall -p blastp -d <db> -i <query> -F "m S" -f 999 -M BLOSUM80 -G 9 -E 2 -e 1e-5
```

WU-BLAST parameters

```
blastp <db> <query> wordmask=seg W=3 T=999 matrix=BLOSUM80 Q=11 R=2 postsw E=1e-5
```

Expected results

Most of your alignments should have high percent identities. You will find some that dip to 30 percent, but this doesn't ensure that you can find such alignments in general. With such insensitive parameters, it is unlikely that you will overrun the output cutoffs, but it's worth checking anyway. Set -v and -b higher (V and B in WU-BLAST), or decrease E as you see fit.

Optimizations and variations

You can't make the NCBI-BLAST search much faster than it is because the parameters are already near optimum. Setting the two-hit distance lower gives a minute increase in speed that isn't worth the loss in sensitivity. You can play around with the WU-BLAST seeding parameters by changing W, T, and hitdist.

Slow, Sensitive Search

If you're having a hard time finding sequences similar to your query or if you're looking for distant relatives, you may have more success with sensitive parameters.

Approach

We recommend lowering T and choosing a scoring matrix designed for greater divergence. The NCBI-BLAST and WU-BLAST scoring parameters are slightly different because they don't have the same built-in estimates for lambda. As usual, we suggest soft masking to align the low-complexity sequence properly; here it's particularly important because we want to make sure that all positive scores are counted. When searching for remote similarities, some real signals can have very low scores. For this reason, even though it will make the report longer, we set E higher. For the same reason, we increase the output reporting parameters.

NCBI-BLAST parameters

```
blastall -p blastp -d <db> -i <query> -f 9 -F "m S" -M BLOSUM45 -e 100 -b 10000 -v
10000
```

WU-BLAST parameters

```
blastp <db> <query> T=9 wordmask=seg  hitdist=60 matrix=BLOSUM50 Q=13 R=1 E=100
B=10000 V=10000
```

Expected results

Whenever you increase sensitivity, expect a decrease in specificity. These parameters are very sensitive, so many of the alignments may be chance similarities and of no biological significance. On the other hand, some biological signals aren't modeled well by BLAST statistics and what may appear as a very low score may be of real interest. Reading a BLAST report containing thousands of alignments isn't always entertaining, so if you're looking for something specific, such as an alignment to a particular region, you may be able to automate the reading with a BLAST parser.

Optimizations and variations

The probability model of BLAST assumes that amino acid pairings are independent of their neighbors. But some domains have characteristic signatures. So if your protein belongs to a family of related proteins, you may be able to find more distant relatives by choosing an algorithm with a position-specific scoring matrix, such as PSI-BLAST or HMMER. However, if your query is a novel protein, the best you can do is make your search parameters more sensitive.

To increase sensitivity even more, turn off the two-hit algorithm. In NCBI-BLAST, set -P 1 and in WU-BLAST, remove hitdist=60.

BLASTX Protocols

BLASTX is generally used to find protein coding genes in genomic DNA or to identify proteins encoded by transcripts. BLASTX runs relatively slowly, and can be the bottleneck in a sequence annotation pipeline. Most BLASTX searches are of the exploring variety. However, it is sometimes necessary to identify nearly identical sequences quickly. The last protocol gives some advice.

Gene Finding in Genomic DNA

Most proteins are related to other proteins. This makes BLASTX a very powerful gene-finding tool. As protein databases become larger and more diverse, BLASTX becomes even more useful because it can identify more and more genes.

Approach

As with any search involving genomic DNA, the sequence must have its repeats masked, and lowercase is preferred to Ns. If possible, low-complexity sequences shouldn't be masked with Ns to avoid terminating extension if a coding region contains a region of low complexity.

Since we want to capture a range of protein similarities, we'll use the default BLOSUM62 scoring matrix, which is a good all-around matrix. We increase the threshold score from its default of 12 to 14, which increases the speed more than twofold and is still quite sensitive.

We use a higher value for E because we don't want to miss low-scoring alignments that may be real genes. We set the output report options very high so that no matches are missed simply by truncation. Some protein families have many members and may fill up a BLASTX report by themselves.

For WU-BLAST, we offer two command lines. The first is similar to the NCBI parameter set, and the second uses a single large word rather than two small words. In our tests, the second set is slightly faster and more sensitive.

NCBI-BLAST parameters

```
blastall -p blastx -d <db> -i <genomic> -F "m S" -U -f 14 -b 10000 -v 10000 -e 100
```

WU-BLAST parameters

```
blastx <db> <genomic> wordmask=seg lcmask hitdist=40 T=14 B=10000 V=10000 E=100
blastx <db> <genomic> wordmask=seg lcmask W=4 T=20 B=10000 V=10000 E=100
```

Expected results

Percent identity is often a good indicator of the reliability of a protein match. Lengthy alignments above 50 percent identity don't occur by chance unless the sequence has some compositional bias. Alignments below 35 percent identity should be met with skepticism, and those below 30 percent aren't very reliable.

The ends of alignments often overrun exon boundaries. If the extensions are too long, they may force an exon into a separate alignment group. If the exon is short, it may not be able to achieve statistical significance when separated. To counteract this phenomenon, you can set the X parameters lower to prevent the extensions from going too far, but this can destroy weak alignments. Another option in WU-BLAST is to use olf and olmax (and their gapped counterparts golf and golmax) to change the overlap rules. These solutions aren't foolproof, so the best approach is to realize that this scenario could happen, and be on the lookout for gaps in coverage.

If your report is very long, you may have some unmasked repeats or low-complexity regions. A graphical report (Appendix D) can help determine where such repeats occur. Look for regions in which the alignment depth is very high. You may have to mask them by hand.

A less obvious problem is associated with GC-rich regions of DNA. These regions tend to have long open reading frames and can match various proteins. If the alignment threshold (Chapter 5) is low, these compositionally biased alignments may be combined to give significant scores. In WU-BLAST, you can set S2 higher, limit alignment groups with topcomboN, or ignore alignment groups with kap. A simpler and more general solution is to raise E.

All gene-finding procedures can be tricked by pseudogenes, and BLASTX is no exception. As discussed in the beginning of the chapter, you can't give stop codons highly negative scores to prevent them from appearing in alignments, that is, unless you use ungapped alignments, which are less sensitive. Rather than trying to remove pseudogenes, try to recognize them quickly. Most pseudogenes have internal stop codons or frame-shifts. While stop codons are easy to find because they appear as a * in an alignment, frame-shifts may not be immediately apparent. Usually, frame-shifts appear as overlapping HSPs in different frames, but they may also appear as HSPs that are very close rather than overlapping. Introns are rarely less than 30 nt, so any HSPs that are closer may result from a frame-shift. The presence of repeats overlapping or abutting an HSP is also a good indicator of a pseudogene. Retro-pseudogenes are derived from mRNAs, so look for poly-A tails or a lack of introns (you may have to do a little research to find out if other versions of the putative gene normally have introns). Also, retro-pseudogenes usually correspond to highly transcribed, conserved genes such as the protein components of the ribosome.

Optimizations and variations

Chapter 12 discusses the serial search strategy as a way to vastly improve the speed of translating BLAST searches without losing sensitivity. It's really the best way to run BLASTX. The protocol here and the serial strategy assume that the proteins are reasonably similar. But what if you want to look for remote coding similarities? You can first try lowering T, which will make the search take longer. However, if you're primarily interested in only a short region, lowering T can identify distant relatives. See the "BLASTP Protocols" section for sensitive searches for appropriate parameters.

Annotating ESTs (and Shotgun Sequence)

Given a collection of ESTs, one of the first analysis tasks is to determine what proteins they encode. The usual procedure is to find the best protein match. Before annotation, the EST may have an identifier such as:

```
>my_EST_001
```

At the end, the EST may be annotated with a FASTA definition line like this:

```
>my_EST_001 similar to Homo sapiens GATA transcription factor
```

While this definition is useful for classifying transcripts, it leads to a transitive annotation problem in which the similarity is eventually misapplied. You should use this procedure with discretion, and please don't submit such descriptions to public databases without good reason. Finally, whatever you do, don't concatenate multiple FASTA definition lines for the annotation because it can become confusing later on.

Many genome sequencing projects begin with a survey of random, whole genome shotgun reads. This protocol also works for shotgun genomic sequence.

Approach

It's a good idea to check your sequences for vector and other contaminants before you begin this search, and if your sequences are genomic in origin, mask repeats as well. ESTs may also contain repeats, but for genomes that have short 3′UTRs and few repeats, this isn't necessary.

This task is much easier to accomplish with a local BLAST installation because you probably have many sequences to classify. If your FASTA file contains multiple sequences, BLAST conveniently processes each one in turn and its output will contain one report for each sequence.

The following alignment parameters are slightly less sensitive than the default parameters and are a good compromise for speed and sensitivity. Since we're really only interested in the description of the top match above some threshold, we set minimal output report parameters and E to 1e-10 (a somewhat arbitrary, but low value to prevent misclassification). Since soft masking can sometimes allow a region of low-complexity to dominate an alignment score, and since we won't look at each alignment, we err on the side of making no inference rather than making the wrong inference. We therefore use ordinary complexity filtering. In keeping with this philosophy, our choice of alignment parameters favors specificity and speed over sensitivity. For WU-BLAST, we offer two command lines. The second is slightly faster and more sensitive.

NCBI-BLAST parameters

```
blastall -p blastx -d <db> -i <ESTs> -U -f 14 -e 1e-10 -b 0 -v 1
```

WU-BLAST parameters

```
blastx <db> <ESTs> filter=seg lcfilter hitdist=40 T=14 E=1e-10 B=0 V=1
blastx <db> <ESTs> filter=seg lcfilter W=4 T=20 E=1e-10 B=0 V=1
```

Expected results

Depending on the source of the sequence, there may not be many matches. With a low E value, most matches should be real similarities.

Optimizations and variations

This is a task that greatly facilitated by the Bioperl tools (see *www.bioperl.org*). Using them simplifies running the BLAST job, parsing the output, editing sequence descriptions, and rewriting the files in FASTA format. BLAST parsers also let you apply other useful criteria for assignment—for example, requiring 40 percent identity. Lacking familiarity with Bioperl, you can pipe your report through common Unix tools. For example, you can capture the first line of the query and its best match with the following grep:

```
blastall -p blastx ... | grep "^Query=\|^>"
```

Unlike the previous protocol, serial searching isn't expected to help much because the first and second searches will find the same alignment.

Super-Fast BLASTX

At times you'll need to quickly map between a genomic sequence and its encoded proteins. This protocol represents the fastest way to find nearly identical matches with BLASTX.

Approach

Our general approach is to set the seeding, extension, and evaluation parameters as insensitively as possible, within reason; we still want to be able to find matches to sequences with allelic differences. We don't bother changing the scoring matrix; it doesn't impact the speed of the search.

The NCBI-BLAST version of BLASTX isn't the best program for quickly finding protein matches to DNA because its maximum word size is 3. The parameters that follow use this size and a minimum distance for the two-hit algorithm (4) for an effective word size of 6 (yes, 4 is a strange way of specifying zero distance between two three-letter words). Oddly, the search runs faster when using maximum gap penalties rather than specifying no gaps with -g F. We don't set lower values for X because in practice, it has almost no impact on speed.

The WU-BLAST search uses a large word size without a neighborhood (automatically turned off at word sizes of 5 and above). The WINK parameter greatly reduces the total number of words and is one of the keys to the speed of this search. With W=6 WINK=6, the effective word size is 12. With such stringent seeding parameters, there is no need to change X or the alignment thresholds (see Chapter 5).

We also include a command line for the classic WU-BLAST 1.4, which works quite well for this task. (The 1.4 version is nearly identical to the 1.4 version of NCBI-BLAST that is no longer available). With this program, a word size of 5 performs best. Lowering X to terminate extensions early and increasing the alignment threshold $S2$ to reduce the computational burden of combined scores are both useful here.

The values for X and $S2$ are calculated based on the default BLOSUM62 matrix. The most negative score is -4, so X=10 allows at least two mismatches. The average match score is about 5, and the average mismatch score is about -1.5 (you can estimate these scores quickly by looking at common amino acids such as alanine and glycine). S2=65 corresponds to a 90 percent identity alignment of 15 amino acids.

NCBI-BLAST parameters

```
blastall -p blastx -d <db> -i <dna> -f 999 -A 4 -G 32767 -E 32767
```

WU-BLAST parameters

```
blastx <db> <dna> filter=seg W=6 WINK=6 nogap
```

WU-BLAST 1.4 parameters

```
blastx <db> <dna> filter=seg W=5 S2=65 X=10
```

Expected results

Not all exons will be hit using such parameters, but with this mapping experiment, the general coordinates are of greatest interest. If you need an accurate alignment, this search can be followed by a more sensitive search using a serial strategy or *bl2seq*.

How much faster are these searches? Speed depends on sequence length and content, but as a general observation for sequences in the 50-200 Kb range, if the default NCBI parameter set is considered 1x, the fastest NCBI-BLAST is 6-8x, WU-BLAST is 100-500x, and the classic WU-BLAST 1.4 is 50-150x.

Optimizations and variations

Other alignment algorithms such as BLAT (yes, the name is nearly identical), index the database as well as the query. They may prove faster, but they may also have larger resource requirements.

TBLASTN Protocols

TBLASTN and BLASTX are very similar in that one sequence is protein and the other is nucleotide. But their usage is different. TBLASTN commonly maps a protein to a genome or searches EST databases for related proteins not yet in the protein databases.

Mapping a Protein to a Genome

Many avenues of investigation focus on a specific protein—for example, medical research on a genetic disease. For many proteins, there exist several closely related homologs, and understanding the role of a particular protein often means studying the near neighbors because they sometimes have interesting properties. The genomic environment of an encoded protein is often of great interest because the genomic sequence contains regulatory elements that determine where and when proteins are expressed. So, in addition to the typical BLASTP search for homologous proteins, it is also useful to do a TBLASTN search against your favorite genomes.

Approach

Even though this is conceptually a mapping experiment, we don't choose extremely insensitive parameters because we also want to identify closely related proteins that may be of interest. The seeding parameters, which require two matching words in a 40 aa window, capture a surprising amount of variability. We'll provide an additional WU-BLAST command line that uses a single, large neighborhood. It's both faster and more sensitive than the two-hit version but takes substantially more memory. We set E to a low value to cut down on the number of low scoring hits that may be prevalent in a large search space, but if your query is especially small, this value should be increased.

NCBI-BLAST parameters

```
blastall -p tblastn -d <genome> -i <protein> -f 999 -e 1e-5
```

WU-BLAST parameters

```
tblastn <genome> <protein> filter=seg T=999 E=1e-5
tblastn <genome> <protein> filter=seg W=5 T=25 E=1e-5
```

Expected results

If all goes well, you'll find your gene in the genome. You may also find several related proteins. If the genome is small, you may not find more than one, but if your source is larger, and more complex, you may find several copies. Genomic sequences in BLAST databases are sometimes not masked, so if your search takes a long time to complete, or if you find hundreds of similar genes, you may be hitting a repeat.

Some of the hits may be to pseudogenes. High stop codon penalties with ungapped extension will not remove all pseudogenes, so in addition to inspecting alignments for the presence of stop codons, also look for overlapping HSPs (from frame shifts) and single HSPs (when multiple exons are expected). Nearby repeats and poly-A tails in the genomic sequence are other useful indicators.

Optimizations and variations

We recommend using the serial search strategy described in Chapter 12 for all translating BLAST searches that employ long sequences. If you can't do this automatically, you can follow up each of the hits found here with *bl2seq*.

For more sensitivity, reduce the value of T to allow neighborhood words. For a less sensitivity and a lot more speed, W=5 T=999 is a useful WU-BLAST setting. It also has the added benefit of using much less memory than W=5 T=25. If you need to do a quick lookup and are only interested in identical matches, you can adapt the protocol found in the "Super-Fast BLASTX" section to TBLASTN.

One way to speed up this procedure is to start with a BLASTP search to identify similar proteins and then follow up each hit in its own genome with near-identity parameters. One disadvantage to this strategy is that you will have more searches to perform and a lot of sequence handling. The assumption that the protein database you're using for your BLASTP search contains all of the genome's genes is also problematic. It's much safer to assume that not all genes have been found and use TBLASTN for your search.

Mining ESTs (and Shotgun DNA) for Protein Similarities

Since ESTs contain fragmentary information and are often unannotated, proteins encoded in ESTs may not appear in protein databases for a while. Therefore, if you're looking for relatives of your favorite protein, search a comprehensive EST database with TBLASTN, in addition to a typical BLASTP search. You can also use this protocol to search shotgun genomic sequence.

Approach

In choosing our alignment parameters, we need to balance sensitivity and speed. We want to be able to identify a range of similar sequences, so we use the default scoring matrix and gap penalties. At the same time, EST databases (and especially shotgun genomic databases) can be quite large, so we use slightly insensitive seeding parameters.

For WU-BLAST, we include four command lines. Number 1 is approximately the same as the NCBI-BLAST parameters. Relative to the first, number 2 is slightly faster and more sensitive, number 3 is about the same speed but much more sensitive, and number 4 has the same sensitivity but is much faster.

We use the default value for E (10) because some of the EST/shotgun matches may contain only a small portion of coding sequence. We set the output parameters high so we don't miss any alignments by report truncation.

NCBI-BLAST parameters

```
blastall -p tblastn -d <est_db> -i <protein> -F "m S" -f 15 -b 10000 -v 10000
```

WU-BLAST parameters

```
tblastn <est_db> <protein> wordmask=seg W=3 T=15 hitdist=40 B=10000 V=10000
tblastn <est_db> <protein> wordmask=seg W=4 T=16 hitdist=40 B=10000 V=10000
```

```
tblastn <est_db> <protein> wordmask=seg W=4 T=20 B=10000 V=10000
tblastn <est_db> <protein> wordmask=seg W=4 T=99 B=10000 V=10000
```

Expected results

Our seeding parameters are on the insensitive side, so if you don't find what you're looking for, the first parameter to change is *T* (-f in NCBI-BLAST). Drop it by one or two points at a time because the search takes longer with each decrement.

Sequencing errors, especially insertions and deletions, may terminate extension. This can lead to multiple HSPs or possibly the loss of smaller HSPs. Check the coordinates of the alignments, and if large regions are missing, they may correspond to out-of-frame coding sequences. They may also be UTRs in a transcript or introns in genomic sequence. Reducing the search space to increase sensitivity enables you to recover shorter HSPs; *bl2seq* is convenient for this task.

Optimizations and variations

If you're looking for near identities, you can make this search much faster. See the section "Super-Fast BLASTX" for parameters. Because the query and database sequences are all short, you can't optimize this search with a serial strategy.

TBLASTX Protocols

As discussed in Chapter 2, coding sequences evolve slowly compared to surrounding DNA. This makes TBLASTX a powerful gene-prediction tool for genomes that are appropriately diverged. What is the proper evolutionary distance? Because genes and organisms change at varying rates, there is no simple answer like "100 million years." If the distance is too great, the similarities may no longer be visible, but if the distance is too small, sequence similarity loses discriminatory power. For example, there is little sense in performing TBLASTX searches between humans and *E. coli* or humans and chimpanzees.

Historically, TBLASTX has not been as popular as the other BLAST programs for several reasons. First, TBLASTX is computationally intensive. Second, until recently, there were not many completely sequenced genomes. Third, when you get a match, you will rarely find a useful description for what was found—just an alignment between two potential coding sequences. As more genomes are sequenced and computer performance continues to rise, TBLASTX will become more useful.

Preventing Stop Codons

The scoring matrices distributed with the BLAST programs give positive scores for aligning stop codons to one another. This is unacceptable for discriminating between coding and noncoding regions. Chapter 10 covers installation of BLAST software and describes how to create derivative scoring matrices with highly negative stop codon scores. If you don't have permission to make these changes, you can create the derivatives in your home directory. In this case, you need to specify the explicit path to your matrix rather than use just the name. WU-BLAST operates a little differently, and it is more convenient to specify alternate scores on the command line. Each protocol gives an example of this. As discussed in Chapter 8, gapped alignment can skip over stop codons. For this reason, consider using ungapped alignment for your TBLASTX searches.

Finding Undocumented Genes in Genomic DNA

Gene prediction is difficult. There are no genomes for which all protein coding genes are completely known. One of the most highly investigated genomes is the human genome, but despite what you read in the news, the number of genes can't be stated with much confidence. Counting genes is easier than determining their exact structure, and as a result, there are many proteins for which the true sequence is in doubt. Many genes are still waiting to be discovered (and many documented genes aren't real genes).

Approach

TBLASTX is computationally expensive because it translates both strands of the query and database sequences in three frames on each strand. To make matters worse, the sequences and databases searched by TBLASTX tend to be large. To counteract these factors we choose insensitive seeding parameters, which is appropriate, considering that the extension algorithm is gapless and therefore also less sensitive.

Like any other search employing genomic DNA, it is always a good idea to mask repeats first. Here we prefer hard masking instead of soft-masking and normal complexity filtering. Our reasoning is that low-complexity sequence is common in genomic DNA and random word hits near low-complexity sequence may result in lengthy extensions, high alignment scores, and misleading statistical significance.

For WU-BLAST, we offer two command lines. The second, which uses a single, large word rather than two small words, is faster and more sensitive, but requires more memory. It also shows how to change scoring matrix values from the command line with the altscore parameter.

NCBI-BLAST

```
blastall -p tblastx -d <db> -i <genomic> -f 999
```

WU-BLAST

```
tblastx <db> <genomic> filter=seg W=3 T=999 hitdist=40 nogap
tblastx <db> <genomic> filter=seg W=5 T=25 nogap altscore="* any -999" altscore="any
* -999"
```

Expected results

This protocol can be used with either genomic or EST databases. However, searching EST databases with BLASTN is usually better. This discussion focuses on genome-genome searches. For genome-EST results and interpretations, see the appropriate BLASTN protocols.

Interpreting TBLASTX alignments isn't straightforward. It's nearly impossible to look at a report full of alignments and determine gene boundaries or the exact coordinates of coding exons. TBLASTX offers testable hypotheses. Regions with strong coding similarities may or may not correspond to real genes, but they are good candidates for experimental biology. Here are a few reasons why TBLASTX might find something missed by other approaches:

Genes in genes
> Most gene-prediction algorithms don't predict genes within genes. However, the fact that large introns contain genes on their opposite strand is a relatively frequent phenomenon. TBLASTX can help identify these genes because the algorithm looks for local alignment similarities and has no bias for overall gene structure.

Alternative splicing
> Some genes have several alternatively spliced forms. This is especially common in certain genomes, such as mammalian ones. Gene prediction algorithms usually find a single, optimal gene structure and no alternate forms. Because TBLASTX has no knowledge of splice sites, this doesn't pose a problem. Spliced variants may also have narrow windows of expression, which makes them difficult to find when using cDNA approaches. TBLASTX is less prone to missing these exons unless they are highly diverged.

Low expression
> Genes expressed at low levels may have odd codon usage, which makes them less visible to gene prediction algorithms. Because the transcripts are rare, they are also less likely to appear in cDNA libraries and EST databases. TBLASTX isn't affected by codon biases or expression levels

Optimizations and variations

This experiment is much more efficiently run as a serial search. In this strategy, a preliminary, insensitive search identifies sequences that are similar, and a second, sensitive search produces the alignments. Chapter 12 discusses this approach. You can try the approach by running *bl2seq* on each sequence identified in the search.

Transcript-Transcript TBLASTX

When presented with a transcript of unknown function, you should first implement a BLASTX search to determine if such a transcript corresponds to a known protein.

But what if it doesn't? One reason why it might not show similarities is because its encoded protein isn't yet in the protein database. It's also possible that the transcript doesn't encode a protein. If it does, though, it might have some undiscovered relatives, and the best place to look for such entities is in EST databases.

Approach

We use the same seeding parameters for the same reasons given in the previous section, "Finding Undocumented Genes in Genomic DNA." We employ soft-masking here, however, because the query sequence is short and probably doesn't contain as much of a low-complexity sequence.

NCBI-BLAST

```
blastall -p tblastx -d <est_db> -i <transcript> -f 999 -F "m S"
```

WU-BLAST

```
tblastx <est_db> <transcript> wordmask=seg W=3 T=999 hitdist=40 nogap
tblastx <est_db> <transcript> wordmask=seg W=5 T=25 nogap altscore="* any -999"
altscore="any * -999"
```

Expected results

Evolutionary distance between the sequences is the key to determining if an alignment really corresponds to a protein. If the sequences are derived from closely related species, similarity isn't much help. In such cases, try aligning the matches with *bl2seq* without extreme stop codon penalties. If you get alignments that cross stop codons, the sequences aren't diverged enough.

If the sequences come from distant species, the alignments correspond to coding regions. This interpretation is even more believable if there are matches from multiple species.

Optimizations and variations

If the sequence has a long open reading frame, it is more efficient to translate this frame first and then search with TBLASTN. Recognizing the true reading frame, though, isn't always easy (see Chapter 8). If in doubt, use this protocol.

Industrial-Strength BLAST

Installation and Command-Line Tutorial

This chapter shows you how to install NCBI-BLAST and WU-BLAST software on your own computer. This is necessary if you want to use BLAST in a high-throughput setting or develop specialized applications. After the installation section, this chapter presents a command-line tutorial that also serves as a test suite to make sure your BLAST installation behaves as expected.

NCBI-BLAST Installation

NCBI-BLAST, as the name implies, is available from the National Center for Biotechnology Information (NCBI). Precompiled binaries and source code are available for free and without restriction. The source code is in the public domain, so there are quite a few derivative works, both commercial and free (see Chapter 12). NCBI-BLAST is currently available as precompiled binaries for 11 popular operating system-hardware combinations. In addition, there is this very generous statement in the *README.bls* file:

> BLAST binaries are provided for IRIX6.2, Solaris2.6 (Sparc) Solaris2.7 (Intel), DEC OSF1 (ver. 5.1), LINUX/Intel, HPUX, AIX, BSD Unix, Darwin, MacIntosh, and Win32 systems. We will attempt to produce binaries for other platforms upon request.

If you have a platform that isn't supported as a precompiled binary, you may wish to take up the offer from the NCBI, or you may be able to find one using an Internet search engine such as Google. You can also compile the executables yourself; the source code may be obtained as part of the NCBI toolbox: *ftp://ftp.ncbi.nih.gov/toolbox/ncbi_tools*. For more information about the toolbox, see *http://www.ncbi.nlm.nih.gov/IEB/ToolBox*.

This chapter will take you through the installation procedures for Unix, Windows, and Macintosh. It doesn't cover how to build the NCBI executables from source. If you are a Windows or Macintosh user, please read the Unix installation first because it has some information that isn't duplicated in the other sections.

Unix Installation

The first step is to download a compressed Unix tape archive, often called a *tarball*, to your computer. Find the appropriate executable for your system at *ftp://ftp.ncbi. nih.gov/blast/executables*. A note of caution here: the files in the tarball aren't contained in a subdirectory so it is a good idea to place the tarball in its own directory before you expand the archive. If you're downloading via a browser, you may have plug-ins that automatically expand the archive. This could leave you with a bunch of files all over your system, or it may create a directory for you. To be safe, if you're using a browser, download the tarball to a new directory, for example, */usr/local/pkg/ ncbi-blast*, or perhaps *ncbi-blast* in your home directory if you don't have root access.

If the archive hasn't already been expanded, you can expand it with this command, where *your_platform_name* will be something like *linux.tar.Z* or *linux.tar.gz*:

```
tar -xzf blast.your_platform_name
```

Not all versions of *tar* support the *-z* option above, in which case you can use the following command line:

```
zcat blast.your_blastform_name | tar -xf -
```

Files and directories

More than 20 files come with the installation. Table 10-1 shows the files and a very brief description in logical order. See the NCBI-BLAST reference in Chapter 13 for comprehensive coverage of each program.

Table 10-1. NCBI-BLAST installation files

File	Description
blastall	The main blast executable. This program runs the five most common BLAST programs: *blastn*, *blastp*, *blastx*, *tblastn*, and *tblastx*.
blastpgp	The executable for running PSI-BLAST and PHI-BLAST searches.
bl2seq	Program to align two sequences with the BLAST algorithms.
megablast	Specialized nucleotide BLAST algorithm optimized to rapidly find nearly identical sequences that differ due to sequencing or other similar errors. This can also be called within the BLASTALL program using the *–n* option.
data/	Directory that contains the scoring matrices and other information necessary for default running of BLAST.
formatdb	Program for formatting BLAST databases from either FASTA or ASN.1 formats.
fastacmd	Program to retrieve sequences from a BLAST database if it was formatted using the *–o* option of *formatdb*.
rpsblast	Reverse PSI-BLAST program. This program searches a query sequence against a database of profiles. This is the reverse of PSI-BLAST, which uses a profile to search against a database of sequences.
seedtop	A companion program to PHI-BLAST that can find the positions of patterns in a sequence and all sequences that contain a particular pattern.

Table 10-1. NCBI-BLAST installation files (continued)

File	Description
blastclust	Program to automatically cluster protein or nucleotide sequences based on pairwise matches.
impala	Integrated Matrix Profiles and Local Alignments. Used to search a database of score matrices (prepared by *copymat*) and produce BLAST-like output.
makemat	Primary profile preprocessor for IMPALA. Converts a collection of binary profiles into ASCII format.
copymat	Secondary profile preprocessor for IMPALA. Converts ASCII matrix profiles, produced by *makemat*, into a database that can be read into memory quickly.
README.bcl	Instruction file for *blastclust* program.
README.bls	Instruction file for *blastall* program.
README.formatdb	Instruction file for *formatdb* program.
README.imp	Instruction file for *impala* program.
README.mbl	Instruction file for *megablast* program.
README.rps	Instruction file for *rpsblast* program.
VERSION	Version and build information.

The .ncbirc file

The next step is to create a resource file that tells *blastall* where to find its scoring matrices and other related files. The contents of the file are just these two lines:

```
[NCBI]
Data="/usr/local/pkg/ncbi-blast/data/"
```

You may also add to this file a line giving the location of the BLAST database files.

```
[BLAST] BLASTDB=path_to_db
```

This file must be named *.ncbirc* (including the leading dot) and should be located in every user's home directory (although it can also be in the directory where *blastall* resides).

Setting the PATH and BLASTDB environment variables

The next step is to make sure the programs can be called without explicit paths— that is, without having to type the full pathname every time you want to run the program. You should either place symbolic links from the executables in */usr/local/bin* or modify your PATH environment variable. If you're not sure how to do this, ask your Unix system administrator to help you or consult an introductory Unix book.

The final step allows you to select databases by name rather than by explicit path. This is more than just a convenience; the abstraction also lets you provide a similar interface on multiple machines where the underlying directory structure may be different. Here is an example of what you might put in your *.cshrc* file if you use *csh* or its derivatives as your shell:

```
setenv BLASTDB /usr/local/blastdb
```

If you're using one of the *sh* derivatives, such as *bash*, use the following:

```
export BLASTDB=/usr/local/blastdb
```

That's it, except that you can't use the software without sequences. If you don't need to know about Mac or Windows installation, skip ahead to the command-line tutorial.

Windows Installation

Download the *blastz.exe* file from *ftp://ftp.ncbi.nih.gov/blast/executable*, and place this in its own directory, such as *C:\ncbi-blast*. This is a self-extracting archive, so you can simply double-click on it, and all the files will be extracted into the current directory. See Table 10-1 for a description of all the files.

The ncbi.ini file

Similar to the Unix install, a special file must be created with the path to the data directory. Create a file called *ncbi.ini* in either the Windows or WINNT directory with the following contents:

```
[NCBI]
Data="C:\ncbi-blast\data"
```

Unlike Unix, rather than setting the BLASTDB environment variable to the location of the BLAST databases, add the following to the *ncbi.ini* file.

```
[BLAST]
BLASTDB="C:\ncbi-blast\db"
```

Setting the PATH environment variable

The PATH environment variable works like its Unix counterpart. The easiest way to set it is to right-click on the My Computer icon, click on the Advanced tab, and then click on the Environment Variables button (Figure 10-1).

This brings up the System Variables window. Select the Path variable to edit and add ;C:\ncbi-blast to the end of the Path (Figure 10-2) Note that there's a semicolon before the C, which is the separator between directories. Now the BLAST executables can be used from any DOS prompt.

Macintosh OS X Installation

MacOS X is Unix under the hood, so you can follow the previous Unix installation procedures (the file is called *blast.darwin.tar.Z* because Darwin is the actual name of the Unix that MacOS X uses). Alternatively, you can use the friendly installer available from the folks at *http://bioteam.net* who have put together a CD containing quite a few common bioinformatics application suites including Apple-Genentech-BLAST

Figure 10-1. Selecting the PATH environment variable

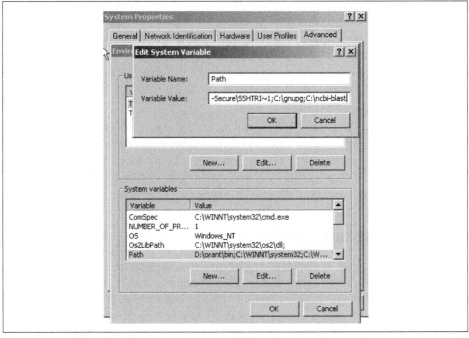

Figure 10-2. Adding the PATH environment variable

(an optimized version of NCBI-BLAST, see Chapter 12). The CD image is located at *http://gm.sonsorol.org:8080/BioInfxToolsInstaller.cdr*.

The installation procedure could not be much simpler. Double-click on the *BioInfxToolsInstaller.cdr* image, open the *BioInfxToolsInstaller* that appears on your desktop, and then double-click the *agncbi12-20-2001.pkg*. This launches a typical installer, and after a few clicks and keystrokes, you're done. At the end, you need to do two more things: add one line to your *.cshrc* file and copy the *.ncbirc* file to your home directory. To do this, open the Terminal application and type the following two lines exactly as they appear here:

```
echo "source/usr/local/biotools/cshrc.biotools" >> ~/.cshrc
cp /usr/local/biotools/.ncbirc ~/.ncbirc
```

Macintosh OS 9 Installation

The OS 9 archive is called *blast.hqx*. If you click on the file icon, your browser will most likely launch the appropriate tools to automatically expand the archive. If not, you can use Stuffit Expander, which is available for free from *http://www.stuffit.com*. The OS 9 applications look completely different from the command-line versions because they all have a graphical interface. Don't worry about this because the interface isn't pretty, and you have to drag the window across your screen several times to see all the buttons and text fields. (You may also experience a few system crashes because OS 9 isn't the ideal environment for BLAST.) You must also create a special file to tell BLAST where to find its data directory. Create a file called *ncbi.cnf* in your system folder that contains the path to the data folder. For example, if the data folder is in a computer named *MyMac* and in a folder called *Blast*, the *ncbi.cnf* file should look like this:

```
[BLAST]
BLASTDB=MyMac:Blast:data
```

Installation instructions for OS 9 are included for completeness, but Apple no longer supports this operating system. You might want to upgrade to OS X or install one of the Linux distributions for PPC. If you install Linux, you may have to compile the executables from the source, but it's worth checking if anyone has already done this. A Google search for "Mac linux BLAST" is a good place to start.

WU-BLAST Installation

Obtaining WU-BLAST software is slightly more complicated than NCBI-BLAST because it requires a license from Washington University in St. Louis. If you are affiliated with an academic institution or a nonprofit organization, the license is free. If you are part of a for-profit enterprise, you must pay a licensing fee. The price is expensive by shrink-wrapped software standards, but is similar to other bioinformatics software packages available from universities. If you find the cost prohibitive, an earlier version of WU-BLAST is available for free. The free version contains fewer features, and is available for a limited number of operating systems, but for most people, it works just fine. If your operating system isn't supported and your specific use doesn't require gapped alignment, a free version of the classic, ungapped BLAST with public domain source code also exists. This older version, 1.4.9, is nearly identical to NCBI-BLAST Version 1.4, which is no longer available from the NCBI.

Should you wish to license WU-BLAST or download the free versions, visit the official site for the WU-BLAST software at *http://blast.wustl.edu*. The free versions can be downloaded with a couple clicks, but more patience is required for the licensed version. After the license is issued, you will be sent a user-specific URL from which to download the software. It's a good idea to save this information because you will use it again to download the free updates. Licensed users are notified by email as new features are added (usually a few times per year).

WU-BLAST is available only for Unix operating systems. If you don't have access to a Unix computer, you can run Linux or FreeBSD under a virtual machine with products such as VMWare (*http://www.vmware.com*) or VirtualPC (*http://www. connectix.com*).

Expanding the tarball

The software comes as a compressed Unix archive, or *tarball*. First, create a directory such as */usr/local/pkg/wu-blast*; if you don't have root access, create a *wu-blast* directory inside your home directory. Next, download the tarball to that directory. If you do this from a browser, the files may be extracted automatically. If not, use the following command, where *your_platform_name* will be something like *linuxi686. tar.Z*:

```
tar -xzf blast2.your_platform_name
```

Not all versions of *tar* support the *-z* option above, in which case you can use the following command line:

```
zcat blast.your_blastform_name | tar -xf -
```

Before you continue with the rest of the installation procedures, look at what's inside the tarball.

Files and Directories

There are a number of files and two subdirectories. The most important items are described very briefly in Table 10-2 in logical, rather than alphabetical, order. See the WU-BLAST reference in Chapter 14 for more information.

Table 10-2. WU-BLAST files and directories

Name	Description
blasta	The WU-BLAST executable. Unlike the free version, which comes with five different BLAST executables, the licensed version has only one.
blastn, blastp, blastx, tblastn, tblastx	Symbolic links (aliases) to *blasta*. *blasta* figures out what kind of program to run based on the name of the symbolic link.
xdformat	Executable for formatting both nucleotide and protein databases.
xdget	Executable that allows you to retrieve sequences by accession number from a WU-BLAST database.
nrdb, patdb	Programs used to create nonredundant databases. *nrdb* keeps only unique sequences and concatenates the descriptions of identical sequences. *patdb* goes a little further and removes sequences that are perfect substrings of other sequences.
gb2fasta, gt2fasta, pir2fasta, sp2fasta	Programs to convert GenBank, SwissProt, and PIR files to FASTA files. *gb2fasta* extracts the nucleotides, and *gt2fasta* extracts the proteins.
filter	Directory containing the complexity filtering programs used by WU-BLAST (*seg, dust,* and *xnu*).
matrix	Directory containing two subdirectories, *aa* and *nt*, which contain, respectively, the amino acid and nucleotide scoring matrices. The amino acid matrices like BLOSUM 62 are singular files, but the nucleotide matrices exist in two forms, with the extension *4.2* or *4.4* that corresponds to 4- and 16-symbol matrices.
setdb, pressdb	Executable used to format protein and nucleotide databases. The *xdformat* executable replaces these programs, but they are included for those who prefer the old interface or require compatibility with older executables.
wu-blastall, wu-formatdb	Perl scripts that mimic the NCBI-BLAST command-line interface while executing the WU-BLAST counterparts.
sysblast	Configuration file that allows administrators to enforce system-level resource limitations on BLAST jobs.

Executables

Let's assume the tarball has been downloaded to */usr/pkg/wu-blast*, and you normally keep your executables in */usr/local/bin*. Issue the following commands to put the executables in your path.

```
ln -s /usr/pkg/wu-blast/blasta /usr/local/bin/blastn
ln -s /usr/pkg/wu-blast/blasta /usr/local/bin/blastp
ln -s /usr/pkg/wu-blast/blasta /usr/local/bin/blastx
ln -s /usr/pkg/wu-blast/blasta /usr/local/bin/tblastn
ln -s /usr/pkg/wu-blast/blasta /usr/local/bin/tblastx
ln -s /usr/pkg/wu-blast/xdformat /usr/local/bin
ln -s /usr/pkg/wu-blast/xdget /usr/local/bin
```

Note, unlike the NCBI program *blastall*, *blasta* can not be executed by its own name, but only through aliases.

Environment Variables

You'll need to set three environment variables: BLASTDB, BLASTMAT, and BLAST-FILTER. These variables correspond to the locations of the databases, scoring matrices, and complexity filters. WU-BLAST environment variables use a colon-delimited list of locations, like the PATH variable. This is especially useful for database files, which can be placed in several locations in the filesystem and then be accessed by name rather than explicit path. This is convenient because it allows computers to access databases on a networked server or on their local disks, and this is invisible to the user. Databases are looked for from a colon-delimited list of locations defined in the BLASTDB environment variable (similar to the PATH variable for executables). If BLASTDB isn't set, *blasta* looks in the current directory and in */usr/ncbi/blast/db*. In these cases, FASTA databases of the same name must be present (or symbolic links to such databases). It's generally a better idea to use the BLASTDB variable because this strategy uses less disk space and is much less confusing.

Two environment variables, BLASTMAT and BLASTFILTER, must be set so *blasta* can find the scoring matrices and complexity filters. These variables also use colon-delimited lists, but there's little reason to have them in more than one location.

Now set the BLASTMAT and BLASTFILTER environment variables to the explicit paths of the *matrix* and *filter* directories (we'll assume that the software was unpackaged in */usr/local/wu-blast*). Here's how to do so in *csh* and its derivatives:

```
setenv BLASTMAT /usr/local/wu-blast/matrix
setenv BLASTFILTER /usr/local/wu-blast/filter
```

And in *sh* and its derivatives:

```
BLASTMAT=/usr/local/wu-blast/matrix
BLASTFILTER=/usr/local/wu-blast/filter
export BLASTMAT BLASTFILTER
```

Setting Resource Limits with /etc/sysblast

WU-BLAST has a special file called */etc/sysblast* that sets systemwide resource limitations for each machine running BLAST jobs. The */etc/sysblast* file currently supports three commands: *nice*, *cpus*, and *cpusmax*. The *nice* value gives BLAST processes a lower priority (*nice* values are generally in the range of 1 to 20, with 20 being the least demanding). If the computer is used for other jobs, such a workstation, setting this to 5 makes the workstation more responsive, but the BLAST job will take over at idle times. The *cpus* value is the default number of CPUs to use, and *cpusmax* defines the maximum number of CPUs allowed. These two should be set on any large, multiprocessor machine. Here is a sample */etc/sysblast* file:

```
nice = 5
cpus = 1
cpusmax = 4
```

The behavior of WU-BLAST on multiprocessor systems is worth discussing, and if you're one of the lucky people who have access to a computer with 16 processors or more, /etc/sysblast will definitely help you. WU-BLAST lets users control the number of CPUs with the *–cpus* command-line parameter. If this parameter isn't given an explicit value, the programs uses all the processors in the computer (except for BLASTN, which reins itself in at four processors). While this may be good for BLAST users, your other users may not be so happy. This is where the /etc/sysblast file is critical because it allows you to modify the default behavior and set limits for CPU usage.

Command-Line Tutorial

Now that you've installed the NCBI-BLAST and/or WU-BLAST software, it's time to try it out. To do this, you will need sequences for both queries and databases. It's generally a good idea to start with something small and make sure it works before attempting to analyze large databases. To begin, download the book's example files from *http://examples.oreilly.com/BLAST*. Copy the *Sequence* directory to a local hard disk. This directory contains several database and sequences in FASTA format. The six files you will need for testing are described in Table 10-3.

Table 10-3. Contents of the Sequence directory

Name	Description
ESTs	2000 nucleotide sequences from the nematode *Caenorhabditis elegans*. These sequences originated from *http://www.wormbase.org*.
EST	A single EST from the previous collection.
globins	1203 protein sequences corresponding to the globin family (Pfam Version 7.6). These sequences and other protein families are available from *http://www.sanger.ac.uk/Software/Pfam*.
globin	A single protein from the previous collection.
AF287139	*Latimeria chalumnae* (Coelacanth) *Hoxa-11* nucleotide sequence.
AAG39070	*Latimeria chalumnae* (Coelacanth) *HoxA-11* protein sequence.
fugu_genomic	*Takifugu rubripes* (Pufferfish) genomic sequence containing globin genes.
chicken_genomic	*Gallus gallus* (Chicken) genomic sequence containing globin genes.
HoxDB	Nine *homeobox* protein sequences from different organisms.
p53	The *Drosophila melanogaster* p53 protein sequence.
p53DB	Twelve p53 homologous protein sequences from different organisms.
hit_file.p53	p53 pattern file for PHI-BLAST search.

NCBI-BLAST

In the following subsections, you'll run the various components of the BLAST software you just installed. You'll see brief descriptions of each program and its arguments, but the programs all have more options those displayed. See Chapter 13 for more information about each program. To begin, change your directory to the sequence directory.

formatdb

We'll start by formatting the ESTs database with the following command:

```
formatdb -i ESTs -p F -l ESTs.logfile -o
```

The -i ESTs indicates the name of the input file. The -p F indicates this isn't a protein database. The -l ESTs.logfile creates a log file. The -o creates indexing files so that sequences may be retrieved from the database. This command creates six files: *ESTs.nhr*, *ESTs.nin*, *ESTs.nsd*, *ESTs.nsi*, *ESTs.nsq*, and *ESTs.logfile*. With the exception of the log file, the files are in binary format and not human-readable. The log file looks like this (the version number will differ depending on your installation):

```
=========================[ Oct 9, 2002 11:40 AM ]=========================
Version 2.2.2 [Jan-08-2002]
Started database file "ESTs"
Formatted 2000 sequences
(END)
```

Now, format the globins database with the following command:

```
formatdb -i globins -p T -l globins.logfile -o
```

The parameters here are similar to those previous, with the exception of -p T because this is a protein database. Because this is the default condition, you can omit -p T. This command also creates six files: *globins.phr*, *globins.pin*, *globins.psd*, *globins.psi*, *globins.psq*, and *globins.logfile*.

blastn

Let's query the ESTs database with a single EST from that database and see if you can find it:

```
blastall -p blastn -d ESTs -i EST > ncbi-blastn_test
```

After the standard header, you should see output identical to this:

```
Query= AU108953 AU108953  Caenorhabditis elegans cDNA clone:yk701a6 :
5' end, single read.
         (322 letters)

Database: ESTs
           2000 sequences; 673,456 total letters

Searching....done
```

```
                                                              Score    E
Sequences producing significant alignments:                  (bits)  Value

AU108953 AU108953  Caenorhabditis elegans cDNA clone:yk701a6 : 5...   632  0.0
AU109042 AU109042  Caenorhabditis elegans cDNA clone:yk702b3 : 5...   567  e-163
AU109359 AU109359  Caenorhabditis elegans cDNA clone:yk705g2 : 5...   436  e-124
AU110478 AU110478  Caenorhabditis elegans cDNA clone:yk718h12 : ...   383  e-107
AU109122 AU109122  Caenorhabditis elegans cDNA clone:yk703d7 : 5...    32  0.040
AU110305 AU110305  Caenorhabditis elegans cDNA clone:yk718a9 : 5...    30  0.16
```

The summary of the report shows that the top sequence has accession number AU108953, which is the same as the query used in the file named *EST*.

If you would like to benchmark the performance of your system as a way to compare different machines, you can search all the ESTs against one another. This will take about 10 minutes on a 1-GHz processor. You'll see this same benchmark in Chapter 12. Read that chapter to understand why this is or isn't a good benchmark for your system. Here is the Unix command line for the benchmarking procedure:

```
time blastall -p blastn -d ESTs -i ESTs > /dev/null
```

megablast

megablast is designed for high-performance *blastn* searches. Do the same two searches as in previous sections.

```
megablast -d ESTs -i EST > megablast-test
```

The default output is tabular. For more information on this format, see Appendix A.

```
'AU108953'=='+AU108953' (1 1 322 322) 0
'AU109042'=='+AU108953' (18 14 324 319) 5
'AU109359'=='+AU108953' (12 58 282 322) 13
'AU109359'=='+AU108953' (12 58 282 322) 13
'AU110478'=='+AU108953' (25 21 240 236) 8
```

If you want to see how much faster *megablast* is than standard *blastn*, time them both. To compare them on equal footing, set the *blastn* word size higher (-W 30) and use tabular output (-m 8).

```
time blastall -p blastn -d ESTs -i ESTs -W 30 -m 8 > /dev/null
time megablast -d ESTs -i ESTs > /dev/null
```

(*megablast* ran about 12 times faster on the Ian's laptop in these tests.)

blastp

Run *blastp* by searching a single protein against a database of proteins:

```
blastall -p blastp -d globins -i globin > ncbi-blastp_test
```

This BLAST report is fairly long, and the following is only part of the summary. The top of your report should look like this:

```
Query= Q9GJY8 Q9GJY8 GAMMA2-GLOBIN.
        (145 letters)

Database: globins
            1203 sequences; 211,084 total letters

Searching...done

                                                            Score     E
Sequences producing significant alignments:                (bits)  Value

Q9GJY8 Q9GJY8 GAMMA2-GLOBIN.                                  293   6e-82
HBG_ATEGE P06891 Hemoglobin gamma chain.                     277   4e-77
HBG1_CALMO Q9GLX4 Hemoglobin gamma-1 chain.                  276   8e-77
HBG_ALOBE P56284 Hemoglobin gamma chain.                     275   1e-76
Q9GJS7 Q9GJS7 GAMMA1-GLOBIN (GAMMA2-GLOBIN).                 274   2e-76
Q9GLX7 Q9GLX7 HYBRID GAMMA1/GAMMA2-GLOBIN.                   273   4e-76
```

You can also benchmark *blastp* in the same way as *blastn*, by doing all-versus-all protein searches. This will take about twice as long to complete as the *blastn* benchmark.

```
time blastall -p blastp -d globins -i globin > /dev/null
```

blastx

It is common to use *blastx* as a gene-finding tool by searching a genomic sequence against a protein database:

```
blastall -p blastx -d globins -i fugu_genomic > ncbi-blastx_test
```

The genomic sequence contains a cluster of alpha globin genes, so you can expect to find quite a few matches to the globins database. Your report should look like this:

```
Query= gi|18463974|gb|AY016024.1| Takifugu rubripes alpha globin gene
cluster, complete sequence
        (35,793 letters)

Database: globins
            1203 sequences; 211,084 total letters

Searching...done

                                                            Score     E
Sequences producing significant alignments:                (bits)  Value

Q9PVU6 Q9PVU6 EMBRYONIC ALPHA-TYPE GLOBIN.                   137   3e-46
HBA_THUTH P11748 Hemoglobin alpha chain.                     119   3e-40
HBA2_NOTCO P16308 Hemoglobin alpha-2 chain.                  130   5e-40
HBA2_TRENE P45719 Hemoglobin alpha-2 chain.                  126   6e-40
Q98974 Q98974 ALPHA-GLOBIN IV.                               119   7e-39
Q98SE6 Q98SE6 ALPHANCP2 (ALPHANCP1).                         140   9e-39
HBA_ELEEL P14520 Hemoglobin alpha chain.                     119   9e-39
```

tblastn

Run *tblastn* in a typical application that searches an EST databases for protein similarities.

```
blastall -p tblastn -d ESTs -i globin  > ncbi-tblastn_test
```

Here's the first alignment of the report in addition to the summary. We'll leave the question of biological and statistical significance as an exercise for you.

```
Query= Q9GJY8 Q9GJY8 GAMMA2-GLOBIN.
        (145 letters)

Database: ESTs
          2000 sequences; 673,456 total letters

Searching....done

                                                            Score    E
Sequences producing significant alignments:                (bits)  Value

AU109565 AU109565  Caenorhabditis elegans cDNA clone:yk708f8 : 5...   28   0.043
AU109149 AU109149  Caenorhabditis elegans cDNA clone:yk703g6 : 5...   27   0.096
AU109370 AU109370  Caenorhabditis elegans cDNA clone:yk705h2 : 5...   25   0.37
AU110425 AU110425  Caenorhabditis elegans cDNA clone:yk716a3 : 5...   24   0.62
AU109448 AU109448  Caenorhabditis elegans cDNA clone:yk706h11 : ...   20   6.9
AU109900 AU109900  Caenorhabditis elegans cDNA clone:yk712d7 : 5...   20   6.9
AU110608 AU110608  Caenorhabditis elegans cDNA clone:yk720c9 : 5...   20   9.0
AU109391 AU109391  Caenorhabditis elegans cDNA clone:yk706b11 : ...   20   9.0

>AU109565 AU109565  Caenorhabditis elegans cDNA clone:yk708f8 : 5' end,
           single read.
           Length = 327

  Score = 27.7 bits (60), Expect = 0.043
  Identities = 12/34 (35%), Positives = 20/34 (58%)
  Frame = -1

Query: 21  VEDAGGETLGRLLVVYPWTQRFFDSFGSLCSPSA 54
           + + G  + R+  V P +QRF  S  ++CSP+A
Sbjct: 144 IREVGESPVIRIFFVLPGSQRFIVSRRAICSPTA 43
```

tblastx

tblastx is commonly used as a gene-finding tool to identify potential coding regions between genomes. You can simulate this by aligning alpha globin clusters from chicken and fish. You haven't formatted the chicken genomic sequence database yet, so do this first and then run the search:

```
formatdb -i chicken_genomic -p F
blastall -p tblastx -d chicken_genomic -i fugu_genomic> ncbi-blastx_test
```

You should see the following error message while your search is running. This warns you that there are more than 200 significant alignments between the two sequences.

You can't increase this number with a command-line switch, and the only workaround is to cut your query sequence into smaller pieces. This limitation applies only in ungapped searches (TBLASTX or any search with the setting -g F).

```
[blastall] WARNING: [000.000] gi|18463974|gb|AY016024.1|: Reached max 200 HSPs in
BlastSaveCurrentHsp, continuing with this limit
```

Since there's only one sequence in the database, look at the first alignment instead of the summary:

```
>gi|17104478|gb|AY016020.1| Gallus gallus alpha globin gene cluster,
            complete sequence
          Length = 103190

  Score =  141 bits (302), Expect = 1e-34
  Identities = 61/73 (83%), Positives = 66/73 (89%)
  Frame = -2 / -3

Query: 25076 ASSDDMTLTSPSMDNSSAELLPGGDSPLNKRITETLLASLSEHERQVILSVPAAQNPEDL 24897
             ASSDDMTLTSPSMDNSSAEL+PGGDSPLNKR+TE LLASL EHER+ IL+VPAAQNPEDL
Sbjct: 5289  ASSDDMTLTSPSMDNSSAELIPGGDSPLNKRMTENLLASLLEHEREAILNVPAAQNPEDL 5110


Query: 24896 RMFAR*NHLSTKC 24858
             RMFAR*  S +C
Sbjct: 5109  RMFAR*EIGSAEC 5071
```

Note the stop codon (*) near the end of the alignment. The scoring matrices distributed with BLAST set the score of all stop codon matches to +1. If you want to terminate alignments at stop codons, you have to edit the scoring matrix. This procedure is described at the end of this chapter.

bl2seq

The previous *tblastx* test used only two sequences. Whenever you want to align just two sequences, you can use the *bl2seq* program to save the effort of having to format one sequence as a database and remove the database files later. Here's the command:

```
bl2seq -p tblastx -j chicken_genomic -i fugu_genomic
```

You won't see a summary, but the rest of the report will be nearly identical to the one in the previous section.

fastacmd

The *fastacmd* program can retrieve one or more FASTA-formatted sequences from a BLAST database. Try this by retrieving a single sequence from the ESTs database:

```
fastacmd -d ESTs -s AU108953 -l 60
```

The -d ESTs designates the database from which you retrieve the sequence. The database must have been formatted with the -o option of *formatdb* for *fastacmd* to work. The -s AU108953 is the string for which to search the database. The -l 60 specifies the sequence line lengths; the default line length is 80. The output from this test should be the following:

```
>lcl|AU108953 AU108953  Caenorhabditis elegans cDNA clone:yk701a6 : 5' end, sing
le read
TGGCCTACTGGANAAAACAACAATGCGTGCTTTACTATTCACCTCTGTTGTTCTTTTGGC
TTTGGCTTTTGTTGAGGCAAAGAAGCAGACTATCACTGTCAAGGGTACAACTATTTGTAA
TAAGAAGAGAATTCAGGCGGAGGTTACCCTTTGGGAGAAAGATACTCTCGACCCCGATGA
CAAGCTCGCCTCAATGCAATCGAACAAAGAAGGAGAGTTCTCACTTACCGGATCCGACGA
CGAGATCACCTCAATCTCTCCATACCTCATAATCACCCACAACAGCAACGTGAAGAAGGC
CGGATGAAGCCGTGTTTCAGAG
```

The beginning of the definition has a prepended lcl|. The lcl| isn't in the original FASTA definition line and doesn't show up in BLAST reports; it shows up here because the database identifier wasn't in NCBI format (see Chapter 11).

fastacmd has several other useful features. It can report a summary of a BLAST database, dump a BLAST database to FASTA format, report a subsequence of a particular sequence, and even display taxonomic information if the databases are downloaded from *ftp://ftp.ncbi.nih.gov/blast/db/*. See Chapter 13 for more information on *fastacmd*.

PSI-BLAST

PSI-BLAST identifies weak amino acid similarities and is executed using the *blastpgp* program. Test it by iteratively searching the *Drosophila melanogaster* p53 protein against a database of p53 homologs. First, format the p53 database, just as you would for any protein database:

```
formatdb -i p53DB -p T -l p53DB.logfile -o
```

Now you can search with your p53 protein{

```
blastpgp -d p53DB -i p53 -j 5 > ncbi-psiblast_test
```

You'll get a report with four iterations. All four rounds of automated searching are concatenated into one report. The following represents the summary section for these four rounds.

In round 1, there are 11 matches out of 12 total database sequences. Notice that there is an insignificant hit to a hypothetical protein at the bottom of the report with a score of 20 and an E-value near 1.

```
Query= gi|7211767|gb|AAF40427.1|AF224713_1 transcription factor p53
[Drosophila melanogaster]
        (385 letters)

Database: p53DB
          12 sequences; 3745 total letters

Results from round 1
```

```
                                                               Score    E
Sequences producing significant alignments:                    (bits) Value

gb|EAA07957.1| agCP1306 [Anopheles gambiae str. PEST]            98    3e-024
gb|AAL99584.1|AF285104_1 p53-like transcription factor p120 [Spi...  75    2e-017
gb|AAA98563.1| p53 tumor suppressor homolog                      70    9e-016
gb|AAC24830.1| p53 homolog [Homo sapiens]                        63    1e-013
gb|AAC37335.1| p53 [Canis familiaris]                            59    1e-012
gb|AAC05704.1| tumor suppressor p53 [Mus musculus]               58    4e-012
gb|AAC60746.1| p53 [Xenopus laevis]                              57    9e-012
gb|AAD12203.1| tumor suppressor protein [Canis familiaris]       43    1e-007
gb|AAF78533.1|AF223793_1 tumor supressor p53 [Oncorhynchus mykiss]  42    2e-007
gb|AAG35765.1|AF209191_1 p53 alternative splice isoform p35/HAS ...  35    4e-005
gb|AAM96822.1| hypothetical protein [Arabidopsis thaliana]       20    0.98
```

In round 2, all 12 sequences from the p53DB have hits better than the E-value threshold of 10. All scores are higher and an annotated p53 peptide fragment from mouse (gb|AAC71764.1|) is now found with a significant score.

```
Results from round 2

                                                               Score    E
Sequences producing significant alignments:                    (bits) Value
Sequences used in model and found again:

gb|AAL99584.1|AF285104_1 p53-like transcription factor p120 [Spi...  293   4e-083
gb|AAC24830.1| p53 homolog [Homo sapiens]                        291   3e-082
gb|AAC05704.1| tumor suppressor p53 [Mus musculus]               279   7e-079
gb|AAC37335.1| p53 [Canis familiaris]                            279   9e-079
gb|AAA98563.1| p53 tumor suppressor homolog                      278   1e-078
gb|AAC60746.1| p53 [Xenopus laevis]                              270   5e-076
gb|EAA07957.1| agCP1306 [Anopheles gambiae str. PEST]            251   3e-070
gb|AAD12203.1| tumor suppressor protein [Canis familiaris]       227   4e-063
gb|AAG35765.1|AF209191_1 p53 alternative splice isoform p35/HAS ...  221   2e-061
gb|AAF78533.1|AF223793_1 tumor supressor p53 [Oncorhynchus mykiss]  127   4e-033

Sequences not found previously or not previously below threshold:

gb|AAC71764.1| p53 protein; Trp53 [Mus musculus musculus]        40    8e-007
gb|AAM96822.1| hypothetical protein [Arabidopsis thaliana]       25    0.028
```

In round 3, the scores of all hits are even better as the position-specific scoring matrix is increasingly tuned to the p53 profile.

```
Results from round 3

                                                               Score    E
Sequences producing significant alignments:                    (bits) Value
Sequences used in model and found again:

gb|AAC60746.1| p53 [Xenopus laevis]                              323   6e-092
gb|AAC05704.1| tumor suppressor p53 [Mus musculus]               309   7e-088
gb|AAA98563.1| p53 tumor suppressor homolog                      306   5e-087
gb|AAC24830.1| p53 homolog [Homo sapiens]                        304   2e-086
```

```
gb|AAL99584.1|AF285104_1 p53-like transcription factor p120 [Spi...   295   1e-083
gb|AAC37335.1| p53 [Canis familiaris]                                 285   2e-080
gb|EAA07957.1| agCP1306 [Anopheles gambiae str. PEST]                 271   2e-076
gb|AAG35765.1|AF209191_1 p53 alternative splice isoform p35/HAS ...   241   2e-067
gb|AAD12203.1| tumor suppressor protein [Canis familiaris]            231   3e-064
gb|AAF78533.1|AF223793_1 tumor supressor p53 [Oncorhynchus mykiss]    124   3e-032
gb|AAC71764.1| p53 protein; Trp53 [Mus musculus musculus]              43   1e-007

Sequences not found previously or not previously below threshold:

gb|AAM96822.1| hypothetical protein [Arabidopsis thaliana]             32   3e-004
```

In round 4, no new sequences are found below the level of significance (0.005). Therefore the search has converged, and no new iterations are performed.

```
Results from round 4

                                                                   Score    E
Sequences producing significant alignments:                        (bits) Value
Sequences used in model and found again:

gb|AAC60746.1| p53 [Xenopus laevis]                                 333   3e-095
gb|AAL99584.1|AF285104_1 p53-like transcription factor p120 [Spi... 319   6e-091
gb|AAC24830.1| p53 homolog [Homo sapiens]                           319   6e-091
gb|AAC05704.1| tumor suppressor p53 [Mus musculus]                  313   5e-089
gb|AAA98563.1| p53 tumor suppressor homolog                         311   3e-088
gb|AAC37335.1| p53 [Canis familiaris]                               289   8e-082
gb|EAA07957.1| agCP1306 [Anopheles gambiae str. PEST]               272   6e-077
gb|AAG35765.1|AF209191_1 p53 alternative splice isoform p35/HAS ... 241   2e-067
gb|AAD12203.1| tumor suppressor protein [Canis familiaris]          230   3e-064
gb|AAF78533.1|AF223793_1 tumor supressor p53 [Oncorhynchus mykiss]  125   2e-032
gb|AAM96822.1| hypothetical protein [Arabidopsis thaliana]           70   1e-015
gb|AAC71764.1| p53 protein; Trp53 [Mus musculus musculus]            44   8e-008

Sequences not found previously or not previously below threshold:

CONVERGED!
```

PHI-BLAST

PHI-BLAST seeds extensions from important regions of a protein—for example, an enzyme active site or a conserved domain. It is also executed with the *blastpgp* program. To specify a PHI-BLAST search, a *hit_file* must be available (-*k*) and the program (-*p*) must be specified as either *patseedp* or *seedp*, with *seedp* specifying a special *hit_file*. You'll run the program using a conserved part of the *Drosophila melanogaster* p53 protein as a pattern seed to search the p53DB. The pattern is designated in *hit_file.p53*:

```
ID  p53 Pattern
PA  [YF]-[ST]-X-X-L-N-K-L-[YF]
```

The following command uses this pattern as a seed in a search of the p53 database:

```
blastpgp -d p53DB -i p53 -k hit_file.p53 -p patseedp > ncbi-phiblast_test
```

In the results, the position of the pattern in the query and the probability of finding the pattern are shown, followed by the summary lines and alignments. In the first alignment, asterisks show the position of the pattern in the query and subject.

```
1 occurrence(s) of pattern in query
 p53 Pattern
 pattern [YF]-[ST]-X-X-L-N-K-L-[YF]
 at position 107 of query sequence
effective database length=3.6e+003
 pattern probability=1.4e-008
lengthXprobability=5.0e-005

Number of occurrences of pattern in the database is 4
WARNING: There may be more matching sequences with e-values below the threshold of
10.000000

                                                           Score      E
                                                          (bits)   Value

Significant matches for pattern occurrence 1 at position 107

gb|AAC37335.1| p53 [Canis familiaris]                       47    2e-014
gb|AAC60746.1| p53 [Xenopus laevis]                         41    2e-012
gb|AAC05704.1| tumor suppressor p53 [Mus musculus]          38    2e-011
gb|AAG35765.1|AF209191_1 p53 alternative splice isoform p35/HAS ...   16    7e-005

Significant alignments for pattern occurrence 1 at position 107

>gb|AAC37335.1| p53 [Canis familiaris]
        Length = 281

 Score = 47.2 bits (132), Expect = 2e-014
 Identities = 56/220 (25%), Positives = 94/220 (42%), Gaps = 27/220 (12%)

Query:  105 WMYSIPLNKLYIRMNKAFNVDVQFKSKMPIQPLNLRVFLCF--SNDVSAPVVRCQNHLSV 162
pattern 107  *********
            W YS LNKL+ ++ K  V +  S P    +R   +  S V+ V RC +H
Sbjct:   16 WTYSPLLNKLFCQLAKTCPVQLWVSSPPPPNTC-VRAMAIYKKSEFVTEVVRRCPHHERC 74
```

Environment variables and .ncbirc

If everything works, make sure the environment variables and data directory function correctly. Now, move to any random directory on your system and attempt one of the previous searches, but substitute the correct path to the query file.

If the executable path is incorrect, you will have an error message such as:

```
blastall: command not found
```

Databases that can't be found produce error messages like the following:

```
[blastall] WARNING: <query> Could not find index files for database <db>
```

If the data directory can't be found, *blastall* reports that it is unable to open the scoring matrix:

```
Searching[blastall] WARNING: <query> [000.000] Unable to open <matrix>
```

WU-BLAST

As in the previous section, you'll run the various components of the WU-BLAST software in typical sequence analysis settings.

xdformat

Start by formatting the ESTs database with the following command. The -n indicates that this is a nucleotide database. This command creates three files: *ESTs.xnd*, *ESTs.xns*, and *ESTs.xnt*.

```
xdformat -n ESTs
```

xdformat also prints some interesting statistics to *stdout*. You can always retrieve this information later with xdformat -n -r ESTs.

```
XDFORMAT-WashU 1.0 [02-Apr-2002] [macosx-ppc-ILP32F64 2002-04-02T01:26:43]
Start:  2002-09-29T12:10:05
Input: "ESTs"
XDF Output Database:  ESTs
 Alphabet:  NCBI2na(1)
 No. of sequences (letters) written:  2000  (673,456)
 Longest sequence written (in database):  933  (933)
 Edit Alphabet:  WUStLna(1)
 Sequences edited for ambiguity codes:  961
 No. of edits (total length) written:  1901  (2102)
 Index entries written (in database):  2000  (2000)
Total cpu time:  0.12u 0.00s 0.12t  Elapsed: 00:00:00
End:  2002-09-29T12:10:05
```

If you use the free version of WU-BLAST, use *pressdb* instead of *xdformat*. The output is quite brief (so it's not shown here). The files are named differently, too: *ESTs.csq*, *ESTs.nhd*, and *ESTs.ntb*.

```
pressdb ESTs
```

Format the globins database with the following command. The -p indicates that this is a file or protein sequences. This command also creates three files: *globins.xpd*, *globins.xps*, and *globins.xpt*.

```
xdformat -p globins
```

If you use the free version of WU-BLAST, use *setdb* and name the files *globins.ahd*, *globins.atd*, and *globins.bsq*:

```
setdb globins
```

blastn

Let's query the ESTs database with a single EST from that database and see if you can find it:

```
blastn ESTs EST > wu-blastn_test
```

The output of your search contains header information and a summary that should look like this:

```
Query=  AU108953 AU108953  Caenorhabditis elegans cDNA clone:yk701a6 : 5' end,
     single read.
        (322 letters)

Database:  ESTs
           2000 sequences; 673,456 total letters.
Searching....10....20....30....40....50....60....70....80....90....100% done

                                                        Smallest
                                                          Sum
                                               High  Probability
Sequences producing High-scoring Segment Pairs: Score  P(N)      N

AU108953 AU108953  Caenorhabditis elegans cDNA clone:yk70... 1603  3.3e-69   1
AU109042 AU109042  Caenorhabditis elegans cDNA clone:yk70... 1507  7.1e-65   1
AU109359 AU109359  Caenorhabditis elegans cDNA clone:yk70... 1203  3.8e-51   1
AU110478 AU110478  Caenorhabditis elegans cDNA clone:yk71... 1052  3.4e-44   1
AU109925 AU109925  Caenorhabditis elegans cDNA clone:yk71...  310  7.9e-11   1
AU110873 AU110873  Caenorhabditis elegans cDNA clone:yk72...  121  0.998     1
```

The query sequence, which was in a file named *EST*, has the accession number AU108953, which is the highest scoring match in the report summary. There were several other hits, and you may want to browse the rest of the file for fun.

If you wish to benchmark your system for comparisons to other systems, you can search all the ESTs against one another. This will take about 10 minutes on a 1-GHz processor. We use this same benchmark in Chapter 12 for NCBI-BLAST; read that chapter to understand why this is or isn't a good benchmark for your system. Don't compare this WU-BLAST benchmark to that produced by NCBI-BLAST because the default parameters produce different results. A proper cross-comparison requires that the results be the same. Here is the command line for the benchmark (note the addition of the *-warnings* flag to suppress warning messages).

```
time blastn ESTs ESTs -warnings > /dev/null
```

blastp

You can run *blastp* as you did *blastn*, by searching a single protein against a database of proteins:

```
blastp globins globin > wu-blastp_test
```

The output of this search is quite a bit longer than the previous EST example. Only part of the summary is shown here:

```
Query= Q9GJY8 Q9GJY8 GAMMA2-GLOBIN.
       (145 letters)


Database: globins
          1203 sequences; 211,084 total letters.
Searching....10....20....30....40....50....60....70....80....90....100% done


                                                       Smallest
                                                         Sum
                                                  High Probability
Sequences producing High-scoring Segment Pairs:  Score  P(N)      N

Q9GJY8 Q9GJY8 GAMMA2-GLOBIN.                        749  1.0e-76   1
HBG_ATEGE P06891 Hemoglobin gamma chain.           710  1.4e-72   1
HBG1_CALMO Q9GLX4 Hemoglobin gamma-1 chain.        707  2.9e-72   1
HBG_ALOBE P56284 Hemoglobin gamma chain.           705  4.7e-72   1
Q9GJS7 Q9GJS7 GAMMA1-GLOBIN (GAMMA2-GLOBIN).       703  7.7e-72   1
Q9GLX7 Q9GLX7 HYBRID GAMMA1/GAMMA2-GLOBIN.         701  1.3e-71   1
```

You can benchmark *blastp* in the same way as *blastn*, however, it takes about twice as long to complete as the *blastn* benchmark.

```
time blastp globins globins -warnings > /dev/null
```

blastx

It is common to use *blastx* as a gene-finding tool by searching a genomic sequence against a protein database:

```
blastx globins fugu_genomic filter=seg  > wu-blastx_test
```

While the search is running, you'll see the following warning message that indicates that some of the default parameters were overrun:

```
WARNING:  Descriptions of 333 database sequences were not reported due to the
          limiting value of parameter V = 500.
WARNING:  HSPs involving 583 database sequences were not reported due to the
          limiting value of parameter B = 250.
```

The top of the report should look like this:

```
Query= gi|18463974|gb|AY016024.1| Takifugu rubripes alpha globin gene cluster,
    complete sequence
       (35,793 letters)

  Translating both strands of query sequence in all 6 reading frames

Database: globins
          1203 sequences; 211,084 total letters.
Searching....10....20....30....40....50....60....70....80....90....100% done
```

```
                                                                   Smallest
                                                                   Sum
                                                      High  Probability
Sequences producing High-scoring Segment Pairs:       Score  P(N)      N

Q9PVU6 Q9PVU6 EMBRYONIC ALPHA-TYPE GLOBIN.            277   7.3e-44    3
HBAA_SERQU Q9PVM4 Hemoglobin alpha-A chain.           275   2.6e-40    3
O13136 O13136 ALPHA-GLOBIN.                           278   8.6e-40    3
Q90487 Q90487 AA1 ALPHA GLOBIN.                       279   1.4e-39    3
HBA_CYPCA P02016 Hemoglobin alpha chain.              278   1.8e-39    3
```

tblastn

It is common to use *tblastn* to search EST databases for protein similarities. Here's the command:

```
tblastn ESTs globin filter=seg  > wu-tblastn_test
```

The top of the report and the first alignment are shown here. You might consider the significance of the alignment as an experiment.

```
Query= Q9GJY8 Q9GJY8 GAMMA2-GLOBIN.
       (145 letters)

Database: ESTs
          2000 sequences; 673,456 total letters.
Searching....10....20....30....40....50....60....70....80....90....100% done


                                                        Smallest
                                                        Sum
                                         Reading  High  Probability
Sequences producing High-scoring Segment Pairs:  Frame Score P(N)    N

AU109565 AU109565  Caenorhabditis elegans cDNA clone:y... -1    60  0.42     1
AU109149 AU109149  Caenorhabditis elegans cDNA clone:y... -1    57  0.75     1
AU109885 AU109885  Caenorhabditis elegans cDNA clone:y... +1    53  0.996    1

>AU109565 AU109565  Caenorhabditis elegans cDNA clone:yk708f8 : 5' end, single
            read.
          Length = 327

  Minus Strand HSPs:

  Score = 60 (26.2 bits), Expect = 0.55, P = 0.42
  Identities = 12/34 (35%), Positives = 20/34 (58%), Frame = -1

Query:    21 VEDAGGETLGRLLVVYPWTQRFFDSFGSLCSPSA 54
             + + G  + R+  V P +QRF  S  ++CSP+A
Sbjct:   144 IREVGESPVIRIFFVLPGSQRFIVSRRAICSPTA 43
```

tblastx

It is common to use *tblastx* as a gene-finding tool to identify potential coding regions between genomes, and you can simulate this by aligning alpha globin clusters from chicken and fish. You haven't formatted the chicken genomic sequence database yet, so do this first. If you're using the free version, substitute *pressdb* for *xdformat* and don't include the -n parameter.

```
xdformat -n chicken_genomic
tblastx chicken_genomic fugu_genomic filter=seg  > wu-blastx_test
```

The following warning is reported during the search, indicating that the number of alignments has passed a default threshold. This can be avoided with *hspmax=0*.

```
WARNING:  hspmax=1000 was exceeded with 1 of the database sequences.
```

The first alignment is shown here:

```
>gb|AY016020.1| Gallus gallus alpha globin gene cluster, complete sequence
        Length = 103,190

  Plus Strand HSPs:

  Score = 183 (69.5 bits), Expect = 9.2e-67, Sum P(14) = 9.2e-67
  Identities = 40/53 (75%), Positives = 44/53 (83%), Frame = +2 / +1

Query: 24479 DWKIEITGSS*LVTTRTLRNLSNSVLRCERLMFSLYMISSRWWCPRK**SSLK 24637
             D K E+TGSS LVTT TLRNLSNS+  CER MFSLYMISS+W  PRK**SSL+
Sbjct:   496 D*KTEMTGSSWLVTTSTLRNLSNSISSCERRMFSLYMISSKWCRPRK**SSLR 654
```

Note that the alignment contains stop codons (*). If you wish to terminate alignments at stop codons, you will have to increase the gap penalties and align without gaps. You will learn more about this topic at the end of this chapter.

xdget

The *xdget* program retrieves sequences from a BLAST database. You can use this only if you have the licensed software, and you must index the databases with *xdformat* before you can use *xdget*. The ESTs database can be indexed by the following command:

```
xdformat -n -X ESTs
```

You'll see some diagnostic output, and there will be an additional file called *ESTs. xni*. You can index at the time of formatting if you include the *-I* flag. The globins database is indexed similarly:

```
xdformat -p -X globins
```

You'll also see some diagnostic output that includes 33 lines similar to the following:

```
*Duplicate ID:  Q17154
```

This indicates that you have duplicate database identifiers in the FASTA database. The duplicates are intentional, and you can remove them with the *nrdb* and *patdb* tools described later. Now retrieve some sequences:

```
xdget -n ESTs AU109017
```

You should see the following output:

```
>AU109017 AU109017  Caenorhabditis elegans cDNA clone:yk701g7 : 5' end, single read.
TGGCCTACTGGGGTTTAATTACCCAAGTTTGAGATGGCTGCTGCTTCAGTGAAAGGCTTT
TTCCAGCGGACCGGAATCAGCATCAAAGAATATTTTAAACGAATGGGAAATGATTATGCT
ACTGTAGCTAGGGAAACTGTCCAAGGATGTAAAGATAGACCTGTTAAAGCTGGAGTTGTT
TTCTCTGGGCTCGGTTTTTTAACCTATGCATATCAGACAAATCCAACAGAGCTGGAAATG
TATGATTATTTATGCGAGAGACGACAAAAGTTAGTTTTGGTCCCGAATTCTGAGCATAAT
CCGGCTACAACTAAAGAATTAACTGCTCGCGA
```

And for proteins, you can rely on a similar action:

```
xdget -p globins HBP_CANLI
```

You should see the following output:

```
>HBP_CANLI P42511 Leghemoglobin.
MGAFSEKQESLVKSSWEAFKQNVPHHSAVFYTLILEKAPAAQNMFSFLSNGVDPNNPKLK
AHAEKVFKMTVDSAVQLRAKGEVVLADPTLGSVHVQKGVLDPHFLVVKEALLKTFKEAVG
DKWNDELGNAWEVAYDELAAAIKKAMGSA
```

nrdb and patdb

The *nrdb* and *patdb* programs are useful for removing the redundant sequences you saw earlier. Use *nrdb* first:

```
nrdb globins > globins_nr
```

The additional output from the program is as follows:

```
          --------- Records ---------  -------------- Residues -----------
Database    Read Duplicate  Written       Read  Duplicate    Written
globins     1203        39     1164    211,084     37,819    173,265

Totals:     1203        39     1164    211,084     37,819    173,265

No. of base word hits:  53 (53 total)
No. of 32-bit hash hits:  39
Total memory allocated:  0.500 MB
Longest comment line read:  184
Longest comment line written:  423
Longest sequence read:  1431
```

The report shows 39 duplicate records. When indexing the globins database, you'll find that there were 33 duplicate identifiers. However, *nrdb* looks for duplicate *sequences* not identifiers. When *nrdb* finds duplicate sequences, it concatenates the identifiers, separating them with a Control-A character. This is normally a whitespace character in a terminal window but is visible in some text editors and pagers.

patdb is even more aggressive than *nrdb* for removing redundancies; it removes identical substrings so the sequences MVLQ and MVLQKP are merged into the same entry.

Environment variables

Now it's time to make sure the environment variables function correctly. To start, move to any random directory on your system and attempt one of the previous searches, substituting the correct path to the query file:

If the executable path is incorrect, you will see an error message such as:

```
blastp: command not found
```

If the databases can't be found, WU-BLAST reports:

```
FATAL:  Could not open the database:  <database name>
```

WU-BLAST offers informative messages when it fails to find scoring matrices and complexity filters:

```
FATAL:  "No such file or directory" error encountered (errno=2), when attempting to
FIND the requested sequence filter program "nseg". Please check the setting of the
BLASTFILTER or WUBLASTFILTER environment variables and the permissions on the
program.
EXIT CODE 32

FATAL:  Could not find or open a substitution matrix file named:  BLOSUM62. Check
file access permissions or the setting of the WUBLASTMAT
(BLASTMAT) environment variable.
EXIT CODE 8
```

For a complete list of errors and messages, see Chapter 14.

Editing Scoring Matrices

The amino scoring matrix files distributed with NCBI-BLAST and WU-BLAST assign a score of +1 to paired stop codons. This doesn't make much biological sense and reduces the ability of TBLASTX to discriminate between coding and noncoding similarities. Therefore, you should edit the scoring matrices to change stop codon pairs to a highly negative score. Be sure to edit the original matrices. The NCBI-BLAST scoring matrices are in the *data* directory. For WU-BLAST, they are in the *matrix/aa* directory. The final line of the scoring matrix files looks like this:

```
* -4 -4 -4 -4 -4 -4 -4 -4 -4 -4 -4 -4 -4 -4 -4 -4 -4 -4 -4 -4 -4 -4  1
```

Just change the final number to -999:

```
* -4 -4 -4 -4 -4 -4 -4 -4 -4 -4 -4 -4 -4 -4 -4 -4 -4 -4 -4 -4 -4 -4 -999
```

You have to do this only once if you remember to keep your edited matrices when updating your BLAST installation.

For any of the translating BLAST programs, you can also change all stop scores to highly negative values. If used in conjunction with ungapped extension, doing so prevents a lot of noncoding sequences from appearing in significant alignments. The following Perl script modifies the standard matrices:

```perl
#!/usr/bin/perl
while (<>) {
    if (/^#|^\s/) {
        print;
    }
    elsif (/^\*/) {
        print '*', ' -999' x 24, "\n";
    }
    else {
        s/\S+\s*$/\-999\n/;
        print;
    }
}
```

Both NCBI-BLAST and WU-BLAST require matrices to have specific names. Unrecognized names cause NCBI-BLAST to terminate the search. WU-BLAST continues searching, but it employs ungapped values for λ, k, and H (it issues a warning to this effect). Try to maintain the names of the matrices, but in a location with an obvious name such as *stop-999-matrices*. Both versions of BLAST look for scoring matrices in the local directory, and on Unix systems, they recognize the BLASTMAT environment variable. Therefore, prior to the search, you can either create a symbolic link (alias) to the scoring matrix of choice or set the BLASTMAT environment variable to point to the location of specialized matrices. In the following examples, the derivative matrices are located in */my_computer/stop-999-matrices*:

```
ln -s /my_computer/stop-999-matrices/BLOSUM62 .
blastall -p tblastx -d db -i query
rm BLOSUM62

setenv BLASTMAT /my_computer/stop-999-matrices
blastall -p tblastx -d db -i query
unsetenv BLASTMAT
```

WU-BLAST users can use the altscore parameter to change the scores of any pair of letters rather than edit the matrix files. See Chapter 14 for more information on the altscore parameter.

CHAPTER 11

BLAST Databases

This chapter shows how to create and maintain BLAST databases—one of the most neglected yet important aspects of using BLAST. We begin with a discussion of the proper use of the FASTA format, and then turns to BLAST database issues. We finish with a general exploration of sequence databases as well as the International Nucleotide Sequence Database.

FASTA Files

Regardless of where you get your sequences, you will eventually want them in FASTA format because it is the standard currency for sequence data. The FASTA format has a very simple specification consisting of two parts: the definition line and the sequence lines.

The *definition line* is a single line that begins with the mandatory > symbol immediately followed by an identifier and then a description. There are no spaces between the > and the identifier. The identifier itself must not contain any whitespace because it is the delimiter between the identifier and the description. The description is free-form text that may contain any characters except an end-of-line character. Figure 11-1 shows a simple definition line in which the identifier is "EcoRI" and the description reads "is a restriction enzyme."

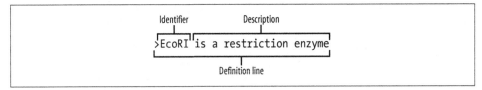

Figure 11-1. The FASTA definition line

The sequence lines follow a very simple format: they may be any length and there may be any number of them. Usually, you'll see 50, 60, or 80 characters per line, but the choice is arbitrary. Some software relies on sequence lines not being too long, so it's generally a good idea to follow the convention of 50 to 80 characters per line.

The first and most important guideline for FASTA definition lines is that the identifier uniquely specifies the sequence in some database. The identifier and description are actually optional. The following is a valid, though confusing, FASTA file because there is no identifier (dumb is the description).

```
> dumb
GAATTC
```

The following definition lines are confusing because the identifier isn't unique:

```
>chromosome 1 sequence 1
>chromosome 1 sequence 2
```

This is easily remedied by replacing the whitespace with some other character:

```
>chromosome_1-sequence.1
>chromosome_1-sequence.2
```

On the surface, these look like good identifiers, but another researcher may have the same identifiers for completely different sequences from another organism. How can you prevent this? You can't, but you can minimize potential conflicts by including a unique tag, based on your name or institution. If your data will be made public, the best solution is to submit your sequences to the public databases and use the accession numbers they provide. If not, choose identifiers you think will be unique (and make sure you read about creating fake GI numbers in the "Alias Databases" section).

The sequencing world is usually very cooperative, and standards have been developed to minimize name conflicts. In particular, there is a tight collaboration between DDBJ, EMBL, and GenBank so that accession numbers among these databases are guaranteed to be unique. But this isn't true of all databases. Although the identifier "AAG39070" points to a specific DDBJ/EMBL/GenBank record, it may also point to a wholly different sequence in another database. A good way to avoid name conflicts is to make sure the identifier specifies a database in addition to some unique tag for the sequence. Let's look at how the NCBI solves this problem.

NCBI Identifier Format

The NCBI identifier format* indicates the name of the database in addition to an accession number. These tokens are separated by the "|" symbol, often called a bar or a pipe. This symbol can be confusing in some fonts, as it may look like a lowercase L or the number one. Try using a constant-width serif font such as Courier if you're having trouble seeing them.

---

* The NCBI identifier format is used by both NCBI-BLAST and WU-BLAST software and is necessary for proper indexing of BLAST databases. You should use it as your standard format.

In general terms, an NCBI definition line has the following specification:

```
>database|identifier
```

A little knowledge can be a dangerous thing, so don't stop reading now and assume that if you follow this syntax you will have valid identifiers. The names of databases are restricted and have particular syntaxes. If you don't follow the proper syntax, you will end up confusing *formatdb* or *xdformat*, which will prevent you performing certain operations such as retrieving sequences by accession number. And you may end up confusing people if you share your data. Table 11-1 shows the current database tokens and their syntax (for an up-to-date list, see the documentation distributed with NCBI-BLAST or WU-BLAST software). For example, if you use the "pat" database token, which corresponds to the patent database, you must supply the country and the patent number as well.

Table 11-1. NCBI identifier syntax

Database name	Syntax
DDBJ	dbj|accession|locus
EMBL	emb|accession|ID
NCBI GenBank	gb|accession|locus
NCBI GenInfo	gi|integer
NCBI Reference Sequence	ref|accession|locus
NBRF Protein Information Resource	pir||entry
Protein Research Foundation	prf||name
SWISS-PROT	sp|accesion|entry
Brookhaven Protein Data Bank	pdb|entry|chain
Patents	pat|country|number
GenInfo Backbone ID	bbs|number
Local	lcl|identifier
General	gnl|database|identifier

Here are some real examples of NCBI identifiers:

```
>gi|21305377
>gb|AAM45611.1|AF384285_1
>ref|NP_104634.1|
```

In the final example, there is no locus, even though this is expected in the syntax. This isn't an error; the locus is just blank.

If you have a collection of your own sequences, with your own names, your best choice is to use the *Local* or *General* databases, which are designed specifically for that purpose. The advantage to using *General* is that you can specify your own sub-namespace in the database field. The following identifier strings are all different from one another (note that identifiers are case-sensitive):

```
>lcl|foo
>lcl|FOO
>gnl|mydatabase|foo
>gnl|yourdatabase|foo
```

If, for some reason, you don't want to use the *Local* or *General* databases, you can omit the database name and just use your own identifiers with the guidelines discussed earlier. If you're using NCBI-BLAST, your sequences are actually stored in the *Local* database, and the following identifiers are therefore identical:

```
>dna.001
>lcl|dna.001
```

If you retrieve sequences from the BLAST database with *fastacmd*, they will have the `lcl|` prepended (even if you didn't specify this), and they will have `no definition line found` if the definition line doesn't include a description.

If you use WU-BLAST, the previous two identifiers aren't considered identical because an additional unnamed database is separate from the *Local* database. Definition lines without descriptions are also reported unmodified.

Compound identifiers

It is typical for the same sequence to be known by various names. The NCBI identifier format supports this by using compound identifiers where individual identifiers are concatenated with a pipe symbol. The following identifiers are examples of such compound identifiers. In databases distributed by the NCBI, the GI number is the first identifier.

```
>gi|11611818|gb|AF287139.1|AF287139
>gi|1708198|sp|P80487|HHP_THICU
>gi|9910844|sp|Q9UWG2|RL3_METVA
>gi|7228451|dbj|BAA92411.1|
>gi|11277201|pir||T44712
```

Concatenated definition lines

If you download the nonredundant protein database from the NCBI or use one of the programs distributed with WU-BLAST that creates nonredundant databases, you will see concatenated definition lines. Each definition is separated with the Control-A character, which is a whitespace character that in text editors or word processors looks like a normal space. When it is forced to be visible, Control-A is often written as ^A (a white character on a black background is also common). You may wonder why you can't just create a larger compound identifier rather than a concatenated definition. The reason is that identical sequences may originate from different organisms or different loci and are therefore not identical in the biological sense; they may have different descriptions, which you may want to see. The following single definition line contains concatenated definitions as well as compound identifiers.

```
>gi|9845511|ref|NP_008839.2| ras-related C3 botulinum toxin substrate 1 isoform
Rac1; rho family, small GTP binding protein Rac1 [Homo sapiens]^Agi|131807|sp|P1
```

```
5154|RAC1_HUMAN Ras-related C3 botulinum toxin substrate 1 (p21-Rac1) (Ras-like
protein TC25)^Agi|68958|pir||TVHUC1 GTP-binding protein rac1 - human^Agi|108115|
pir||G36364 GTP-binding protein rac2 - dog^Agi|280956|pir||A60347 GTP-binding pr
otein rac1 - mouse^Agi|14277763|pdb|1I4D|D Chain D, Crystal Structure Analysis O
f Rac1-Gdp Complexed With Arfaptin (P21)^Agi|14277766|pdb|1I4L|D Chain D, Crysta
l Structure Analysis Of Rac1-Gdp In Complex With Arfaptin (P41)^Agi|922|emb|CAA3
9801.1| rac2 [Canis familiaris]^Agi|53886|emb|CAA40545.1| ras-related C3 botulin
ium toxin substrate [Mus musculus]^Agi|190824|gb|AAA36537.1| ras-related C3 botu
linum toxin substrate^Agi|249582|gb|AAB22206.1| rac1 p21=small GTP-binding prote
in [human, HL60, Peptide, 192 aa]^Agi|3184510|gb|AAC18960.1| GTPase cRac1A [Gall
us gallus]^Agi|6007014|gb|AAF00714.1|AF175262_1 GTPase [Bos taurus]^Agi|8574038|
emb|CAB53579.5| Rac1 protein [Homo sapiens]^Agi|12843555|dbj|BAB26027.1| RAS-rel
ated C3 botulinum substrate 1~data source:MGD, source key:MGI:97845, evidence:IS
S~putative [Mus musculus]^Agi|13277918|gb|AAH03828.1| ras-related C3 botulinum t
oxin substrate 1 (rho family, small GTP binding protein Rac1) [Mus musculus]^Agi
|15919905|dbj|BAB69451.1| RAS-related C3 botulinum substrate 1~data source:MGD,
source key:MGI:97845, evidence:ISS~putative [Mus musculus]^Agi|20379102|gb|AAM21
111.1|AF498964_1 small GTP binding protein RAC1 [Homo sapiens]
```

Most concatenated definitions aren't this long. This particular protein is highly conserved and is identical from human to chicken (*Gallus gallus*). You might take a moment to appreciate that in the eons during which continents have split apart and converged, this protein has remained completely unchanged.

Descriptions

While you should use the NCBI identifier format, there isn't a publicly recognized standard for descriptions. Some people choose to omit descriptions entirely, while others load up the definition line with the entire contents of a GenBank file. The best descriptions are both brief and informative. Descriptions from the NCBI include a short description and the species names in square brackets at the end of the line. This is a reasonably good practice, but you should be wary of trying to reliably parse descriptions that don't come from a controlled vocabulary. The following identifier is a real example of a difficult-to-parse description:

```
>gi|20820984|ref|XP_140836.1| similar to DiGeorge syndrome critical region gene DGSI
protein [Homo sapiens] [Mus musculus]
```

It's hard to tell if this is a human or mouse sequence. In reality, it's a mouse sequence similar to a human protein that originates from a region involved with the genetic disease called DiGeorge Syndrome. If you use a regular expression to find all *Homo sapiens* sequences and you don't bind the pattern match to the end of the line, this description can fool you. This kind of problem isn't limited to FASTA files; you'll also find fields in GenBank records that have embedded GenBank tags. It's both confusing and annoying. Unfortunately, automatically generating descriptions from transitive associations is a common practice. One way to cope with this problem is to rigorously construct your own definition lines from a controlled vocabulary. Another way is to trust only the identifiers, and when you need biological information, such as the species, retrieve it directly from the parent biological database.

BLAST Databases

The mechanics of creating BLAST databases is quite simple; just run *formatdb* or *xdformat* with the proper syntax. Chapter 10 discussed this topic, and you'll find the command summaries in Chapters 13 and 14. There are, however, subtleties that make this process more complicated than it may appear.

Large Databases

One of the most common database complications occurs with large files. Most computers today use 32-bit operating systems and 32-bit filesystems. This puts a physical limit of 4 GB on the amount of RAM and 4 GB on the size of any particular file. (You may find that you are actually limited to less than 4 GB in both cases, and a 2-GB limit is quite common.) Most computers these days don't have or need 4-GB RAM. However, most hard disks are quite a bit larger than 4 GB, and files can sometimes exceed these limits. Therefore many operating systems have the option of using 64-bit filesystems. Unfortunately you can't just change the filesystem and expect everything to work. Making software applications aware of large files often means recompiling them with special flags, and the process of migrating to a 64-bit filesystem can be painful because the applications don't tell you useful things like "I'm not large-file-aware." Instead, they just sit there quietly burning CPU time while they run in endless loops.

Large NCBI databases

The standard protocol for formatting a database is to run *formatdb* on a FASTA database:

```
formatdb -p F -i fasta_db -o
```

NCBI-BLAST databases are physically limited to 4 GB of sequence, which corresponds to about 4 billion amino acids or 16 billion nucleotides (nucleotides are compressed 4:1). On a 32-bit filesystem, the previous approach won't let you use all this space because the FASTA file can't contain more than 2 or 4 billion letters. Creating a database larger than 2 or 4 billion letters requires piping sequence to *formatdb*.

```
cat fasta1 fasta2 fasta3 | formatdb -p F -i stdin -n my_db -o
```

But what if you happen to have more than 16 billion letters? This isn't a problem because *formatdb* automatically segments individual BLAST databases to files containing 16 billion nucleotides and creates something called an alias database that stitches them all together. This is really convenient because it means that you can search enormous databases even on 32-bit filesystems. Alias databases are discussed in more detail later in this chapter.

It's still possible to run into file size issues by piping FASTA files to *formatdb* because the filesystem maximum may be 2 GB and the implicit BLAST maximum is 4 GB.

Fortunately, *formatdb* lets you set the size of each database volume with the *-v* parameter. The following example sets this size this to 2 billion and includes a bit more realism by piping the FASTA files from a compressed format.

```
zcat file*.gz | formatdb -i stdin -p F -o -n my_db -v 2000000000
```

A word of caution: be precise. If you accidentally leave off one of the zeroes, you can create 10 times as many files. For large databases, this can be a problem because the maximum number of volumes is 100.

Large WU-BLAST databases

WU-BLAST doesn't use alias databases, so the only way to create a database larger than 4 GB is on a 64-bit filesystem. If you're accessing or distributing databases over a network, the network must also be 64-bit aware. To index a large number of compressed files, use a command such as the following:

```
zcat file* | xdformat -n -I -o ESTs -- -
```

In the typical Unix command line syntax, the double-dash indicates the end of the command line options, and the single-dash denotes standard input rather than a file.

If you're stuck with a 32-bit filesystem and need to search large BLAST databases, you can use virtual databases, which are explained next. If you use the free version of WU-BLAST, there is no large file support and no virtual database mechanism. Your best solution is to create several databases within the limits of your filesystem, search each independently and then merge the results.

Virtual Databases

Virtual databases let you combine multiple databases and use them as if they were one. It's as simple as including the various databases in quotes on the command line. Here's how it looks for NCBI-BLAST:

```
blastall -p blastp -d "db1 db2 db3" -i query
```

And here is the equivalent WU-BLAST command line:

```
blastp "db1 db2 db3" query
```

Virtual databases are useful for grouping related searches. Let's say you want to search individually against an EST and an mRNA database, as well as a transcripts database that combines the two. You can create each database individually, but there is some duplication in data. Alternatively, you can just create the EST and mRNA databases and use the virtual database EST mRNA for transcripts. Virtual databases behave just like normal databases. You can even retrieve sequences from virtual databases with *fastacmd* (this feature isn't yet available for *xdget*, but see the end of this chapter for a workaround).

One thing you probably don't want to do is to combine databases with redundant sequences. For example, you wouldn't want to group the NCBI *nr* database with

SWISSPROT because *nr* already includes SWISSPROT. Duplicated sequences decrease the statistical significance of matches and can be confusing in the output.

Alias Databases

Alias databases are a unique and powerful feature of NCBI-BLAST. You've already seen that *formatdb* creates alias databases when splitting large files, but alias databases also have other uses. Alias databases can be used as static virtual databases for any combination of databases; all you have to do is create a file with the proper name and syntax. Here's a simple alias file, *transcripts.nal*, that combines the previous ESTs and mRNAs example to create a transcripts databases:

```
TITLE transcripts
DBLIST ESTs mRNAs
```

The TITLE is the name of the database and the DBLIST is simply a list of the databases to merge. Using alias databases you can, for example, organize sequences by organism. All you have to do is create the individual databases and combine them in various ways with alias files to create more comprehensive sets.

Not only can you join databases, but you can also use alias files to restrict searches to particular sequences from a database. Let's say you create a comprehensive EST database and then want to create a human-only EST database. The alias file for such a database looks something like this:

```
TITLE humanESTs
DBLIST ESTs
GILIST human.gi
```

The GILIST specifies a list of files that contains the GI numbers of the sequences to search. There are a few complexities when working with GI lists. First, using a GI list assumes that your sequences have GI numbers. If your original FASTA identifiers don't include GI numbers, you can't use this feature. It is unfortunate that the file of GI numbers isn't a file of accession numbers, but that's the way it is. If you want to use GI lists for sequences without GI numbers, you have to add fake GI numbers to your identifiers. The following script counts backward from the maximum possible GI number and thus minimizes the potential conflict with real GI numbers:

```perl
#!/usr/bin/perl

$i = 2147483648;
while (<>) {
    if (/^>/) {
        $i--;
        print ">gi|$i (fake-gi) ", substr($_, 1);
    }
    else {
        print;
    }
}
```

To use this script, *fake-gi.pl*, simply place it upstream of *formatdb* in your pipe:

```
zcat file*.gz | fake-gi.pl | formatdb -i stdin -p F -o -n my_db -v 2000000000
```

Creating an alias database restricted to GI numbers is a bit more complicated than just merging databases. First you need to get a list of GI numbers for your sequences of interest. There are a number of ways you can do this, but the easiest is to use NCBI Entrez. If you have a GI list called *human.gi.list*, the next step is to convert it to binary form using *formatdb* (this step isn't actually required, but it does improve performance).

```
formatdb -F human.gi.list -B human.gi
```

Finally, create the alias file. You can do this yourself, but you might as well let *formatdb* do it for you because it also adds the number of sequences and their length to the information in the alias file.

```
formatdb -p F -i ESTs -L humanESTs -F human.gi
```

-L identifies the name of the alias database to create, and -F is the name of the binary file of GI numbers.

As you can see, alias databases are a powerful way to join and split databases. As BLAST development continues, you should expect to see more structure in BLAST databases and greater control of sequences subsets.

Removing Redundancy

One way to improve the efficiency of your BLAST searches is to remove redundant sequences. Consider what happens when you search a redundant database. The statistical significance of a database hit depends on the size of the database. Each redundant sequence artificially increases the size of the database and therefore reduces the statistical significance of any hit. In addition, redundancy makes the search slower.

The *nrdb* program that comes with the licensed version of WU-BLAST concatenates the definition lines of all identical sequences. This program isn't available with the free version, and the NCBI distribution doesn't include such a program in the BLAST distribution. WU-BLAST also includes *patdb*, which is a bit more aggressive because it concatenates identical subsequences. Both programs are very efficient. You can find examples of their use in Chapter 10. You can also write your own database purifier using Bioperl tools. (Some entertaining discussions about the "best" way to do this may be found in the Bioperl mailing list archives at *http://bioperl.org*). Here's one way:

```perl
#!/usr/bin/perl
use Bio::SeqIO;

my %NR;
my $file = Bio::SeqIO->new(-fh => \*ARGV);
while (my $fasta = $file->next_seq){
```

```
    my $def = $fasta->id ." " .$fasta->desc;
    $NR{$fasta->seq}{$def} = 1;
}
for my $seq(keys %NR){
    print ">",join(chr(1),keys
    %{$NR{$seq}}),"\n",$seq,"\n";
}
```

It's more common to collapse redundant proteins than redundant nucleotide sequences. One reason is because nucleotide sequences are rarely identical to one another. Another is that nucleotide sequences can be very large, and the procedure becomes impractical with off-the-shelf hardware. Most importantly, it is better to assemble genomic fragments into chromosomes and ESTs into full-length transcripts. Because these tasks are complicated and compute-intensive, these feats of bioinformagic are best left to the experts.

Standard BLAST Databases

Every BLAST search is an experiment and should be planned as such. Just as you wouldn't want to use the same query for every BLAST search, you wouldn't want to use the same database for every BLAST search. However, a few databases are used so frequently that they have become standards. All databases described in this section are available from the NCBI at *ftp://ftp.ncbi.nih.gov/blast/db/*. The most important is the nonredundant protein database, *nr*. This database combines all translations from GenBank records (including RefSeq) with proteins from the SWISS-PROT, PIR, and PDB databases. If you want to do a comprehensive search against all known proteins, this is the database to use. Not all of the protein sequences have been verified experimentally, so you should expect some errors.

There are several essential nucleotide databases. The *ecoli* and *vector* databases may sound like uninteresting databases, but they're actually quite important. The procedures used to sequence DNA require various molecular biology techniques that rely on the *E. coli* bacterium and various vector sequences for carrying DNA. Because of this, many common sources of data contamination are from *E. coli* and vector sequences. Screening nucleotide sequences against these databases is a good way to detect these pollutants. Another database that is useful for detecting contaminants in genomic DNA is the *mito* database of mitochondrial sequences. The *est* database is also one of the most popular ones. It contains all the expressed sequence tags from DDBJ/EMBL/GenBank. Many undiscovered proteins lurk in the *est* database.

The NCBI FTP site includes several other databases. For those interested in the business side of bioinformatics, the *pataa* and *patnt* databases contain patented amino acid and nucleotide sequences. The *sts* database contains sequence tagged sites, which are mostly PCR amplimers that uniquely identify a region of a genome and are used in genome mapping. The *gss* sequences correspond to genome survey sequences. These are random-ish sequences from various organisms. Some sequences may not have been processed to remove sequencing vectors or low quality reads, so the quality of the sequences varies. Finally, the *htg* database contains all high-throughput genomic sequences that correspond to large genomic fragments from various organisms.

Custom BLAST Databases

In many cases, using a custom database rather than a standard database is more efficient. For example, if you're only interested in searching against human sequences, there's no point in including the rest of the public database. But the total cost of a BLAST search also includes creating the database, so it isn't always more efficient to use a custom database. Suppose you've just cloned a dog gene with mutations that bear some similarity to a human disease, and you want to know which human proteins correspond to the dog protein. You can build a human protein database and search it, or you could search against *nr* and ignore anything that isn't human. If this is the only experiment you're going to perform, it's probably more efficient to search *nr* than build a custom database.

If you occasionally want to make custom databases, it's worth getting to know one of the batch retrieval systems available on the Internet. You can make custom databases easily using these web-based systems. If you find yourself making custom databases frequently and find limitations with using web-based systems, you will probably want to have an in-house database. This can be a nontrivial task involving many hours of work and expensive computers, or it can be a relatively simple operation. It depends on the kind of performance and features you want. You will learn more about this topic in just a bit, but let's first discuss sequence databases in general.

Sequence Databases

The sequences in BLAST databases come from sequence databases. But what are sequence databases and where do you get them? The answers to these simple questions are surprisingly complex. Sequence databases come in many shapes and sizes. Some are just collections of raw sequence data from genome sequencing projects, while others contain comprehensive information about the origin and function of the sequences. Unfortunately, there isn't a one-stop shopping place to get all the information you may want, but there is one particular service worth mentioning above all others: the International Nucleotide Sequence Database.

International Nucleotide Sequence Database

Probably the most important molecular biology resource is the public sequence database maintained by the International Nucleotide Sequence Database (INSD). It is composed of three parties: the DNA Data Bank of Japan (DDBJ, *http://www.ddbj.nig.*

ac.jp), the European Molecular Biology Laboratory, (EMBL, *http://www.embl.org*), and GenBank from the National Center for Biotechnology Information (NCBI, *http:// ncbi.nlm.nih.gov/GenBank*). This consortium collaborates to form the largest public repository for DNA and protein sequences in the world. Because it is such an important resource, this chapter spends some time exploring it.

Database Growth

The amount of publicly available sequence has been growing geometrically, doubling approximately every 14 months (see Figure 11-2). Fortunately, computer technology has also kept pace. While it seems scary that GenBank is currently approaching 100 GB and will be half a terabyte in a few years, it's nice to know that this isn't going to be a problem. Not every database grows so fast, though. Organism-specific databases such as the *Saccharomyces* Genome Database, WormBase, and FlyBase are growing at a more moderate pace, principally because the sequence of their genomes is complete. But many new genome projects are just getting started, and they will probably grow very quickly.

Flat Files

Sequence databases usually offer their data in several different formats. The FASTA format is universally accepted for operating on sequences, but many sequence databases record a lot more data than just the sequence. Such extra information is commonly presented in a human-readable format called a *flat file*. The INSD uses two kinds of flat files. The DDBJ and GenBank flat file formats are identical, while the EMBL format is slightly different. The following DDBJ/GenBank record corresponds to a fragment of the Hoxa-11 gene from the coelacanth (the ancient fish on the cover of the book):

```
LOCUS       AF287139                 606 bp    DNA     linear   VRT 10-DEC-2000
DEFINITION  Latimeria chalumnae Hoxa-11 gene, partial cds.
ACCESSION   AF287139
VERSION     AF287139.1  GI:11611818
KEYWORDS    .
SOURCE      Latimeria chalumnae.
  ORGANISM  Latimeria chalumnae
            Eukaryota; Metazoa; Chordata; Craniata; Vertebrata; Euteleostomi;
            Coelacanthiformes; Coelacanthidae; Latimeria.
REFERENCE   1  (bases 1 to 606)
  AUTHORS   Chiu,C.H., Nonaka,D., Xue,L., Amemiya,C.T. and Wagner,G.P.
  TITLE     Evolution of Hoxa-11 in lineages phylogenetically positioned along
            the fin-limb transition
  JOURNAL   Mol. Phylogenet. Evol. 17 (2), 305-316 (2000)
  MEDLINE   20538275
   PUBMED   11083943
REFERENCE   2  (bases 1 to 606)
```

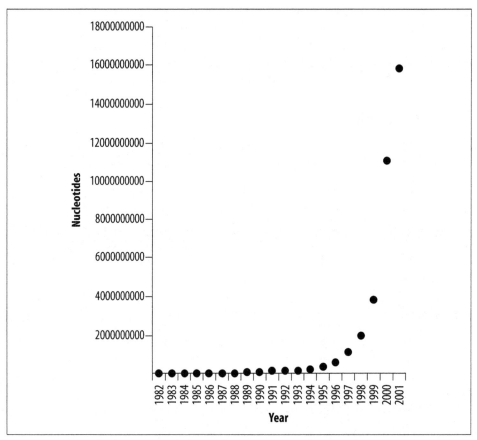

Figure 11-2. Growth of DDBJ/EMBL/GenBank

```
AUTHORS    Chiu,C.-H. and Wagner,G.P.
TITLE      Direct Submission
JOURNAL    Submitted (14-JUL-2000) Ecology and Evolutionary Biology, Yale
           University, 165 Prospect St., New Haven, CT 06520-8106, USA
FEATURES             Location/Qualifiers
   source            1..606
                     /organism="Latimeria chalumnae"
                     /db_xref="taxon:7897"
   CDS               <1..>606
                     /codon_start=1
                     /product="Hoxa-11"
                     /protein_id="AAG39070.1"
                     /db_xref="GI:11611819"
                     /translation="YLPSCTYYVSGPDFSSLPSFLPQTPSSRPMTYSYSSNLPQVQPV
                     REVTFRDYAIDTSNKWHPRSNLPHCYSTEEILHRDCLATTTASSIGEIFGKGNANVYH
                     PGSSTSSNFYNTVGRNGVLPQAFDQFFETAYGTTENHSSDYSADKNSDKIPSAATSRS
                     ETCRETDEKERREESSSPESSSGNNEEKSSSSSGQRTRKKRC"
BASE COUNT     173 a    169 c    129 g    135 t
```

```
ORIGIN
        1 tacttgccaa gttgcaccta ctacgtttcg ggtcccgatt tctccagcct cccttctttt
       61 ttgccccaga ccccgtcttc tcgccccatg acatactcct attcgtctaa tctaccccaa
      121 gttcaacctg tgagagaagt taccttcagg gactatgcca ttgatacatc caataaatgg
      181 catcccagaa gcaatttacc ccattgctac tcaacagagg agattctgca cagggactgc
      241 ctagcaacca ccaccgcttc aagcatagga gaaatctttg ggaaaggcaa cgctaacgtc
      301 taccatcctg gctccagcac ctcttctaat ttctataaca cagtgggtag aaacgggggtc
      361 ctaccgcaag cctttgacca gtttttcgag acggcttatg gcacaacaga aaaccactct
      421 tctgactact ctgcagacaa gaattccgac aaaatacctt cggcagcaac ttcaaggtcg
      481 gagacttgca gggagacaga cgagaaggag agacgggaag aaagcagtag cccagagtct
      541 tcttccggca acaatgagga gaaatcaagc agttccagtg gtcaacgtac aaggaagaag
      601 aggtgc
//
```

The next example is the same record in the slightly different EMBL format. Most of the data is identical between the two formats, but there are a few important differences. The VERSION field of the DDBJ/GenBank record includes a GI number (discussed below) that isn't in the EMBL record. The EMBL record contains both a creation date and a modification date, while the DDBJ/GenBank record contains only a modification date.

```
ID   AF287139    standard; DNA; VRT; 606 BP.
XX
AC   AF287139;
XX
SV   AF287139.1
XX
DT   11-DEC-2000 (Rel. 66, Created)
DT   11-DEC-2000 (Rel. 66, Last updated, Version 1)
XX
DE   Latimeria chalumnae Hoxa-11 gene, partial cds.
XX
KW   .
XX
OS   Latimeria chalumnae (coelacanth)
OC   Eukaryota; Metazoa; Chordata; Craniata; Vertebrata; Euteleostomi;
OC   Coelacanthiformes; Coelacanthidae; Latimeria.
XX
RN   [1]
RP   1-606
RX   PUBMED; 11083943.
RA   Chiu, Ch, Nonaka D., Xue L., Amemiya C.T., Wagner G.P.;
RT   "Evolution of Hoxa-11 in Lineages Phylogenetically Positioned along the
RT   Fin-Limb Transition";
RL   Mol. Phylogenet. Evol. 17(2):305-316(2000).
XX
RN   [2]
RP   1-606
RA   Chiu C.-H., Wagner G.P.;
RT   ;
RL   Submitted (14-JUL-2000) to the RL   Ecology and Evolutionary Biology, Yale
University, 165 Prospect St., New
```

```
RL      Haven, CT 06520-8106, USA
XX
DR      SPTREMBL; Q9DDT9; Q9DDT9.
XX
FH      Key             Location/Qualifiers
FH
FT      source          1..606
FT                      /db_xref="taxon:7897"
FT                      /organism="Latimeria chalumnae"
FT      CDS             <1..>606
FT                      /codon_start=1
FT                      /db_xref="SPTREMBL:Q9DDT9"
FT                      /product="Hoxa-11"
FT                      /protein_id="AAG39070.1"
FT                      /translation="YLPSCTYYVSGPDFSSLPSFLPQTPSSRPMTYSYSSNLPQVQPVR
FT                      EVTFRDYAIDTSNKWHPRSNLPHCYSTEEILHRDCLATTTASSIGEIFGKGNANVYHPG
FT                      SSTSSNFYNTVGRNGVLPQAFDQFFETAYGTTENHSSDYSADKNSDKIPSAATSRSETC
FT                      RETDEKERREESSSPESSSGNNEEKSSSSSGQRTRKKRC"
XX
SQ      Sequence 606 BP; 173 A; 169 C; 129 G; 135 T; 0 other;
        tacttgccaa gttgcaccta ctacgtttcg ggtcccgatt tctccagcct cccttctttt        60
        ttgccccaga ccccgtcttc tcgccccatg acatactcct attcgtctaa tctaccccaa       120
        gttcaacctg tgagagaagt taccttcagg gactatgcca ttgatacatc caataaatgg       180
        catcccagaa gcaatttacc ccattgctac tcaacagagg agattctgca cagggactgc       240
        ctagcaacca ccaccgcttc aagcatagga gaaatctttg ggaaaggcaa cgctaacgtc       300
        taccatcctg gctccagcac ctcttctaat ttctataaca cagtgggtag aaacggggtc       360
        ctaccgcaag cctttgacca gtttttcgag acggcttatg gcacaacaga aaaccactct       420
        tctgactact ctgcagacaa gaattccgac aaaatacctt cggcagcaac ttcaaggtcg       480
        gagacttgca gggagacaga cgagaaggag agacgggaag aaagcagtag cccagagtct       540
        tcttccggca acaatgagga gaaatcaagc agttccagtg gtcaacgtac aaggaagaag       600
        aggtgc                                                                 606
//
```

Note that the sequence data is only one part of the record; there's a lot of other useful information in here including the organism, the taxonomic classification, the authors, a reference to the scientific literature, and a feature table indicating the translation of the DNA. This is great stuff, and INSD is full of these kinds of records. But there is a downside to using the public databases. They're a bit like public parks: huge, beautiful, inexpensive to use, and valuable, but there's always someone who doesn't pick up their trash. Some sequences are erroneous, and the ancillary information is sometimes wrong and misleading. But overall, the databases are high-quality resources, and you should take a moment to applaud the scientists who contribute their sequences to the INSD, as well as the administrators and curators at DDBJ/EMBL/GenBank who do an outstanding job. Now let's take a closer look at some parts of the sequence record.

ACCESSION, LOCUS, VERSION, and GI

One of the most important parts of any sequence record is its database identifier, which is often called its accession number. (Although it's called a number, it may be a mixture of letters, numbers, and other symbols, but not spaces.) This tag uniquely identifies the sequence in a database. There isn't necessarily a one-to-one correspondence between sequences and tags because sequences are sometimes known by multiple unique names. The DDBJ/GenBank ACCESSION (or AC in EMBL) is the primary name for a sequence record. Another unique name is the LOCUS (or ID in EMBL). The locus is supposed to be a "short mnemonic name for the entry, chosen to suggest the sequence's definition." For example, "HSMG01" is the locus name for the database entry containing *Homo sapiens* myoglobin exon 1. Over time, like the names of celestial objects, locus names have become less descriptive and are often just duplicates of the accession numbers.

Sequence records can also change over time. This often happens when the record is edited to correct a sequence error. The accession number and locus don't change, but the version number is increased (VERSION in DDBJ/GenBank and SV in EBML). In this way, an ACCESSION.VERSION points to a particular record at a particular time. It's a good idea to always refer to sequences in this way and not by ACCESSION alone or by LOCUS or ID.

DDBJ/GenBank records include an additional token called the GI number, which is a numeric identifier that points to a particular ACCESSION.VERSION. The GI number is especially important because NCBI-BLAST relies on it as an additional mechanism for indexing BLAST databases. This topic was covered in the section "Alias Databases."

DEFINITION, KEYWORDS, and SOURCE

The DEFINITION is a concise description of the origin and function of a sequence, and is typically what you find a FASTA description. The text is structured, meaning that there are rules that define how it is produced. However, it doesn't use a controlled vocabulary, which means you can't be sure which words will or won't appear.

KEYWORDS are a historical relic like the locus name and aren't used in modern sequence records. Avoid the temptation to believe that keywords are meaningful.

The common name for an organism is often found in the SOURCE, or in parentheses after the OS in EMBL format. The scientific name is on the ORGANISM line (OS in EMBL) and the complete taxonomic classification is given on the following lines (OC in EMBL). The complete taxonomy may be abbreviated if it's especially long.

FEATURES

The FEATURES (FT in EMBL) list specific regions of importance on the sequence such as genes or repetitive elements. The general syntax of features is fairly simple; each has a key and location, and optional qualifiers. The *key* tells what kind of feature it is (e.g., a gene), the *location* (e.g., from nucleotide 100 to nucleotide 200), and the *qualifiers* include additional information, such as specific names, database cross references, and experimental notes. A detailed discussion of the feature table is beyond the scope of this book. See *http://www.ncbi.nih.gov/projects/collab/FT* for more information.

Other Common Databases

INSD is just one of many important databases. Some other favorites are listed in Table 11-2.

Table 11-2. Popular biological databases

Database	Description
RefSeq	RefSeq provides reference sequences that represent the highest quality information about a particular sequence. Each record may be constructed from several INSD records, which makes the database nonredundant. All RefSeq accession numbers are preceded by two letters and an underscore, for example XP_102310. Some types of RefSeq records have been inspected manually by curators, and they are the highest quality records (indicated below).

Prefix	Molecule	Description
NC_	Genomic	Curated complete genomic molecules including genomes, chromosomes, organelles, and plasmids.
NG_	Genomic	Curated incomplete genomic region; primarily supplied for *Homo sapiens* and *Mus musculus* to support the NCBI Genome Annotation pipeline.
NM_	mRNA	Curated mRNAs.
NR_	RNA	Curated noncoding transcripts including structural RNAs, transcribed pseudogenes, and others.
NP_	Protein	Curated proteins.
NT_	Genomic	Intermediate genomic assemblies of BAC sequence data.
NW_	Genomic	Intermediate genomic assemblies of Whole Genome Shotgun sequence data.
XM_	mRNA	*Homo sapiens* model mRNA provided by the Genome Annotation process; sequence corresponds to the genomic contig.
XR_	RNA	*Homo sapiens* model noncoding transcripts provided by the Genome Annotation process; sequence corresponds to the genomic contig.

http://www.ncbi.nlm.nih.gov/LocusLink/refseq.html

Table 11-2. Popular biological databases (continued)

Database	Description
Pfam	Pfam is a collection of multiple sequence alignments and hidden Markov models (HMMs) for many common protein domains and families. If you are interested in a particular family, such as globins, or a particular domain, such as WD-40, this is a great resource. HMMs are probabilistic models that describe how whole domains evolve, which is quite different from a scoring matrix employed by BLAST that treats each amino acid of a protein independently.
	http://pfam.wustl.edu , http://www.sanger.ac.uk/pfam
SWISS-PROT	The SWISS-PROT Protein Knowledgebase is a curated protein sequence database that provides a high level of annotation (such as the description of protein function, domains structure, post-translational modifications, variants, etc.), a minimal level of redundancy, and high level of integration with other databases.
	http://www.ebi.ac.uk/swissprot
TrEMBL	The TrEMBL database contains translations of all coding sequences (CDS) present in the INSD, which aren't yet integrated into SWISS-PROT. TrEMBL is split into two main sections: SP-TrEMBL contains entries expected to be included in SWISS-PROT, and REM-TrEMBL contains those that aren't expected to be included.
	http://www.ebi.ac.uk/tremble
UniGene	UniGene is an experimental system for automatically partitioning GenBank sequences into a non-redundant set of gene-oriented clusters. Each UniGene cluster contains sequences that represent a unique gene, as well as related information such as the tissue types in which the gene has been expressed and the map location. UniGene sets are available for most genomes with a lot of EST sequences.
	http://www.ncbi.nlm.nih.gov/UniGene
MGC	The goal of the Mammalian Gene Collection (MGC) is to provide a complete set of full-length (open reading frame) sequences and cDNA clones of expressed mammalian genes. The current focus is limited to human and mouse.
	http://mgc.nci.nih.gov
SGD	SGD is a scientific database of the molecular biology and genetics of the yeast *Saccharomyces cerevisiae*, which is commonly known as baker's or budding yeast. *S. cerevisiae* was the first eukaryotic genome sequenced.
	http://genome-www.stanford.edu/Saccharomyces
WormBase	WormBase is a comprehensive database dedicated to the biology and genome of the nematode *Caenorhabditis elegans*. *C. elegans* was the first multicellular organism to have its genome sequenced.
	http://www.wormbase.org
FlyBase	FlyBase is a comprehensive database for information on the genetics and molecular biology of *Drosophila*. It includes data from the *Drosophila* Genome Projects and data curated from the literature. FlyBase is a joint project with the Berkeley *Drosophila* Genome Project.
	http://www.flybase.org
TAIR	The *Arabidopsis* Information Resource (TAIR) provides a comprehensive resource for the scientific community working with *Arabidopsis thaliana*, a widely used model plant.
	http://www.arabidopsis.org

Sequence Database Management Strategies

There are many useful public sequence databases, and you may have access to some private ones as well. Because this is a book about BLAST, we assume you want to use these collections of sequences in BLAST searches. Some sequences may be used as queries, and others in databases. How are you going to manage them all in a rational way? Several possible strategies exist, and the correct one for you depends on your needs and resources. To demonstrate some of the issues, let's review a typical sequence analysis scenario.

Suppose a colleague of yours has just found the gene that makes cats go crazy for catnip. She wants to learn more about this gene and comes to you for help because you are a BLAST expert. The first thing she wants to do is a BLAST search to find out what vertebrate proteins are similar to this one. Where are you going to get such a database of proteins? Once you perform the BLAST search, you find several interesting similarities. Your colleague tells you that these are probably all part of a family of proteins, and she would like to build a phylogenetic tree to determine their relationships to one another. How are you going to get the individual sequences? Finally, she decides she wants more information about the human sequences, and to do that, she would like references to the scientific literature like the ones she would find in a DDBJ/EMBL/GenBank report. How are you going to retrieve such information? You could just refuse to help her because these aren't really BLAST problems, but these are the kinds of tasks many BLAST users must face. Let's take a look at how they can be solved.

This example has basically two solutions to each question: the first is to use tools available on the Internet. The second is to build the tools yourself. In general, it is much easier to use the Internet, but for high speed or high-throughput operations you'll want a local solution. After you read this chapter, you may decide that you want some services to be provided locally, while others are Internet-only operations. This section begins with a brief review of databases.

Queries, Indexes, and Reports

The most common database operation is a query. One person may want to retrieve a particular sequence. Another may want all human sequences. As you have seen, sequence records have quite a bit of useful information, and a user may request non-sequence information such as all the MEDLINE references for all sequences with the word *disease* in the description.

The efficiency with which a query is executed depends a lot on how the database is indexed. If there is no indexing, a query must operate on every record of the database. So, for example, if you want to find all the coelacanth sequences, you would have to look through millions of records to find the handful whose sequences originate from the coelacanth. Clearly, this isn't going to be efficient, so databases usually have indexes that, for example, keep lists of species and all the sequences for each species.

The most straightforward kind of indexing occurs when there is a unique relationship between a property and a sequence. This is called a *one-to-one mapping*, and an example would be an accession number. A more complex indexing occurs when a property points to many sequences. This is called a *one-to-many mapping*, and an example is a species name that is shared by millions of records.

Once a query is executed, the data must be reported in some format. For sequences, this is usually the FASTA format. For other kinds of data, there are other appropriate formats, such as lists, tables, and graphs.

Local Database Considerations

Having a local sequence database has some real advantages. First, local databases are faster and more reliable because they don't rely on an Internet connection. If you're involved in high-throughput research, these reasons are sufficient. Another compelling reason is that you can combine several databases, and even include your own sequences that aren't in the public databases. The downside to creating a local sequence database is the amount of work it takes. Depending on the scale of the operation, it can be a full-time job. Here are six important issues to address when building a local sequence database:

Downloading
> Each database you support must be downloaded from time to time to keep the data current. For example, GenBank has five to six major releases each year, as well as daily updates. Other databases have their own update schedule. Managing updates can be a chore if you download a lot of databases, so automating the procedure is a good idea. In addition, you may want to take measures to ensure that during updates, which can take some time, the database that's presented to users isn't actually changing. This may require keeping a mirror of some data. Notice that having a local database doesn't mean you can completely insulate yourself from the Internet.

Processing records
> Each database you support must have a parser to read the various fields of each record. This may be as simple as pulling out the accession number for a sequence, or it may be much more complicated, such when you record specific keywords. You can build your own parsers but it takes less time to use one already created, such as a parser from the Bioperl project.

Storing data
> Your database schema will determine how each record is stored and what kinds of relationships exist between various pieces of data. Designing an appropriate schema is a difficult problem because it takes people who understand the data

(biologists), the data models (software engineers), and the storage/backup of the data (systems administrators).

Indexing

The efficiency of queries will largely depend on what data is indexed. You may choose to index everything, but your indexes could grow much larger than your data. So you may have to make compromises. This is another place where users and engineers must interact to determine the appropriate solution.

Querying

Not all databases are queried in the same way. Relational databases usually employ SQL as the query language, but many popular databases have their own querying mechanisms. The details of how you interacts with the database may depend on what kind of database you use. Regardless of the underlying architecture, you may decide to present a different interface to users, such as a form in a web browser or a script/program interface that connects directly to the database.

Formatting

You'll definitely want to create FASTA files, but what other report formats will you want to support? The DDBJ/EMBL/GenBank flat file formats are sometimes used to exchange data, so this would be useful, as would tabular format and some kind of HTML that looks good in browsers. For each output format, you may need some specialized code to generate the report.

As you can see, building a local database isn't trivial. But it doesn't have to be a full-time job if you only want a subset of the information. For example, if all you want is to retrieve records by accession number, you don't need to invest more than a couple hours of work. The following section explores the common techniques for managing sequence data.

Retrieving FASTA Files by Accession

The task of retrieving FASTA files by accession number is so common and has such an easy solution that it should be a local resource. If you're using NCBI-BLAST, the *fastacmd* program retrieves sequences from BLAST databases singly or in batches. If you're using WU-BLAST, the *xdget* program does the same thing. To use these features, you must index the databases when you format them, which is as simple as including the *-o* or *-I* option (see the command-line tutorial in Chapter 10, the reference sections for *formatdb* and *fastacmd* in Chapter 13, and *xdformat* and *xdget* in Chapter 14). One limitation of this approach is that the sequences are stored in a case-insensitive format in the database. If you use lowercase to denote regions containing repeats, for example, that information will be lost. If this is a serious problem for you, use one of the flat-file indexing schemes described later.

NCBI-BLAST users take note that unless you use the NCBI FASTA definition line format discussed earlier in this chapter, your definition lines may not look exactly the same when they come out of the database. For example, if you have a definition line such as this:

```
>FOO
```

When you retrieve it with *fastacmd*, it looks like:

```
>lcl|FOO no definition found
```

You can easily avoid such inconsistencies by using the recommended identifier format and by including descriptions on the definition line.

WU-BLAST users take note: *xdget* doesn't support virtual databases. You can work around this limitation with a simple script, such as this one:

```perl
#!/usr/bin/perl -w
use strict;

my (@DB, $i);
for ($i = 0; $i < @ARGV; $i++) {
    if ($ARGV[$i] =~ /\s/) {
        @DB = split(/\s+/, $ARGV[$i]);
        last;
    }
}

exec("xdget @ARGV") unless @DB;

my @pre = splice(@ARGV, 0, $i);
my @post = splice(@ARGV, 1);
foreach my $db (@DB) {
    system("xdget @pre $db @post");
}
```

Flat File Indexing

One of the most common procedures used to manage sequence data is called *flat file indexing*. In this approach, you keep concatenated sequence reports in their native format and store the starting position of each record in a separate file. One advantage of this approach is that you don't have to do any work when you want to reproduce the data in flat file format. Another reason why flat file indexing is so common is that it is simple to implement, at least for one-to-one mappings. To illustrate the process, we'll show you how to index identifiers in FASTA files. Here is an example of a very short FASTA file:

```
>FOO
GAATTC
>BAR
ATAGCGAAT
```

This file has two records with identifiers FOO and BAR, and they begin at bytes 0 and 12, respectively (count the letters and don't forget to add one for the end of line—in Windows, the end of line is actually two characters, and this will change the positions to 0 and 14). You can now create an index file that tells where each record begins in the file:

```
BAR 12
FOO 0
```

To use this index file, simply find the identifier of interest in the index and *seek* to the appropriate position in the FASTA file. Note that you sorted the lookup file alphabetically by identifier. This makes it much more efficient to find the record because you can use a binary search to find the identifier. If you have an index file containing 1 million records, on average, a linear search looks through 500,000 records, but a binary search looks at only 20.

You can make a couple of improvements to this simplistic indexing scheme. The first is to allow the index file to support more than one FASTA file. This is a trivial modification because you can just add a filename to your index file:

```
BAR file-A 12
FOO file-A 0
XYZ file-B 0
```

Another easy improvement is to use a persistent indexed data structure such as a Perl tied-hash. The Bioperl project uses this strategy in its `Bio::Index` classes.

A slightly more complicated approach manages the indices with one of the many free or commercial database applications, such as MySQL, PostgreSQL, FileMaker, Microsoft Access, or whatever you happen to be familiar with. If you're going to do this, you might as well store a bit more data. For illustrative purposes, imagine you create a schema like that in Table 11-3. In addition to the accession number, file, and offset, this schema provides for a species and a molecule type (moltype). The actual sequence in the schema was not provided because some applications can't handle data this large. If you wish to store sequences as well, test the performance of the system with realistic data to see if the system scales well.

Table 11-3. Sequence database example

Accession	Species	Moltype	File	Offset
A	Homo sapiens	AA	file-1	12024
B	Homo sapiens	AA	file-1	250
C	Homo sapiens	DNA	file-2	28223
AF287139	Latimeria chalumnae	cDNA	file-3	0

Using such a database you can don't only the simple accession number retrievals, but also the one-to-many relationships such as all human sequences or all DNA sequences. All you have to do is query the database and seek to the appropriate place in the appropriate file for every record. Organizing the data this way has a number of advantages over just downloading DDBJ/EMBL/GenBank by division. For example, if you want to make a database of all human transcripts, you need to identify the human ESTs from the EST division, as well as all the mRNAs from the PRI (primate) division. But if you've designated all ESTs and mRNAs as the cDNA moltype, getting all human transcripts is as easy as retrieving all records in which the species is *Homo sapiens* and the moltype is cDNA. You can add several more fields to the database, like date created, division, keywords, etc., and get quite a bit of functionality without much more complexity.

Overall, flat file indexing is a very good strategy for sequence management because it is simple, fast, and retains the data in its original format. You don't even have to write any software, as both free and commercial software packages are designed specifically for managing flat file data. Check out the Bioperl project at *http://bioperl.org*, MyGenBank at *http://sourceforge.net/projects/mgb*, and SRS (see Table 11-4).

Commercial Sequence Management Software

Several commercial software packages are designed for managing biological sequence data. The database software is generally part of a much larger software suite that includes sequence analysis tools such as BLAST and visualization tools to make interpretation easier. The companies that develop these packages expend a great deal of effort to make the various sequence analysis tasks interoperable and user friendly. Table 11-4 gives a brief description of the software.

Table 11-4. Commercial sequence management software

Company	Product and description
Accelrys	The popular Wisconsin GCG package is now owned by Accelrys, which provides the SeqStore software for managing sequence data. The system uses an Oracle database and allows daily/weekly updates. To install and maintain the system, you must have personnel with experience in Unix systems administration and Oracle database administration. Accelrys recommends a computer with at least 4 CPUs, at 4-GB RAM, and 40- GB disk space. *http://www.accelrys.com*
Informax	The Genomax software suite provides sequence management along with a comprehensive set of interoperable tools. Informax recommends a project manager, a Unix systems administrator, and an Oracle database administrator to manage and maintain the system, as well as a life sciences expert to respond to users' questions. Informax uses a three-tiered architecture and recommends that the three computers be configured with 4 CPUs and 4-8 GB RAM, and the database server have 400-GB disk space. *http://www.informaxinc.com*
LION Biosciences	LION Biosciences offers the Sequence Retrieval System (SRS). SRS is probably the most popular sequence management software in use today and is used by both DDBJ and EMBL. SRS is free for academic users. LION produces a separate, related product PRISMA2, which is an automatic databank-updating and maintenance tool. SRS requires a person with competent Unix skills to install and maintain and a server with enough storage for the various databases and indexes. *http://lionbioscience.com*

As you can see from the descriptions of the personnel and hardware requirements, using these comprehensive sequence analysis systems requires a serious commitment. For these reasons, these packages aren't recommended for small research groups. For larger groups, though, these products can save a lot of time and money. It's easy to underestimate the effort required to develop your own sequence management system, so take caution before embarking on such a task, and give the professionals a chance to show you their wares.

Tools on the Internet

There are good reasons to use web-based tools for sequence management rather than building a local database. First, you don't have to download more data than you need. Mirroring the entire public database isn't efficient if you need only a slice of it. Second, database providers take care of the most time-consuming and expensive tasks, namely processing, storing, and indexing the data. Third, the databases are self-updating, which means that you can always get the latest and most accurate information. Best of all, the service is completely free. Well, maybe not completely free since the databases are supported from taxes, but let's all thank the various governments and funding agencies for putting our hard-earned money toward a worthy cause, and let's especially recognize all the people that make it actually happen.

The downside to using web-based tools is that you have to spend time learning how to query the database efficiently and accurately, but that's going to be true of any sequence management system, even your own. A more serious issue is that you will depend on the computers and network between you and the database provider, but this will improve over time. Still, even if you have to put up with a few glitches here and there, the total cost in time and money is probably cheaper than building your own local mirror.

## CHAPTER 12

Hardware and Software Optimizations

This chapter explores how to optimize BLAST searches for maximum throughput and will help you get the most out of your current and future hardware and software. The first rule of BLAST performance is *optimize your BLAST parameters*. Incorrect settings can cause BLAST to run slowly, and you can often achieve surprising increases in speed by adjusting a parameter or two. Chapter 9 can help you choose the correct parameters for a particular experiment. If you're already running BLAST efficiently and want to get the most BLAST performance possible, read on.

The Persistence of Memory

Modern operating systems cache files. You may hear it referred to as RAM cache or disk cache, but we'll just call it cache. Once a file is read from the filesystem (e.g., hard disk), the file is kept in memory even after it is no longer used, assuming there's enough free RAM to do so. Why cache files? It's frequently the case that the same file is requested repeatedly. Retrieving from memory is much faster than from a disk, so keeping it in memory can save a lot of time. Caching can be very important in sequential BLAST searches if the database is located on a slow disk or across a network. While the first search may be limited by the speed that the database can be read, subsequent searches can be much faster.

The advantage of caching is most appreciable for insensitive BLAST searches, such as BLASTN with a large word size. In more sensitive searches, retrieving sequences from the database becomes a smaller fraction of the total elapsed time. In Table 12-1, note how the speed increase from caching is a function of sensitivity (here, word size).

Table 12-1. How caching benefits insensitive searches

Program	Word size	Search 1	Search 2	Speed increase
BLASTN	W=12	12 sec	7 sec	1.71 x
BLASTN	W=10	33 sec	28 sec	1.18 x

Table 12-1. How caching benefits insensitive searches (continued)

Program	Word size	Search 1	Search 2	Speed increase
BLASTN	W=8	57 sec	52 sec	1.10 x
BLASTN	W=6	243 sec	238 sec	1.02 x

BLAST itself doesn't take much memory, but having a lot of memory assists caching. Look at the amount of RAM in your current systems and the size of your BLAST databases. As a rule, your RAM should be at least 20 percent greater than the size of your largest database. If it isn't and you do a lot of insensitive searches, a simple memory upgrade may boost your throughput by 50 percent or more. However, if most of your searches are sensitive searches or involve small databases, adding RAM to all your machines may be less cost-effective than purchasing a few more servers.

BLAST Pipelines and Caching

If you're running BLAST as part of a sequence analysis pipeline involving several BLAST searches and multiple databases, you may want to consider how caching will affect the execution of the pipeline. For example, look at the typical BLAST-based sequence analysis pipeline for ESTs depicted in Figure 12-1. The most obvious approach is to take each EST and pass it through each step. But is this the most efficient way?

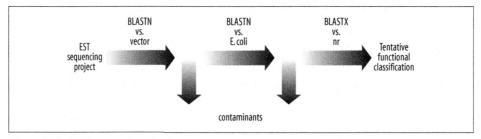

Figure 12-1. EST annotation pipeline

It's common to design sequence analysis pipelines with the following structure:

```
for each sequence to analyze {
    for each BLAST search in the pipeline {
        execute BLAST search
    }
}
```

However, you can switch the inner and outer loops to achieve this structure:

```
for each BLAST search in the pipeline {
    for each sequence to analyze {
        execute BLAST search
    }
}
```

The problem with the first pipeline is that if the BLAST databases are large, they may not all be cached. Each BLAST database can bump out the previously cached file if you don't have enough RAM, and then you get no benefit from caching. The second structure keeps the same BLAST database in memory for all the sequences. Before you tear apart your current pipeline, however, remember that caching isn't going to help much with sensitive searches. If most of your searches are sensitive, it is a waste of effort to optimize the already fast parts of your pipeline. As in any tuning procedure, optimize the major bottlenecks first.

CPUs and Computer Architecture

The clock speed of a CPU isn't necessarily an accurate indicator of how fast it will run BLAST. There are other complicating factors such as the amount of L2 cache, the memory latency and the speed of the front-side bus. Unfortunately, there is no good rule to predict how fast BLAST will perform on a particular computer except for the obvious within-family predictions—for example, that a 1-GHz Pentium III will be faster than an 800-MHz Pentium III. The best you can do is to benchmark a bunch of systems or contact people who have already done so.

Two benchmarks are provided Table 12-3. Before reading the description, please understand that you should use extreme caution whenever interpreting any benchmarks because the benchmarking protocol may be very different from your everyday tasks, and therefore may not reflect real-world performance. The best benchmark procedure should mimic your daily routine. In addition, if you use benchmarks to decide what hardware to purchase, you may be in for a nasty surprise, as other important considerations may override a simplistic interpretation of the "most BLAST for the buck." Total cost of ownership is a complicated equation that includes maintenance, support, facilities, cooling, and interfacing with legacy equipment and culture.

Table 12-2 shows the performance on various platforms when searching all members of a database against themselves. There are two databases, and both can be found at *http://examples.oreilly.com/BLAST*. The tests were performed using default parameters for NCBI-BLAST. The following command lines were used:

```
time blastall -p blastn -d ESTs -i ESTs > /dev/null
time blastall -p blastp -d globins -i globins > /dev/null
```

Table 12-2. Performance benchmarks of various systems

CPU; clock speed	blastn test		blastp test	
	Time (sec)	Giga-cycles	Time (sec)	Giga-cycles
Macintosh G4: 550 MHz	1011	556	1599	879
Sun Ultra Sparc III; 750 MHz	835	626	1427	1070
Intel Pentium III; 1 GHz	649	649	1187	1187

Table 12-2. Performance benchmarks of various systems (continued)

CPU; clock speed	blastn test		blastp test	
	Time (sec)	Giga-cycles	Time (sec)	Giga-cycles
Intel Pentium IV Xeon; 1.8 GHz	469	844	788	1418
AMD Athlon 1800+; 1.533 GHz	416	638	741	1136

Multiprocessor Computers

One way to speed up BLAST is to employ multiprocessor computers. BLAST is a multithreaded application and can utilize the additional processors. Adding additional processors to a computer is sometimes cheaper than purchasing multiple machines because you don't have to duplicate all the other components. That said, once outside the commodity computer market, prices rise steeply, and a computer with 32 CPUs is likely to cost you much more than 16 dual-CPU computers. The improvement with multiple processors isn't completely linear, and it depends on the type of search.

If you want a single BLAST job to complete quickly, it's best to use as many CPUs as possible. On NCBI-BLAST, you can increase the number of processors with the *-a* option, and on WU-BLAST you use the *-cpus* option (see Chapters 13 and 14 for more information). However, for best aggregate performance, it is better to use only 1 CPU for each BLAST job and load up the machine with as many jobs as there are processors. If you are searching multiple databases, you may need a lot of RAM if you wish to keep them all cached.

Operating Systems and Compilers

Even on the same hardware, BLAST may run faster under different operating systems. Due to the complex interactions between operating systems, compilers, and computer architecture, it is difficult to predict what the optimal combination will be. If you have the time and inclination, you might be able to eke out as much as an extra 5 percent in speed. However, choosing an operating system based entirely on BLAST performance may not be a wise choice, so this is probably the last thing to consider.

Compute Clusters

The price and performance of commodity computer hardware and the sophistication of modern free operating systems have made it very attractive to set up computer clusters rather than purchase a multiprocessor behemoth. Clusters don't have to be dedicated rack-mounted towers of blinking lights and buzzing drives; they can also be a mixture of desktop computers that use their idle time to run jobs. There are two fundamental kinds of clusters: Beowulf-style clusters and compute farms.

Beowulf clusters act as a single computer, sharing memory and CPU cycles to cooperatively solve the same problem. *Compute farms* don't share memory or CPU cycles and solve separate, but possibly related problems. The field of bioinformatics has algorithms that are appropriate for both kinds of clusters, but BLAST is really a job that is best suited to compute farms. There are two major reasons for this: (1) BLAST is more data-intensive than compute-intensive, and (2) large-scale BLAST searches consist of many small jobs that are easily parallelized on separate machines.

If you wish to build your own cluster, be prepared for quite a bit of work. There are plenty of considerations outside the normal window-shopping for the best price-performance ratio. For example, one of the most common problems is having sufficient power and cooling. It doesn't do much good to have a super computer that is constantly overheating and burning out its components. Total cost of ownership is a complicated equation, and you're better off not trying to solve this entirely on your own. Your best bet is to talk with people who build clusters for a living. Several companies will sell you prepackaged compute farms for running BLAST. For those who like getting their hands dirty, the bioclusters mailing list at *http://bioinformatics.org* has plenty of useful information in their archives and helpful members who will gladly give advice.

Remote Versus Local Databases

When designing a cluster, one of the most important decisions is where to put your BLAST databases. There are two general choices: (1) store the database on a file server and let the cluster access it remotely over a network, or (2) keep a local copy of the database on each computer. Both methods have their advantages and disadvantages, so there is no simple way to determine which is better.

Remote databases

It's simpler to manage the files on one computer than on multiple computers. This is particularly true if you update your BLAST databases on a frequent, perhaps daily basis. So this is one good reason to use remote databases. If you run your compute nodes diskless, it is really the only choice. The main concerns with this approach are network bandwidth and the speed of the file server. Most computers today have 100-Mbps network interfaces. This translates to 12.5 MBps. Fast computers performing insensitive searches (e.g., BLASTN) can actually exceed this transfer rate. In this case, the compute nodes will sit idle, waiting for data. But what happens when multiple computers are all connected to the same database server? Unfortunately, they must all share the same network bandwidth from the server, so if 10 compute nodes are connected to a database server, each one may get only data at 1.25 MBps. Not good. But remember that if the compute nodes have enough RAM and the databases aren't falling out of cache, subsequent searches will be very fast because they can read the database directly from memory.

One obvious improvement is to employ faster networking. Doing so increases the cost of each compute node a little and significantly increases the cost of network switches because gigabit network switches are still quite expensive. However, it is possible to use a hybrid solution in which the database server is connected to a hybrid network switch via a gigabit line and the compute nodes are connected to the switch via the more common 100-Mb interface. This is much cheaper than using gigabit everywhere, and, because exceeding 12.5 MBps is rare, it doesn't hinder performance too much.

When building file servers, people often neglect to put in enough RAM. For BLAST database servers, though, you really want as much RAM as possible. Caching applies on the file-server end, too, and if several computers request data from the file server, it's much better if it can be served from memory rather than from disk. If you're thinking of using autonomous network attached servers as a BLAST database server, think again. Most don't have gigabit networking or enough RAM.

Local databases

Keeping local copies of your BLAST databases on each node of the cluster will make access to the data very fast. Most hard disks can read data at 20 to 30 MB per second or about double what you could get from common networking. If your network is slow, your cluster is large, or your searches are really insensitive, it's much better to have local copies of databases. The main concern with this approach is keeping the files synchronized and updated with respect to a master copy. This can be done via *rsync* or other means. However, if all the nodes update their databases at the same time across a thin pipe, this operation could take a long time, and the compute nodes may sit idle.

A lesser concern is the disks themselves. They cost money and are a potential source of hardware failure (for this reason, some people advocate running the compute nodes diskless). When discussing disks, there's a great deal of debate over IDE versus SCSI. Drives using the IDE interface are generally slower and less reliable, but are much less expensive. Experts on both sides of the debate will argue convincingly that buying one type of drive makes more sense than buying the other. However, for optimal performance, you really should access the database from cache rather than disk, and therefore the disk shouldn't really matter. Those who choose IDE or SCSI aren't necessarily fools, but people who fail to put enough RAM in their boxes are.

Distributed Resource Management

If you're running a lot of BLAST jobs, one problem to consider is how to manage them to minimize idle time without overloading your computers. Being organized is the simplest way to schedule jobs. If you're the only user, you can use simple scripts to iterate over the various searches and keep your computer comfortably busy. The problem starts when you add multiple users. In a small group, it's possible for users to cooperate with one another without adding extra software. Sending email saying "hey, stay off blast-server5 until I say so" works surprisingly well. But if you have a large group or irresponsible users, you'll want some kind of distributed resource management (DRM) software.

There are a number of DRM software packages, both free and commercial. But even the free ones will cost you time to install and maintain, and users need training to use the system. Table 12-3 lists some of the most popular packages in the bioinformatics community. Condor is an established DRM that is downloadable for free. It is rare in that it supports Windows and Unix. LSF is a mature product with many bioinformatics users. It is, however, expensive. For large groups, however, the robustness makes the cost justifiable. Parasol is purpose-built for the UCSC kilocluster and throws out some of the generalities for increased performance. PBS and ProPBS are popular DRMs, and if you're an academic user, you can get ProPBS for free. SGE is a relative newcomer but has a strong following, partly due to the fact that it's an open source project.

Table 12-3. DRM software

Product	Description (as advertised)
Condor	Condor is a specialized workload management system for compute-intensive jobs. Like other full-featured batch systems, Condor provides a job-queuing mechanism, scheduling policy, priority scheme, resource monitoring, and resource management. Users submit their serial or parallel jobs to Condor; Condor then places them into a queue, chooses when and where to run the jobs based upon a policy, carefully monitors their progress, and ultimately informs the user upon completion. *http://www.cs.wisc.edu/condor*
LSF	• Platform LSF 5 is built on a grid-enabled, robust architecture for open, scalable, and modular environments. • Platform LSF 5 is engineered for enterprise deployment. It provides unlimited scalability with support for over 100 clusters, more than 200,000 CPUs, and 500,000 active jobs. • With more than 250,000 licenses spanning 1,500 customer sites, Platform LSF 5 has industrial-strength reliability to process mission-critical jobs reliably and on time. • A web-based interface puts the convenience and simplicity of global access to resources into the hands of your administrators and users. • Platform LSF 5, with its open, plug-in architecture, seamlessly integrates with third-party applications and heterogeneous technology platforms. *http://www.platform.com*
Parasol	Parasol provides a convenient way for multiple users to run large batches of jobs on computer clusters of up to thousands of CPUs. Parasol was developed initially by Jim Kent, and extended by other members of the Genome Bioinformatics Group at the University of California Santa Cruz. Parasol is currently a fairly minimal system, but what it does, it does well. It can start up 500 jobs per second. It restarts jobs in response to the inevitable systems failures that occur on large clusters. If some of your jobs die because of your program bugs, Parasol can also help manage restarting the crashed jobs after you fix your program. *http://www.soe.ucsc.edu/~donnak/eng/parasol.htm*

Table 12-3. DRM software (continued)

Product	Description (as advertised)
PBS	The Portable Batch System (PBS) is a flexible batch queuing and workload management system originally developed by Veridian Systems for NASA. It operates on networked, multiplatform UNIX environments, including heterogeneous clusters of workstations, supercomputers, and massively parallel systems. Development of PBS is provided by the PBS Products Department of Veridian Systems. *http://www.openpbs.org*
ProPBS	The PBS Pro Version 5.2 workload management solution is the professional version of the Portable Batch System. Built on the success of OpenPBS, PBS Pro goes well beyond it with the features and support you expect in a mission-critical commercial product, such as: • Shrink-wrapped, easy-to-install binary distributions • Support on every major version of Unix and Linux • Enhanced fault tolerance and scalability • Enhanced scheduling algorithms • Computational grid support • Direct support from the team that created PBS • New, rewritten documentation • Source code availability *http://www.propbs.com*
SGE	The Grid Engine project is an open source community effort to facilitate the adoption of distributed computing solutions. Sponsored by Sun Microsystems and hosted by CollabNet, the Grid Engine project provides enabling distributed resource management software for wide-ranging requirements from compute farms to grid computing. *http://gridengine.sunsource.net*

Software Tricks

In addition to choosing appropriate BLAST parameters and optimizing your hardware set, you can use a few software tricks to increase your BLAST performance. Most of these tricks involve splitting or concatenating sequences into optimal-sized pieces because very large and very small sequences are inefficiently processed by BLAST.

Multiplexing/Query Packing

Input and output (I/O) can become a large fraction of the overall CPU load when the search parameters are insensitive, such as when running BLASTN. If you find yourself running a lot of BLASTN searches, you can pack multiple queries together and reduce the overhead of reading the database repeatedly. For example, let's say you have a collection of 100,000 ESTs from your favorite organism and you want to search them against all other ESTs in the public database. If you search them one at a time, you will perform 100,000 BLAST searches and therefore have to read the database 100,000 times. It should go without saying that caching is essential in such a task.

But what if you glue the sequences together in groups of 100? Well, you've just cut your database I/O down to 1 percent of what it used to be, which can be a significant savings. For ESTs and other sequences of this length, the speed up is typically tenfold. This technique is called *multiplexing* or *query packing*. It isn't as simple as it sounds because there must be a way to prevent alignments from bridging the sequences, the coordinates must be remapped, and the statistics need to be recalculated. MegaBLAST, part of the NCBI-BLAST distribution, is a specialized version of BLASTN that multiplexes queries and includes a variety of other optimizations. It's really fast, and anyone doing a lot of BLASTN searches should use this program. You can find more information about MegaBLAST in Chapters 9 and 13. Query packing can also be accomplished with a single, sophisticated Perl script (see MPBLAST at *http://blast.wustl.edu*).

Query Chopping

Larger sequences require more memory to search and align. This can blow away your cached database, or worse, cause the computer to start swapping (using the disk for RAM). In addition, for a variety of reasons, larger query sequences are processed less efficiently. One way to solve this problem is to divide the query sequence into several segments, search them independently, and then merge the results back together. This is called *query chopping* and is effectively the opposite of query packing. The main difficulty with query chopping is dealing with alignments that cross the boundaries between segments.

Both NCBI-BLAST and WU-BLAST let you specify that only a subsequence of a large query sequence is to be searched (see the -L parameter in Chapter 13 and the newstart and nwlen parameters in Chapter 14). Currently, this works a little better for WU-BLAST because alignments seeded in a restricted region can extend outside this region, so there's no need to stitch together the alignments between neighboring segments. The following Perl script searches chromosome-sized sequences in 100-KB segments using WU-BLAST. All coordinates and statistics are identical to a search with an entire chromosome. Note that complexity filters are currently applied to the whole sequence, so apply these filters ahead of time.

```perl
#!/usr/bin/perl -w
use strict;
die "usage: $0 <wu-blast command line>\n" unless @ARGV >= 3;
my ($BLAST, $DB, $Q, @P) = @ARGV;
die "ERROR ($0): single FASTA files only\n" if `grep -c ">" $Q` > 1;
my $params = "@P";
die "ERROR ($0): filter ahead of time\n" if $params =~ /filter|wordmask/;
open(FASTA, $Q) or die;
my $def = <FASTA>;
my $count = 0;
while (<FASTA>) {$count += length($_) -1}
my $segment = 100000;
```

```
for (my $i = 1; $i <= $count; $i += $segment) {
    system("$BLAST $DB $Q  nwstart=$i nwlen=$segment");
}
```

Database Splitting

If you have a computer cluster and a lot of individual BLAST jobs to run, you can easily split the jobs among the nodes of your cluster. But what if you have a single, slow BLAST job that you want to spread out over several computers? If your sequence is very large, you can use query chopping as described earlier and assign each computer a separate segment. But what if your sequence isn't so large? A good solution is to have each computer search only part of the database. You'll need to do a little statistical manipulation to set the effective search space to the entire database, as well as some post-processing to merge all the reports together, but overall the process is pretty simple. The hard part is making sure the database is properly segmented on the various computers.

If you're using NCBI-BLAST, you can create database slices using alias databases as described previously. This allows a great deal more flexibility than physically splitting the databases into various parts. But remember that alias databases require that you use GI numbers in the FASTA identifier.

If you're using WU-BLAST, you can split the database dynamically. WU-BLAST has command-line parameters called dbrecmin and dbrecmax that describe the minimum and maximum database records. You can assign each node of the cluster a different subsection of the database by simply assigning dbrecmin and dbrecmax. For example, if your database contains 100 records and you have 10 nodes, node 1 gets records 1 to 10, node 2 gets records 11 to 20, etc. To benefit from caching, each node should be assigned the same database slice.

Serial BLAST Searching

As discussed in Chapter 5, the best way to speed up BLAST searches is by making the seeding more stringent. The only problem is that low-scoring alignments may be lost. High scoring alignments, however, are relatively resistant to changes in seeding parameters. The serial strategy takes advantage of this property; it uses an insensitive search to identify database matches and then a sensitive search to generate the alignments. An intuitive way to think about this with genomic sequence is "if I can hit just one exon, I can get the whole gene." The procedure has three steps and can be carried out with a simple script:

1. Run BLAST with insensitive parameters.
2. Build a BLAST database from the matches.
3. Run BLAST with sensitive parameters on just the matches.

NCBI-BLAST doesn't currently offer a wide range of word sizes, so serial searching is best carried out with WU-BLAST. Example 12-1 shows a script that wraps up the entire procedure.

Example 12-1. A script for serial BLAST searching

```
#!/usr/bin/perl -w
use strict;
die "usage: $0 <database> <query> <wordsize> <hitdist>\n" unless @ARGV == 4;
my ($DB, $Q, $W, $H) = @ARGV;
$H = $H ? "hitdist=$H" : "";
my $tmpdir = "/tmp/tt-blastx.tmpdir";
END {system("rm -rf $tmpdir") if defined $tmpdir}
system("mkdir $tmpdir") == 0 or die "ERROR ($0): can't create $tmpdir\n";
my $STD = "B=100000 V=100000 wordmask=seg";

# search
system("blastx $DB $Q W=$W T=999 $H $STD > $tmpdir/search") == 0 or die;

# collect names
my @name;
open(NAME, ">$tmpdir/names") or die;
open(SEARCH, "$tmpdir/search") or die;
while (<SEARCH>) {print NAME "$1\n" if /^>(\S+)/}
close SEARCH;
close NAME;

# build second stage database
system("xdget -p -f $DB $tmpdir/names > $tmpdir/database") == 0 or die;
system("xdformat -p $tmpdir/database") == 0 or die;

# align
system("blastx $tmpdir/database $Q $STD") == 0 or die;
```

To demonstrate the performance of the serial strategy, the script in Example 12-1 performs a search of a *Caenorhabditis briggsae* genomic fragment (c009500587. Contig4) against all *C. elegans* proteins (wormpep97). To minimize the effect of chance similarities, only alignments with at least 30 amino acids and 35 percent identity are analyzed. The search parameters, search speed, and number of HSPs found are displayed in Table 12-4. The first two rows correspond to standard, nonserial searches. Using the parameters recommended in Chapter 9 (row 2) BLASTX runs seven times faster than the very sensitive WU-BLAST default parameters (row 1). This speed is paid for by a loss in sensitivity (number of HSPs). The serial searches (rows 3 and above) offer varying levels of speed and sensitivity. Only a few combinations of W and T are presented; there are many useful combinations. Of particular interest is row 4, which has approximately the same sensitivity as row 1, but runs 18 times faster. Not bad for a short script. Because BLAST is under active development, perhaps you'll see serial searching become a standard part of BLAST software.

Table 12-4. Serial BLAST performance

#	First search	Second search	Speed	Elapsed time (sec)	HSPs
1	W=3 T=12	None	1 x	883.3	251
2	W=3 T=14 hitdist=40	None	7 x	121.4	186
3	W=3 T=999 hitdist=40	W=3 T=12	14 x	62.1	230
4	W=4 T=999	W=3 T=12	18 x	49.1	248
5	W=5 T=999	W=3 T=12	50 x	17.6	219
6	W=4 T=999 hitdist=40	W=3 T=12	80 x	11.1	137
7	W=5 T=999 hitdist=40	W=3 T=12	110 x	7.9	116

Optimized NCBI-BLAST

The source code for NCBI-BLAST is in the public domain, and anyone can modify it without restriction (*ftp://ftp.ncbi.nih.gov/toolbox/ncbi_tools*). It's therefore not surprising that there are a number of variants. The rest of this chapter discusses three of them.

Apple/Genentech BLAST

Macintosh G4 computers have an additional vector processing unit called Velocity-Engine or Altivec that can process several similar instructions in parallel. Apple Computer and Genentech collaborated to rewrite portions of NCBI-BLAST to take advantage of the Altivec processor. These modifications affect the seeding phase of BLASTN. The result, AG-BLAST, significantly outperforms NCBI-BLAST under certain conditions.

Table 12-5 shows an experiment in which a *Caenorhabditis elegans* transcript (F44B9.10) was searched against the *Caenorhabditis briggsae* genome using various word sizes but otherwise default parameters (the hardware is a 550-MHz Power-Book). For cross-species work, it's generally a good idea to employ word sizes slightly smaller than the default 11 to minimize the chance of missing meaningful similarities. Here, AG-BLAST has a significant speed advantage over NCBI-BLAST. AG-BLAST also runs faster at very large word sizes, which is useful if you are matching sequences that are expected to be identical or nearly identical (e.g., mapping ESTs to their own genome).

Table 12-5. Apple/Genentech BLAST

W	NCBI-BLAST (sec)	AG-BLAST (sec)	Speed increase
8	56.9	37.9	1.5 x
9	50.0	9.5	5.3 x
10	46.6	5.5	8.5 x
11	2.9	2.8	1.0 x
15	2.1	2.1	1.0 x
20	1.4	1.0	1.4 x
30	1.4	0.6	2.3 x
40	1.4	0.5	2.8 x

AG-BLAST does have a few disadvantages. First, the version may be slightly out of date with respect to NCBI-BLAST. The current version of AG-BLAST is based on 2.2.2, while NCBI-BLAST is up to Version 2.2.6. Not all changes are backward-compatible; for example, the latest preformatted databases require Version 2.2.5. Second, AG-BLAST doesn't work with multiple CPUs. You can execute more than one job at a time, but you can't use the -a option to increase the number of CPUs used by a single process. Finally, the minimum word size on AG-BLAST is 8, or one greater than the NCBI-BLAST minimum. See *http://developer.apple.com/hardware/ve/acgresearch.html* for more information.

Paracel-BLAST and BlastMachine

Paracel makes an NCBI-BLAST derivative called Paracel-BLAST and sells it with a prepackaged computer cluster called a BlastMachine. This product takes all the high performance hardware and software tricks and puts them into a single, easy-to-use product. The hardware is a rack of Linux-Intel machines, and the DRM software is Platform LSF. Large query sequences are chopped, small ones are packed, and data is distributed so the search comes back as fast as possible. This is really convenient because it lets users concentrate on what they want to do and not how they have to do it. In the end, more science and less frustration is a good thing.

See *http://www.paracel.com* for more information.

TimeLogic Tera-BLAST

TimeLogic uses an entirely different approach to optimizing BLAST. The BLAST algorithm is soft-wired into a special kind of chip called a *field programmable gate array* (FPGA). Each FPGA executes the search very quickly and multiple FPGA boards reside in a single computer called a DeCypher accelerator. The end result is a specialized computer that is limited in what it can do, but what it does, it does astonishingly well. A single DeCypher accelerator running Tera-BLAST (the name for their

NCBI-BLAST-derived algorithm) is the equivalent of about 100 general-purpose computers. Shockingly, it all fits in a standard server case. Such technology doesn't come cheaply. However, if you do a lot of BLAST searches (or use some of the other algorithms they provide), it may be far cheaper than a huge cluster, especially when you consider power consumption and maintenance.

One hidden cost in specialized systems such as a DeCypher accelerator is the time and effort required to integrate them with more general systems you may already have. If you have a stepwise sequence-analysis pipeline already worked out, it may be difficult to adapt it to Tera-BLAST. Tera-BLAST works most efficiently with big jobs, and to take advantage of this requires giving it a whole bunch of sequences at once. Thus, you might have to restructure your pipeline in much the same way as discussed earlier with respect to caching.

TimeLogic also offers a completely new variant of BLAST called Gene-BLAST. This algorithm strings together HSPs by dynamic programming (an affine Smith-Waterman with two levels of gap scoring schemes) to achieve a better model of exon-intron structure. Gene-BLAST works with both nucleotide- and protein-level alignments and appears to be a welcome new addition to the BLAST family. Unfortunately, the only way to run Gene-BLAST is on TimeLogic hardware. See *http://www.timelogic. com* for more details.

## PART V

BLAST Reference

## CHAPTER 13

NCBI-BLAST Reference

This chapter describes the parameters and options for the NCBI suite of BLAST programs. The NCBI distribution includes the *blastall* program, plus several ancillary programs that are either necessary for *blastall* (e.g., *formatdb*) or provide other BLAST-like searches that aren't included within *blastall* (e.g., *blastpgp and blastclust*). This reference also describes the various command-line parameters for the most important executables.

Usage Statements

If you forget the syntax for a particular parameter, you can view a usage statement from most programs by typing the program name followed by a dash (in some cases the dash isn't required, but it's easier to remember to use a dash with all programs). For example:

```
blastall -
formatdb -
fastacmd -
megablast -
bl2seq -
blastpgp -
blastclust -
```

Command-Line Syntax

All parameters for NCBI-BLAST programs are single letters and must be preceded by a single dash. Unlike many common Unix programs, the parameters for NCBI programs are never concatenated. All parameters may take arguments, including those that operate as true/false (T/F) switches. For such switches, the T/F is case-insensitive, and the argument may be omitted, in which case the switch is set to T. Finally, the space between the parameter and the argument is optional. The following commands are all identical.

```
formatdb -i db -o T -V t
formatdb -i db -o -V
formatdb -idb -ot -VT
formatdb -idb -o -V
```

The following command, however, is illegal because it tries to set -o to a value of V.

```
formatdb -idb -oV
```

blastall Parameters

blastall is controlled by several parameters. Many of the parameters have default settings and don't need to be explicitly assigned. Consider this simple command:

```
blastall -p blastp
```

Behind the scenes, this command is converted to:

```
blastall -p blastp -d nr -i stdin -e 10 -m 0 -o stdout -F T -G 11 -E 2 -X 15 -v 500
-b 250 -f 11 -g T -a 1 -M BLOSUM62 -W 3 -z 0 -K 0 -Y 0 -T F -U F -y 0.0 -Z 0 -A 40
```

You can see that many parameters are set without your express knowledge. These parameters affect the results of your experiment and, as reinforced many times throughout the book, you should try to understand these parameters and set them to fit each experiment.

The following reference section explains all the parameters available for *blastall* and lists the default values that are used if not explicitly set. The table was compiled according to the default values for the five basic programs. Although *megablast* can be run from within *blastall* (-n T), you should use the standalone program. The parameters for it are presented later in the chapter.

-a [integer]

Default: 1   Programs: All

Sets the number of processors to use on of processors. If you have multiple queries, you will get better throughput by executing multiple BLAST searches. For insensitive searches such as default BLASTN, setting -a to a higher value may not appreciably improve speed if disk I/O is the bottleneck.

-A [integer]

Default: *blastn* 0, others 40   Programs: All

Sets the multiple-hit window size. When BLAST is set to two-hit mode, this option requires two word hits on the same diagonal to be within [integer] letters of each other in order to extend from either one. The larger the [integer], the more sensitive BLAST will be. Setting [integer] to 0 sets the default behavior of 40, except for *blastn*, whose default is single word hit. To specify one-hit behavior, set -P 1.

-b [integer]

Default: 250   Programs: All

Truncates the report to [integer] number of alignments. There is no warning when you exceed this limit, so it's generally a good idea to set [integer] very high unless you're interested only in the top hits.

-B [integer]

Default: Optional   Programs: *blastn, tblastn*

Sets the number of queries to concatenate in a single search. Concatenating queries accelerates the search because the database is scanned just one time. This is the principle underlying *megablast*, but the implementation is different in *blastall*.

This option is new in Version 2.2.6 and still experimental. The specified [integer] must be the number of sequences in the query file. If it's less, only the first set of [integer] sequences is used. Also, the output is very different than you would expect. All the query names are listed, and then all the one-line summaries are given, followed by the alignments, and finally, one footer is produced for the whole report. Given this format, it's very difficult to discern which alignments belong to which query. This option should not be used in its current implementation.

-d [database]

Default: nr   Programs: All

Identifies the database to search. [database] must already be formatted by *formatdb*. BLAST looks for [database] in the following order: the local directory, the BLASTDB environment variable (Unix only), and finally, the location specified in the *.ncbirc* file.

You can merge multiple databases into a single virtual database by putting the individual databases in quotes. For example, to merge the *nt* and *est* databases, use: -d "nt est". You can't mix nucleotide and amino acid databases. The statistics reported are based on the sizes of the combined databases. Virtual databases may exceed file size limits imposed by the operating system.

-D [1..23]

Default: 1   Programs: *tblastn, tblastx*

The genetic code to use for translation of the database nucleotide sequence. See *http:// www.ncbi.nlm.nih.gov/htbin-post/Taxonomy* for updates.

Options

1   Standard Nuclear Genetic Code
2   Vertebrate Mitochondrial
3   Yeast Mitochondrial
4   Mold, Protozoan, and Coelocoel Mitochondrial

5	Invertebrate Mitochondrial
6	Ciliate Nuclear
9	Echinoderm Nuclear
10	Euplotid Nuclear
11	Bacterial and Plant Plastid
12	Alternative yeast nuclear
13	Ascidian Mitochondrial
14	Flatworm Mitochondrial
15	Blepharisma Nuclear
16	Chlorophycean Mitochondrial
21	Trematode Mitochondrial
22	Scenedesmus Obliquus Mitochondrial
23	Thraustochytrium Mitochondrial

-e [real number]

Default: 10   Programs: All

Sets the threshold expectation value for keeping alignments. This is the E from the Karlin-Altschul equation that describes how often an alignment with a given score is expected to occur at random.

-E [integer]

Default: *blastn* 2, others 1   Programs: All

The penalty for each gap character. The -G parameter controls the initial cost of opening a gap. Note that -E 0 is synonymous with the default behavior and, it's impossible to set -E to zero unless -g F is set, which turns gapping off. The default gap cost, for programs other than *blastn*, depends on the scoring matrix. The value shown here is for the default BLOSUM62 matrix. See Appendix C for a complete list of default and legal gap penalties.

-f [integer]

Defaults: *blastp* 11, *blastx* 12, *tblastn* 13, *tblastx* 13   Programs: *blastp, blastx, tblastn, tblastx*

Neighborhood word threshold score. Only those words scoring equal to or greater than [integer] will seed alignments.

-F [T/F], -F [string]

Default: T, but see below   Programs: All

Filters the query sequence for low-complexity subsequences. The default setting is T. Complexity filtering is generally a good idea, but it may break long HSPs into several smaller HSPs due to low-complexity segments. This can cause some alignments to fall below the significance threshold and be lost. To prevent this, either turn off filtering (not recommended) or use soft masking, in which the filter is used only in the word seeding phase, but not the extension phase.

The parameter argument's [string] form follows a nonintuitive syntax. If the string begins with an m, soft masking is turned on. Filtering programs are specified by a single capital letter: D for *DUST*, R for human repeats, V for vector sequences, S for *SEG*, and C for *coiled-coil*. D, R, and V are used only for *blastn* searches, and S and C are used for all other programs. More than one filter may be specified, and additional parameters may be passed to the programs. See the following tables and the -U parameter used for filtering lowercase letters in the query sequence.

To use R or V, the correct database files must be downloaded and installed in the BLASTDB directory. For human repeats, three databases are needed: *humlines.lib*, *humsines.lib*, and *retrovir.lib*. For vector filtering, use the *UniVec_Core* database (*ftp://ftp.ncbi.nih.gov/pub/UniVec/*).

String options for blastn

Behavior	Parameter format
No complexity filter	-F ""
Default (*DUST*)	-F "D"
Soft masking	-F "m D"
Lowercase soft masking	-F "m" -U
Soft masking of *DUST* and lowercase letters	-F "m D" -U
Mask human repeats	-F "R"
Mask vector sequences	-F "V"
Soft-masking of human repeats and vector	-F "m R;V"

String options for blastp, blastx, tblastn, and tblastx

Behavior	Parameter format
No complexity filter	-F ""
Default (*SEG*)	-F "S"
Soft masking	-F "m S"
Lowercase soft masking	-F "m" -U
Coiled-coil	-F "C"
SEG plus coiled-coil	-F "S;C"
SEG with settings for *windowsize*, *locut*, and *hicut*	-F "S 10 1.0 1.5"
As above, plus coiled coil and soft masking (including lowercase)	-F "m S 10 1.0 1.5; C" -U

-g [T/F]

Default: T   Programs: *blastn, blastp, blastx, tblastn*

Performs gapped alignment. Setting this to F invokes the older, ungapped style of alignment. You can't perform gapped alignments with *tblastx*, regardless of this setting.

-G [integer]

Defaults: *blastn* 5, others 11   Programs: All

Initial penalty for opening a gap of length 0. Penalties for extending the gap is controlled by parameter -E. -G 0 invokes the default behavior, and setting -G to zero is impossible, unless -g F is set, which turns gapping off. The default gap costs for programs other than *blastn* depend on the scoring matrix; the value here is for the default BLOSUM62 matrix. See Appendix C for a complete list of default and legal gap penalties.

-i [input file]

Default: *stdin*   Programs: All

If -i isn't included on the command line, BLAST expects input from *stdin* (i.e., it will wait indefinitely for you to type in a FASTA file from the keyboard). The following commands are therefore equivalent:

```
blastall -p blastn -d nt -i query
blastall -p blastn -d nt < query
cat query | blastall -p blastn -d nt
cat query | blastall -p blastn -d nt -i stdin
```

If the input file contains multiple sequences, BLAST will be run on each sequence in order, and the resulting output will contain concatenated BLAST reports.

-I [T/F]

Default: F   Programs: All

Shows GenInfo Identifier (GI) numbers in definition lines. A GI is a unique numeric identifier assigned for a sequence in GenBank. A GI corresponds to an accession version pair.

-J [T/F]

Default: F   Programs: All

Believe the query defline.

-K [integer]

Default: 0 - Off   Programs: All

The number of best hits from a region to keep. This option is useful when you want to limit the number of alignments that might pile up in one section of the query. This is most useful if the settings of -b or -v are low, and the abundant alignments push lower scoring alignments off the end of the report. If set, a value of 100 is recommended.

-l [file]

Default: Optional   Programs: All

Restricts database search to a list of GIs found in [file]. The database sequences must have NCBI-compliant identifiers, including GI numbers, and the database must be indexed (by running *formatdb* with the -o option). The [file] must be in the same directory as the database or in the directory from which *blastall* is called. [file] may be in text format with one GI per line or in binary format (see the -B parameter for *formatdb*).

-L [string]

Default: Optional   Programs: All

The location on query sequence. This lets you limit the search to a subsequence of the query sequence. For example, to search just the letters from 21 to 50, add the following parameter:

    -L "21,50"

The alignments won't extend outside the specified region. In older versions of BLAST, -L set the size of the region under control of the -K parameter.

-m [0..11]

Default: 0   Programs: All

Sets the alignment viewing options. Appendix C gives examples of these display options.

Options

0   Pairwise

1   Query-anchored, showing identities, no gaps in query (gaps are shown as a tree-like thing in subjects), identities shown as ".", positives uppercase, negatives lowercase

2   Query-anchored, no identities, no gaps in query, negatives lowercase

3   Flat query-anchored, show identities, padding through all sequences

4   Flat query-anchored, no identities, padding through all sequences

5   Query-anchored, no identities and blunt ends, (dashes [-]are used to blunt the ends)

6   Flat query-anchored, no identities and blunt ends, ([-] to ends)

7   XML output

8   Tabular

9   Tabular with comment lines

10 ASN.1 in text format ([-] must be set for this option to work)

11 ASN.1 in binary format ([-J] must be set for this option to work)

-M [matrix file]

Default: BLOSUM62   Programs: All except *blastn*

Designates a protein similarity matrix. This is used in all BLAST programs except *blastn*. Matrices are sought in the following order: in the local directory, in the location specified in the *.ncbirc* file, in a local data directory, and finally, in the BLASTMAT environment variable (only on Unix systems). Other matrices included in the standard distribution include BLOSUM45, BLOSUM80, PAM30, and PAM70.

You can use custom matrix files, but it requires modifying the source code and defining the new matrix with all of its associated statistics for different affine gap combinations and recompiling the binary. Using these custom files isn't recommended because it requires the arduous task of calculating gapped values for lambda and maintaining a derivative branch of the source code.

-n [T/F]

Default: F   Programs: *megablast*

Sets the *blastn* program to the *megablast* mode, which is optimized to find near identities very quickly. The following lines are equivalent:

```
blastall -p blastn -n T -d est -i my_file
megablast -d est -i my_file -D 2
```

More program options are available if you run the *megablast* executable (see the section "megablast Parameters").

-o [output file]

Default: Optional   Programs: All

Designates an output file for the search results. If not used, output is printed to *stdout*. The following commands are equivalent:

```
blastall -p blastn -d nr -i query -o output
blastall -p blastn -d nr -i query > output
```

-p [program name]

Default: None, required parameter   Choices: *blastn, blastp, blastx, tblastn, tblastx, psitblastn*

When choosing *psitblastn*, the -R [checkpoint file] must also be specified. This special use of *blastall* uses the output PSSM checkpoint file of PSI-BLAST (see *blastpgp* -C option), combined with the protein query sequence, to implement a *tblastn* search against a nucleotide database.

-P [0/1]

Default: *blastn* 1, others 0   Programs: All

Specifies the two-hit or single-hit algorithm. The two-hit option requires two word hits on the same diagonal to extend from either one. When set to two-hit mode, the -A parameter specifies how close the two hits have to be to trigger extension.

Options

0   Two hit
1   Single hit

-q [negative integer]

Default: -3   Programs: *blastn* only

Sets the penalty for a nucleotide mismatch. Also see -r. The choice of [integer] for -q and -r are very important because they determine your target frequencies. The default values -r 1 -q -3 are most effective for aligning sequences that are 99 percent identical. See Appendix B for more information on nucleotide scoring schemes.

-Q [1..23]

Default: 1   Programs: *blastx, tblastx*

Genetic code to use for translation of the query nucleotide sequence. See the -D parameter for list of genetic codes.

-r [integer]

Default: 1   Programs: *blastn* only

Sets the score of a nucleotide match. See the -q parameter and Appendix B.

-R [checkpoint file]

Default: Optional   Programs: *psitblastn*

Designates the PSI-BLAST checkpoint file to be used in the *psitblastn* search. -p must be set to *psitblastn*. The input must be a protein sequence and be the same one used with *blastpgp* -C to generate the [checkpoint file].

-S [1..3]

Default: 3   Programs: *blastn, blastx, tblastx*

Chooses which strand of DNA-based queries is searched.

Options

1 Top strand

2 Bottom strand

3 Both strands

For example, the following command searches only the query's top strand.

```
blastall -p blastn -d nr -i query -S 1
```

-t [integer]

Default: 0

Length of the largest intron allowed in *tblastn* for linking HSPs. A default of 0 means that linking is turned off.

-T [T/F]

Default: F   Programs: All

Produces HTML output with <anchor> links from the summary at the top of the report to the alignments farther below. This option should be used only with the standard report format (-m 0).

-v [integer]

Default: 500   Programs: All

Sets the number of database sequences for which to show the one-line summary descriptions at the top of a BLAST report. You won't be warned if you exceed [integer]. Also see the -b parameter.

-w [integer]

Default: 0   Programs: *blastx only*

Sets the frame shift penalty for the Out Of Frame (OOF) algorithm of *blastx*. When -w is set, it invokes the OOF mode of BLAST, which lets alignments proceed across reading frames. The expect values calculated from OOF *blastx* are only approximate, and BLAST issues the following warning when OOF is invoked:

```
[NULL_Caption] WARNING: test500: Out-of-frame option
selected, Expect values are only approximate and
calculated not assuming out-of-frame alignments
```

The out-of-frame alignments are signified by slashes that indicate the +1(/),+2(//), -1(\), and -2(\\) frameshifts. The following is a sample OOF alignment:

```
Query: 23  PLIRNSL/YCINC\\A//QSIIRAHVKGPYLTRWVVNC/E\TCSKGYAKTPGASTDLLLL 160
           PLIRNSL YCINC    QSIIRAHVKGPYLTRWVVNC    TCSKGYAKTPGASTDLLLL
Sbjct: 1   PLIRNSL YCINC  X  QSIIRAHVKGPYLTRWVVNC X  TCSKGYAKTPGASTDLLLL 53
```

```
Query: 161 YKTRNSLTSASSLSPVRSQRMI/N\SFPRFQGHLVVSG/S\SAHNR/FS\FNRDSPRGSG 322
            YKTRNSLTSASSLSPVRSQRMI   SFPRFQGHLVVSG   SAHNR F  FNRDSPRGSG
Sbjct:  54 YKTRNSLTSASSLSPVRSQRMI X SFPRFQGHLVVSG X SAHNR FX FNRDSPRGSG 107

Query: 323 SYCSREPMGQIKIRRTHTDDKLFR/ND\SRHTRAGDGLNI//TLA\\RDPSFLSRVYNAN 484
            SYCSREPMGQIKIRRTHTDDKLFR     SRHTRAGDGLNI    L    RDPSFLSRVYNAN
Sbjct: 108 SYCSREPMGQIKIRRTHTDDKLFR XX SRHTRAGDGLNI XLX  RDPSFLSRVYNAN 161

Query: 485 SYLHI 499
            SYLHI
Sbjct: 162 SYLHI 166
```

-W [integer]

Defaults: *blastn* 11, others 3   Programs: All

Sets the word size for the initial word search. The minimum word size for *blastn* is 7. Word sizes for *blastp, blastx, tblastn,* and *tblastx* are 2 or 3.

-X [integer]

Default: *blastn* 30, others 15   Programs: All, except *tblastx*

Sets the X2 dropoff value for gapped alignments. The value is measured in bits. Smaller values of X2 result in earlier termination of extensions. Adjusting this parameter is generally unnecessary.

-y [integer]

Default: *blastn* 20; other 7   Programs: All

Sets the X1 dropoff value (in bits) for extensions. The lower X1 is set, the shorter the extension will be. It's rarely necessary to adjust this parameter.

-Y [real number]

Default: 0   Programs: All

The effective length of the search space. This is the size of the database multiplied by the size of the query or MN from the Karlin-Altschul equation.

If -Y is unset or set to 0, the actual size of the database and query is used.

-z [real number]

Default: 0   Programs: All

The effective length of the database. This option is useful for maintaining consistent statistics over time as databases grow.

If -z is unset or set to 0, the actual effective length of the database is used.

-Z [integer]

Default: 25   Programs: All

Sets the *X3* dropoff value (in bits) for extensions but is bounded by the value for *X2*. It's generally not necessary to adjust this parameter.

formatdb Parameters

formatdb turns FASTA files into BLAST databases (ASN.1 format is also acceptable, but because it isn't commonly used, it isn't covered in this book. You can find more information about ASN.1 at *http://www.ncbi.nlm.nih.gov/Sitemap/Summary/asn1. html/*). Chapter 11 discusses the typical methods for building BLAST databases and examines the NCBI identifier syntax required for some aspects of *formatdb* and *blastall*. Here are a few sample command lines:

```
formatdb -i protein_db
formatdb -p F -i nucleotide_db
zcat est*.gz | formatdb -p F -i stdin -o -n est -v 2000000000
```

The following reference lists the default value for each *formatdb* parameter.

-B [file]

Default: Optional

Specifies a binary GI output file. The advantage of using a binary GI file is that it's smaller than a corresponding text file and can be read directly into memory without being parsed. See the -F option.

To convert a text GI file to binary, use the following command:

```
formatdb -F text_gi_list -B binary_gi_list
```

-F [file]

Default: Optional

Specifies a GI file, either text or binary. This is used for creating an alias database that doesn't contain sequences, but pointers to sequences stored in another database (which may be an alias database as well). See the -L parameter. The databases must use the NCBI FASTA identifier syntax, include GI numbers, and be indexed with -o.

-i [file]

Default: Required

Sets the input FASTA file. You may specify that input come from *stdin* with -i stdin, but you must also set the -n parameter to give it a name. If you wish to make a single BLAST database from multiple FASTA files, pipe them to *formatdb* as follows:

```
cat file1 file2 file3 | formatdb -i stdin -n my_db
```

-l [file]

Default: *formatdb.log*

Specifies an output log file. Log messages are appended to this file.

-L [file]

Default: Optional

Creates an alias database, which has several uses. It can be a simple synonym for another database, a selection of specific records from a database (see the -F option), or a static virtual database. Alias databases have the *.pal* or *.nal* extension, depending on whether they are proteins or nucleotides.

To create an alias database with a selected set of GI numbers:

```
formatdb -i db -F gi_list -L alias_name -p [T/F]
```

To merge databases, first create a synonymous alias and then edit it to include additional database names. Chapter 11 covers this process in more detail.

-n [string]

Default: Optional, required with -i stdin

Sets the base name for the BLAST database. If not specified, the name of the FASTA file will be used. If the input is from *stdin*, this parameter must be set.

-o [T/F]

Default: Optional

Creates indexes. Indexing the databases isn't required but is recommended. Alias databases that use GI lists (see -F and -L options) and the *blastall* -1 option require indexed databases. Additionally, some *blastall* output options specified with the -m parameter require indexing. Indexing adds four files with extensions *.nnd*, *.nni*, *.nsd*, and *.nsi* for nucleotides and *.pnd*, *.pni*, *.psd*, and *.psi* for proteins. If you know you don't need indexes, you can save space by omitting -o.

If GI numbers are included and more than one sequence has the same GI number, *formatdb* terminates with an error. If accession numbers aren't unique, an error won't be issued (see -V).

-p [T/F]

Default: T

Specifies the type of type of file being formatted. By default, *formatdb* assumes the file is protein, so you must set -p F whenever you format nucleotide databases.

-s [T/F]

Default: Optional

Creates indexes for accessions but not locus names. Must be used in conjunction with the -o parameter. For many sequences from DDBJ/GenBank/EMBL, the locus name and accession number are identical and some disk space can be saved by not including redundant information. In general, locus names are historical relics, so always include -s.

-t [string]

Default: Optional

The title for a database file. If this parameter isn't set, the title of the database will be the name of the FASTA file or the argument of -n, if it was set. -t lets you use more descriptive names that you might not want as filenames. For example:

```
formatdb -i proteins -t "my favorite human proteins"
```

In the BLAST report, this is reported in the header as:

```
Database: my favorite human proteins
```

Using this parameter can be confusing, because backtracking from reports to databases might be difficult.

-v [integer]

Default: Optional

The maximum number of sequence bases to be created in a volume. Values range from 1 to 2147483647 (2 billion in powers of two). This parameter is useful if the filesystem doesn't support large files. Volumes with greater than [integer] letters are automatically split, and an alias is created. See Chapter 9 for more information.

-V [T/F]

Default: F

Reports warning messages if sequence identifiers aren't unique. Requires the -o option.

fastacmd Parameters

fastacmd retrieves sequences, individually or in batches, from BLAST databases. When using it, you don't have to keep FASTA files on your file system after you've formatted the BLAST database. Sequences are stored in a case-insensitive format, however, so if you use lower- and uppercase for semantic purposes, this information will be lost.

Here are a few sample command lines using *fastacmd*:

```
fastacmd -d nr -s P02042
fastacmd -d nr -s 12837002,P02042
fastacmd -d nr -D
fastacmd -d est -i file_of_gi
cat file_of_gi | fastacmd -d est -i stdin
```

The following reference lists the default value for each *fastacmd* parameter.

-a [T/F]

Default: F

Retrieves all accessions even duplicates when using -s or -i to retrieve sequences. If -a isn't set, only the first accession of duplicates is retrieved.

-c [T/F]

Default: F

Uses Control-A as a nonredundant definition line separator. This parameter applies only to nonredundant databases with concatenated definition lines. By default, a normal space is used as the separator. Using Control-A unambiguously separates sequence definitions.

-d [string]

Default: nr

The database from which to retrieve sequences.

-D [T/F]

Default: F

Dumps the entire database in FASTA format.

-i [file]

Default: Optional

A batch retrieval. The format of the text file is one GI or accession per line. *stdin* is a valid file.

```
cat file_of_gi | fastacmd -d est -i stdin
```

-I

Default: Optional

Prints information about a formatted database. Overrides all other retrieval options. Needs to be used with -d.

```
fastacmd -d my_db -I
```

-l [integer]

Default: 80

Sequences line length. The most common values are 50 (a nice round number), 60 (evenly divisible by 3), and 80 (a traditional terminal width).

-L [integer],[integer]

Default: 0,0

Extracts a region of the sequence. Using 0 as the start coordinate indicates the actual beginning of the sequence. Using 0 as the end coordinate indicates the end of the sequence. A colon and the sequence range are appended to the identifier to signify the region extracted.

```
fastacmd -d nr -s AAG39070 -L 10,50

>gi|11611819:10-50 (AF287139) Hoxa-11 [Latimeria chalumnae]
SGPDFSSLPSFLPQTPSSRPMTYSYSSNLPQVQPVREVTFR
```

-o [file]

Default: *stdout*

Sends the output to the named file or *stdout*, if none is named.

-p [T/F/G]

Default: G

Options

G   Guess. Look for a protein first, and then a nucleotide.

T   Protein.

F   Nucleotide.

-P [integer]

Default: Optional

Retrieves sequences with this PIG.

-s [string]

Default: Optional

An identifier of the sequence to retrieve. The identifier may be a GI or accession. To retrieve multiple sequences, the identifiers must be separated by commas as follows:

```
fastacmd -d nr -s AAG39070,11611819
```

To retrieve a large number of sequences, using the -i parameter is more convenient, especially since there may be limits on the length of command-line strings.

-S [1..2]

Default: 1

The strand on subsequence. Only used with nucleotide sequences.

1 Top strand

2 Bottom strand

-t [T/F]

Default: F

The definition line should contain target GI only. This parameter applies only to nonredundant databases. When set, only the definition line corresponding to the GI is reported, not the redundant definition lines. No such mechanism exists for accession numbers; redundancies are always reported.

-T [T/F]

Default: F

Gets taxonomy information from an NCBI-formatted BLAST database. The downloadable FASTA files don't allow this feature; only the preformatted will work. The preformatted databases can be found at *ftp://ftp.ncbi.nlm.nih.gov/blast/db/FormattedDatabases/*.

megablast Parameters

megablast is similar to *blastn* but optimized to find near identities very quickly. It's much faster than the standard *blastn*, partly because it uses query packing. The extension algorithm differs from the standard *blastn* and isn't designed for cross-species searches. Many parameters are identical between *megablast* and *blastall*, but some are unique to one program or the other, and some parameters with the same symbol do different things.

Here are a few example command lines:

```
megablast -d my_db -i my_query -F "m D"
megablast -d my_db -i my_query -D 2 -t 18 -W 11
```

-a [integer]

Default: 1

The number of processors; same as *blastall*.

-A [integer]

Default: 40

The two-hit algorithm window size; same as *blastall*.

-b [integer]

Default: 250

The number of database sequences to show; same as *blastall*, if -D 2 is set.

-d [string]

Default: nr

The database; same as *blastall*.

-D [0..3]

Default: 0

The type of output. The -m option applies only if -D 2 is set here.

Options

0   One-line output for each alignment in the form of:

```
'subject-id'=='[+-]query-id' (s_beg q_beg s_end q_end) Score
```

For example:

```
'AF071362'=='+AF071357' (1 715 200 920) 8
```

Score for non-affine gapping parameters (the default) is the total number of differences (mismatches + gaps); it's the actual raw score when using affine gapping.

1   Same as the output of -D 0, but additionally shows the endpoints and percent identity for each ungapped segment in the alignment.

```
#'>AF071362'=='+AF071357' (1 715 200 920) 8
a {
  s 8
  b 1 715
  e 200 920
  l 1 715 26 740 (96)
  l 27 742 27 742 (100)
  l 28 744 47 763 (100)
  l 48 765 50 767 (100)
  l 51 769 60 778 (100)
  l 61 780 133 852 (100)
  l 134 854 200 920 (99)
}
```

s   Score.

b   Begin coordinates for the subject and query, respectively.

e   End coordinates for subject and query, respectively.

l   Coordinates for each ungapped segment with the percent identity in parentheses at the end.

2   A traditional BLAST output.

3   A tab-delimited, one-line format. The 12 reported tab-delimited fields are as follows:
>   Query
>   Subject
>   Percent identity
>   Alignment length
>   Mismatches
>   Gap openings
>   Query start
>   Query end
>   Subject start
>   Subject end
>   E value
>   Bit score

-e [real number]

Default: 1,000,000

The expectation value; same as *blastall*. However, it's set to a very large number, so there is effectively no cutoff.

-E [integer]

Default: 0

Setting -E and -G turns on affine gapping (same as standard *blastall*). This causes *megablast* to use more memory and isn't necessary when the sequences are expected to be nearly identical. When -E and -G aren't set, the gap extension penalty is calculated from the match (-r) and mismatch (-q) so that $E = r/2 - q$. E is rounded down to the nearest integer. So, for the default +1/-3 matrix, the gap extension penalty equals 3.

-f [T/F]

Default: F

Shows full IDs of the database sequences in the output. The default is only the accession, or just the GI if no accession is given. Applies to -D 0, -D 1, and -D 3.

-F [T/F] [string]

Default: T

Filters the query sequence; same as *blastall*.

-G [integer]

Default: 0

Setting -E and -G turns on affine gapping (same as standard *blastall*). This causes *megablast* to use more memory and isn't necessary when the sequences are expected to be nearly identical.

-H [integer]

Default: 0

The maximum number of HSPs to save per database sequence. The default of 0 means "unlimited."

-i [file]

Default: *stdin*

The query file; same as *blastall*.

-I [T/F]

Default: F

Shows GI numbers in database deflines; same as *blastall*.

Can be used only with -D 2.

-l [file]

Default: Optional

Restricts search to a list of GI numbers; same as *blastall*.

-L [string]

Default: Optional

The location on query sequence; same as *blastall*.

-m [0..11]

Default: 0

Alignment view options. Must set -D 2, then it's the same as *blastall*.

-M [integer]

Default: 20000000 (20 million)

The maximum total length of queries for a single search. Reducing this number reduces the amount of memory required by *megablast*.

-n [T/F]

Default: F

Uses dynamic programming extension for affine gap scores. The default is to use a greedy algorithm for an extension.

-N [0,1,2]

Default: 0

The type of discontiguous template. To use discontiguous seeding, -t must be set to 16, 18, or 21, and -W must be 11 or 12.

Discontiguous templates don't require the usual exact word match employed by the other BLAST programs, but use a template pattern that must be matched to seed an alignment. If a template is specified by 1s and 0s, for example, with 1 representing required matches and 0 representing residues that need not match, then you can represent a template size 16 with a word size of 11 as:

```
1,110,010,110,110,111
```

Options

0   Coding template. This discontiguous template uses a pattern of 110 to match coding sequence where the third codon position is variable (and therefore set to 0 and not required to match). Here are all coding template combinations:

```
110,110,110,110,110,1        [11 of 16]
111,110,110,110,110,1        [12 of 16]
10,110,110,010,110,110,1     [11 of 18]
10,110,110,110,110,110,1     [12 of 18]
10,010,110,010,110,010,110,1 [11 of 21]
10,010,110,110,110,010,110,1 [12 of 21]
```

1   Optimal. This template pattern tries to minimize the correlation between successive words. Here are all optimal template combinations:

```
1,110,010,110,110,111        [11 of 16]
1,110,110,110,110,111        [12 of 16]
111,010,010,110,010,111      [11 of 18]
111,010,110,010,110,111      [12 of 18]
111,010,010,100,010,010,111  [11 of 21]
111,010,010,110,010,010,111  [12 of 21]
```

2   Simultaneous optimal and coding. This option increases sensitivity by allowing seeding from a match to either template at a given position.

-o [file]

Default: Optional

Output file; same as *blastall*.

-p [real number]

Default: 0

Percent identity cutoff. Alignments less than [real number] aren't reported. If using -D 0, all alignments are kept regardless of percent identity (no trace-back is performed, so percent identity can't be calculated).

-P [integer]

Default: 0

The maximum number of positions for a hash value. If set to nonzero, redundant subsequences will be masked in the word seeding phase. This allows a simple type of filtering by masking out subsequences that occur in the query sequences more than [integer] times. When the word size (-W) is set to 16 or higher, -P applies to subsequences of length 12; it applies to subsequences of length 8 when -W is set less than 16.

-q [negative integer]

Default: -3

Mismatch penalty; same as *blastall*.

-Q [file]

Default: Optional

Masked query output. Each query sequence is reported to [file], but with any region hit turned to Ns. This works only in conjunction with -D 2.

-r [integer]

Default: 1

Match score; same as *blastall*.

-R [T/F]

Default: Optional

Reports a short log message at the end of the run.

-s [integer]

Default: Optional

The minimum hit score to report. All alignments scoring less than [integer] aren't reported. By default, this is set to the word size, which results in all hits being reported.

-S [0..3]

Default: 3

The strands to search; same as *blastall*.

-t [16,18,21]

Default: Optional

Sets discontiguous template size. This, combined with the word size (-W) of either 11 or 12 and the template type (-N), sets discontiguous *megablast*.

-T [T/F]

Default: F

The HTML output; same as *blastall*, but is active only if -D 2 is set.

-U [T/F]

Default: F

Lowercase filtering; same as *blastall*.

-v [integer]

Default: 500

The number of one-line descriptions. Same as *blastall* if -D 2 is set.

-W [integer]

Default: 28

Word size. The default word size is very high because sequences aligned by *megablast* are expected to be nearly identical. For discontiguous searches (-t), word size can be only 11 or 12. *megablast* generates words every four bases (similar to the WU-BLAST wink parameter), so using a word size divisible by four assures that all words of that size will be found.

-X [integer]

Default: 20

The X dropoff value for a gapped alignment; same as *blastall*.

-y [integer]

Default: 10

The X dropoff value for an ungapped extension; same as *blastall*.

-z [real number]

Default: 0

The effective length of a database; same as *blastall*.

-Z [integer]

Default: 50

The X dropoff value for a dynamic programming gapped extension.

bl2seq Parameters

bl2seq runs the basic BLAST searches on two sequences. Many parameters are identical between *bl2seq* and *blastall*, but some are unique to one program or the other, and some parameters with the same symbol do different things.

Here are a few sample command lines:

```
bl2seq -p blastp -i protein1 -j protein2
bl2seq -p blastn -i nucleotide1 -j nucleotide2 -F F -D 1
bl2seq -p blastx -i nucleotide -j protein
bl2seq -p tblastn -i protein -j nucleotide
bl2seq -p tblastx -i nucleotide1 -j nucleotide2
```

The following reference describes the parameters for *bl2seq*.

-a [file]

Default: Optional

Specifies the *SeqAnnot* output file. The [file] will be in the Abstract Syntax Notation 1 (ASN.1) format for import into and use with the NCBI toolbox.

-A [T/F]

Default: F

Input sequences are NCBI identifiers. When set to T, the program makes an online connection to the NCBI databases to retrieve the FASTA sequences.

```
bl2seq -A -p blastx -i AF287139 -j AAG39070
```

(This function was just enabled in the 2.2.6 release.)

-d [real number]

Default: 0

Sets the theoretical size of the database. This is useful for maintaining consistent E-values between *blastall* and *bl2seq* searches. Identical to the *blastall* -z parameter. If -d isn't set, the database size is set to the length of the -j sequence.

-D [0/1]

Default: 0

Sets the output format to tabular, which corresponds to the *blastall* setting -m 8. The other -m report options available in *blastall* aren't available in *bl2seq*.

Unlike the *blastall* parameter of the same name, -D doesn't set the genetic code for translating database sequences. All *bl2seq* translations use the standard nuclear genetic code.

Options

0   Traditional

1   Tabular

-e [real number]

Default: 10

The expectation value; same as *blastall*.

-E [integer]

Default: 1

The gap extension value; same as *blastall*.

-F [T/F] [string]

Default: T

Complexity filtering; same as *blastall*.

-g [T/F]

Default: T

The gapped alignment; same as *blastall*.

-G [integer]

Defaults: *blastn* 5, others 11

The gap initiation penalty; same as *blastall*.

-i [file]

Default: Required

Sets the input (query) file for the search. For *blastx*, [file] must be nucleotide, and for *tblastn*, [file] must be protein. Setting [file] to *stdin* or using multisequence files isn't recommended.

-l [integer],[integer]

Default: 0,0

The location on the input sequence defined by -i. Follows the *blastall* -L syntax.

-j [file]

Default: Required

Sets the database file for the search. For *blastx*, [file] must be protein, and for *tblastn*, [file] must be nucleotide. Setting [file] to *stdin* or using multisequence files isn't recommended.

-J [integer],[integer]

Default: 0,0

The location on a sequence defined by -j. Follows the *blastall* -L syntax.

-m [T/F]

Default: F

Sets a *blastn* search to *megablast* mode; same as *blastall* -n.

-M [string]

Default: BLOSUM62

The scoring matrix, same as *blastall*.

-o [file]

Default: Optional

The output file; same as *blastall*.

-p [string]

Default: None, required parameter

The program name; same as *blastall*.

-q [negative integer]

Default: -3

The nucleotide mismatch score; same as *blastall*.

-r [integer]

Default: 1

The nucleotide match score; same as *blastall*.

-S [1..3]

Default: 3

The search strand; same as *blastall*.

-t [integer]

Default: 0

The longest intron allowed in *tblastn* for linking HSPs; same as *blastall*.

-T [T/F]

Default: F

HTML output; same as *blastall*.

-U [T/F]

Default: F

Lowercase masking; same as *blastall*.

-W [integer]

Defaults: *blastn* 11, others 3

The word size; same as *blastall*.

-X [integer]

Default: *blastn* 30, others 15

The extension cutoff; same as *blastall*.

-Y [real number]

Default: 0

The search space; same as *blastall*.

blastpgp Parameters (PSI-BLAST and PHI-BLAST)

blastpgp is the program used to run PSI-BLAST and PHI-BLAST. These programs are specialized protein BLAST comparisons that are more sensitive than the standard BLASTP search. PSI-BLAST considers position-specific information when searching for significant hits. PHI-BLAST uses a pattern, or profile, to seed an alignment, which is then extended by the normal BLASTP algorithm.

PSI-BLAST

PSI-BLAST (position-specific iterated BLAST) uses a specialized scoring matrix that assigns scores to each position (hence, position-specific) in the query sequence based on alignments defined by consecutive iterations of searches (hence, iterated). The specialized matrix is a position-specific scoring matrix (PSSM) that assigns a score for every amino acid at each position in the query sequence (See Figure 13-1).

```
        A   R   N   D   C   Q   E   G   H   I   L   K   M   F   P   S   T   W   Y   V
 1 Y   -2  -2  -2  -3  -2  -1  -2  -3   2  -1  -1  -2  -1   3  -3  -2  -2   2   7  -1
 2 L   -1  -2  -3  -4  -1  -2  -3  -4  -3   2   4  -2   2   0  -3  -2  -1  -2  -1   1
 3 P   -1  -2  -2  -2  -3  -2  -1  -2  -2  -3  -3  -1  -3  -4   8  -1  -1  -4  -3  -3
 4 S    1  -1   0  -1   0   0  -1  -1  -3  -3   0  -2  -3  -1   5   1  -3  -2  -2
 5 C   -1  -4  -3  -4   9  -3  -4  -3  -3  -2  -2  -3  -2  -3  -3  -1  -1  -3  -3  -1
 6 T    0  -1   0  -1  -1  -1  -1  -1  -2  -2  -3  -1  -2  -3  -1   4   3  -3  -2  -2
 7 Y   -2  -3  -3  -4  -3  -2  -3  -4   1  -1  -1  -3  -1   5  -4  -2  -2   1   7  -2
 8 Y   -1  -1  -1  -1  -2   0  -1  -2   6  -2  -1  -1  -1   1  -1  -1   0   5  -2
 9 V   -1  -2  -2  -2  -1  -2  -2  -2  -2   1   2  -2   0  -1  -2  -2  -1  -2  -1   4
10 S   -1  -1  -1  -1  -3   3   3  -2  -1  -2   1   0  -1  -2  -2   2  -1  -3  -2  -2
```

Figure 13-1. PSSM for the first 10 amino acids of the coelacanth HoxA11 protein

Figure 13-1 shows a portion of a PSSM calculated for the coelacanth Hoxa11 protein (AAG39070). The query amino acids are numbered in the left column with the position-specific scores for each of the 20 amino acids shown across each row. The diverse scores of the three Tyrosines (Y) at positions 1, 7, and 8 highlight the position-specific aspect of this scoring scheme compared to traditional BLAST matrices, which would contain the same scores for Y in all three positions.

The PSSM, or checkpoint file, is created internally by PSI-BLAST, but it can also be exported to a file using the -C option of *blastpgp*. This option is extremely useful. You can use the checkpoint file in subsequent PSI-BLAST (*blastpgp*) searches or as a database entry for the RPS-BLAST program. You can also use the PSSM in a specialized *tblastn* search in *blastall* by using the -p psitblastn and -R <checkpoint file> options with a nucleotide database.

To run PSI-BLAST, the -j parameter must be set to something greater than 1. The default of -j 1 means that there are no iterations and that it's therefore the same as a single BLASTP search. Setting -j sets the maximum number of iterations to run, with the program stopping beforehand if the search comes to convergence. Convergence occurs when no new sequences are found that are better than the E value threshold set by the -h parameter.

Here are a few sample command lines:

```
blastpgp -d nr -i my_protein -s T -j 5
blastpgp -d nr -i my_protein -R my_protein.ckp -d nr -j 5 -h 0.001
```

PHI-BLAST

PHI-BLAST stands for pattern-hit initiated BLAST. The program uses an input sequence and a defined pattern to query a protein database. The pattern is defined in PROSITE format (*http://ca.expasy.org/prosite/*) and is used as the seed for the alignment. The pattern is used instead of the words that are usually generated for seeding alignments in BLASTP. Here's a sample profile:

```
ID  HoxA11 pattern1
PA  Y-S-[SA]-X-[LVIM]
```

The profile's syntax has a line starting with ID, followed by two spaces and the name of the pattern. The name is free text. The next line should start with PA, followed by two spaces, and then the pattern in PROSITE format. The PROSITE format is simple. A dash (-) separates letters, an X means any letter, and the brackets ([]) specify a choice of amino acids. You can find more information on the pattern syntax in the *README.bls* file that comes with the NCBI-BLAST distribution.

Additionally, if the pattern occurs more than once in the query and you would like to limit which occurrences are used as seeds, specify those locations by using the HI (hit initiation) tag in the pattern file. You set -p to *seedp* instead of *patseedp* (explained in the reference section that follows). The following example specifies that the pattern starting at position 143 should be used. (In this case, there's also an occurrence at 34, which is ignored.)

```
ID  HoxA11 pattern2
PA  Y-S-[SA]-X -[LVIMK]
HI  143
```

PHI-BLAST can also be a jumping-off point for a PSI-BLAST run. In the following command line, the pattern in *hit_file* initiates the first iteration of PSI-BLAST for the development of the PSSM, followed by normal rounds of PSI-BLAST iterations.

```
blastpgp -d nr -i my_protein -k hit_file -p patseedp -j 5
```

Here are a few sample PHI-BLAST command lines:

```
blastpgp -d nr -i my_protein -k hit_file -p patseedp
blastpgp -d nr -i my_protein -k multi_hit_file -p seedp
blastpgp -d HoxDB.pep -i AAG39070.pep -k hit_file.hox -p patseedp
```

The following reference describes parameters used with *blastpgp*, which executes PSI- and PHI-BLAST searches.

-a [integer]

Default: 1

The number of processors to use; same as *blastall*.

-A [integer]

Default: *blastn* 0, others 40

The multiple-hit window size; same as *blastall*.

-b [integer]

Default: 250

The number of alignments to show; same as *blastall*.

-B [file]

Default: Optional   Program: PSI-BLAST only

The input alignment file for a PSI-BLAST restart. It allows a PSI-BLAST run to start with a curated multiple sequence alignment instead of allowing the program to generate it from the first round of database alignments. For example:

```
blastpgp -i query -B multiple_alignment -j 5 -d nr
```

The alignment file must be based on the Clustal format but without the header and footer. The file should have a row for each sequence and can be broken into blocks separated by one or more blank lines. The query file (specified by -i) must be included in the alignment (though it doesn't need to be the first one), and all rows must be padded with dashes (---) to make them equal lengths. Also, each column must contain either all uppercase or lowercase letters. An uppercase letter signifies that the column should be given a position-specific score; a lowercase letter means that the matrix (specified by -M) score should be used. Here is a portion of the example alignment file included in README.bls (the query is 26SPS9_Hs, in this case):

```
26SPS9_Hs     IHAAEEKDWKTAYSYFYEAFEGYdsidspkaitslkymllc
F57B9_Ce      LHAADEKDFKTAFSYFYEAFEGYdsvdekvsaltalkymll
YDL097c_Sc    ILHCEDKDYKTAFSYFFESFESYhnltthnsyekacqvlky
YMJ5_Ce       LYSAEERDYKTSFSYFYEAFEGFasigdkinatsalkymil
FUS6_ARATH    KNYIRTRDYCTTTKHIIHMCMNAilvsiemgqfthvtsyvn
COS41.8_Ci    SLDYKLKTYLTIARLYLEDEDPVqaemyinrasllqnetad
644879        KCYSRARDYCTSAKHVINMCLNVikvsvylqnwshvlsyvs
YPR108w_Sc    IHCLAVRNFKEAAKLLVDSLATFtsieltsyesiatyasvt
eif-3p110_Hs  SKAMKMGDWKTCHSFIINEKMNGkvw---------------
T23D8.4_Ce    SKAMLNGDWKKCQDYIVNDKMNQkvw---------------
YD95_Sp       IYLMSIRNFSGAADLLLDCMSTFsstellpyydvvryavis
```

```
KIAA0107_Hs    LYCVAIRDFKQAAELFLDTVSTFtsyelmdyktfvtytvyv
F49C12.8_Hs    LYRMSVRDFAGAADLFLEAVPTFgsyelmtyenlilytvit
Int-6_Mm       KFQYECGNYSGAAEYLYFFRVLVpatdrnalsslwgklase

26SPS9_Hs      kimlntpedvqalvsgklalryagrqtealkcvaqasknr
F57B9_Ce       ckvmldlpdevnsllsaklalkyngsdldamkaiaaaaqk
YDL097c_Sc     mllskimlnliddvknilnakytketyqsrgidamkavae
YMJ5_Ce        ckimlneteqlagllaakeivayqkspriiairsmadafr
FUS6_ARATH     kaeqnpetlepmvnaklrcasglahlelkkyklaarkfld
COS41.8_Ci     eqlqihykvcyarvldyrrkfleaaqrynelsyksaihet
644879         kaestpeiaeqrgerdsqtqailtklkcaaglaelaarky
YPR108w_Sc     glftlertdlkskvidspellslisttaalqsissltisl
eif-3p110_Hs   ----------------------------------------
T23D8.4_Ce     ----------------------------------------
YD95_Sp        gaisldrvdvktkivdspevlavlpqnesmssleacinsl
KIAA0107_Hs    smialerpdlrekvikgaeilevlhslpavrqylfslyec
F49C12.8_Hs    ttfaldrpdlrtkvircnevqeqltggglngtlipvreyl
Int-6_Mm       ilmqnwdaamedltrlketidnnsvssplqslqqrtwlih
```

-c [integer]

Default: 9   Program: PSI-BLAST only

Sets a constant in pseudocounts for PSSM. It's generally not necessary to change this parameter.

-C [file]

Default: Optional   Program: PSI-BLAST only

Outputs a file for PSI-BLAST checkpointing. This outputs the final PSSM for a multipass run of PSI-BLAST. The checkpoint file can then be used in a PSI-BLAST restart (see -R), in a *blastall -p psitblastn* run (also see -R), or as an entry in an RPS-BLAST database.

```
blastpgp -d nr -i my_protein -j 5 -C my_protein.ckp
```

-d [string]

Default: nr

The database name; same as *blastall*.

-e [real]

Default: 10

The expectation value; same as *blastall*.

-E [integer]

Default: *blastn* 2, others 1

The penalty to extend a gap; same as *blastall*.

-f [integer]

Default: 11

The threshold for extending a hit; same as *blastall*.

-F [string]

Default:

Filters the query sequence; same as *blastall*.

-g [T/F]

Default: T

Performs gapped alignment; same as *blastall*.

PHI-BLAST requires gapping and therefore forbids -g F.

-G [integer]

Defaults: *blastn* 5, others 11

The penalty to open a gap; same as *blastall*.

-h [real number]

Default: 0.005   Program: PSI-BLAST only

The E-value threshold for inclusion in PSSM. All alignments better than this threshold are used in constructing the PSSM.

-H [integer]

Default: -1

The end of the required region in query. The default of -1 indicates the actual end of the query. This option can be used in combination with -S to specify a particular region to use

-i [file]

Default: *stdin*

The query file; same as *blastall*.

-I [T/F]

Default: F

Shows GIs in defline; same as *blastall*

-j [integer]

Default: 1

The maximum number of passes to use in a multipass version. The default of 1 is just a regular BLASTP search.

-J [T/F]

Default: F

Believes the query definition line; same as *blastall*.

-k [file]

Default: *hit_file*   Program: PHI-BLAST only

Specifies the file containing the PROSITE pattern to be used for seeding in a PHI-BLAST run. If -k isn't specified when running PHI-BLAST (e.g. -p patseedp or -p seedp), the program looks for a file called *hit_file*.

-K [integer]

Default: 0 - Off

The number of best hits from a region to keep; same as *blastall*.

-l [string]

Default: Optional

Restricts the search of the database to a list of GIs; same as *blastall*.

-L [integer]

Default: 0 (disabled)

The cost to decline an alignment.

-m [0..9]

Default: 0

Alignment view options; same as *blastall*.

-M [string]

Default: BLOSUM62

The matrix; same as *blastall*.

-N [real number]

Default: 22.0

The number of bits required to trigger gapping.

-o [file]

Default: Optional

The output file for alignment; same as *blastall*.

-O [file]

Default: Optional

A *SeqAlign* file output; same as *blastall*.

-p [string]

Default: *blastpgp*

Specifies whether to run in PSI- or PHI-BLAST mode.

Options

blastpgp
    PSI-BLAST mode
patseedp
    PHI-BLAST mode. Uses all occurrences of the *hit_file* pattern to seed alignments. Any HI tags (see later) in the *hit_file* are ignored.
seedp
    PHI-BLAST mode. The specified pattern is found more than once in the query, and the *hit_file* specifies which to use as seeds. The specific pattern(s) occurrences to use is specified with the HI tag in the *hit_file*. For example, the following *hit_file* designates seeding from a pattern that occurs at position 143 of the coelacanth HoxA11 protein:

```
ID  HoxA11 pattern2
PA  Y-S-[SA]-X-[LVIMK]
HI  143
```
seedp throws an exception if the *hit_file* doesn't contain the HI tags.

-Q [file]

Default: Optional

Output file for a PSI-BLAST matrix in ASCII format. This [file] can't be used in any subsequent programs. Use -c to output a matrix for subsequent searches.

-R [file]

Default: Optional

Input checkpoint file for PSI-BLAST restart. Uses the checkpoint file. Output with -c.

-s [T/F]

Default: F

Calculates locally optimal Smith-Waterman alignments. Because of the heuristic nature of BLAST, it sometimes produces nonoptimal local alignments. This option causes BLAST to run the full Smith-Waterman alignment algorithm on subjects found by the normal BLAST heuristic. There may be some speed cost using this option, but it helps guarantee high-quality alignments, which are important in PSSM generation. Setting -s T is highly recommended.

-S [integer]

Default: 1

The start of the required region in query. Used in combination with -H, this sets a specific region of the query to be used when generating the PSSM.

-t [T/F]

Default: T

Uses composition-based statistics. With this set to T, the score is adjusted based on composition biases in the query and subject sequences. Using it helps avoid possible corruption of the PSSM because it introduces low-entropy false positives in the multiple sequence alignment.

-T [T/F]

Default: F

Produces HTML output; same as *blastall*.

-U [T/F]

Default: F

Uses lowercase filtering of a query sequence; same as *blastall*.

-v [integer]

Default: 500

The number of one-line descriptions to show; same as *blastall*.

-W [1..3]

Default: 3

The word size; same as *blastall*.

-X [integer]

Default: 15

The X dropoff for gapped alignments; same as *blastall*.

-y [real number]

Default: 7.0

X dropoff for ungapped extensions; same as *blastall*

-Y [real number]

Default: 0

The effective length of the search space; same as *blastall*.

-z [real number]

Default: 0

The effective database size; same as *blastall*.

-Z [integer]

Default: 25

The X dropoff for final gapped alignment; same as *blastall*.

blastclust Parameters

blastclust clusters a database of protein or nucleotide sequences. It outputs rows of sequence identifiers from the database with clustered sequences occurring on the same row and clusters sorted from largest to smallest. The program can generate a list of clusters for input into another program (e.g., an alignment program such as PHRAP); however, it should be used only on a relatively small number of sequences (10-1000) because it runs only on a single computer, and the RAM requirements quickly exceed most capacities.

Here are a few sample command lines:

```
blastclust -i my_nucdb -p F -o my_nucdb.clusters
blastclust -i my_pepdb -o my_pepdb.clusters -L 0.7 -S 90
```

The following reference describes parameters used with *blastclust*.

-a [integer]

Default: 1   Programs: All

Specifies the number of CPUs to use on a multiprocessor machine.

-b [T/F]

Default: T

Requires coverage on both sequences. If set to T, the program requires both sequences to pass the coverage criteria set with -L before they are called neighbors and clustered together.

-c [file]

Default: Optional

Specifies a configuration file with advanced options. The configuration file is simply a list of the options that you commonly use.

-C [T/F]

Default: F

The crash recovery option. Set it to complete unfinished clustering. Set to T if using the -r option with a file to restore the clustering. Use the same command line as the crashed run with the same -s, with only -C, T, and -r being added. This restarts the run using the hit list file specified by -r and then appending to it (as specified by -s).

-d [file]

Default: Optional

The input file is a BLAST database, not a FASTA file.

-e [T/F]

Default: F

Enables ID parsing in the database-formatted report.

-i [file]

Default: stdin

Specifies the FASTA input file for clustering.

-I [file]

Default: Optional

Restricts the reclustering to the IDs specified in [file]. It can be useful when you have a very large FASTA database and wish to cluster a subset of sequences.

-L [real number]

Default:0.9

Specifies the length of coverage threshold.

-p [T/F]

Default: T

Input sequences are proteins. Set to F for nucleotides.

-r [file]

Default: Optional

Specifies the file used to restore neighbors for reclustering. Set -C to T. This file is created by the -s command of a previous run. Use it if the program crashes during a run.

-s [file]

Default: Optional

Specifies the file in which to save the hit list. This file can restore a crashed run and is the input file specified by -r.

-v [file]

Default: *stdout*

Prints progress messages. Progress is reported to standard output if no file is specified.

-W [integer]

Default: Protein 3, Nucleotide 32

The word size; same as *blastall*.

## CHAPTER 14

WU-BLAST Reference

WU-BLAST was developed and is maintained entirely by Warren Gish. He was one of the original authors of BLAST while at the NCBI but is now at Washington University in St. Louis (where the *WU* comes from). Development began in 1994 at Version 1.4, before BLAST had gapped alignments. Quite a lot has changed since then. Paradoxically, WU-BLAST is more similar to the original BLAST than the current NCBI version.

WU-BLAST is useful because it has more command-line parameters that allow advanced users to control the program with more precision. It is also faster. Table 14-1 displays features unique to WU-BLAST or significantly different from NCBI-BLAST.

Table 14-1. WU- and NCBI-BLAST feature differences

Feature	WU-BLAST	NCBI-BLAST
Word size	Any word size for any program mode. Neighborhood words are turned off for word sizes of 5 or greater, but may be activated by setting an explicit value for T.	*blastn* has a minimum word size of 7. *blastp*, *blastx*, *tblastn*, and *tblastx* have word sizes of 2 or 3. Neighborhood words are never used for *blastn*.
Nucleotide scoring	Choice of match/mismatch or scoring matrix.	Only match/mismatch scoring.
Nucleotide statistics	Karlin-Altschul parameters are available for several match/mismatch values and gap costs.	Karlin-Altschul parameters are always computed without respect to gap costs. Reported E-values may greatly overestimate significance.
altscore	Allows score modification for any matrix (e.g., to set stop scores lower).	Nothing similar.
H, K, L, gapH, gapK, gapL	Especially useful when using unsupported scoring schemes; allow the provision of values for Karlin-Altschul parameters.	Nothing similar. Unsupported scoring schemes are fatal errors.
Alias databases	No, but virtual databases offer similar functionality.	Yes, both alias and virtual databases are supported.
Gapped alignment	All programs.	All programs except *tblastx*.

Table 14-1. WU- and NCBI-BLAST feature differences (continued)

Feature	WU-BLAST	NCBI-BLAST
/etc/sysblast	Allows systems administrators to set system-wide resource restrictions.	Nothing similar.
Database subset selection	Yes, via dbrecmin and dbrecmax.	No, but alias databases can be used for static splitting.
Restricted region of query	The nwstart and nwlen parameters restrict seeding but not alignment.	-L restricts both seeding and alignment.
links	Displays the order of alignments in a group.	Nothing similar.
topcomboN	Allows restriction of number alignment groups. Groups are clearly labeled.	Nothing similar.
kap	Computes significance without sum statistics.	Nothing similar.
olf, golf, olmax, golmax	Allows setting of overlap rules for HSP consistency.	Fixed internally.
notes, warnings, errors	Descriptive messages at various levels of caution.	Most error messages are terse and not user friendly.
Output formats	Only the standard format.	Multiple output report formats including HTML, ASN.1, XML, tabular, and anchored multiple alignments. See Appendix A.

To use the most recent version of WU-BLAST, you must have a site license from Washington University in St. Louis. The product is free for academic use, but commercial users must pay a fee. Unlike NCBI-BLAST, the source code isn't freely available. For the latest information on WU-BLAST, visit the official site at *http://blast. wustl.edu*. If you want to try WU-BLAST, an early version is available without license.

Usage Statements

All WU-BLAST programs provide usage statements if they are executed without any arguments. They are sometimes lengthy, so it's best to pipe them through a pager such as *less* or *more*.

```
blastn | more
xdformat | less
xdget | less
```

Command-Line Syntax

WU-BLAST command-line syntax isn't uniform between all programs. The BLAST programs *blastn*, *blastp*, *blastx*, *tblastn*, and *tblastx* use a slightly different syntax than do *xdformat*, and *xdget*.

The BLAST program options come after the mandatory arguments of database and query sequence. The command-line structure is as follows:

```
[program name] [blast database] [query sequence] [parameters]
```

The parameter names in the BLAST programs and their arguments have some flexibility. The following command lines are all identical:

```
blastn db query E=10
blastn db query -E 10
blastn db query E 10
blastn db query -E=10
```

This book uses the first form to avoid confusion with NCBI-BLAST.

xdformat and *xdget* use the traditional Unix syntax where the parameters precede the mandatory arguments:

```
[program name] [parameters] [mandatory arguments]
```

The *xdformat* and *xdget* options are all single letters preceded by a single dash. For parameters that require a value, a space between the parameter and its value is optional. As is typical for Unix programs, a double dash indicates the end of command-line options and a single dash signifies *stdin*.

```
xdformat -p protein_db
xdformat -n -I nucleotide_db
zcat fasta.*.gz | xdformat -n -o my_db -- -
```

WU-BLAST Parameters

WU-BLAST has many control parameters, some of which are esoteric and rarely useful. The most important parameters are listed here.

altscore=[string]

Default: Off

Defines an alternate scoring system for any pair of letters. For example, `altscore="M M -3"` changes the score of M-M pairs to -3, and `altscore="A C 4"` gives a score of 4 if the query is A and the subject is C. Letters may be designated as any to change an entire row or column. The score can be given as *min* or *max* for the minimum and maximum scores in the matrix or *na* to make the score infinitely low. To set the score of all rows and columns containing stop codons to negative infinity, set `altscore="* any na"` and `altscore="any * na"`. If you change the scoring parameters, you may also want to adjust gapL, gapH, and gapK.

See also   nogap, gapL, gapH, gapK

B=[integer]

Default: 250

Sets the number of database hits to report. A warning is issued if this number is exceeded. It is typical to set this parameter to a very high value, such as B=100000, to ensure that no alignments are missed.

bottom

Default: Off   Programs: *blastn, tblastx, blastx*

Search only the bottom strand of the query.

See also   top

cpus=[integer]

Default: 4 for *blastn*; all for *blastp, blastx, tblastn,* and *tblastx*

Sets the number of processors to use. If not set, all processors on the system may be used except *blastn*, which will limit itself to 4. See Chapter 10 for information on the */etc/sysblast* file used for setting systemwide resource limitations.

dbrecmax=[integer]

Default: Last database record

Last database record number to search.

See also   dbrecmin, qrecmin, qrecmax

dbrecmin=[integer]

Default: 1

First database record number to search. For example, by setting dbrecmin=1 dbrecmax=10, only the first 10 database sequences are searched.

See also   dbrecmax, qrecmin, qrecmax

E=[number]

Default: 10

This is the E from the Karlin-Altschul equation. Database hits whose E-value is greater than this threshold will not be reported. If both E and S are set, the more restrictive parameter is used.

See also   S

E2=[number]

Default: Variable; calculated from scoring parameters

Sets the alignment threshold for ungapped alignments. When E2 and S2 are set, the more restrictive parameter is used.

See also   S2, gapE2, gapS2

echofilter

Default: Off

Prints out the query sequence after all filtering is performed. This is useful for troubleshooting when there are no database hits, and you suspect the filtering is too aggressive.

See also   filter, wordmask, maskextra

errors

Default: Off

Suppress nonfatal error messages. It is generally a good idea to pay attention to the error messages, but at times it is useful to block them.

See also   nonnegok, novalidctxok

filter=[string]

Default: Off

Processes the query sequence with the specified filtering method. Letters are replaced with X and N for proteins and nucleotides, respectively.

seg
    Identifies low-complexity regions in both nucleotide and amino acid sequences.
dust
    The standard low-complexity filter for nucleotide sequences. Generally less sensitive than seg.
xnu
    Finds short repeats in protein sequences.
seg+xnu
    Combines both seg and xnu.
ccp
    Coiled-coil filter for proteins.

Multiple filtering methods may be specified on the same command line; for example:

    blastp nr query filter=seg filter=ccp filter=xnu

See also   echofilter, maskextra, wordmask

gapE2=[number]

Default: Variable; calculated from scoring parameters

Expectation threshold for saving individual gapped alignments. When gapE2 and gapS2 are set, the more restrictive parameter is used.

See also   gapS2, E2, S2

gapH=[number]

Default: Variable; depends on scoring parameters

Sets the value of H (information per aligned letter) for gapped alignments. If a particular combination of scoring matrix (or match/mismatch scores) and gap values doesn't already have precomputed values for gapH, gapK, and gapL, WU-BLAST uses ungapped statistics. In this case, the resulting E-values may be much too low. A warning is issued when this is the case. Computing proper values for gapped Karlin-Altschul parameters requires simulations with random sequences that determine what ungapped scoring scheme is most similar to the gapped scoring scheme.

See also   H, K, gapK, L, gapL, warnings

gapK=[number]

Default: Variable; depends on scoring parameters

Sets the value of the Karlin-Altschul K parameter for gapped alignments. See the description for gapH.

See also   H, gapH, K, L, gapL

gapL=[number]

Default: Variable; depends on scoring parameters

Sets the value of the Karlin-Altschul parameter lambda (information per unit score) used for gapped alignments. See the description for gapH.

See also   H, gapH, K, gapK, L

gapS2=[integer]

Default: Variable; calculated from scoring parameters

Score threshold for saving individual gapped alignments. Alignments below the threshold aren't reported.

See also   gapE2

gapsepqmax=[int]

Default: Unlimited

Maximum separation allowed between gapped alignments along the query.

See also   gapsepsmax, hspsepqmax, hspsepsmax

gapsepsmax=[int]

Default: Unlimited

Maximum separation allowed between gapped alignments along the subject.

See also   gapsepqmax, hspsepqmax, hspsepsmax

gapX

Default: Variable; depends on scoring parameters

Sets the alignment extension cutoff for gapped alignment.

See also   X

gi

Default: Off

Displays the GenInfo identifiers of database hits, if present.

golf=[number]

Default: 0.1

Maximum fractional length overlap for gapped alignment consistency. See the description for olf.

golmax=[integer]

Default: Unlimited

Maximum absolute length of overlap for gapped alignment consistency. See the description for olf.

gspmax=[integer]

Default: 1,000

Sets the maximum number of gapped alignments per subject sequence. gspmax is bounded by hspmax. A value of 0 implies no limit.

See also   hspmax

H=[number]

Default: Variable; depends on scoring parameters

Sets the value of the Karlin-Altschul parameter H.

See also   gapH, K, gapK, L, gapL

hspmax=[integer]

Default: 1000

Sets the maximum number of ungapped alignments per subject sequence. A warning is issued if this limit is exceeded. A value of 0 implies no limit.

See also   gspmax

hitdist=[integer]

Default: 0, off

Maximum distance between word hits for the two-hit seeding algorithm. WU-BLAST uses one-hit seeding by default.

hspsepqmax=[int]

Default: Unlimited

Maximum separation allowed between alignments along the query.

hspsepsmax=[int]

Default: Unlimited

Maximum separation allowed between alignments along the subject.

K=[number]

Default: Variable; depends on scoring parameters

Sets the value for K from the Karlin-Altschul equation.

See also   gapK, H, gapH, L, gapL

kap

Default: Off

Assesses individual alignment scores with Karlin-Altschul statistics rather than using sum statistics on groups of alignments.

L=[number]

Default: Variable; depends on scoring parameters

Sets lambda (nats per unit score) from the Karlin-Altschul equation.

See also   gapL, H, gapH, K, gapK

lcfilter

Default: Off

Filters lowercase letters in the query sequence. The lowercase letters are treated as if they had been filtered out by one of the filtering programs.

See also   echofilter, filter, wordmask, lcmask

lcmask

Default: Off

Masks lowercase letters in the query sequence for seeding only. Lowercase letters in the query sequence aren't used in the initial word search but are available for alignment during the extension stage; known as soft masking.

See also   echofilter, filter, wordmask, lcfilter

links

Default: Off

Display group information. Parentheses indicate the placement of the alignment in the group. The following example shows three alignments in the group. The score of the second reported alignment is 159, the last alignment in the chain.

```
Score = 159 (61.0 bits), Sum P(3) = 2.7e-38
Identities = 26/39 (66%), Positives = 32/39 (82%)
Links = 1-3-(2)
```

See also   topcomboN

M=[integer]

Default: +5 *blastn*

Sets the match score. This parameter is usually used for *blastn* only but may be used for other programs.

See also   N

maskextra=[integer]

Default: Off

Extends masking an extra distance of [integer] letters.

See also   echofilter, filter, wordmask, lcfilter, lcmask

matrix=[file]

Default: BLOSUM62   Programs: *blastp, blastx, tblastn, tblastx*

Specifies a scoring matrix file. The default is BLOSUM62. A large number of scoring matrices are distributed with WU-BLAST in the *matrix/aa* directory. Nucleotide matrices for use with *blastn* are in *matrix/nt*.

N=[integer]

Default: *-4 blastn*

Sets the mismatch score. This parameter is usually used for *blastn* only but may be used for other programs.

See also   M

nogap

Default: Off

Turns off gapped alignment. This parameter is useful in conjunction with altscore to prevent stop codons.

See also   altscore

nonnegok

Default: Off

Under Karlin-Altschul statistics, the expected score, must be negative. WU-BLAST normally exits with a fatal error if this isn't the case. Sometimes scoring schemes with positive expected scores are useful, and setting nonnegok silences the error condition.

See also   novalidctxok, errors

nosegs

Default: Off

WU-BLAST doesn't allow alignments to cross hyphen characters that act as query segment boundaries (e.g., for draft sequence). nosegs effectively converts hyphens to Ns.

notes

Default: Off

Suppresses informational messages. For example, if you are intentionally searching for a low-complexity sequence, you may wish to disable the message that suggests that a low-complexity filter would help remove meaningless alignments.

See also   errors, warnings

novalidctxok

Default: Off

If a sequence can't generate any significant HSPs, WU-BLAST normally exits with an error that says there are no valid contexts. You may see encounter such an error when searching a collection of sequencing reads, some of which are mostly (or completely) Ns. Setting novalidctxok allows you to continue without error.

See also   nonnegok, errors

nwlen=[integer]

Default: End of sequence

Sets the length of region for seeding.

See also   nwstart

nwstart=[integer]

Default: 1

Sets the starting position for seeding alignments. nwstart and nwlen indicate that a specific region of the query should be seeded. Alignments may extend outside of this region. For example, nwstart=500 nwlen=200 seeds positions 500 to 700 of the query sequence.

See also   nwlen

o=[file]

Default: *stdout*

Write results to this file instead of to *stdout* (the screen).

olf=[number]

Default: 0.125

Maximum fractional length of overlap for alignment consistency.

Consistent alignments must be ordered and have minimal overlap (see Chapter 5). The amount of permitted overlap is expressed as both a relative fraction and an absolute number. The default setting, 0.1, prevents alignments whose overlap length is more than 10 percent of the length of either alignment from being in the same group. The golf parameter plays the same role for gapped alignments. The olmax and golmax parameters control the absolute length of the overlap.

olmax=[integer]

Default: Unlimited

Maximum absolute length of overlap for alignment consistency. See the description for olf.

postsw

Default: Off   Programs: *blastp*

Performs Smith-Waterman alignment after initial BLAST alignment to return the single maximum-scoring pair rather than several high-scoring pairs.

Q=[integer]

Default: 10 *blastn*, 9 *blastp, blastx, tblastn, tblastx*

Sets the cost for the first gap character.

See also   R

qoffset=[integer]

Default: 0

Adjusts the query numbering by this amount—for example, if you search with a sequence that was known to have a vector sequence in the first 25 bases. By setting this parameter to 25, your numbering will be based on the insert sequence.

qrecmax=[integer]

Default: 1

Last query sequence to search. See the description for qrecmin.

Qrecmin=[integer]

Default: 1

By default, WU-BLAST produces one BLAST report for each query sequence in a FASTA files with multiple sequences. Setting qrecmin and qrecmax allows you to select a subset of query sequences in much the same way as dbrecmin and dbrecmax.

See also   qrecmax, dbrecmin, dbrecmax

R=[integer]

Default: 10 *blastn*, 2 *blastp*, *blastx*, *tblastn*, *tblastx*

Sets the cost for the second and remaining gap characters.

See also   Q

restest

Default: Off

blastp and *blastx* statistical tests are based on the number of residues (letters) in the database. If Z is set in conjunction with restest, *blastn*, *tblastn*, and *tblastx* will also be based on the number of letters.

See also   seqtest, Z

S=[integer]

Default: Variable; calculated from *E*

Sets the final score threshold. Since *S* and *E* are interconvertible through the Karlin-Altschul equation, setting S effectively sets E, and vice versa. When both are set, the more restrictive one is used.

See also   E

mS2=[integer]

Default: Variable; depends on scoring parameters

Score threshold for individual ungapped alignments. If both S2 and E2 are set, the more restrictive one is used.

See also   E2, gapS2, gapE2

seqtest

blastn, *tblastn*, and *tblastx* statistical tests are based on the number of sequences in the database. If Z is set in conjunction with seqtest, *blastp* and *blastx* will also be based on the number of sequences.

See also   restest, Z

span, span1, span2

Default: span2

WU-BLAST normally discards HSPs that are contained completely within a larger, higher-scoring HSP. This behavior is called span2. If span1 is set, alignments are thrown out if they are subsets of the query or subject (unlike span2, both conditions aren't required). This is useful if the sequences contain many repeats. To prevent discarded alignments, set span. The output may become very large.

T=[integer]

Default: 11 *blastp*, 12 *blastx*, 13 *tblastn*, 13 *tblastx*

Sets the neighborhood word threshold score. Setting this value extremely high removes neighborhood words and makes seeding require matching words. T, W, and hitdist are the most effective parameters for controlling the sensitivity and speed of BLAST searches.

See also   W, hitdist

top

Default: Off   Programs: *blastn, tblastx, blastx*

Searches only the top strand of the query.

See also   bottom

topcomboN=[integer]

Default: Off

Reports the number of consistent, or collinear, HSP combinations.

V=[integer]

Default: 500

Controls the number of one-line summaries.

See also   B

warnings

Default: Off

WU-BLAST reports various warning conditions. This parameter turns them off.

See also   notes, errors

wink=[integer]

Default: 1

Words are created by sliding a window of width W by wink letters at a time. If W equals wink, words don't overlap.

See also   W, T, hitdist

wordmask=[method]

Default: Off

Filters the query sequence for seeding only. Low-complexity region in the query sequence isn't used in the initial word search but is available for alignment during the extension stage; called soft masking.

See also   filter, lcfilter, lcmask, echofilter, maskextra

W=[integer]

Default: 11 *blastn*, 3 others

Sets the word size for seeding alignments.

See also   T, hitdist, wink

X=[integer]

Default: Variable; depends on scoring parameters

Controls the alignment extension cutoff for ungapped alignments.

See also   gapX

Y=[number]

Default: Variable; depends on scoring parameters

Sets the size of the query sequence.

See also   Z

Z=[number]

Default: Variable; depends on scoring parameters

Sets the size of the database in letters (restest is assumed), but Z may also be used to mean the number of sequences if seqtest is set.

See also   Y, seqtest, restest

xdformat Parameters

xdformat formats BLAST databases from FASTA files. It also reports descriptive information about the database and dumps the entire content to FASTA format.

Here are some examples:

```
xdformat -n files
xdformat -p files
zcat fasta.*.gz | xdformat -o my_db -n -- -
xdformat -n -i database
xdformat -n -r datatbase > fasta_file
```

-A [0..2]

Default: 2

When indexing accession.version identifiers, you have three indexing options:

0   Accession only; version isn't stored

1   Stored as accession.version

2   Stored as both accession only and accession.version

-a [database]

Appends sequences to the named database. If the database is indexed, the appended sequences will also be indexed.

-c [character]

Default: Off

If an invalid letter is encountered, *xdformat* terminates and reports an error message. If this occurs, check the sequence file for errors. After checking, you may either skip illegal characters with -k or change them to a legal character with -c. The typical operation for nucleotides is to set -c N, and for proteins -c X.

See also   -k

-D [integer]

Default: Unlimited

Sets the maximum length for definition lines.

-d [string]

Default: None

Sets a user-defined release date for the database. The date may have 63 characters at most.

See also   -v

-e [file]

Default: *stderr*

Appends information and errors to the named file.

-G

Default: Off

Prefaces each sequence with the database record number in the format of gnl|xdf|#.

-i

Default: Off

Reports descriptive information about a BLAST database. This is useful for determining when a database was created, how many sequences it contains, and if it is indexed.

-K [integer]

Default: Unlimited

Sets the maximum number of identifiers with Control-A separators. This is useful for trimming highly redundant sequences created with *nrdb* or another redundancy purifier that uses Control-A separators.

-k

Default: Off

If an invalid letter is encountered, *xdformat* terminates. If this occurs, you can either skip illegal characters with -k or change them to a legal letter with -c. Check the errors to ensure the input file is formatted properly.

See also   -c

-L [number]

Default: 100000000 (100 million letters)

Sets the maximum sequence length. For optimal performance, break up large sequences into smaller fragments no larger than 1 million letters.

-l [number]

Default: 0

Sets the minimum sequence length.

-M [number]

Default: 96m

Sets the cache size for indexing. For faster indexing, the size may be increased (for example, -M 512m).

-O [4..8]

Default: 4

Sets the number of bytes of precision. The default value allows databases of up to 4 billion amino acids or 16 billion nucleotides. If you expect a database to contain more than this limit, increasing precision by one level multiplies the limit by 256. Setting -O is necessary only if you append to the database because the precision automatically increases appropriately when databases are created.

-P [integer]

Default: 60

This option applies only when dumping the entire content of a database with -r. -P controls the length of the sequence lines; -P 0 puts the whole sequence on one line.

See also   -r

-q [0..3]

Default: 0

Certain files may contain numerous nonfatal errors in their identifier format. -q quiets these errors.

0   No silencing
1   Silences field1 errors
2   Silences field 2 errors
3   Silences all fields

-r

Default: Off

Reports (dumps) the entire database content to *stdout* in FASTA format.

-T [string]

Default: Off

This option lets you restrict indexing of identifiers to a particular database name or tag. The [string] has two parts: part 1 is the name of the database (e.g., gb for GenBank or emb for EMBL—see Chapter 10), and part 2 is either blank or a number.

blank

> Index all identifiers.

0   Don't index.

1   Index only field 1.

2   Index only field 2.

Here are some examples:

> -T emb0 doesn't index EMBL records.
> -T gb1 indexes GenBank accession but not locus.
> -T gb2 indexes GenBank locus but not accession.
> -T gb index both accession and locus of GenBank records.

-v

Default: Off

Sets a user-defined version string for the database (a maximum of 63 characters).

See also   -d

-X

Default: Off

Databases that are formatted but not indexed may be indexed or re-indexed (e.g., with a different indexing scheme) with -X. In the following examples, the two commands on Line 1 are equivalent to the one on Line 2.

```
xdformat -n nt_db ; xdformat -n -X nt_db
xdformat -n -I nt_db
```

xdget Parameters

xdget retrieves files in FASTA format from databases formatted with *xdformat* (not *formatdb*, *pressdb*, or *setdb*). The database must have been indexed prior to using *xdget* (see -I and -X in the previous section "xdformat Parameters").

Here are a few example command lines. If identifiers contain vertical bars, as in the second example, you have to enclose the string in quotes to prevent the shell form interpreting them as pipes. This isn't required for identifier files.

```
xdget -n db 12345
xdget -p nr 'gi|11611819|gb|AAG39070.1|'
xdget -n -f db files_of_ids
```

-A [n, 0]

Default: n

Given an accession number without a version, *xdget* retrieves the latest version number. This parameter is set explicitly with -A n. If -A 0 is set, the earliest version number is retrieved.

See also   -d, -N

-a [integer]

Default: 1

The -a and -b parameters retrieve a subsequence. For example, if you want to retrieve just nucleotides 1 to 100, include -a 1 -b 100. For nucleotide sequences, if -b is greater than -a, the sequence is returned as its reverse-complement.

See also   -b, -r, -t

-b [integer]

Default: 0, end of sequence

See -a above.

-d

Default: Off

Ordinarily, when duplicate identifiers are present, only one is retrieved. With -d, all duplicates are reported. Having duplicate identifiers is generally not a good idea.

See also   -A, -N

-D [integer]

Default: Unlimited

Sets the maximum definition line length. Using definition lines to store arbitrary sequence data is common. This option is useful when you don't need the whole definition line.

-e [file]

Default: *stderr*

Appends messages and errors to log file.

-F

Default: Off

Flushes the output stream after each request. This is useful for preventing I/O deadlocks between communicating processes.

-f

Default: Off

Indicates that files of identifiers are given on the command line. The file format is one identifier per line.

-G

Default: Off

Prefaces each definition line with its record number using the *gnl* namespace. The format is gnl|xdf|#.

-o [file]

Default: *stdout*

Reports FASTA files to the named file rather than *stdout*.

-N [0, n]

Default: 0

For sequences with duplicate identifiers, the first one is retrieved by default. It is set explicitly with -N 0. Setting -N n retrieves the last one. Accession numbers with version numbers have different rules.

See also   -A, -d

-P [integer]

Default: 60

Sets the maximum line length for sequence data. Setting -P 0 puts the entire sequence on one line.

-r

Default: Off

Returns the reverse complement for nucleotide sequences.

-T [string]

Default: Off

This option lets you restrict the lookup of identifiers to a particular database name or tag. For example, to look only in GenBank sequences, use -T gb. For only local, use -T lcl. For tags with multiple identifiers, a numeric suffix identifies which one to select. For example, -T gb1 selects accessions and -T gb2 selects loci. To prevent lookups in a database name, use zero. For example, -T gb0 omits GenBank records.

-t

Default: Off

Translates nt seq.

## PART VI

Appendixes

NCBI Display Formats

NCBI-BLAST has several options for displaying sequence alignments. These options are available for the five basic BLAST programs (BLASTN, BLASTP, BLASTX, TBLASTN, TBLASTX), PSI-BLAST, PHI-BLAST, and MegaBLAST. For all programs, these formats are selected by using the –m option; however, in MegaBLAST, the formats must first be set with the –D 2 option to use classic BLAST formatting. The next section gives a brief description of each option, followed by a detailed explanation and an example.

Brief Descriptions

The alignment display format is set with the –m option followed by a number from 0 to 11 as you can see in the following table.

Option number	Brief description
0	The default pairwise display. Classic BLAST format.
1-6	Various types of query-anchored multiple sequence alignments. The query is anchored and the aligned regions of the subjects are displayed underneath.
7	eXtensible Markup Language (XML) output.
8	Tabular output, without header lines.
9	Tabular output, with header lines.
10	ASN.1 text
11	ASN.1 binary

Detailed Descriptions and Examples

This section includes detailed descriptions of each format, followed by an example. To create the examples, the authors performed a BLASTP search of the coelacanth HoxA11 protein sequence (AAG39070) versus the *HoxDB.pep* database, which is included in the online supplement.

Option 0: Pairwise Alignments

Option 0 is the default alignment and the classic BLAST format. The definition line of the subject is given at the top of each entry, marked with the greater-than sign (>) and followed with the subject's total length. For each HSP of a subject, the score, expect, identities, positives, and gaps are reported and followed by a pairwise alignment. For the pairwise alignment in Figure A-1, the query sequence is shown on the first row and the subject on the third row. Gaps are represented in each as a dash (-). Between the query and subject lies the alignment row, which shows the residue for identities, a plus (+) for positive scoring alignments, and a dot (.) for mismatches. In BLASTN alignments, the middle row has vertical bars (|) for identities and nothing for mismatches.

```
>HoxA11_chick gi|399992|sp|P31258|HXAB_CHICK Homeobox protein Hox-A11 (Ghox-1I)
             (Chox-1.9)
             Length = 297

 Score =  318 bits (816), Expect = 4e-091
 Identities = 163/216 (75%), Positives = 178/216 (82%), Gaps = 14/216 (6%)

Query: 1    YLPSCTYYVSGPDFSSLPSFLPQTPSSRPMTYSYSSNLPQVQPVREVTFRDYAIDTSNKW 60
            YLPSCTYYVSGPDFSSLPSFLPQTPSSRPMTYSYSSNLPQVQPVREVTFR+YAID S+KW
Sbjct: 15   YLPSCTYYVSGPDFSSLPSFLPQTPSSRPMTYSYSSNLPQVQPVREVTFREYAIDPSSKW 74

Query: 61   HPRSNLPHCYSTEEILHRDCLATTTASSIGEIFGKGNANVY-HPGSSTSSNFYNTVGRNG 119
            HPR+NLPHCYS EEI+HRDCL +TT +S+GE+FGK  ANVY HP ++ SSNFY+TVGRNG
Sbjct: 75   HPRNNLPHCYSAEEIMHRDCLPSTTTASMGEVFGKSTANVYHHPSANVSSNFYSTVGRNG 134

Query: 120  VLPQAFDQFFETAYGTTENHSS-DYSADKNSDKIP-----SAATSRSE------TCRETD 167
            VLPQAFDQFFETAYGT EN SS DY  DK+ +K P     +AATS SE
Sbjct: 135  VLPQAFDQFFETAYGTAENPSSADYPPDKSGEKAPAAAGATAATSSSEGGCGGAAAAAGK 194

Query: 168  EKERREES-SSPESSSGNNEEKSSSSSGQRTRKKRC 202
            E+ RR ES SSPESSSGNNEEKS SSSGQRTRKKRC
Sbjct: 195  ERRRPESGSSPESSSGNNEEKSGSSSGQRTRKKRC 230
```

Figure A-1. Option 0: Standard pairwise alignment

Query-Anchored Alignments

All query-anchored formats (1-6) are multiple-sequence alignments. They share the same general form, with the query repeated at the top of each line and all matching subjects aligned on subsequent lines. The difference between showing identities and not showing them is counterintuitive. For the options that show identities (1 and 3), identical residues are symbolized with a dot (.), similar amino acids are in uppercase, and mismatches are in lowercase. For the options without identities (2, 4, 5 and 6) every residue is shown with identities and similar residues in uppercase and mismatches are in lowercase.

Option 1: Query-Anchored Showing Identities

In the format shown in Figure A-2, the identical residues are represented by a dot (.) and insertions and deletions are represented in the subject sequences, but not the query.

```
QUERY         1  YLPSCTYYVSGPDFSSLPSFLPQTPSSRPMTYSYSSNLPQVQPVREVTFRDYAIDTSNKW 60
HoxA11_chick 15  ..............................................E....p.S.. 74
HoxA11_human 14  ..............................................E...EpAT.. 73
HoxA11_mouse 15  ..............................................E...EpAT.. 74
HoxD11_shark  2  ..........A.....VsT...p.t.cQ-..Fp......a......LS....GLEhpT.. 60
HoxD11_chick 15  ...G.A....ps...Tk....s.S-..cq..Fp......H.......A..E.GLErG-.. 72
HoxD11_newt  15  ...G.A....psE..Tkt...s.g-..c.V.Fp......H......MA..E.Gwrr-.. 72
HoxC11_human 33  ........M--.E..TVs.....A..-.qIS.p..AQV.---.....S----.GLEp.G.. 83
HOxD11_mouse  2  ...G.A...Aps..A.k....s.-...cq..Fp......H.......A....GLErA-.. 60
                                                              \
                                                              |
                                                              A

HoxD11_human 15  ...G.A...Aps..A.k....s.-...cq..Fp......H.......A....GLErA-.. 73
                                                              \
                                                              |
                                                              A
```

Figure A-2. Option 1: Query-anchored showing identities

Option 2: Query-Anchored, No Identities

This format (Figure A-3) is the same as Option 1 (Figure A-2), but all residues are shown with identities and positives in uppercase and mismatches in lowercase. As with Option 1, insertions and deletions are represented in the subject sequences, but not the query.

```
QUERY         1  YLPSCTYYVSGPDFSSLPSFLPQTPSSRPMTYSYSSNLPQVQPVREVTFRDYAIDTSNKW 60
HoxA11_chick 15  YLPSCTYYVSGPDFSSLPSFLPQTPSSRPMTYSYSSNLPQVQPVREVTFREYAIDpSSKW 74
HoxA11_human 14  YLPSCTYYVSGPDFSSLPSFLPQTPSSRPMTYSYSSNLPQVQPVREVTFREYAIEpATKW 73
HoxA11_mouse 15  YLPSCTYYVSGPDFSSLPSFLPQTPSSRPMTYSYSSNLPQVQPVREVTFREYAIEpATKW 74
HoxD11_shark  2  YLPSCTYYVSAPDFSSVsTFLPpTtScQ-MTFpYSSNLaQVQPVRELSFRDYGLEhpTKW 60
HoxD11_chick 15  YLPGCAYYVSpsDFSTkPSFLsQS-SScqMTFpYSSNLPHVQPVREVAFREYGLErG-KW 72
HoxD11_newt  15  YLPGCAYYVSpsEFSTktSFLsQg-SScPVTFpYSSNLPHVQPVREMAFREYGwrrS-KW 72
HoxC11_human 33  YLPSCTYYM--PEFSTVsSFLPQAPS-RqISYpYSAQVP---PVREVS---YGLEpSGKW 83
HOxD11_mouse  2  YLPGCAYYVApsDFASkPSFLsQ-PSScqMTFpYSSNLPHVQPVREVAFRDYGLErA-KW 60
                                                              \
                                                              |
                                                              A

HoxD11_human 15  YLPGCAYYVApsDFASkPSFLsQ-PSScqMTFpYSSNLPHVQPVREVAFRDYGLErA-KW 73
                                                              \
                                                              |
                                                              A
```

Figure A-3. Option 2: Query-anchored, no identities

Option 3: Flat Query-Anchored Showing Identities

Same as Option 1 (Figure A-2), but insertions or deletions in Figure A-4 are padded in the query, rather than shown in the subjects. This is a more compact format than the nonflat one, which has residues dangling down to represent insertions within the subject sequences.

```
QUERY        1  YLPSCTYYVSGPDFSSLPSFLPQTPSSRPMTYSYSSNL-PQVQPVREVTFRDYAIDTSNK 59
HoxA11_chick  15  ................................................-...........E....p.S. 73
HoxA11_human  14  ................................................-...........E....EpAT. 72
HoxA11_mouse  15  ................................................-...........E...EpAT. 73
HoxD11_shark   2  ..........A.....VsT...p.t.cQ-..Fp.....-a.......LS....GLEhpT. 59
HoxD11_chick  15  ...G.A...ps...Tk....s.S-..cq..Fp.....-.H.......A..E.GLErG-. 71
HoxD11_newt   15  ...G.A...psE..Tkt...s.g-..c.V.Fp.....-.H.......MA..E.Gwrr.-. 71
HoxC11_human  33  ........M--.E..TVs....A..-.qIS.p..AQV-.-----...S---.GLEp.G. 82
HOxD11_mouse   2  ...G.A...Aps..A.k....s.-...cq..Fp.....a.H.......A....GLErA-. 59
HoxD11_human  15  ...G.A...Aps..A.k....s.-...cq..Fp.....a.H.......A....GLErA-. 72
```

Figure A-4. Option 3: Flat query-anchored showing identities

Option 4: Flat Query-Anchored, No Identities

This format is the same as Option 2 (Figure A-3), but insertions or deletions in Figure A-5 are padded in the query, rather than shown in the subjects. Thus, the entire multiple sequence alignment is flat, without subject insertions dangling down.

```
QUERY        1  YLPSCTYYVSGPDFSSLPSFLPQTPSSRPMTYSYSSNL-PQVQPVREVTFRDYAIDTSNK 59
HoxA11_chick  15  YLPSCTYYVSGPDFSSLPSFLPQTPSSRPMTYSYSSNL-PQVQPVREVTFREYAIDpSSK 73
HoxA11_human  14  YLPSCTYYVSGPDFSSLPSFLPQTPSSRPMTYSYSSNL-PQVQPVREVTFREYAIEpATK 72
HoxA11_mouse  15  YLPSCTYYVSGPDFSSLPSFLPQTPSSRPMTYSYSSNL-PQVQPVREVTFREYAIEpATK 73
HoxD11_shark   2  YLPSCTYYVSAPDFSSVsTFLPpTtScQ-MTFpYSSNL-aQVQPVRELSFRDYGLEhpTK 59
HoxD11_chick  15  YLPGCAYYVSpsDFSTkPSFLsQS-SScqMTFpYSSNL-PHVQPVREVAFREYGLErG-K 71
HoxD11_newt   15  YLPGCAYYVSpsEFSTktSFLsQg-SScPVTFpYSSNL-PHVQPVREMAFREYGwrrS-K 71
HoxC11_human  33  YLPSCTYYM--PEFSTVsSFLPQAPS-RqISYpYSAQV-P---PVREVS---YGLEpSGK 82
HOxD11_mouse   2  YLPGCAYYVApsDFASkPSFLsQ-PSScqMTFpYSSNLaPHVQPVREVAFRDYGLErA-K 59
HoxD11_human  15  YLPGCAYYVApsDFASkPSFLsQ-PSScqMTFpYSSNLaPHVQPVREVAFRDYGLErA-K 72
```

Figure A-5. Option 4: Flat query-anchored, no identities

Option 5: Query-Anchored, No Identities, and Blunt Ends

Blunt-end options extend the HSPs out to the beginning and end of the entire query sequence so that each HSP is shown in all lines of the alignment. In Figure A-6, the HoxD11_chick and HoxD11_human entries have additional HSPs that are seen later in the alignment (not shown). You see the dashes (-) at the beginning of the second HSP of each, which makes the entry blunt.

Option 6: Flat Query-Anchored, No Identities, and Blunt Ends

Same as Option 5 (Figure A-6), but the insertion and deletion characters in Figure A-7 are inserted into the query, making it flat, without any dangling insertions in the subject alignment lines.

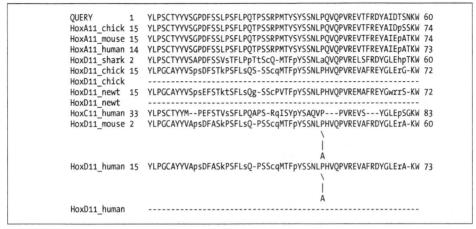

```
QUERY         1  YLPSCTYYVSGPDFSSLPSFLPQTPSSRPMTYSYSSNLPQVQPVREVTFRDYAIDTSNKW 60
HoxA11_chick 15  YLPSCTYYVSGPDFSSLPSFLPQTPSSRPMTYSYSSNLPQVQPVREVTFREYAIDpSSKW 74
HoxA11_mouse 15  YLPSCTYYVSGPDFSSLPSFLPQTPSSRPMTYSYSSNLPQVQPVREVTFREYAIEpATKW 74
HoxA11_human 14  YLPSCTYYVSGPDFSSLPSFLPQTPSSRPMTYSYSSNLPQVQPVREVTFREYAIEpATKW 73
HoxD11_shark  2  YLPSCTYYVSAPDFSSVsTFLPpTtScQ-MTFpYSSNLaQVQPVRELSFRDYGLEhpTKW 60
HoxD11_chick 15  YLPGCAYYVSpsDFSTkPSFLsQS-SScqMTFpYSSNLPHVQPVREVAFREYGLErG-KW 72
HoxD11_chick     -----------------------------------------------------------
HoxD11_newt  15  YLPGCAYYVSpsEFSTktSFLsQg-SScPVTFpYSSNLPHVQPVREMAFREYGwrrS-KW 72
HoxD11_newt      -----------------------------------------------------------
HoxC11_human 33  YLPSCTYYM--PEFSTVsSFLPQAPS-RqISYpYSAQVP---PVREVS---YGLEpSGKW 83
HoxD11_mouse  2  YLPGCAYYVApsDFASkPSFLsQ-PSScqMTFpYSSNLPHVQPVREVAFRDYGLErA-KW 60
                                               \
                                                |
                                                A


HoxD11_human 15  YLPGCAYYVApsDFASkPSFLsQ-PSScqMTFpYSSNLPHVQPVREVAFRDYGLErA-KW 73
                                               \
                                                |
                                                A

HoxD11_human     -----------------------------------------------------------
```

Figure A-6. Option 5: Query-anchored, no identities and blunt ends

```
QUERY         1  YLPSCTYYVSGPDFSSLPSFLPQTPSSRPMTYSYSSNL-PQVQPVREVTFRDYAIDTSNK 59
HoxA11_chick 15  YLPSCTYYVSGPDFSSLPSFLPQTPSSRPMTYSYSSNL-PQVQPVREVTFREYAIDpSSK 73
HoxA11_mouse 15  YLPSCTYYVSGPDFSSLPSFLPQTPSSRPMTYSYSSNL-PQVQPVREVTFREYAIEpATK 73
HoxA11_human 14  YLPSCTYYVSGPDFSSLPSFLPQTPSSRPMTYSYSSNL-PQVQPVREVTFREYAIEpATK 72
HoxD11_shark  2  YLPSCTYYVSAPDFSSVsTFLPpTtScQ-MTFpYSSNL-aQVQPVRELSFRDYGLEhpTK 59
HoxD11_chick 15  YLPGCAYYVSpsDFSTkPSFLsQS-SScqMTFpYSSNL-PHVQPVREVAFREYGLErG-K 71
HoxD11_chick     -----------------------------------------------------------
HoxD11_newt  15  YLPGCAYYVSpsEFSTktSFLsQg-SScPVTFpYSSNL-PHVQPVREMAFREYGwrrS-K 71
HoxD11_newt      -----------------------------------------------------------
HoxC11_human 33  YLPSCTYYM--PEFSTVsSFLPQAPS-RqISYpYSAQV-P---PVREVS---YGLEpSGK 82
HoxD11_mouse  2  YLPGCAYYVApsDFASkPSFLsQ-PSScqMTFpYSSNLaPHVQPVREVAFRDYGLErA-K 59
HoxD11_human 15  YLPGCAYYVApsDFASkPSFLsQ-PSScqMTFpYSSNLaPHVQPVREVAFRDYGLErA-K 72
HoxD11_human     -----------------------------------------------------------
```

Figure A-7. Option 6: Flat query-anchored, no identities and blunt ends

Option 7: XML

The BLAST eXtensible Markup Language (XML) is specified by the Data Type Definition (DTD) file, *NCBI_BlastOutput.dtd*, which is located at *http://www.ncbi.nlm.nih.gov/dtd/*. This format isn't meant to be human-readable, but Figure A-8 shows the first few lines from the BLASTP search so you can get a feel for how XML looks.

Option 8: Tabular, Without Comment Lines

Tabular formats are very nice for easy parsing. All fields in Figure A-9 are tab-delimited. The fields are query id, subject id, percent identity, alignment length, mismatches, gap openings, query start, query end, subject start, subject end, e-value, and bit score.

```
<?xml version="1.0"?>
<!DOCTYPE BlastOutput PUBLIC "-//NCBI//NCBI BlastOutput/EN" "NCBI_BlastOutput.dtd">
<BlastOutput>
  <BlastOutput_program>blastp</BlastOutput_program>
  <BlastOutput_version>blastp 2.2.5 [Nov-16-2002]</BlastOutput_version>
  <BlastOutput_reference>~Reference: Altschul, Stephen F., Thomas L. Madden, Alejandro
A. Schaffer, ~Jinghui Zhang, Zheng Zhang, Webb Miller, and David J. Lipman (1997),
~&quot;Gapped BLAST and PSI-BLAST: a new generation of protein database
search~programs&quot;,  Nucleic Acids Res. 25:3389-3402.</BlastOutput_reference>
  <BlastOutput_db>HoxDB_custom.pep</BlastOutput_db>
  <BlastOutput_query-ID>lcl|QUERY</BlastOutput_query-ID>
  <BlastOutput_query-def>AAG39070 gi|11611819|gb|AAG39070.1| Hoxa-11 [Latimeria
chalumnae]</BlastOutput_query-def>
  <BlastOutput_query-len>202</BlastOutput_query-len>
  <BlastOutput_param>
    <Parameters>
      <Parameters_matrix>BLOSUM62</Parameters_matrix>
      <Parameters_expect>10</Parameters_expect>
      <Parameters_gap-open>11</Parameters_gap-open>
      <Parameters_gap-extend>1</Parameters_gap-extend>
      <Parameters_filter>m S</Parameters_filter>
    </Parameters>
  </BlastOutput_param>
```

Figure A-8. Option 7: XML format

```
AAG39070  HoxA11_chick  75.46  216   39   5   1   202   15   230   3.8e-091   318.9
AAG39070  HoxA11_human  65.67  233   49   6   1   202   14   246   3.8e-083   292.4
AAG39070  HoxA11_mouse  64.66  232   52   6   1   202   15   246   7.1e-082   288.1
AAG39070  HoxD11_shark  50.25  203   94   5   1   202   2    198   3.2e-050   183.0
AAG39070  HoxD11_chick  44.39  205  105   7   1   202   15   213   5.7e-039   145.6
AAG39070  HoxD11_newt   41.87  203  110   5   1   202   15   210   9.1e-037   138.3
AAG39070  HoxC11_human  38.79  214  110   9   1   202   33   237   1.1e-034   131.3
AAG39070  HOxD11_mouse  33.85  260  109  11   1   202   2    256   2.5e-026   103.6
AAG39070  HoxD11_human  63.93   61   19   3   1    60   15    73   2.1e-017   73.94
AAG39070  HoxD11_human  36.67  120   54   4  102   202  155   271   2.2e-014   63.93
```

Figure A-9. Option 8: Tabular, without comment lines

Option 9: Tabular, with Comment Lines

The format of Figure A-10 is the same as that in Option 8 (Figure A-9), except it
includes four header lines at the top of each query that describe the BLAST program,
the query, the database, and the fields of the alignment.

Option 10: ASN.1 Text Format

Abstract Syntax Notation One (ASN.1) is an International Standards Organization
(ISO) data format. ASN.1 is used to mark up data for reliable, robust exchange. Like
XML, it isn't meant to be human-readable, but Example A-1 shows the first few lines

```
                # BLASTP 2.2.5 [Nov-16-2002]
                # Query: AAG39070 gi|11611819|gb|AAG39070.1| Hoxa-11 [Latimeria chalumnae]
                # Database: HoxDB_custom.pep
                # Fields: Query id, Subject id, % identity, alignment length, mismatches, gap
                openings, q. start, q. end, s. start, s. end, e-value, bit score
                AAG39070  HoxA11_chick  75.46  216  39   5   1  202  15  230  3.8e-091  318.9
                AAG39070  HoxA11_human  65.67  233  49   6   1  202  14  246  3.8e-083  292.4
                AAG39070  HoxA11_mouse  64.66  232  52   6   1  202  15  246  7.1e-082  288.1
                AAG39070  HoxD11_shark  50.25  203  94   5   1  202   2  198  3.2e-050  183.0
                AAG39070  HoxD11_chick  44.39  205  105  7   1  202  15  213  5.7e-039  145.6
                AAG39070  HoxD11_newt   41.87  203  110  5   1  202  15  210  9.1e-037  138.3
                AAG39070  HoxC11_human  38.79  214  110  9   1  202  33  237  1.1e-034  131.3
                AAG39070  HOxD11_mouse  33.85  260  109  11  1  202   2  256  2.5e-026  103.6
                AAG39070  HoxD11_human  63.93   61   19  3   1   60  15   73  2.1e-017  73.94
                AAG39070  HoxD11_human  36.67  120   54  4  102  202 155  271  2.2e-014  63.93
```

Figure A-10. Option 9: Tabular, with comment lines

of a BLASTP search so you can get a feel for the syntax. For more information on the
NCBI use of ASN.1, see *http://www.ncbi.nlm.nih.gov/Sitemap/Summary/asn1.html.*

Example A-1. ASN.1 text format

```
Seq-annot ::= {
   desc {
     user {
       type
         str "Hist Seqalign" ,
       data {
         {
           label
             str "Hist Seqalign" ,
           data
             bool TRUE } } } ,
     user {
       type
         str "Blast Type" ,
       data {
         {
           label
             str "BLASTP" ,
           data
             int 2 } } } } ,
   data
     align {
       {
         type partial ,
         dim 2 ,
         score {
           {
             id
               str "score" ,
             value
               int 699 } ,
           {
             id
```

```
            str "e_value" ,
          value
            real { 139321249, 10, -85 } } ,
        {
          id
            str "bit_score" ,
          value
            real { 273862735, 10, -6 } } ,
        {
          id
            str "num_ident" ,
          value
            int 140 } } ,
```

Option 11: ASN.1 Binary Format

This option produces the same ASN.1 output as Option 10, but in binary format. It isn't readable and therefore isn't shown.

Nucleotide Scoring Schemes

Nucleotide scoring schemes are often summarized by their target frequency, which is the expected frequency of nucleotide pairs. This frequency is usually expressed as the expected percent identity. For example, the +1/-1 match/mismatch values have a target frequency of 75 percent identity. But this is true only for ungapped alignments between sequences of infinite length. Short sequences and gapped alignment change the true target frequency. In the following table, the target frequencies for a variety of match (+), mismatch (-), and simple gap costs (gap) are calculated for pairs of sequences of length 100, 500, and 1,000 by performing local alignments of random nucleotide sequences of unbiased composition. The theoretical target frequency (TF) is included for comparison.

+	-	Gap	TF	100	500	1,000
1	1	1	75	55	49	49
1	1	2	75	79	70	69
1	1	3	75	85	79	79
1	2	2	95	93	89	88
1	2	3	95	98	96	96
1	2	4	95	98	97	97
1	3	3	99	99	99	98
5	4	4	65	51	48	48
5	4	5	65	53	49	49
5	4	6	65	55	50	49
5	4	7	65	59	51	50
5	4	8	65	62	52	50
5	4	9	65	64	55	53
5	4	10	65	67	59	57
5	4	11	65	69	61	60
5	4	12	65	71	63	62

+	-	Gap	TF	100	500	1,000
5	5	5	75	55	49	49
5	5	6	75	59	51	50
5	5	7	75	64	55	53
5	5	8	75	70	61	59
5	5	9	75	72	65	64
5	5	10	75	79	70	69
5	5	11	75	80	73	71
5	5	12	75	81	75	74
5	5	13	75	82	76	76
5	5	14	75	82	77	77
5	5	15	75	85	79	79
5	6	6	82	62	53	51
5	6	7	82	69	60	58
5	6	8	82	75	67	65
5	6	9	82	79	73	71
5	6	10	82	83	77	75
5	6	11	82	85	79	79
5	6	12	82	87	81	81
5	6	15	82	90	85	84
5	6	18	82	90	87	86
5	7	7	87	73	64	63
5	7	8	87	78	72	70
5	7	9	87	83	77	76
5	7	10	87	87	82	81
5	7	11	87	89	84	83
5	7	12	87	90	86	85
5	7	13	87	91	88	87
5	7	14	87	91	88	87
5	7	21	87	93	91	90
5	8	8	90	81	75	73
5	8	9	90	85	80	79
5	8	10	90	89	85	84
5	8	11	90	91	87	86
5	8	12	90	92	89	88
5	8	13	90	93	90	89
5	8	14	90	93	91	90
5	8	15	90	94	92	91

+	-	Gap	TF	100	500	1,000
5	8	16	90	94	93	92
5	8	24	90	95	94	93
5	9	9	93	86	82	81
5	9	10	93	90	86	85
5	9	11	93	92	89	89
5	9	12	93	93	91	90
5	9	13	93	93	92	91
5	9	14	93	94	92	91
5	9	15	93	95	93	92
5	9	16	93	95	94	93
5	9	17	93	95	94	93
5	9	18	93	95	94	94
5	9	27	93	96	95	94
5	10	10	95	93	89	88
5	10	11	95	94	92	90
5	10	12	95	95	93	91
5	10	13	95	95	94	93
5	10	14	95	95	94	96
5	10	15	95	98	96	96
5	10	20	95	98	97	97
5	10	30	95	98	98	97

NCBI-BLAST Scoring Schemes

'Statistical parameters for gapped alignment are determined empirically from random sequence alignments. NCBI-BLAST provides several combinations of scoring matrices and gap costs. These are the only combinations of gap penalties that can be used with a given matrix. The default values for each matrix are in boldface in the following table. If your BLAST distribution doesn't have all the listed matrices, you can find more at *ftp://ftp.ncbi.nih.gov/blast/matrices*.

NCBI-BLAST Matrices and Gap Costs

Matrix	G	E	λ	K	H
BLOSUM62	32767	32767	0.318	0.134	0.401
	11	2	0.297	0.082	0.27
	10	2	0.291	0.075	0.23
	12	1	0.283	0.059	0.19
	9	2	0.279	0.058	0.19
	8	2	0.264	0.045	0.15
	11	**1**	**0.267**	**0.041**	**0.14**
	10	1	0.243	0.024	0.10
	7	2	0.239	0.027	0.10
	6	2	0.201	0.012	0.061
	9	1	0.206	0.010	0.052
BLOSUM80	32767	32767	0.343	0.177	0.657
	25	2	0.342	0.17	0.66
	13	2	0.336	0.15	0.57
	9	2	0.319	0.11	0.42
	11	1	0.314	0.095	0.35
	8	2	0.308	0.090	0.35

Matrix	G	E	λ	K	H
	10	**1**	**0.299**	**0.071**	**0.27**
	7	2	0.293	0.070	0.27
	9	1	0.279	0.048	0.20
	6	2	0.268	0.045	0.19
BLOSUM90	32767	32767	0.335	0.190	0.755
	9	2	0.310	0.12	0.46
	11	1	0.302	0.093	0.39
	8	2	0.300	0.099	0.39
	7	2	0.283	0.072	0.30
	10	**1**	**0.290**	**0.075**	**0.28**
	6	2	0.259	0.048	0.22
	9	1	0.265	0.044	0.20
BLOSUM50	32767	32767	0.232	0.112	0.336
	16	2	0.215	0.066	0.20
	13	3	0.212	0.063	0.19
	19	1	0.212	0.57	0.18
	15	2	0.210	0.058	0.17
	12	3	0.206	0.055	0.17
	18	1	0.207	0.050	0.15
	14	2	0.202	0.045	0.14
	11	3	0.197	0.042	0.14
	17	1	0.198	0.037	0.12
	13	**2**	**0.193**	**0.035**	**0.12**
	10	3	0.186	0.031	0.11
	16	1	0.186	0.025	0.10
	12	2	0.181	0.025	0.095
	9	3	0.172	0.022	0.082
	15	1	0.171	0.015	0.063
BLOSUM45	32767	32767	0.229	0.092	0.251
	13	3	0.207	0.049	0.14
	16	2	0.210	0.051	0.14
	15	2	0.203	0.041	0.12
	19	1	0.205	0.040	0.11
	12	3	0.199	0.039	0.11
	18	1	0.198	0.032	0.10
	14	**2**	**0.195**	**0.032**	**0.10**
	11	3	0.190	0.031	0.095

Matrix	G	E	λ	K	H
	13	2	0.185	0.024	0.084
	17	1	0.189	0.024	0.078
	10	3	0.179	0.023	0.075
	16	1	0.176	0.016	0.063
	12	2	0.171	0.016	0.061
PAM250	32767	32767	0.218	0.0877	0.287
	15	3	0.205	0.049	0.13
	17	2	0.204	0.047	0.12
	14	3	0.200	0.043	0.12
	21	1	0.204	0.045	0.11
	16	2	0.198	0.038	0.11
	20	1	0.199	0.037	0.10
	13	3	0.194	0.036	0.10
	15	2	0.191	0.031	0.087
	12	3	0.186	0.029	0.085
	19	1	0.192	0.029	0.083
	14	**2**	**0.182**	**0.024**	**0.073**
	18	1	0.183	0.021	0.070
	11	3	0.174	0.020	0.070
	13	2	0.171	0.017	0.059
	17	1	0.171	0.014	0.052
PAM30	32767	32767	0.336	0.277	1.82
	10	1	0.309	0.15	0.88
	7	2	0.305	0.15	0.87
	6	2	0.287	0.11	0.68
	9	**1**	**0.294**	**0.11**	**0.61**
	5	2	0.264	0.079	0.45
	8	1	0.270	0.072	0.40
PAM70	32767	32767	0.328	0.222	1.11
	8	2	0.301	0.12	0.54
	11	1	0.305	0.12	0.52
	7	2	0.286	0.093	0.43
	10	**1**	**0.291**	**0.91**	**0.41**
	6	2	0.264	0.064	0.29
	9	1	0.270	0.060	0.28

blast-imager.pl

blast-imager.pl creates a graphical summary of a BLAST report using Thomas Boutell's GD graphics library (*http://www.boutell.com/gd*), which has been ported to Perl by Lincoln Stein (*http://stein.cshl.org/WWW/software/GD*). The latest versions support PNG or JPEG format, but not GIF. Depending on which GD installation you have, you may want to edit the output section in the program. Just toggle the comments from one output to another.

To use the *blast-imager.pl* program, the data must be in NCBI tabular format (-m 8) as described in Appendix A. Appendix E presents a program for converting standard BLAST output to tabular format. The simplest way to use *blast-imager.pl* is to have it read an entire BLAST report (but not concatenated BLAST reports).

```
blast-imager.pl blast_table > blast.gif
```

In Figure D-1, a *Takifugu rubripes* genomic sequence (AY016024.1) containing an alpha globin gene cluster was used to search the *nr* protein database. The output of the BLASTX report was converted to tabular format with *blast2table.pl* in the region of 34,000 to 35,000.

```
blast2table.pl -m 34000 -n 35000 report | blast-imager.pl > fugu.gif
```

Database matches and alignments are shown in the order they appear in the report. Only the best alignments are color-coded (the exact number is limited by the image size). Query coordinates are given above the subject coordinates for each alignment. A minus strand is indicated by a hyphen (-) at the subject end (as shown in Figure D-1). The number of alignments at each position in the query is given by the thin black lines under the query sequence. Each line in this figure represents 90 alignments. This scale changes as necessary.

The complete program is listed here and may be downloaded from *as blast-imager.pl* from this book's web site.

```
#!/usr/bin/perl -w
# blast-imager.pl
use strict;
use GD;
```

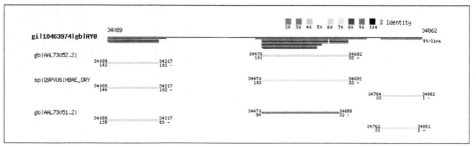

Figure D-1. Selected region of a BLASTX report

```
# Parse tabular data
my ($Q, %S, @S);
my ($MAX, $MIN, $HSPs) = (0, 1e20, 0);
while (<>) {
    my ($q, $id, $p, $l, $m, $g, $qb, $qe, $sb, $se, $e, $b) = split;
    $Q =$q;
    if ($qb > $qe) {($qb, $qe, $sb, $se) = ($qe, $qb, $se, $sb)}
    $MAX = $qe if $qe > $MAX;
    $MIN = $qb if $qb < $MIN;
    push @S, $id if not defined $S{$id};
    push @{$S{$id}}, [$qb, $qe, $sb, $se, $p];
    $HSPs++;
}

# Setup graph
my ($L, $B, $R, $H, $F) = (150, 600, 50, 40, 20); # graph regions
my ($W, $Hsep, $Ssep) = (3, 14, 18); # line width and spacing
my $vsize = $H + $F + $Hsep * $HSPs + $Ssep * (keys %S);
$vsize = 100 if $vsize < 100;
$vsize = 600 if $vsize > 600;
my $hsize = $L + $B + $R;
my $SCALE = $B / ($MAX - $MIN + 1);
my $image = new GD::Image($hsize, $vsize);

# Colors
my @Color;
my @data = ([0,0,0], [196,0,255], [0,0,255], [0,255,255], [0,255,0],
    [255,255,0], [255,196,0], [255,0,0], [128,128,128]);
for (my $i = 0; $i < @data; $i++) {
    $Color[$i] = $image->colorAllocate(@{$data[$i]});
}
my $White = $image->colorAllocate(255,255,255);
my $Black = $Color[0];

# Header
$image->filledRectangle(0, 0, $hsize, $vsize, $White);
$image->string(gdMediumBoldFont, 5, $H-8, substr($Q,0,18), $Black);
$image->line($L, $H, $L+$B, $H, $Black);
$image->string(gdSmallFont, $L, $H-20, $MIN, $Black);
$image->string(gdSmallFont, $L+$B, $H-20, $MAX, $Black);
```

```perl
# Percent identity key
$image->string(gdSmallFont, 670, 5, "% Identity", $Black);
for (my $i = 20; $i <= 100; $i += 10) {
    my $x = $L+$B/2 + $i*2;
    $image->filledRectangle($x, 5, $x+10, 15, colormap($i));
    $image->string(gdTinyFont, $x, 17, $i, $Black);
}

# Alignments
my @Depth;
my $v = 0;
foreach my $id (@S) {
    $v += $Ssep;
    $image->string(gdSmallFont, 10, $H+$v+9, substr($id,0,18), $Black);
    foreach my $hsp (@{$S{$id}}) {
        $v += $Hsep;
        my ($qb, $qe, $sb, $se, $pct) = @$hsp;
        my $strand = $sb < $se ? '+' : '-';
        my ($x1, $x2, $y) = (scale($qb), scale($qe), $H+$v);
        foreach my $x ($x1..$x2) {$Depth[$x]++}
        my $c = colormap($pct);
        $image->filledRectangle($x1, $y, $x2, $y+$W, $c);
        $image->string(gdTinyFont, $x1 -(5*length($qb)), $y-5, $qb, $Black);
        $image->string(gdTinyFont, $x2+2, $y-5, $qe, $Black);
        $image->string(gdTinyFont, $x1 -(5*length($sb)), $y+2, $sb, $Black);
        $image->string(gdTinyFont, $x2+2, $y+2, "$se $strand", $Black);
    }
}

# Alignment depth
my $MaxDepth = 0;
foreach my $d (@Depth) {$MaxDepth = $d if defined $d and $d > $MaxDepth}
my $Dscale = int($MaxDepth/10) +1;
$image->string(gdTinyFont, $L+$B+2, $H+2, "$Dscale/line", $Black);
for (my $i = 0; $i < @Depth; $i++) {
    next unless defined $Depth[$i];
    my $level = $Depth[$i]/$Dscale +1;
    for (my $j = 0; $j < $level; $j++) {
        $image->line($i, $H+$j*2, $i, $H+$j*2, $Black);
    }
}

# Output (edit this for your installation/taste)
print $image->png;
# print $image->jpg;
# print $image->gif;

sub colormap {
    my ($value) = @_;
    my $n = ($value >= 100) ? 0: int((109 - $value) / 10);
    return defined $Color[$n] ? $Color[$n] : $Color[@Color-1];
}
```

```
sub scale {
    my ($x) = @_;
    my $scale = ($x - $MIN) * $SCALE + $L;
    return $scale;
}
```

blast2table.pl

It's often useful to have both the standard report and tabular data for the same search. This program converts standard WU-BLAST or NCBI-BLAST output to the NCBI tabular format (-m 8) described in Appendix A. It supports concatenated BLAST reports and is more efficient than most full-featured BLAST parsers. *blast2table.pl* can be used either on a file or in a pipe:

```
blast2table.pl my_blast_output > my_table_output
blastp nr query | blast2table.pl > table_from_wu-blast
```

The Unix *tee* program can create both the standard output and a table at the same time:

```
blastall -p blastp -d nr -i query | tee standard | blast2table.pl > table
```

blast2table.pl also has a few useful filtering options (see Table E-1). The following command displays only those with an alignment of over 50 percent identity and with a bit score greater than 20:

```
blast2table.pl -p 50 -b 20 blast_output
```

Table E-1. blast2table.pl options

Option	Description
-b	Minimum number of bits for each alignment
-e	Maximum E-value for each alignment or alignment group
-m	Minimum coordinate of the query sequence
-n	Maximum coordinate of the query sequence
-p	Minimum percent identity for each alignment

The complete program is listed next and may be downloaded as *blast2table.pl* from this book's web site.

```
#!/usr/bin/perl -w
use strict;
use Getopt::Std;
```

```perl
use vars qw($opt_p $opt_b $opt_e $opt_m $opt_n);
getopts('p:b:e:m:n:');
my $PERCENT = $opt_p ? $opt_p : 0;
my $BITS    = $opt_b ? $opt_b : 0;
my $EXPECT  = $opt_e ? $opt_e : 1e30;
my $START   = $opt_m ? $opt_m : 0;
my $END     = $opt_n ? $opt_n : 1e30;

my ($Query, $Sbjct);
my $HSP = "";
while (<>) {
    if    (/^Query=\s+(\S+)/) {outputHSP(); $Query = $1}
    elsif (/^>(\S+)/)         {outputHSP(); $Sbjct = $1}
    elsif (/^ Score = /) {
        outputHSP();
        my @stat = ($_);
        while (<>) {
            last unless /\S/;
            push @stat, $_
        }
        my $stats = join("", @stat);
        my ($bits) = $stats =~ /(\d\S+) bits/;
        my ($expect) = $stats =~ /Expect\S* = ([\d\-\.e]+)/;
        $expect = "1$expect" if $expect = ~/^e/;
        my ($match, $total, $percent)
            = $stats =~ /Identities = (\d+)\/(\d+) \(((\d+)%\)/;
        my $mismatch = $total - $match;

        $HSP = {bits => $bits, expect => $expect, mismatch => $mismatch,
            percent => $percent, q_begin => 0, q_end => 0, q_align => "",
            s_begin => 0, s_end => 0, s_align => ""};
    }
    elsif (/^Query:\s+(\d+)\s+(\S+)\s+(\d+)/) {
        $HSP->{q_begin}  = $1 unless $HSP->{q_begin};
        $HSP->{q_end}    = $3;
        $HSP->{q_align} .= $2;
    }
    elsif (/^Sbjct:\s+(\d+)\s+(\S+)\s+(\d+)/) {
        $HSP->{s_begin}  = $1 unless $HSP->{s_begin};
        $HSP->{s_end}    = $3;
        $HSP->{s_align} .= $2;
    }
}
outputHSP();

sub outputHSP {
    return unless $HSP;
    return if $HSP->{percent}  < $PERCENT;
    return if $HSP->{bits}     < $BITS;
    return if $HSP->{expect}   > $EXPECT;
    return if ($HSP->{q_begin} < $START or $HSP->{q_end} < $START);
    return if ($HSP->{q_begin} > $END   or $HSP->{q_end} > $END);
    print join("\t", $Query, $Sbjct, $HSP->{percent},
```

```
            length($HSP->{q_align}), $HSP->{mismatch},
            countGaps($HSP->{q_align}) + countGaps($HSP->{s_align}),
            $HSP->{q_begin}, $HSP->{q_end}, $HSP->{s_begin}, $HSP->{s_end},
            $HSP->{expect}, $HSP->{bits}), "\n";
        $HSP = "";
    }

sub countGaps {
    my ($string) = @_;
    my $count = 0;
    while ($string =~ /\-+/g) {$count++}
    return $count;
}
```

Glossary

1°

The abbreviation for primary. 1° sequence refers to the letters of DNA, RNA, or protein. 1° transcript refers to an unprocessed RNA that still contains its introns.

2°

The abbreviation for secondary. Most frequently used for generalizing protein and RNA structures; for example, the α-helix and hair-pin are common 2° structures.

3′

The end of a nucleic acid sequence; often used with UTR.

5′

The start of a nucleic acid (DNA or RNA) sequence; often used in conjunction with UTR (e.g., 5′UTR). Nucleotide sequences are conventionally written with the 5′ end at the left. DNA molecules are usually double-stranded but when written, usually only the 5′ to 3′ strand is displayed. The complementary strand has reversed polarity (3′ to 5′).

aa

The abbreviation for an amino acid that is often used when describing the length of a protein (e.g., the average protein is about 300 aa long).

allele

A form of a gene. Typically, the most common form is called *wild-type*, and each allele is given a specific (and often obscure) name.

amino acid

The basic building block for all proteins. There are 20 common amino acids.

Arabidopsis thaliana

Known by its common name, thale cress, this mustard weed is a favorite organism for plant genetics and molecular biology. It was the first plant with a complete genomic sequence. For more information, see *http://www.arabidosis.org*.

bit

The contraction for binary digit. The base-2 logarithm of a number is in units of bits.

BLOSUM

The abbreviation for a blocks substitution matrix. Matrix names are followed by a number (e.g., BLOSUM62) that indicate the minimum percent identity between any two aligned sequences.

bp

The abbreviation for base pair. The length of DNA is usually given in bp or nt, Common measures include Kb, Mb, and Gb for thousands, millions, and billions of bp, respectively.

C-terminus

The end of a protein. In text form, the C-terminus of the protein is always at the right.

Caenorhabditis elegans

A nematode (also called a roundworm) that is about 1 mm long and has about

1,000 cells as an adult. *C. elegans* was the first animal to have its complete genome sequenced. See *http://www.wormbase.org.*

CDS

The abbreviation for a coding sequence. CDS isn't synonymous with exon, since exons may contain noncoding sequence.

codon

Three contiguous letters of DNA or RNA. Each of the 64 codons specifies either an amino acid or a translation stop.

complement

The complement of a DNA sequence is the sequence on the other strand. For example, the complement of ACCCGT is TGGGCA. To complement a sequence in Perl, use either of the following:

```
# 4-letter alphabet
$dna =~ tr/ACGT/TGCA/;
# 15-letter alphabet
$dna =~ tr[ACGTRYWSKMBDHV]
         [TGCAYRSWMKVHDB];
```

Drosophila melanogaster

The common fruit fly. This is one of the most famous organisms for genetic research and was one of the first animals whose complete genomic sequence was determined. See *http://www.fruitfly.org.*

dynamic programming

A common technique that reduces the computational complexity of a problem by finding and extending a partial optimization.

E. coli

Eschericia coli. A common bacteria normally found in your gut and a favorite organism for molecular biology research. Some variants cause food poisoning.

effective length

Karlin-Altschul statistics assume sequences of infinite length. To adjust for edge effects in real sequences, the search space is reduced by adjusting the true lengths of the sequences to effective lengths.

entropy

Randomness; disorder; unpredictability.

eukaryote

Organisms with intracellular membranous organelles such as the nucleus and mitochondria are called eukaryotes.

frame-shift mutation

A mutation that causes an insertion or deletion of nucleotides that isn't a multiple of three, and therefore causes the reading frame to change.

gene

A functional unit of the genome. When not specifically stated, "gene" is usually considered a "protein-coding" gene, but many genes don't contain the instructions for proteins (e.g., various RNA genes).

genetic code

The mapping of codons to amino acids. See Table 2-3.

genetic drift

The tendency of sequences to change over time by accumulating random mutations.

genome

The complete genetic material for an organism. For eukaryotes, the genome refers to the nuclear genome and doesn't include organelles.

global alignment

An alignment algorithm that requires every letter of each sequence to appear in the alignment. Globally aligning sequences of different lengths may lead to very strange alignments.

homologous

In sequence analysis, homologous means derived from a common ancestor. Sequences are either homologous or they aren't. It is incorrect to say that sequences are 80 percent homologous unless you mean that there is an 80 percent chance of common ancestry. Use percent identity to describe the similarity of alignments.

hydrophilic

Literally, "likes water." Water is a polar molecule that mixes well with other polar molecules. The charged amino acids K, R, D, and E, are examples of hydrophilic amino acids.

hydrophobic

Literally, "fears water." Nonpolar molecules (like those in oils) don't mix well with water. The amino acids L, I, V, and F are particularly hydrophobic.

Karlin-Altschul

The standard local alignment theory is often called Karlin-Altschul statistics after its founding authors.

lambda, λ

The Karlin-Altschul statistical parameter that converts a raw score to a normalized score.

local alignment

An alignment algorithm that finds the optimal subsequence alignment. The alignment may include all letters of each sequence, but it isn't required to do so.

low-complexity sequence

Regions of sequences that are highly predictable—for example, a region that is 90 percent A or T.

methionine

One of the 20 common amino acids. Methionine is abbreviated as M or Met, and is especially important because all proteins begin with a methionine. There is only one codon for this amino acid: ATG.

mutation

Any change in sequence to a DNA molecule.

N-terminus

The start of a protein. In text form, a protein's N-terminus is always at the left.

nat

Contraction for natural log digits. The base e logarithm of a number is in units of nats.

natural selection

A theory founded by Charles Darwin that explains how organisms change over time to better fit their environment. It is based on the principles of variation, heritability, and differential reproduction.

ncRNA

The abbreviation for noncoding RNA. Some RNAs, like tRNAs or rRNAs, don't contain information for protein sequences.

Needleman-Wunsch

Global alignment is often called Needleman-Wunsch after the authors who first described the algorithm.

nucleotide

The basic building block of nucleic acid sequences (DNA and RNA). DNA is made from A, C, G, or T, while RNA contains A, C, G, or U.

nt

The abbreviation for nucleotide.

O(n)

The computational complexity of an algorithm is often described by its asymptotic behavior. O(n) problems grow linearly with the size of the input. $O(\log_2 n)$ grow much more slowly, and $O(n^2)$ grow much more quickly.

ORF

Abbreviation for open reading frame. Each strand of DNA has three frames. Any subsequence that doesn't contain stop codons in a particular frame is an open reading frame.

ortholog

Genes that are separated by speciation (i.e., the same gene in different species). This is often approximated as the best reciprocal match between two complete genomes or proteomes.

palindrome

A palindrome in DNA is a sequence that is read the same on the plus and minus strands. For example, the sequence GAATTC is a palindrome. Palindromes and near-palindromes are often sites for DNA-protein interaction. Proteins scanning along DNA "see" a palindrome as the same sequence regardless of which direction they are moving.

PAM

An acronym for Percent or Point Accepted Mutation. PAM scoring matrix names are usually followed by a number (e.g., PAM200), which indicates how many iterations of multiplication were used starting with the PAM1 matrix. The higher number indicates a more distant similarity.

paralogs

Genes that are duplicated within a single genome. Duplication sometimes allows one of the genes to take on a specialized function.

phylogenetics

The study of evolutionary relationships among organisms.

prokaryotes

Organisms that don't contain intracellular organelles. All bacteria are prokaryotes.

proteome

The complete set of all proteins produced by a particular organism. Many proteins undergo post-translational modifications that add or subtract features from a protein. Therefore, a particular mRNA might have many different protein isoforms.

pseudogene

A sequence that looks like a gene but isn't. Most pseudogenes are derived from mRNAs that have been reverse-transcribed back to DNA and inserted into the genome. They have the hallmarks of RNA processing—notably a poly-A tail and no introns.

relative entropy

The average number of bits (or nats) per aligned letter for a given scoring scheme.

repeat

Any class of a sequence that appears multiple times in a genome. Usually, gene families aren't called repeats and the term is used for junk DNA. Some of the most common repeats in the human genome include the *ALU* and *LINE* families.

reverse transcriptase

A protein that creates DNA from an RNA template.

RNA

Ribonucleic acid. RNA is chemically similar to DNA but not used strictly for storage. Many RNA molecules have important functions in the cell and may even have enzymatic properties. Some of the most

common functional RNA molecules include rRNAs and tRNAs.

RNA polymerase

A protein or multiprotein complex that creates RNA from a DNA template.

ribosome

A complex macromolecule made up of proteins and rRNAs. Ribosomes are responsible for translating mRNAs into proteins.

rRNA

Ribosomal RNA. The ribosome is composed of many specific RNA molecules, and these components are called rRNAs. rRNAs are some of the most abundant RNAs in a cell.

Smith-Waterman

Local alignment is often referred to as Smith-Waterman, after the authors who first described the algorithm.

start codon

ATG. Codes for the amino acid methionine. Many proteins have N-terminal post-translational modifications, and the first amino acid of the mature protein may therefore not be methionine.

stop codon

TAA, TGA, and TAG are the three codons that terminate translation.

sum statistics

A method that determines the aggregate statistical significance of multiple local alignments.

target frequency

The expected frequencies of individual letter pairings. For nucleotide scoring matrices, the target frequency is often summarized by the expected percent identity in sequences with unbiased composition.

transcriptome

The complete set of transcripts for a particular genome. This term is often used to mean the mRNAs of protein coding genes and their alternatively spliced variants.

tRNA

The abbreviation for transfer RNA. tRNAs transfer individual amino acids to the ribosome. Each tRNA molecule has an anti-codon the matches the reverse-complement of the amino acid it carries.

UTR

The abbreviation for an untranslated region. The 5´ and 3´ ends of an mRNA have untranslated regions. These regions sometimes play regulatory roles that change the mRNA's stability, translatability, or localization.

Index

We'd like to hear your suggestions for improving our indexes. Send email to *index@oreilly.com*.

alignment (*continued*)
  determining significance, 111
  ESTs and, 138
  gaps and, 65
  insensitive search, 146
  mapping and, 130
  number expected by chance, 119
  overcalling and, 142
  percent identity and, 148
  query chopping and, 221
  repeats and, 143
  score metric, 55
  search space and, 65
  stop codons, 124, 158, 184
  sum score, 102
  TBLASTN, 93
  TBLASTX, 93
  vectors, 142
alignment groups
  BLAST report, 94
  exons and, 148
  links and topcomboN, 128
  WU-BLAST, 128
alignment threshold, 84, 120
Alignments option (report), 9
allele frequencies, 30
alleles, 29, 31
Altivec, 224
Altschul, Stephen, 65
altscore parameter (WU-BLAST), 187, 269
amino acid similarity, 57–59, 64
amino acids (aa)
  databases, 197
  difficulty sequencing, 123
  genetic code, 25
  PHI-BLAST and, 257
  proteins and, 22, 25
  PSI-BLAST and, 176
  scoring matrices, 60
  symbols listed, 22–24
annealing, 131
annotating
  concatenating lines and, 150
  ESTs, 149, 151
Apple Computer, 224
Archaea, 33
arginine (R), 24, 58
ASCII format, 262
ASN.1 (Abstract Syntax Notation One)
  bl2seq parameter, 252
  format, 296, 298

formatdb parameter, 240
  reports and, 12
asparagine (N), 24
aspartate (D), 22
asterisk (*), 149, 184
ATG (start codon), 26

B

B= parameter (WU-BLAST), 270
Bacteria, 33
bandwidth, 52
base pair (bp), 21, 126, 134
Basic Local Alignment Search Tool
        (see BLAST)
batch retrieval systems, 198
benchmarking
  blastn, 215
  blastp, 172, 182, 215
  EST search, 181
  systems, 215
Beowulf clusters, 217
big-O notation, 50
biological sequences, 35–38, 64
  (see also evolution; genes; genomes;
        molecular biology)
Bioperl
  annotating ESTs, 151
  clustering and, 141
  database purifiers, 196
  parsing, 126–127
  repeat masking and, 143
bit score
  defined, 100
  Expect and, 101, 103
  lambda and, 111
bitScoreToExpect function, 102
bl2seq (NCBI-BLAST)
  BLASTX and, 152, 158
  exons and, 126, 134, 152
  functionality, 175
  HSPs and, 153, 155
  installation files, 162
  parameter, 252–255
BLAST algorithm
  evaluation, 84–87
  extension, 81–84
  overview, 76, 77
  seeding, 77–81
BLAST (Basic Local Alignment Search Tool)
  custom databases, 198
  functionality, 3
  implementation, 79

sequences (*continued*)
    transcripts for proteins, 36
    xdget, 184
serial searches
    accurate alignment, 152
    BLAST and, 222–224
    BLASTX and, 149
    long sequences, 153
    undocumented genes, 157
serine (S), 24
setdb (WU-BLAST), 168, 180
SGD database, 204
SGE distributed resource management, 219
Shannon, Claude, 56
Shannon's Entropy, 56
shotgun sequence, 141, 149, 151
silent mutations, 28
SIM4 program, 135
similarity
    biological sequences and, 38
    patterns of, 27
    vectors, 142
    weak, 117
simple repeats, 37
Smith-Waterman algorithm
    alignment endpoints, 81
    BLAST statistics compared, 102
    blastpgp parameter, 263
    gold standard, 76
    (see also local alignment)
soft masking
    BLASTP searches, 145
    case sensitivity and, 133
    cross-species exploration, 135
    functionality, 120
    low-complexity and, 150
    seeding and, 81, 233
    sensitive searches, 146
software
    optimization, 220–224
    sequence management, 211, 212
source code (NCBI-BLAST), 161, 224
source, message and symbols from, 56
SOURCE (sequence record), 203
sp2fasta (WU-BLAST file), 168
span parameter (WU-BLAST), 279
span1 parameter (WU-BLAST), 279
span2 parameter (WU-BLAST), 279
species, 134
specificity, 131, 133, 147
SPIDEY program, 135

splicing
    alternative, 157
    coding sequences and, 36
    regulation and, 138
    transcript clustering, 140
SRS (Sequence Retrieval System), 211
stacking, 139
start codons, 26
statistics
    massaging, 128, 129
    redundant sequences and, 196
    statistical outliers, 128
    (see also specific methods)
Stein, Lincoln, 305
stop codons
    alignment and, 124, 158, 184
    BLASTX, 149
    defined, 26
    mutation and, 28
    preventing, 155
    prokaryotic genes, 36
    pseudogenes, 38, 124, 153
    TBLASTX search, 175
storage considerations, 207
strandedness
    BLAST, 92
    BLASTX, 93
    TBLASTX, 93
sts database, 197
Stuffit Expander, 166
substitution matrix (see scoring matrix)
substitution, nonconservative, 28
sum score
    alignments and, 102
    calculating, 106
    Expect and, 103, 104
    overview, 67–70, 104
sumScore function, 106
suppressors, 36
SWISS-PROT database, 197, 204
symbolic links, 163
symbols, message and, 56
synonymous mutations, 28
synteny, 136

T

T= parameter (WU-BLAST), 280
tabular format
    blast-imager.pl, 305
    BLASTN and, 133
    converting to, 118, 309
    megablast and, 172

NCBI and, 295, 296
parsing, 132
TAIR (The Arabidopsis Information
        Resource), 204
tar command, 162, 167
tarball (tape archive), 162, 167
target frequency (TF)
    cross-species, 119
    lambda, 61, 62
    match-mismatch scoring, 63, 64, 131
    nucleotide scoring schemes, 299
    overview, 60–64
    relative entropy, 62
    report differences, 113
taxonomic classification, 33, 202, 203
Taxonomy browser (NCBI toolbox), 4
TBLASTN
    alignment, 93
    BLAST program, 75
    display formats, 291–298
    features, 174, 183
    searches, 152–155
    strandedness, 92
    ungapped alignment, 124
TBLASTX
    alignment, 93
    BLAST program, 75, 76
    cross-species exploration, 136
    display formats, 291–298
    gapped alignment and, 234
    genomic DNA/ESTs, 139
    NCBI-BLAST features, 174, 175
    searches, 155–158
    strandedness, 92
    ungapped alignment, 124
    WU-BLAST features, 183, 184
tee program (Unix), 309
templates, discontiguous, 249, 251
Tera-BLAST, 225, 226
T/F (true/false) switches, 229
threonine (T), 24
thymine (T), 20
TimeLogic, 225, 226
top parameter (WU-BLAST), 280
topcomboN parameter (WU-BLAST), 94,
        128, 280
trace-back, 44–46
transcripts
    aligning to genome, 53
    BLASTX searches, 147, 157, 158
    clustering and extension, 139, 140
    ESTs, 137, 197

low-complexity regions, 138
mapping between species, 134
transfer RNA (tRNA), 22, 37
translation
    BLASTX and, 108
    inferences from, 123
    to protein sequence, 25
    reading frames, 27
transposons, 37
TrEMBL database, 204
tRNA (transfer RNA), 22, 37
tryptophan (W), 24, 58
tutorials
    NCBI-BLAST, 170–180
    WU-BLAST, 180–186
twilight zone, 117
two-hit algorithm
    blastall parameter, 230, 237
    BLASTX search, 151
    defined, 79
    insensitive search, 146
    megablast parameter, 246
    WU-BLAST parameter, 274
tyrosine (Y), 24, 58

U

undercalling, 142, 143
ungapped alignments
    depicted, 76
    finding, 86
    HSPs and, 84
    reporting lengths, 113
    usage, 124
UniGene database, 4, 9, 204
Unix environment
    dashes, 194
    DRMs, 219
    NCBI-BLAST installation, 162–164
    WU-BLAST installation, 166–170
unordered-sum score, 68
untranslated regions (UTRs), 36, 123, 155
uracil (U), 20, 22
UTRs (untranslated regions), 36, 123, 155

V

V= parameter (WU-BLAST), 120, 280
valine (V), 24, 58
variables (see environment variables)
variation, selection and, 29, 30, 32

xdformat
  BLAST and, 184, 193
  FASTA files, 208
  features, 184
  parameters, 281–285
  Unix syntax, 269
  WU-BLAST and, 168, 180
xdget
  FASTA files, 208
  features, 168, 184, 185
  parameters, 285–288
  Unix syntax, 269
  virtual databases, 208
XML (eXtensible Markup Language), 12, 295

Y

Y= parameter (WU-BLAST), 281
Yersinia pestis, 33

Z

Z= parameter (WU-BLAST), 281

About the Authors

Ian Korf received his B.A. from Cornell University and his Ph.D from Indiana University. His formal training is in molecular biology, but he has had a fondness for computer programming since his early teens. His post-doctoral research at Washington University in St. Louis and at The Wellcome Trust Sanger Institute in the United Kingdom has focused on genomic sequence analysis with an emphasis on comparative genomics and gene prediction. His goal in life is to follow genomes, wherever they happen to take him.

Mark Yandell received his Ph.D in molecular, cellular, and developmental biology from the University of Colorado, Boulder. After graduation, he joined the Genome Sequencing Center at Washington University, where he pursued postdoctoral studies in computational biology, genome annotation, and SNP discovery. In 1999, he joined Celera Genomics, where he wrote much of the software used by Celera to annotate and analyze the drosophila, human, mouse, and mosquito genomes. He recently joined the Berkeley Drosophila Genome Project.

Joseph Bedell received his B.S. in genetics from the University of Georgia in 1991, then worked on mosquito genetics at the Centers for Disease Control and Prevention in Atlanta. He went on to complete a Ph.D. in human genetics at the University of California, Irvine in 1999. Joey, like his coauthors, completed a postdoc in mammalian gene annotation with Warren Gish, one of the original developers of BLAST. He is currently the Director of Bioinformatics for Orion Genomics in St. Louis where he spends his days (and nights) using BLAST to answer important biological and phylogenetic questions about plants.

Colophon

Our look is the result of reader comments, our own experimentation, and feedback from distribution channels. Distinctive covers complement our distinctive approach to technical topics, breathing personality and life into potentially dry subjects.

The animal on the cover of *BLAST* is a coelacanth. The modern coelacanth, *Latimeria chalumnae*, is the sole living representative of *Actinista*, an ancient family of lobe-finned fish. The first live coelacanth was discovered off the east coast of South Africa in 1938 and caused a stir in the scientific community because they were believed to have been extinct for approximately 80 million years. A second, closely related species of coelacanths was found off the coast of Sulawesi in 1998.

Coelacanths grow to about 6 feet long; weigh up to 150 pounds; and are covered with bony, dark blue scales flecked with white. Coelacanths are unlike other living fish in that they have a three-lobed tail, fleshy fins, and a partially developed vertebral column. They are the only living vertebrate with a functional intercranial joint. It's this joint that allows the coelacanth's jaws to open exceptionally wide when inhaling its prey. Coelacanths are opportunistic predators (they eat whatever they can find) and are ovoviviparous (they give birth to live young).

From an evolutionary perspective, coelacanths are unique, and they provide a key perspective on the evolution of many different genes in vertebrate species. With their front and rear paired fins, which move in a similar fashion to the arms and legs of land vertebrates, coelacanths may be one of the closest links to those vertebrates that first crawled out of the sea to live on land more than 350 million years ago.

Mary Anne Weeks Mayo was the production editor and proofreader, and Ann Schirmer was the copyeditor for *BLAST*. Derek DiMatteo, and Darren Kelly provided quality control. Lucie Haskins wrote the index.

Emma Colby designed the cover of this book, based on a series design by Edie Freedman. The cover image is an original illustration created by Lorrie LeJeune. Emma produced the cover layout with QuarkXPress 4.1 using Adobe's ITC Garamond font.

David Futato designed the interior layout. This book was converted by Julie Hawks to FrameMaker 5.5.6 with a format conversion tool created by Erik Ray, Jason McIntosh, Neil Walls, and Mike Sierra that uses Perl and XML technologies. The text font is Linotype Birka; the heading font is Adobe Myriad Condensed; and the code font is LucasFont's TheSans Mono Condensed. The illustrations that appear in the book were produced by Robert Romano and Jessamyn Read using Macromedia FreeHand 9 and Adobe Photoshop 6. This colophon was compiled by Lorrie LeJeune.

CPSIA information can be obtained at www.ICGtesting.com
Printed in the USA
BVOW10s1410211015

423520BV00021B/333/P